Praise for Homebrewing For Dummies

"Marty Nachel has penned an outstanding, surefire guide for homebrewers at every level of expertise."

— Tom Dalldorf, Publisher, *Celebrator Beer News*

"Homebrewing For Dummies clearly fills a void in the homebrewing how-to arena. Marty Nachel has very effectively communicated his extensive knowledge of the brewing process and his passion for the subject."

— Tom Sweeney, America's Brewing Co.

"Homebrewing For Dummies is written as if Marty Nachel is standing right next to you in the brewery, always ready to let you tap into his vast experience. Whether contemplating your first batch, or ready to move up to advanced brewing, Marty's there to help you along."

— Gregg Smith, Managing Editor,
Beer and Tavern Chronicle and Author

"Homebrewing For Dummies tells you all you need to know about homebrewing — from a simple first batch to the most advanced procedures, it's all there."

— Jim Dorsch, Co-chair,
North American Guild of Beer Writers

"This book is by far the most thorough homebrewing book I have ever seen."

— Bill Owens, Brewmaster and Publisher

"Most people don't know that homebrewing is easy and fun, with incredible awards. With a little care and attention, anyone can make beer at home as good as, if not better than, the big commercial brewers. Beginning with the basics, Marty outlines all the steps needed, and all the pitfalls, in making great beer. With Marty as your guide, you'll be making great beer in your own kitchen in no time at all."

— Daniel Bradford, Publisher,
All About Beer Magazine

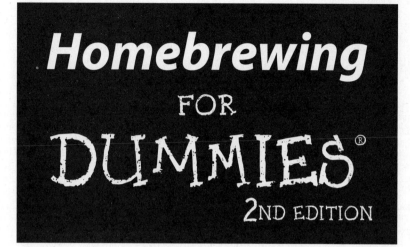

Homebrewing FOR DUMMIES®

2ND EDITION

by Marty Nachel

John Wiley & Sons, Inc.

Homebrewing For Dummies®, 2nd Edition

Published by
John Wiley & Sons, Inc.
111 River St.
Hoboken, NJ 07030-5774
www.wiley.com

For general information on our other products and services, please contact our Customer Care Department within the U.S. at 877-762-2974, outside the U.S. at 317-572-3993, or fax 317-572-4002.

For technical support, please visit www.wiley.com/techsupport.

Wiley publishes in a variety of print and electronic formats and by print-on-demand. Some material included with standard print versions of this book may not be included in e-books or in print-on-demand. If this book refers to media such as a CD or DVD that is not included in the version you purchased, you may download this material at http://booksupport.wiley.com. For more information about Wiley products, visit www.wiley.com.

Library of Congress Control Number: 2008922656

ISBN 978-0-470-23062-6 (pbk); ISBN 978-0-470-37418-4 (ebk); ISBN 978-0-470-37416-0 (ebk); ISBN 978-1-118-05244-0 (ebk)

Manufactured in the United States of America

10 9 8

WILEY

About the Author

An occasional welder and steel fabricator, **Marty Nachel** is also a freelance writer on beer and brewing. As a member of the North American Guild of Beer Writers, in September 1996 Marty was voted one of the three best beer writers in the United States at the N.A.G.B.W. Quill & Tankard Awards at the Great American Beer Festival in Denver.

A former President of the Chicago Beer Society and founding member of the Brewers Of South Suburbia (B.O.S.S.) homebrew and beer appreciation club, Marty has been brewing his own award-winning beers since 1985. In 1986, he was the first person in the state of Illinois to become a Certified Beer Judge. In addition to his homebrew judging duties, Marty served on the panel of beer evaluators at the prestigious Beverage Testing Institute in Chicago, home of the World Beer Championships, as well as the Great American Beer Festival in Denver, Colorado.

Marty has been the writer of the newsletters that accompany monthly shipments of microbrewed beer from Beer Across America since October 1992. His articles have also appeared in *All About Beer* magazine, *Brew Magazine, Brew Your Own* magazine, *Celebrator Beer News, Drink* magazine, *Fine Cooking* magazine, *Zymurgy Magazine,* and Epicurious.com. In 1998 Marty was also tapped to write the beer and brewing entries for the latest edition of Microsoft's Encarta Encyclopedia. His first book on the microbrewing industry, *Beer Across America* (Storey Communications), was published in July of 1995. Marty's second book, *Beer For Dummies* (Wiley Publishing), was a huge hit when it was published in August of 1996.

Travel in search of good beer has taken Marty to over 200 breweries and brewpubs and assorted beer festivals and shrines throughout Europe and North America. When he can find the time, Marty also likes to collect breweriana.

Dedication

Were it not for my wife, Patti, and the 32 years she has dedicated to her career, I would not know the pleasure of writing about beer for a living. Though she and our two children reap secondary dividends from our professional/domestic arrangement, no one benefits more from it than I. Thank you, Dear, from the bottom of my pint glass.

Author's Acknowledgments

My sincere thanks to all the people at John Wiley & Sons for creating this unique opportunity. I would especially like to thank Acquisitions Editor Tracy Boggier for her part in making this all happen, as well as for giving me the proper focus in the early stages of this project. I also enjoyed working with my talented Copy Editor, Megan Knoll, and I'm grateful for her amazing attention to detail. A big thanks also to my Editorial Program Coordinator Erin Calligan Mooney, who helped re-secure all of the permissions for the recipes that appear in this book. Finally, heartfelt thanks to the Composition Services crew for all their behind-the-scenes help and effort. I owe you all a round of my best brew!

Most importantly, I would like to thank my Project Editor, Alissa Schwipps, for her patience, focus, and direction (did I mention patience?) — all of which created a comfortable and confident working relationship that made the writing and editing of this book much easier and more enjoyable.

Again, I would like to thank my agent and book producer Steve Ettlinger for his boundless energy and enthusiasm while working on *Beer For Dummies,* a project which subsequently paved the way for this book. I am indebted to him for his vision, guidance, and professionalism.

Over the years I have been fortunate to meet and befriend many beer-knowledgeable people who have influenced me and my brewing ability. One of these people is Mike Pezan, a dedicated homebrewer-turned-professional brewer and Beer Geek of the highest order. His technical know-how pumped life into the more advanced chapters of this book and his quick wit and sense of humor helped infuse these otherwise dry subjects with much needed levity.

Speaking of technical know-how, many thanks to Dr. Joe Formanek, my Technical Editor. Dr. Formanek is well respected in homebrewing circles, especially in the Midwest, where he continues to win scores of awards for his incredibly tasty homebrew. A couple of Joe's award-winning beer recipes can be found in the recipe section of this book.

Thanks also to Jim Dudley, sales manager at Northwestern Extract Co. Jim was kind enough to share his database of homebrew recipes with me for this project. And my sincere thanks to Steve Kamp, Joe Formanek, Tim Reiter, Mark Merisco, and Tom Dennis, who graciously responded to my call for some last-minute beer and mead recipes — I think you'll really like the award-winning brews they provided.

Too numerous to mention by name are the many gifted homebrewers in the Chicago Beer Society, the Urban Knaves of Grain, and the Brewers Of South Suburbia (B.O.S.S.) whose talents inspired me to take up homebrewing in the first place and continue to challenge me to new brewing heights each and every year. Through this book, may their enthusiasm infect you all. . . .

Publisher's Acknowledgments

We're proud of this book; please send us your comments through our Dummies online registration form located at www.dummies.com/register/.

Some of the people who helped bring this book to market include the following:

Acquisitions, Editorial, and Media Development

Senior Project Editor: Alissa Schwipps

    (Previous Edition: Jennifer Ehrlich)

Acquisitions Editor: Tracy Boggier

Copy Editor: Megan Knoll

    (Previous Edition: Michael Bolinger, William A. Barton)

Editorial Program Coordinator: Erin Calligan Mooney

Technical Editor: Joseph A. Formanek, PhD

Senior Editorial Manager: Jennifer Ehrlich

Editorial Assistants: Joe Niesen, Leeann Harney, David Lutton

Cover Photos: © iStockphoto.com / PLAINVIEW

Cartoons: Rich Tennant (www.the5thwave.com)

Composition Services

Project Coordinator: Patrick Redmond

Layout and Graphics: Reuben W. Davis, Melissa K. Jester, Erin Zeltner

Proofreaders: Laura Albert, John Greenough, Christine Sabooni

Indexer: Broccoli Information Management

Publishing and Editorial for Consumer Dummies

    Kathleen Nebenhaus, Vice President and Executive Publisher

    Kristin Ferguson-Wagstaffe, Product Development Director

    Ensley Eikenburg, Associate Publisher, Travel

    Kelly Regan, Editorial Director, Travel

Publishing for Technology Dummies

    Andy Cummings, Vice President and Publisher

Composition Services

    Debbie Stailey, Director of Composition Services

About the AHA

The rules, guidelines, and beer styles used in this book follow those provided by the American Homebrewers Association (AHA) and the Beer Judge Certification Program (BJCP). For more information on homebrewing, beer styles, beer evaluation, publications, or the American Homebrewers Association National Homebrew Competition, please contact the American Homebrewers Association at (phone) 303-447-0816, (fax) 303-447-2825, or visit the AHA's Web site at www.beertown.org.

The following recipes have been reprinted with written permission of the American Homebrewers Association and Brewers Publications. The original recipes appear in *Victory Beer Recipes* (Brewers Publications) and are winning recipes from the American Homebrewers Association National Homebrew Competition:

Ales: "Bridge House Bitter," Andy Leith, p.161; "A Peek Under the Kilt," Jim Campbell, p.165; "Scotch Ale," Jerry Bockmore, p.165; "Cedar Mountain Brown Ale," Jim Dilldine, p.171; "Southeast Texas Northern Brown Ale," Steve Daniel, p.171; "Coal Porter" Dennis Kinvig, p.175; "Entirely Yours," Paddy Giffen, p.175; "New Years Day," Paddy Giffen, p.181; "D & J Stout," Brian and Linda North, p.183; "New Stout II," David and Melinda Brockington, p.185; "Fountainhead Black Magic," Rande Reed, p.187; "Rose's Russian Imperial Stout," Dick Van Dyke, p.187; "Cream City Abbey Ale," Robert Burko, p.197; "Ester the Molester," Brian Bliss, p.203; "Boobs Barleywine," Chuck Boyce, p.209; Lagers: "Butt Scratcher," Steve Daniel, p.213; "Meltdown Lager," Brian and Linda North, p.215; "Helles," Dave Miller, p.215; "Grain-n-Beerit," Norman Dickenson, p.217; "Yellow Dogs Pilsner," Matthew Holland, p.219; "Dominion Day Oktoberfest," John Janowiak, p.221; "(unnamed)," Dennis and Cindy Arvidson, p.221; "League City Dark," Steve Daniel, p.223; "Lady of the Morning," Ross Herrold, p.225; "Stu Brew," Stu Tallman, p.225; "Basically Bock," Phil Rahn, p.229; "Dopplebock Two," Thomas Griffith, p.231; "Scintillator," Steve Dempsey, p.231; Mixed Styles: "Arlington Ale No. 33," Richard Schmit, p.235; "Colby's Cream Ale," Rodney Howard, p.235; "Great Wheat," Jack H. Denny, p.239; "Fat Brothers Original American," Stephen Morelli, p.241; "Memphis Steamer," Phil Rahn, p.241; "League City Alt Part 3," Steve and Christina Daniel, p.243; "Pale Moon Rizen Weizen," Paddy Giffen, p.249; "Cherry Ale," David G. Hammaker, p.251; "Leftover Strawberry Ale," Dan Robinson, p.251; "Herb Alpert," Ron Page, p.253; "Anne's Choice Christmas Ale," Phillip Fleming, p.255; "Chocolate Chambord Stout," Ron Page, p.255; "Beech Beer," James Cannon, p.257.

In Memoriam

In 1985, a talented brewer by the name of Russell Schehrer won the coveted "Homebrewer of the Year" award at the National Homebrew Competition in Boulder, Colorado. Using that accomplishment as a springboard, Russell launched a short but brilliant career as a brewer and brewing consultant in the fledgling microbrewing industry.

I had the pleasure of meeting Russell Schehrer briefly one summer afternoon several years ago. Amidst his busy brewing schedule, he took the time to show me around his brewhouse at Wynkoop Brewing Company in Denver. The impromptu tour included a visit to the lagering cellar downstairs, where he proudly proffered samples of his beers fresh from the fermenters. Once back at the bar, he casually chatted with me as I tasted my way through a complimentary flight of house brews.

Though our meeting was brief, it gave me a short insight into Russ's love of good beer and his dedication to his craft. And it was cause for me to mourn his sudden passing in 1996 at the age of 38. Russ's spirit and enthusiasm sparked both the homebrewing and craft brewing communities in the United States; he has, likewise, been missed by both.

Contents at a Glance

Introduction 1

Part 1: First Things First 9
Chapter 1: Welcome to the Wonderful World of Wort 11
Chapter 2: Setting Up Your Beeraphernalia 17
Chapter 3: Creating Your Own Department of Sanitation 33

Part 11: 1t's in There: The Nuts and Bolts of Beer 41
Chapter 4: Malt: A Tale of Two Sources (Grain and Extract) 43
Chapter 5: Hop Heaven 51
Chapter 6: Yeast and Fermentation 63
Chapter 7: On the Water Front 73
Chapter 8: Adjuncts and Flavorings 81
Chapter 9: Making Your Brew Bionic: Additives, Preservatives,
   Finings, and Clarifiers 91

Part 111: Ready, Set, Brew! 97
Chapter 10: Beginner Brewing Directions 99
Chapter 11: Intermediate Brewing Directions 107
Chapter 12: Homebrewing Directions for the Serious Beer Geek 117
Chapter 13: Bottling Your Brew 135
Chapter 14: Kegging: Bottling's Big Brother 149

Part 1V: Homebrew Recipes 157
Chapter 15: Ale Recipes 159
Chapter 16: Lager Recipes 211
Chapter 17: Mixed-Style Recipes 233

Part V: Alternative Brewing 263
Chapter 18: In-Cider Information 265
Chapter 19: A Meading of the Minds 273
Chapter 20: Going Green: Being an Eco-Friendly Homebrewer 283
Chapter 21: Gluten-Free Brewing 293

Part VI: Putting Your Brew to the Test........................299

Chapter 22: Storing and Pouring 301
Chapter 23: You Can't Judge a Bock by Its Cover: Evaluating Beer 309
Chapter 24: Troubleshooting 319
Chapter 25: Homebrew Competitions........................333

Part VII: The Part of Tens................................341

Chapter 26: Ten (or so) Ways to D.I.G.I.B.I.Y. (Do It, Grow It, Build It Yourself)......343
Chapter 27: Ten Gizmos That Can Make Your Brewing Easier 353
Chapter 28: Just the FAQs: Ten (or so) Frequently Asked Questions........................357

Appendix: Ingredients: The Building Blocks of Beer......361

Index 395

Table of Contents

Introduction 1

About This Book 2
Conventions Used in This Book 3
What You're Not to Read 3
Foolish Assumptions 4
How This Book Is Organized 4
    Part I: First Things First 4
    Part II: It's in There: The Nuts and Bolts of Beer 5
    Part III: Ready, Set, Brew! 5
    Part IV: Homebrew Recipes 5
    Part V: Alternative Brewing 5
    Part VI: Putting Your Brew to the Test 5
    Part VII: The Part of Tens 6
Icons Used in This Book 6
Where to Go from Here 7

Part 1: First Things First 9

Chapter 1: Welcome to the Wonderful World of Wort ... 11

Homebrewers Abound! 11
All the Right Stuff 12
    Gathering the equipment you need 12
    Tracing the homebrewing timeline 13
    Adding ingredients galore! 14
    Preparing wisely 15
    All done — now what? 16

Chapter 2: Setting Up Your Beeraphernalia 17

Sniffing Out Sources 18
Square One: Equipment for the Beginning Brewer 19
    So much equipment, so little time 19
    What do I do with all these gadgets? 20
Square Two: Equipment for the Intermediate Brewer 25
    Now what do I need? 25
    What do these gizmos even do? 27
Square Three: Equipment for the Advanced Brewer 28
    I need even more stuff? 29
    What else could I possibly need another doodad for? 30

Chapter 3: Creating Your Own Department of Sanitation **33**

No Dirty Words: Sanitation Lingo...33
Battling Bacteria (and Fungi)...34
Soaps for Suds: Cleansers and Sanitizers 35
Cleaning Up Your Act: Equipment Cleaning Practices 37
Bottle Cleanliness Is a Virtue..38

Part II: It's in There: The Nuts and Bolts of Beer............41

Chapter 4: Malt: A Tale of Two Sources (Grain and Extract) **43**

Going with Grain...43
  Malting 44
  Mashing 45
  Mixing it up with other grains 45
  Manipulating grain: Kilning and milling...46
Enjoying the Ease of Extracts 47
  Graduating to other malty methods 49
  Comparing liquid versus dry malt extract......................................50

Chapter 5: Hop Heaven **51**

Seeing the Hop Flower up Close...52
Hopping with Variety 55
Selecting the Best Hops..57
  Freshness is fundamental...57
  Bittering potential is important too..58
Taking Note of Top Hops 60

Chapter 6: Yeast and Fermentation **63**

There's a Fungus among Us 63
The Magic of Fermentation 65
  It's cyclical...65
  Factoring in fermentation variables..65
  Liquid yeast versus dry yeast: A foamenting debate 67
  Propagating yeast 69
  Yeast energizers and nutrients 71
Considering Alcohol Content 71
  ABV versus ABW 71
  N/A (nonalcoholic) beer is n/a (not achievable)............................72

Chapter 7: On the Water Front **73**

H₂OH: Understanding How Water Chemistry Affects
  Your Homebrew 74
Something Is in the Water 74
  pHundamentals of pH balance..75
  Antibacterial agents 75

Hard facts, fluid concepts 76
Mineral ions 77
Trace metals..78
Buying Brew-Friendly Bottled Water 78

Chapter 8: Adjuncts and Flavorings ....**.81**
Adjuncts: Sugar, Sugar . . . Aw, Honey, Honey.............82
Flavoring Your Brew with Flavorings.........................84
Funky flavorings: The exotic and the esoteric 85
Herbs and spice and everything nice 87

**Chapter 9: Making Your Brew Bionic: Additives,
Preservatives, Finings, and Clarifiers** ....**.91**
To Add and Preserve 92
A Little Clarification, Please.....................................93
The Acid Test 96

Part III: Ready, Set, Brew! **97**

Chapter 10: Beginner Brewing Directions ....**.99**
Gathering the Tools You Need................................100
Brewing Your First Batch 101
Taking Hydrometer Readings 104
Brewing day reading 104
Prebottling reading..104

Chapter 11: Intermediate Brewing Directions ....**.107**
Taking Control of Your Beer...................................107
Fooling Around with Ingredients............................108
Grain and strain..108
Hop to it..109
Yeasty beasties 110
Conditioning for Better Beer 111
Secondary fermentation 111
Tertiary fermentation 115

**Chapter 12: Homebrewing Directions
for the Serious Beer Geek** ....**.117**
Yes, We Have No Potatoes: Mashing Procedures...................118
Three important variables 118
Gimme some water: Simplified water treatment for mashing 119
And then there were three: Mashing types 120
The aftermash or mash-out..................................122
Easing into Mashing with a Partial Mash 124
Going All Out with All-Grain Brewing 128
Increasing Your Batch Size....................................131
Harvest Time: Reusing Your Yeast.........................133

Chapter 13: Bottling Your Brew 135
Picking Out Bottles 135
Ready, Set, Bottle! 136
Tanks a Lot! Bottling Kegged Beer 142
Carbon-aid: Sharing kegged beer in plastic bottles 142
Counterintelligence: Flowing from keg to bottle
for competition 143
A Primer on Priming 144
Getting ready to prime 144
Deciding which and how much primer to use 145
Exploring alternative primers 146
Crowning Achievements 147

Chapter 14: Kegging: Bottling's Big Brother 149
Roll Out the Barrel: Buying Your Kegging Equipment 149
Getting Your Keg Up and Flowing 151
Clean 'em out and fill 'em up: Sanitizing and
racking procedures 151
Making bubbles: Carbonating procedures 154
Enjoying Your Brew: Tapping and Lapping Procedures 156

Part IV: Homebrew Recipes *157*

Chapter 15: Ale Recipes 159
Extra Special/Strong Bitter (E.S.B.) (8-c) 160
Irish Red Ale (9-d) 162
Strong Scotch Ale (9-e) 164
American Pale Ale (10-a) 166
American Amber Ale (10-b) 168
American Brown Ale (10-c) 170
Northern English Brown Ale (11-c) 172
Brown Porter (12-a) 174
Robust Porter (12-b) 176
Baltic Porter (12-c) 178
Dry Stout (13-a) 180
Sweet Stout (13-b) 182
Foreign-Style Stout (13-d) 184
Imperial Stout (13-f) 186
English India Pale Ale (IPA) (14-a) 188
American India Pale Ale (IPA) (14-b) .190
Imperial India Pale Ale (IPA) (14-c) .192
White (Wit) (16-a) 194
Belgian Pale Ale (16-b) 196
Dubbel (18-b) 198
Tripel (18-c) 200
Belgian Golden Strong Ale (18-d) 202
Belgian Dark Strong Ale (18-e) 204
Old Ale (19-a) 206
English-Style Barley Wine (19-b) 208
Fun Label Ideas 210

Chapter 16: Lager Recipes **211**
American Premium Lager (1-c)........................212
Münchner-Style Helles (1-d) 214
Dortmunder/European-Style Export (1-e)............216
Bohemian-Style Pilsener (2-b) 218
Märzen/Oktoberfest (3-b) 220
American Dark Lager (4-a) 222
Munich Dunkel (4-b) 224
German-Style Helles Bock/Maibock (5-a)............226
Traditional Bock (5-b) 228
Doppelbock (5-c) 230
Fun Label Ideas.................................232

Chapter 17: Mixed-Style Recipes **233**
Cream Ale (6-a) 234
Blonde Ale (6-b) 236
American Wheat (6-d) 238
California Common Beer (7-b) 240
Düsseldorfer-Style Altbier (7-c)....................242
Weizen/Weissbier (15-a) 244
Dunkelweizen (15-b) 246
Weizenbock (15-c) 248
Fruit Beer (20) 250
Herb, Spice, and Vegetable Beer (21-a) 252
Christmas/Winter/Specialty Spiced Beer (21-b) 254
Smoked Beer (22-b)..............................256
Wood-Aged Beer (22-c) 258
Specialty Beer (23) 260
Fun Label Ideas.................................262

Part V: Alternative Brewing *263*

Chapter 18: In-Cider Information **265**
Exploring the Cider Option........................265
Comparing apples to apples 266
Sorting cider styles 267
Making Cider....................................269
Cider Considerations: Recipes 270
Common Cider (27-a) 270
New England-Style Cider (28-a) 271
Specialty Cider (28-d) 272

Chapter 19: A Meading of the Minds **273**
Mulling Over the Mead Option.....................273
The honey bunch: Appreciating honey 273
The honey-brew list: Mead styles................275
Sweet Success: Making Magnificent Mead 277
Choosing your honey..........................278
Mead-iocre? Not! Fermenting your Mead 278

I Mead a Drink: Mead Recipes 280
Traditional Mead (24-a) 280
Open Category Mead (26-c) 281
Pyment (grape melomel) (25-b) 282

Chapter 20: Going Green: Being an Eco-Friendly Homebrewer 283
Brewing Green Beer: It's Not Just for St. Patrick's Day Anymore...........283
Reduce 284
Reuse...285
Recycle..286
Organically Speaking 286
Why use organic ingredients?.....................................287
Tracking the trend..288
Certifiably nuts: Determining what's really organic....................289

Chapter 21: Gluten-Free Brewing 293
Getting to Know Gluten 293
From Intolerant to Tolerable: Brewing Gluten-Free Beer at Home 294
Readying your equipment 294
Substituting safe ingredients 294
Brewing gluten-free beers from all grain 296
Last, but not yeast...297

Part VI: Putting Your Brew to the Test 299

Chapter 22: Storing and Pouring 301
Storing Your Suds..301
How do I store it?..302
Where do I store it?..302
How long do I store it?..303
Pouring Procedures 303
Out of the bottle. 303
. . . and into the glass 304
Dirty Deeds: Cleaning Beer Glassware 307
Storing Your Steins...308

**Chapter 23: You Can't Judge a Bock
by Its Cover: Evaluating Beer 309**
Tuning In to Your Beer..309
Evaluating One Sense at a Time 310
The nose knows..311
Seeing is beer-lieving 313
In good taste 314
From Observations to Reflections 317
Relaying the Results: Homebrew Lingo, Jargon, and Vernacular...........317

Chapter 24: Troubleshooting **319**

Fermentation Lamentations..319
No fermentation...320
Stuck fermentation 321
Never-ending fermentation 321
In Bad Taste: Off Flavors and Aromas 322
Butter/butterscotch flavors 322
Sour/tart flavors 323
Medicinal/plastic/smoky flavors 323
Papery/cardboard/sherry-like flavors (oxidation) 324
Dry/puckering mouthfeel (astringency)............................324
Harshness/hotness...325
Metallic flavor 325
Skunk aroma..325
Sulfury odors 326
Vegetal flavors and aromas 326
Flavor and Aroma Therapy Quick References.........................326
Conditioning and Appearance Problems 329
Flat out of gas..330
Thar she blows! Overcarbonated beers 330
In a haze: Cloudy beers..331
Poor head, bad body...331

Chapter 25: Homebrew Competitions **333**

What's Involved in Homebrewing Competitions?....................334
How are the entries judged? 334
How do I enter a homebrew competition,
and what are the rules?...336
How do I send my beer? 337
Becoming a Barrister of Beer..337
What it takes to become a beer judge 337
Advancing to supreme quart justice.................................339

Part VII: The Part of Tens.............................341

**Chapter 26: Ten (or so) Ways to D.I.G.I.B.I.Y.
(Do It, Grow It, Build It Yourself)** **343**

Banking Yeast..343
Preparing to open your own bank......................................344
Creating yeast 344
Handling Grain..345
Roast-a-rama 345
Smoke 'em if you got 'em..346
Di-vine Intervention: Growing Hops 346
Here we grow!..347
Pick a hop, any hop..347
Drying and storing your hops...348

Building Brewing Equipment 348
    Chillin' out: Immersion wort chillers 348
    Tuns of fun: Lauter tun 349
    Pot o' plenty: Large-volume brewpot..351
    Cold feat: Lagering cellar 351

Chapter 27: Ten Gizmos That Can Make Your Brewing Easier 353
Digital Thermometer and pH Meter...353
Wort Aeration System..354
Auto Siphon 354
Counterpressure Bottle Filler 354
Beer Filter...354
Germicidal Lamp...355
Wort Transfer Pump 355
Refractometer...355
Mashing Sparge Arm 355
Counterflow Wort Chiller 356

**Chapter 28: Just the FAQs: Ten (or so)
Frequently Asked Questions 357**
How Much Is Taking Up Homebrewing Going to Cost? 357
How Much Does the Average Batch of Beer Cost?..................................358
Where Can I Buy Homebrewing Supplies? 358
How Long Does Making a Batch of Homebrew Take?..............................358
Is Homebrewed Beer Better Than Commercially Made Beer? 359
How Do You Carbonate Homebrew?...359
How Do I Add Alcohol to Homebrew? 359
Can I Distill Homebrew into Whiskey?..359
Can I Sell Homebrew? 360
Why Shouldn't I Age Beer in the Plastic Primary Fermenter?................360
Do I Have to Worry About Things Blowing Up in My House?..................360

Appendix: Ingredients: The Building Blocks of Beer 361
Malt: Grainy Names and Extract Excerpts 361
    Producers of grains...362
    Types of grains 363
    Malt extract brands...369
Top Hops: Hop Varieties and Descriptions 370
Yeast: Dry and Liquid 379
    Liquid top-fermenting yeast (Ales)...380
    Liquid bottom-fermenting yeast (Lagers).....................................382
    Advanced liquid yeast (Ales)..384
    Liquid top-fermenting yeast (Ales)...386
    Specialty/Belgian yeast...388
    Bottom-fermenting yeast (Lagers) 390
    Suggested strains for specific beer styles....................................391
    Mead and cider yeast...393

Index...395

Introduction

Homebrewing is one of the most sublime hobbies. Like growing vegetables in your backyard garden or baking bread in your own kitchen, homebrewing enables you to recapture the hands-on rusticity of the olden days while producing something that's an absolute delight to consume. Just as nothing can substitute for layering a salad with tomatoes and cucumbers picked fresh from your own garden, nothing is as gratifying as sipping a fresh beer brewed on your own kitchen stove.

In addition to the personal enjoyment you can gain from drinking your own beer, you can't deny the deep sense of gratification that accompanies the kudos and congratulations of friends, family, and coworkers who equally enjoy your homebrewing efforts. Perhaps best of all is the widespread recognition that comes from winning awards — often quite valuable — in acknowledgment of your brewing prowess and expertise. This list of benefits is a just a glimmer of what homebrewing is like today.

The hobby hasn't always been this way. Modern homebrewing in the United States wasn't even a legal enterprise until 1979. Even after it became legal, homebrew still bore the disparaging mantle of *bathtub booze* and other such pejoratives, a residue of the illicit beer-making days during national prohibition.

Fortunately, we've come full circle. Homebrewers have been rightly credited with being the catalyst of the recent American brewing renaissance. The early homebrew pioneering spirits, longing for a beer more satisfying than the homogenous mass-market brands, were the ones who went on to open the first of the *microbreweries* that are so popular today. And as more of these craft-brewing operations open across the country and throughout the world, they expose more and more people to small-brewery quality and diversity. Inspired by the craft-brewing ethic and enthusiasm, many more people are now interested in brewing beer at home.

Following in footsteps far greater than my own, I began brewing my own beer in 1985. I didn't start homebrewing for lack of good beer, because plenty of good, locally available commercial beers were available. I chose to brew my own beer because I wanted to personally experience the magic of the beer making process. After I started homebrewing, I quickly became hooked and realized only much later that as much as I was consuming the hobby of homebrewing, it was also consuming me.

So I had my own reasons for homebrewing — but why should you start? Because homebrewers tend to develop a love and enjoyment and respect for beer beyond its simple consumption. Homebrewers are ethereally connected to both the brewing past and the brewing future; they're champions of both a medieval art and an advanced science. Plus, the homebrewing community-at-large shares a common sense of purpose — of sharing information and ideas, of promoting education as part of the hobby, and of enriching and enlightening the general public by improving its collective perception of beer.

And despite anything you may have seen or heard or assumed on your own, facial hair isn't a prerequisite to being a good homebrewer. On the other hand, growing wild hair now and again is strongly encouraged among those who brew their own beer at home.

About This Book

I've written this book primarily with brewer wannabes in mind — those who have always stood on the sidelines wondering what it's like to play in the game. But unlike baseball, football, soccer, or any other team game of physical ability, homebrewing is more like a singles card game — one in which you can improve your skill through repetitive play (and at your own pace).

But this book isn't just a primer on the joy of playing Solitaire (if you'll excuse the analogy). This book tells you everything you need to know about this particular deck of cards, how to shuffle the deck, how to deal the cards, how to play various card games at different levels of difficulty, and finally, how to find and associate with others who share your interest.

Unlike other how-to books, *Homebrewing For Dummies,* 2nd Edition is arranged in such a way that you need not read it in order, cover to cover. Using the many cross-references provided within the text enables you to jump around to those sections that are of greatest interest to you. Please notice, however, that certain chapters deal with topics that depend on your having read some previous chapters for basic comprehension. But don't worry; where this sort of thing occurs, I make the point clear.

Whether you've ever made a homebrew — or even tasted one, for that matter — isn't important for you to read and appreciate this book. Even with so many different beers to make and so many different ways to make them, you should eventually be able to master them all after reading *Homebrewing For Dummies,* 2nd Edition. This book not only provides all the parameters of tried-and-true beer styles but also encourages you, the reader, to go off on your own brewing tangent. Be bold, be daring; invent a beer style all your own — just be ready and willing to share it with others.

Conventions Used in This Book

The following conventions are used throughout the *For Dummies* series to make things consistent and easy to understand:

- ✔ All Web addresses appear in `mono font`.
- ✔ New terms appear in *italic* and are closely followed by an easy-to-understand definition.
- ✔ **Bold** is used to highlight the action parts of numbered steps.

I use many additional conventions throughout this book, and I think I should explain them to you:

- ✔ **All recipes and text assume that the batch size is 5 gallons:** Unless I say otherwise, you can assume that all recipes create a 5-gallon batch of beer. The same goes for any other times that I discuss quantities or aspects of a batch of beer.
- ✔ **The text and recipes use U.S. measurements:** Every weight and liquid measurement is given in standard pounds, gallons, and ounces. See the Cheat Sheet at the front of this book for conversions.
- ✔ **All beer styles and beer-style parameters are based on the American Homebrewers Association Beer Style Guidelines:** This hierarchical listing of major beer-style classifications and substyles (which you can find on the Cheat Sheet at the front of this book) was established by the AHA for recipe formulation and evaluation purposes.

What You're Not to Read

I've written this book to help you achieve your dream of becoming a world-class homebrewer. I made a special effort to include as much information about homebrewing as possible. However, you may consider some of this information nonessential and choose to skip certain parts. Here are some parts you may want to pass over, at least until you've had a chance to read the more important stuff.

✔ **Text in sidebars:** The sidebars are the shaded boxes that appear occasionally throughout the book. They share anecdotal information and observations, but aren't necessary reading.

✔ **Technical Stuff icons:** This information is geared toward those folks who thrive on tech-heavy details about homebrewing.

✔ **Any of the fine print**: None of this hard-to-read information is going to help you brew good beer anyway.

Foolish Assumptions

I wrote this book with some thoughts about you in mind. Here's what I assume about you, my reader:

✔ You like beer.

✔ You want to brew your own beer at home.

✔ You weren't convinced brewing good beer at home was possible.

✔ You want to impress your friends and family with your new hobby.

✔ You've already brewed your own beer but want to make it even better.

✔ You're already a homebrewer, but you're looking for all the latest tips, trends, and recipes available.

How This Book Is Organized

I've organized this book into eight parts and crammed several chapters into each part. Feel free to check out the table of contents to find the subject that interests you most (or, more likely, is giving you the most fits). No matter how you decide to use this book, the following sections give you a general idea of what you find between its yellow and black covers.

Part 1: First Things First

When you're ready to begin brewing, you gotta start somewhere. This part gives you the basic homebrewing overview and equipment list so you can get started making your own beer. It also includes the all-important chapter on how to keep your home brewery and equipment clean and sanitized in order to make good beer. After you start brewing and are looking to progress in your hobby, c'mon back to Part I to check out the upgraded equipment lists — you'll be glad you did.

Part II: It's in There: The Nuts and Bolts of Beer

Beer is made with four basic ingredients: barley (malt), hops, yeast, and water. In keeping with this breakdown, I dedicate an entire chapter to each of these gems. Because these ingredients are the very being of beer, I'm sure you'll want to savor every word of these chapters (and every drop of the beer they create). Having said this, however, you'll also find many more ingredients and additives and such that you can use to your advantage when brewing beer at home. That's why I've included an additional two chapters in this part.

Part III: Ready, Set, Brew!

From making your very first kit beer to brewing an entire batch from scratch, the chapters in this part walk you through the various steps necessary at the Beginner, Intermediate, and Advanced levels of homebrewing. And then, of course, you'll need to keep your beer in something until you're ready to drink it, so I've added another couple of chapters to explain options for packaging your beer.

Part IV: Homebrew Recipes

This part is your ticket to paradise. More than 100 recipes at three levels of difficulty are here for you to try and enjoy; many of them are proven award-winners. I also include many beer-style profiles. Bottoms up!

Part V: Alternative Brewing

Sometimes the same-old, same-old doesn't always work for people. That's why I've included some chapters on making alternative beverages by using the equipment you already have. Most of these beverages are about options and personal choice, but at least one chapter deals with making a beverage that addresses important dietary restrictions.

Part VI: Putting Your Brew to the Test

Is your homebrew good? How do you know? Part VI not only helps you to discern quality homebrew on your own but also points you to outside sources of helpful feedback on your beer. Ultimately, this part is about making better beer and about maximizing your brewing and drinking pleasure.

Part VII: The Part of Tens

In the *For Dummies* tradition, the Part of Tens is a small collection of valuable information designed to help answer vexing questions or provide direction to even more helpful information found elsewhere. If you happen to get a chuckle along the way, so much the better.

This book wouldn't be complete without the appendix. I've compiled tons of important homebrewing information for your benefit, and I cross-reference this information often throughout this book. Don't miss it!

Icons Used in This Book

In keeping with the traditional *For Dummies* style, this book uses icons — those little pictures in the margins — to serve as guideposts for various kinds of information. You can use them to pick out information customized to your needs.

Explains technical subjects that are important only if you're really getting into homebrewing (or you're a techno-head). Those who are neither of these can skip these sections altogether.

Flags information that, if not read carefully, can cause you to botch a batch of beer.

Shows pointers, suggestions, and recommendations that can make your homebrewing go more smoothly.

Draws your attention to important information you should remember for future reference. Sometimes it flags material that I've already mentioned elsewhere but that you should read again (for good measure).

Highlights some highly recommended products, services, or techniques. Try 'em — you'll be glad you did!

The "things that make you go 'huh!' " member of the icon family. Tells funny, intriguing, or just plain interesting beer trivia or lore. Excellent material for homebrewing banter with your friends, if you're into that sort of thing.

Where to Go from Here

Now that you have a quick overview of what to expect from this book, you can begin your trek through the world of homebrewing. Go ahead, flip through the book or begin with Chapter 1 — it doesn't matter to me. All I ask is that you have fun with your hobby and never take yourself or your brew too seriously.

Still here? What are you waiting for?

Part I
First Things First

"Great homebrew! By the way, whatever happened to that buddy of yours, the Tin Man?"

In this part . . .

Homebrewing is a fun and enjoyable hobby, but you can't join in the fun until you have a little understanding of the craft as well as the necessary equipment. Chapters 1 and 2 give you just the information you need to get started. Chapter 3 tells you how to keep your brewery and all your equipment good and clean, and a good, clean brewery means good, clean beer.

Chapter 1

Welcome to the Wonderful World of Wort

In This Chapter

▶ Why brew at home?

▶ Do I have what it takes?

*O*ne vexing question for the homebrewer wannabe is "why go through the trouble of brewing beer at home when I can just buy it at the local store?"

Well, for starters, brewing beer at home is no trouble if you enjoy what you're doing, and with the help of this book, you can certainly enjoy homebrewing. Secondly, homebrewed beer can be every bit as good as — if not better than — a lot of commercial beer, with more flavor and character than most. In fact, avoiding mass-market beer was the original inspiration for homebrewing. Thirdly, homebrewing is a hobby that pays many dividends, from having your own house brand of beer to hanging colorful award ribbons on your wall to earning the undying admiration of your beer-drinking buddies. (***Warning:*** Admiration can be addictive.)

In this chapter, I give you an overview of the topics covered in detail in the rest of the book as well as a bit of the history of homebrewing and its recent surge in popularity.

Homebrewers Abound!

Becoming a homebrewer means you're in good company. According to the American Homebrewers Association (AHA) in Boulder, Colorado, an estimated 1 million homebrewers are brewing in the United States. That's a lot of brewers. And the hobby continues to expand every year. Recent estimates indicate that over 1,000 homebrew supply retailers and several hundred homebrewing clubs have popped up in response to homebrewing's growing popularity. Most of these clubs are small, but the national group (AHA) boasts 15,000 members. Homebrewing associations are growing worldwide, too.

The explosive growth in homebrewing has been closely mirrored by a tremendous increase in small, craft breweries in the U.S. — this is no coincidence. Since homebrewing became legal almost 30 years ago, the interest in hand-crafted beer has blossomed, and over 1,500 brewpubs and microbreweries have opened in this same period of time. The growth in the American craft-brewing industry has been so dynamic that even European countries with long and respected brewing histories have had no choice but to sit up and take notice. Small, craft breweries have begun opening up in Canada, England, Germany, and elsewhere in Europe.

In the more than 20 years that I've been involved in homebrewing, I've had the pleasure of meeting and speaking with hundreds of people who share a common interest in beer and homebrewing. Here are some of the reasons so many folks seem to enjoy brewing their own beer:

- To participate in the do-it-yourself homebrewing trend — what other hobby allows you to drink the fruits of your labor?
- To make beers comparable to hard-to-find microbrews and expensive brews from around the world.
- To share homebrewed beer with friends and family members (beware of mooches).

All the Right Stuff

New homebrewers are no different from other hobbyists; they're champing at the bit (or foaming at the mouth) to get started with their hobby. Although this unbridled enthusiasm is good, jumping headlong into the unknown isn't. You need to incorporate some degree of planning into your decision to home-brew. What kind of equipment do I need, and where can I find it? How much time do I need to dedicate to this whole process? What kind of ingredients do I need, and where can I buy them? What other preparations do I need to make? What do I do with the beer when I finish brewing? Can I take a homebrewer's deduction on the IRS 1040 long form? These are the questions you need to ask (and answer!) before you make the plunge. Conveniently, all the answers you need are right here in this book. (And no, the IRS doesn't give a home-brewer's tax deduction. Sorry.)

Gathering the equipment you need

Like having the right tools to do work around your house, having the right equipment for brewing your beer is essential.

Although the equipment needed at the beginner level is relatively inexpensive, you may want to try your hand at brewing beer without the cost commitment of buying the equipment first. If you're fortunate enough to live near one, try brewing a batch of beer at a *Brew On Premises* (BOP), using the BOP's equipment and facilities. (BOPs are breweries at which individuals can brew their own batch of beer.) If you happen to know of other homebrewers in your area, ask to participate in one of their brews so you can get a feel for the hobby, or search out local homebrew clubs for assistance.

If you're ready to commit to buying your own equipment, check out Chapter 2 for all the details on the equipment required to get started and pursue each level of brewing thereafter.

Tracing the homebrewing timeline

Homebrewing wannabes are understandably concerned with how much of a time commitment is necessary to brew beer at home. To someone not familiar with the fermentation processes, this takes a little extra explaining. First, you have the hands-*on* part of brewing: the actual cooking of the *wort* (unfermented beer; rhymes with *dirt*) on the stovetop, the *fermentation* (conversion of sugars to alcohol and CO_2 by yeast) and *aging* (maturation) processes, and then the bottling of the beer. What most people aren't aware of is the hands-*off* part of brewing — the stage when the brewer does nothing but wait patiently. This part not only constitutes the longest segment of the timeline, but it also represents a test of the brewer's patience and self-restraint.

At the beginner level, you need at least two or three hours on brewing day to properly sanitize the equipment, brew and cool the wort, *pitch* the yeast (add it to your wort), seal the fermenter, and clean up whatever mess you made. (Part III details the brewing day process.) You need to set aside the same amount of time on the day you bottle the beer. (Chapter 13 provides all you need to know about bottling.)

In between the brewing and bottling days, however, you face the little matter of fermentation. The yeast needs at least seven days to complete the fermentation cycle — sometimes more, depending on extenuating circumstances. You need do nothing more than wait patiently for the yeast to complete its task. Even after you've bottled your beer, you still need to wait patiently while your brew conditions in the bottles — two weeks is the recommended minimum length of this conditioning process.

At the beginner level, if you brew on a Saturday your brewing timeline may look something like the following:

1. Brew day (S). **Ferment the beer Su-M-T-W-Th-F.**
2. Bottle day (S). **Condition the beer Su-M-T-W-Th-F-S-Su-M-T-W-Th-F.**
3. **Drink the beer!**

As you begin to employ different ingredients, equipment, and processes in your beer-making repertoire, expect the timeline to expand. Secondary fermentation (a helpful extra aging step — see Chapter 11) adds another two weeks to the timeline, and advanced brewers, for example, may spend as many as eight to ten hours in a single day brewing their beer from grain (see Chapter 12).

Please note that homebrewing is a pursuit that requires a higher degree of dedication than, say, su doku puzzles, but the rewards are considerable (and tasty!) In addition to personal gratification, quality homebrew can inspire a certain respect from your fellow brewers, awe in nonbrewers, and other intangibles that make all the effort worthwhile.

Adding ingredients galore!

Like various kinds of bread, all beer styles consist of the same basic ingredients. The difference is that the ingredients vary slightly in attributes and quantities required from one beer style to the next. Although wheat bread may look and taste different than rye bread, they're very much alike and made in very much the same way.

At the commercial level, brewing uses grain (mostly malted barley), hops, yeast, and water (see Chapters 4 through 7). Thanks to many stores and Internet sites that specialize in homebrewing supplies, homebrewers today have access to most of the same ingredients used by corporate brewhouses everywhere. Of course, these shops don't just provide the everyday ingredients for the average beer; different hop varieties and yeast strains from around the world are now available in the homebrewing market.

With the help of specially made products, such as malt syrup derived from grain (see Chapter 4), beginner homebrewers can easily produce beers that emulate those made commercially. Intermediate- and advanced-level homebrewers may even make their beer with the same grains used by their favorite commercial brewers.

Beyond the four basic building blocks of beer, dozens of other flavorings and additives can contribute different flavors and textures to your brew (see Chapter 8), and a number of other agents can affect the appearance of your brew (see Chapter 9).

Although thriftiness is a virtue, you need high-quality ingredients to produce high-quality beer — so loosen your grip on the purse strings when buying homebrew ingredients.

Not all of these ingredients are necessary to make great beer, but they exist for you, the brewer, to use if you're so inclined. In your house, you're the Head Brewer — you make the choices (but read about 'em in Parts II and III first).

Like home cooking, homebrewing doesn't come with an automatic guarantee of quality. Certain responsibilities and expectations are squarely on the brewer to ensure that each batch of beer turns out right. Failure to heed simple rules and suggestions can result in a less-than-perfect brew and a waste of time, effort, and money.

Preparing wisely

Good homebrew starts with good preparation, and good preparation starts with a complete list of ingredients. Nothing is more aggravating than starting your brewing procedures only to find that you're missing a necessary ingredient. Before you head off to your homebrew supply shop or submit a mail-order form, consider all your needs. Occasionally, homebrewers fail to look beyond the beer recipe and forget something as simple — but essential — as bottle caps.

Another important preparation consideration is having the brewery in order — clearing your workspace of clutter and having all your equipment present and accounted for (see Chapter 2). Removing free-roaming pets to another part of the house is always a good idea.

Sanitizing your equipment is also high on the preparation checklist (see Chapter 3); you never want your brew to come in contact with equipment that isn't properly clean and sanitized to protect against beer-ruining bacteria.

All done — now what?

So, say your beer is done and ready to drink — what next? Well, grab a bottle opener, a clean beer glass, and a seat, because it's time to revel in your success. While you're admiring the brew in your glass and savoring its flavor on your palate, consider how you can best commemorate your efforts:

- ✔ Invite a bunch of your closest (and thirstiest) buddies over to sample it.

- ✔ Give it away as gifts to close friends and family members deserving of your time and talent.

- ✔ Increase your good standing with bosses and other influential people by presenting them with a bottle of beer of your own making.

- ✔ Swap a couple of bottles with other homebrewers in your area.

- ✔ Submit some entries to homebrew competitions around the country. (See Chapter 25 to find out more about homebrew competitions.)

One of the most incredible awards is having your homebrew replicated and sold by a nationally distributed brand — kinda like your mom's chocolate chip cookies being made by Sara Lee. Several well-known microbrewers solicit homebrew entries to their own annual, sponsored competitions. The winners may receive a cash award and royalties or have their beer recipe reproduced as a one-time-only specialty beer and sold to the public. For example, every year the Boston Beer Company hosts the Samuel Adams LongShot competition. Two winners get their beer brewed, packaged, and nationally distributed for a limited time in the LongShot Variety Pack. Check out `http://www.samuel adams.com/promotions/LongShot/Default.aspx` for more information on entering this contest.

Or you can do as I do when I'm particularly pleased with a batch of brew — hoard it, hide it, jealously guard it, and only take a bottle out to celebrate the most sublime accomplishments in life — like making another batch of great beer!

Chapter 2

Setting Up Your Beeraphernalia

In This Chapter

▶ Shopping for homebrew shops

▶ Understanding the three levels of equipment and equipment prices

▶ Deciding what equipment you need and when

Forget any preconceived notions you may have about shiny copper kettles and coils taking up your whole kitchen and huge wooden vats bubbling and churning in the cellar — those notions are the product of vivid imaginations and vintage Hollywood movies. Human civilization is well into the stainless-steel and plastic age, where everything is smaller, more durable, and lighter weight.

Every homebrewer is a first-time brewer at least once, which means that every homebrewer needs to start with at least the minimum amount of equipment. With its barest essentials, homebrewing requires three tools: a *brewpot* in which you boil the *wort* (the German term for beer before it's fermented), a container in which you ferment the beer (the *fermenter*), and bottles in which you package the beer.

If this list sounds overly simplistic, that's because it is. Actually, the proper brewpot needs to conform to specific acceptable parameters, the fermenter must be airtight and yet be able to vent carbon dioxide, and the bottles require bottle caps, which in turn require a bottle-capping device. And your list of needs has only begun.

You also want a number of smaller (but no less important) items that all brewers need to have in their breweries. And as you may find out, brewers who continue to brew beer are likely to continue to buy or build additional time- and effort-saving equipment as they need it. This chapter discusses the necessary equipment at all levels of homebrewing because more advanced equipment is required to produce the more advanced beer styles found later in the book.

Don't panic — just follow along at your own pace. You don't need to progress to levels you're not comfortable with. Although some brewers feel compelled to advance as rapidly as possible, others find their niche and stick with it. Above all else, homebrewing should be an enjoyable undertaking.

Sniffing Out Sources

The first step in your homebrewing expedition is to locate your local home-brew supply retailer. I suggest that you start with the phone book; try looking under "Hobbies" or "Beer." Stop in at your local homebrew supply shop and ask for a catalog and price list (if they have one). Take a look at the equipment and supplies; ask questions about the stock — especially the ingredients. To the first-timer, the vast quantities of equipment and ingredient choices can be somewhat intimidating.

You may find (as many people have) that you don't have a local retailer in your area, in which case mail order is the next best thing. Many mail-order shops have toll-free phone numbers or Web sites for ordering, and most offer free catalogs, many of which are both extensive and information-packed. Homebrewing equipment varies, as shown in Figure 2-1, and any homebrew supply shop worth its salt can get you just about anything you need or desire (for homebrewing, that is!)

Figure 2-1:
Many homebrew shops sell this basic equipment as a start-up kit.

Square One: Equipment for the Beginning Brewer

Square one generally denotes a starting point (although it's also been used to describe this author), and this section is no different: It serves as the starting point in your homebrewing career. Before you can embark on this career path, however, you need to buy the tools of the trade.

So much equipment, so little time . . .

For the benefit of beginning homebrewers, in this section I recommend and discuss only the minimal amount of equipment needed; however, I may mention additional convenient and time- and effort-saving pieces along the way. Thrift is also a consideration; I typically recommend cheaper alternatives over more expensive equipment and methods.

Many homebrew equipment suppliers sell prepackaged starter kits that can range from the bare-bones to the top-of-the-line — all-inclusive starter kits can run up to $200. All these kits include the basic equipment essentials, but some kits also throw in books, videos, or other unnecessary items that just inflate the price. Before you buy a kit, consider what you need and what you want to spend. To help you get the wheels turning, Table 2-1 gives you a starter list of necessary items and their approximate costs.

If you go high-end on all your equipment, your cost adds up to well over a couple hundred dollars, not including the cost of bottles (see the section "What do I do with all these gadgets?" in this chapter for more information about bottles and their cost). If you buy the smaller brewpot and a two-handed capper to cut some corners, you can save about 25 bucks.

Table 2-1	Beginner Brewing Equipment and Its Cost
Equipment	**Approximate Cost**
Brewpot, 16 qt. minimum	$40/20 qt., $80/30 qt.
Brew spoon (HDPE plastic)	$4 or less
Primary fermenter (HDPE plastic) with spigot, lid	$20 or less
Airlock	$2 or less
Drilled rubber stopper for airlock	$2 or less
3 to 4 feet of food-grade plastic hose, ½ inch in diameter	$3

(continued)

Table 2-1 *(continued)*

Equipment	Approximate Cost
Bottling or "priming" bucket (HDPE plastic) with spigot	$15 or less
Bottles (must be the reusable type that don't use twist-off caps)	$20–$30 for one batch of beer (5 gallons); the exact number of bottles depends on their size: 12 oz., 16 oz., 22 oz., or 1 qt.
Bottle rinser	$12
Bottle brush	$3
Bottling tube (HDPE plastic) with spring valve	$4 or less
Bottle capper	$35 (bench-type) or $15 (two-handed)
Hydrometer (triple scale) with cylinder	$10 ($5 or less for the cylinder)

What do I do with all these gadgets?

Okay, you've read the list in Table 2-1 and made your own list of what equipment you need. You're ready to go shopping, right? Not so fast. You probably want to understand a little bit about what it is you're buying. The following list gives you some insights into what all these gadgets do so you can be a more informed consumer.

- ✔ **Brewpot:** Chances are you already have a large pot of some sort in your kitchen, but if your brewpot is made of enamel-coated metal, make sure it's not chipped where it may come in contact with your beer. Your brewpot also needs to have a minimum 16-quart capacity, but I highly recommend you go ahead and upgrade to the 20- or 30-quart pot listed in Table 2-1.

   The more of your wort you boil, the better for your finished beer. So, when it comes to brewpots, the bigger the better.

- ✔ **Brew spoon:** Regardless of how well equipped your kitchen is, every homebrewer needs to have a spoon dedicated for brewing beer and nothing else. A brew spoon needs to be stainless steel or HDPE (food-grade) plastic, and it needs to have a long handle — 18 inches or more. Avoid wooden spoons because they can't be kept thoroughly sanitized (and they can splinter).

✔ **Primary fermenter:** The *primary fermenter* is where you pour the cooled wort shortly after you're done brewing. You must be able to seal this vessel airtight for the duration of the fermentation. A primary fermenter needs to have a minimum capacity of 7 gallons and an airtight lid with a hole in it (to accommodate an airlock with an attached rubber stopper). These specially made plastic fermenters come with removable plastic spigots positioned near the bottom for easy use.

The kinds of plastics used in homebrewing are of the same quality and standards as those plastics used in the food industry. In fact, another name for *HDPE (high-density polyethylene)* is *food-grade plastic.* Unlike lesser grades of plastic, HDPE restricts gaseous transfer through the plastic (though not completely).

✔ **Airlock:** An *airlock* is an inexpensive (but incredibly simple and efficient) tool that allows the carbon dioxide gases to escape from the fermenter during fermentation without compromising the antiseptic environment within. Filled halfway with water, this setup lets gas escape without allowing any air (and, therefore, germs) into the fermenter. A similar contraption, called a *bubbler,* is a two-chambered device that works on the same principle. The difference is that you can easily clean and sanitize the inside of an airlock (unlike the totally enclosed bubbler). Both mechanisms work equally well otherwise, but the airlock, shown in Figure 2-2, is my first choice.

Figure 2-2: An airlock allows carbon dioxide to escape from the fermenter.

Bubbler   3-Piece airlock

✓ **Drilled rubber stopper:** You need a rubber stopper to fit over the stem of the airlock or bubbler to act as a wedge when you insert the airlock into the hole in the fermenter lid. These drilled stoppers come in numbered sizes (for example, a #3 stopper). Be sure you buy a stopper that fits the opening in your fermenter lid. (Your homebrew equipment supplier can determine what you need.)

✓ **Plastic hose:** Flexible plastic hosing is a multifunctional piece of equipment you use to transfer your beer from vessel to vessel or from vessel to bottle. It's an important part of your equipment package and one that you need to always keep clean and undamaged. You want to have 3 to 5 feet of hosing.

✓ **Bottling bucket:** The *bottling bucket* is a vessel you need on bottling day. It doesn't require a lid, but it's considerably more efficient if you buy a bucket with a removable spigot at the bottom. The bottling bucket is also called a *priming vessel* because you prime your fermented beer with corn sugar just prior to bottling. (I discuss the priming process in detail in Chapter 13.)

✓ **Glass bottles:** Your bottles must be the thick, heavy, returnable kind. Don't use any bottle with a threaded (twist-off) opening — a bottle cap doesn't seal properly across the threads. You need enough bottles to hold 5 gallons of beer: 54 12-ounce bottles, 40 16-ounce bottles, or any combination of bottles that adds up to 640 ounces. You can buy brand-new bottles from a homebrew supply shop, but you can get used bottles much more cheaply from commercial breweries.

Find out whether a local liquor store sells any beer in returnable bottles (not the cheap recyclable kind). If it does, buy a couple of cases, drink the beer, and voilà! You have 48 bottles (not to mention a swollen bladder and a nasty headache).

Another alternative, albeit an initially more expensive one, is to buy the self-sealing *swing-top* bottles. See the sidebar "Swingtime" in Chapter 13 for more information.

✓ **Bottling tube:** A *bottling tube* is a hard plastic tube that's about a foot long and comes with a spring-loaded valve at the tip. You attach the bottling tube to the plastic hosing (which you then attach to the spigot on the bottling bucket) and insert the tube in the bottles when filling them.

✓ **Bottle brush:** A *bottle brush* is another inexpensive but important piece of equipment. You need this soft-bristle brush to properly scrub the inside of the bottles prior to filling.

✓ **Bottle rinser:** A *bottle rinser* is a curved plastic or brass apparatus that you attach to a faucet. It works as an added convenience for rinsing bottles. This device isn't an absolute necessity, but for the money it's a good investment.

If you buy a bottle rinser, take note of which faucet in your home you plan to use. Utility faucets usually have larger hose threads and others, such as bathroom and kitchen faucets, have fine threads where an adapter may be needed. Make sure the bottle rinser and any adapters have a rubber washer (gasket) in place.

✔ **Bottle capper:** You need a *bottle capper* to affix new bottle caps to the filled bottles. These come in all shapes, sizes, and costs.

Most cappers work equally well, but I suggest that you choose a bench-type capper, like the one shown in Figure 2-3, over the two-handed style. A *bench capper* is free-standing and can be attached to a work surface (permanently, if you like), which leaves one hand free to hold the bottle steady.

✔ **Triple-scale hydrometer:** A *hydrometer* is a fragile glass measuring device used to calculate the density of your beer as well as the amount of alcohol that the yeast has produced in your homebrew. *Triple scale* refers to the three different measuring scales within the hydrometer (see the sidebar "Of liquid density and hydrometers . . ." in this chapter).

Some people argue that a hydrometer isn't a necessary piece of equipment at the beginner level. I disagree. A hydrometer isn't very expensive, it's easy to use, and anyone who wants to progress in the world of homebrewing needs to learn how to use one. Therefore, I recommend adding a hydrometer to your initial shopping list — and be sure to buy a plastic cylinder to go with it.

Figure 2-3:
You can attach a bench-type bottle capper to a work surface for easy use.

Of liquid density and hydrometers . . .

A hydrometer is a long, cylindrical, narrow glass device designed to measure liquid density. It's weighted at the bottom and has a numeric scale or scales inside for measuring purposes. With the weighted end submerged in the liquid, the calibrated stem projects out of the liquid; the density of the liquid determines the height of this projection.

A triple-scale hydrometer features three separate scales. Two of them — the *specific gravity scale* and the *Balling scale* — measure *liquid density* (the density of liquids in relation to the density of water), but the third measures potential alcohol. Ordinary water has a specific gravity of 1.000 at 60 degrees Fahrenheit. (For comparison's sake, at the same temperature, gasoline has a specific gravity around 0.66, whole milk is about 1.028, and mercury is 13.600!)

The Balling scale performs the exact same function as the specific gravity scale, except that it reads in different incremental numbers called *degrees Plato.* A homebrew with a specific gravity of 1.048 has a density of 12.5 degrees Plato. (The difference between these two measurement scales is similar to the difference between the Fahrenheit and Celsius temperature scales; homebrewers seem to prefer the specific gravity scale.)

So, what's the point? Measuring the density of your brew accomplishes two goals: It tells you when your brew is done fermenting (and thus, when it's time to bottle your beer), and it allows you to calculate the alcohol potential of your brew. Of course, potential alcohol and actual alcohol are two different things, which is why you need to take two different hydrometer readings. Taking a hydrometer reading before you ferment the wort gives you the *original gravity;* it tells you the *alcohol potential.* Taking a second

hydrometer reading after fermentation is over gives you the *final gravity* (also called *terminal gravity)* and a *final alcohol potential.* Subtracting the F.G. (final gravity) from the O.G. (original gravity) on one scale and the final alcohol potential from the initial alcohol potential on the other scale tells you, in mathematical terms, how much of the sugar your yeast ate and how much alcohol is in your brew.

When yeasts eat sugar they produce alcohol, so any decrease in gravity results in a reciprocal increase in alcohol.

A few things to remember:

✔ Although a hydrometer is a very reliable method of measuring specific gravities and figuring alcohol potentials, the readings skew if the liquid temperature is not near 60 degrees Fahrenheit at reading time. Hot wort readings are lower than they should be and cold bottling readings are higher than they should be due to the temperature-sensitive nature of liquid density. Therefore, always measure at 60 degrees Fahrenheit (or use a *temperature correction scale* — ask your homebrew retailer for details).

✔ Alcohol potential readings are measured in *alcohol by volume* (ABV), not *alcohol by weight* (ABW) (see Chapter 6).

✔ Surface tension in liquids causes something called a *meniscus effect.* The tendency of liquids to cling to other surfaces creates a meniscus. The *meniscus* is the concave appearance of the beer between the wall of the cylinder and the exterior of the hydrometer. Be sure to sight your reading at the lowest point of the meniscus.

✔ A hydrometer, like the one shown in the figure, can also call attention to possible fermentation problems. Average healthy yeasts consume at least 65 percent of available sugars (usually more); if the final gravity reading of your beer is not 35 percent or less of the original gravity, a lot of sugar may still be in the beer (see Chapter 10 for details on taking hydrometer readings).

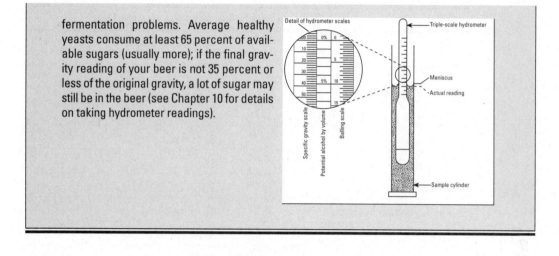

Square Two: Equipment for the Intermediate Brewer

Okay, you've mastered homebrewing techniques at the novice level and you're looking for a bigger challenge. Well, you've come to the right place. This section is for the budding homebrewer who intends to get more personally involved in the brewing processes. A more hands-on approach to anything calls for more specialized equipment (a car owner intending to do her own vehicle maintenance can't get far without the right tools). A lot of different procedures await you at the intermediate level of homebrewing, each with its own degree of difficulty (see Chapter 11).

Now what do I need?

The list of equipment in Table 2-2 is based on the additional needs of the homebrewer who endeavors to try all of the procedures outlined in Chapter 11. Those brewers who aren't compelled to try all the intermediate brewing procedures need to pick and choose the items that best suit their needs and levels of confidence. Figure 2-4 shows a couple of the more important items you need.

Table 2-2	Intermediate Equipment and Its Cost
Equipment	*Approximate Cost*
Glass carboy (5 gallon)	$23 or less
Another airlock	$2 or less
Rubber stopper for carboy (drilled)	$2 or less
Carboy brush	$5 or less
Racking tube or cane	$3
8-inch plastic funnel	$10 or less
Kitchen strainer	$10 or less
Sparge bags	$5 (reusable nylon)
	$.50 (throw-away)
Lab immersion thermometer (or similar)	$8
Grain mill	$100 and up
Kitchen or postal scale	$20–$30

Figure 2-4:
A glass carboy and a hand-cranked grain mill are important additions that you may want to make to your home brewery.

Glass carboy

Hand-cranked grain mill

What do these gizmos even do?

New challenges in homebrewing often call for new equipment. Before you take off on this new adventure, take a gander at the following list so you know exactly what you need and why you need it.

- ✔ **Glass carboy:** *Carboys* are the large cylindrical jugs that water delivery companies used for years until they switched to the plastic carboys used today. Because plastic carboys aren't really appropriate for homebrewing use, you need to purchase a glass carboy from your local homebrew supply store. The principal use for a glass carboy in homebrewing is as a secondary fermenter, where you age and mature your beer.

  Carboys may come in 3- to 15-gallon capacities, but the 5-gallon size best matches the typical batch of homebrew; therefore, it's probably the best choice for homebrewing purposes.

- ✔ **Rubber stopper:** If you intend to use the carboy as a fermenter, you need another drilled rubber stopper to fit the carboy's neck (usually a #6 or #7 stopper). As with the plastic primary fermenter, the carboy needs to be sealed with an airlock while the beer inside is aging.

- ✔ **Airlock:** You may not actually need another airlock in the brewery, but you may find you like to have a spare one around — besides, it costs less than a couple of bucks!

  Having a second airlock allows you to brew two batches in quick succession. While one batch is aging in the carboy, another can be fermenting in the primary fermenter.

- ✔ **Carboy brush:** If you want to continue to use the carboy as a fermenter, you need a carboy brush. This heavy-duty, soft-bristle brush is specially designed to reach every curve and corner of the carboy during cleaning.

- ✔ **Racking tube:** *Racking* is the act of transferring beer from one vessel to another, or into bottles, while leaving yeast sediment and particulate matter behind. Because carboys don't offer the convenience of a spigot, you need a hard-plastic, curved racking tube — also called a *cane* — to siphon the beer out.

- ✔ **Funnel:** Because the opening of the carboy is so small, a good funnel is a handy thing to have around. I recommend one with an opening at least 8 inches in diameter.

- ✔ **Kitchen strainer:** With the addition of loose grain, hops, and other ingredients to your brewpot, a strainer with a handle becomes a necessary piece of equipment. Food-grade steel mesh is better than plastic; don't settle for a strainer with a diameter of less than 10 inches or one without a strong handle. You may have to go to a culinary specialty store to find the right one.

✔ **Sparge bags:** Regardless of whether you have a strainer, *sparge bags* are effective for steeping grain or keeping whole-leaf hops under control in the brewpot. You can buy reusable nylon bags with drawstrings, or you can buy the inexpensive throw-away kind.

✔ **Lab immersion thermometer:** Because temperature control becomes more and more important in brewing at the intermediate level, you probably want to have an immersion thermometer in your brewery. A lab-quality immersion thermometer is capable of temperature readings above the boiling point (212 degrees Fahrenheit or 100 degrees Celsius at sea level) and as low as 40 degrees Fahrenheit (or 4.4 degrees Celsius).

✔ **Grain mill:** A *grain mill* is one of the more expensive items you need. You use the grain mill to crack the grain prior to brewing with it. You can buy precracked grain, but many homebrew stores don't crack it properly (and precracked grain can also go stale more quickly). The mill-less homebrewer can find inventive ways to crack the grain, such as putting it into a large sealable plastic bag and rolling it with a rolling pin or baseball bat.

Whatever you do, don't use a coffee grinder to do your grain milling. If you do, your grain ends up looking like sawdust — and how it looks is just the beginning of your problems. Grinding your grain too finely causes your beer to have an unpleasant, bitter, astringent taste.

✔ **Kitchen or postal scale:** After you start to brew beer according to specific recipes, you may find that you need many ingredients in small quantities. A good kitchen or postal scale is vital to getting these quantities just right because it can measure fractions of ounces.

Square Three: Equipment for the Advanced Brewer

Some homebrewers become so completely engrossed and absorbed in their hobby that their craving for homebrewing information is only surpassed by their need to take full control of the brewing processes they perform. Welcome to the world of advanced homebrewing (also known as homebrewing geekdom).

What separates this level of homebrewing from the intermediate level (besides this mania) is that you produce wort from grain only — just like the commercial brewers make beer. To do so, you must master the process known as *mashing*. Mashing is the method of producing your wort from raw grain instead of using malt syrup. (See Chapter 12 for more on mashing.) And even though the learning curve is pretty steep, mashing allows you to make cheaper and potentially more-flavorful beer.

I need even more stuff?

As you progress even farther up the homebrewing evolutionary ladder, you need to obtain the proper equipment for your brewing needs. Table 2-3 shows you the additional items that are necessary to perform the brewing procedures outlined in the advanced brewing chapter (Chapter 12). You may have already purchased some of these items for the intermediate level of brewing, which means you're ahead of the game. If you kept your wallet close to your hip at the beginner and intermediate levels, here's where the cost is gonna catch up to you.

Table 2-3	Advanced Equipment and Its Cost
Equipment	*Approximate Price*
Large-volume brewpot (7+ gallons)	$80 or more
12–20 qt. brewpot (to mash in)	$0 (you should already have one at this brewing level)
Lauter tun	$20
3–8 qt. stock pot (for holding sparge water)	$0 (you should already have one at this brewing level)
Immersion wort chiller	$50 or less
pH papers	$4
Lab immersion thermometer	$8
Grain mill (if not using preground malt)	$100 and up
Kitchen or postal scale	$20–$30
Gypsum (calcium sulfate)	$2 or less
Calcium carbonate (food-grade chalk)	$2 or less
Calcium chloride	$2 or less

Note: These items are absolutely necessary for all-grain brewing (making your beer from nothing but grain), but not necessarily for partial-mash brewing (making your beer primarily from extract but adding more fermentable ingredients by also using grain).

In addition to these brewery-specific items, you need a set of ordinary measuring spoons for some of the testing techniques.

What else could I possibly need another doodad for?

Okay, you've handled all the intermediate homebrewing procedures with ease. Now you really want to brew beer like the pros, but you need the equipment that helps you do that. Study this list (and double-check the balances on your credit cards).

Check out Chapter 26 to find out how to make many of these items inexpensively. Chapter 12 discusses many of these items and processes in greater depth.

- ✔ **Large-volume brewpot:** Because all-grain brewing requires you to boil the entire volume of beer, you need a brewpot that is large enough to hold 7 gallons or more of wort (which eventually boils down to 5 gallons) with room to spare at the top. Purchased new, this item can be a major expense. Check local garage sales and thrift stores. You can also find cheaper, large-volume ceramic-lined pots from other equipment sources (or simply make the brewpot yourself by following the directions in Chapter 26).

- ✔ **Mashing brewpot (12-20 quarts):** If you already have a smaller brewpot left from your beginner days, that's all you need here.

- ✔ **Lauter tun:** A *lauter tun* is a fairly simple device that allows you to drain the wort away from the grain after the mashing process. It basically acts as a large-volume strainer or colander. See Chapter 26 for instructions on building your own lauter tun.

- ✔ **Stock pot (4-8 quarts):** You use this pot to heat water for sparging purposes. *Sparging* is pouring hot water through the bed of grain in your lauter tun to recapture all the malt sugars still contained within it. You can use any household pot capable of holding this volume of water.

- ✔ **Immersion wort chiller:** An *immersion wort chiller* is basically a coil of ⅜- to ½-inch copper tubing with a fitting on one end that connects to a water source. As the coil is immersed in the hot wort, cold water flowing through the tubing removes the heat by thermal conductivity. The hot water flowing out the opposite end can be recaptured and used for various purposes. Check out Chapter 26 for information on building an immersion wort chiller.

- ✔ **pH papers:** These disposable test papers are absolutely necessary for the mashing processes described in the advanced brewing chapter. pH papers measure the acidity and alkalinity of your water. Simply dip the test strip into your wort for about one minute and then compare the strip to the color comparison chart. (See Figure 2-5.)

Always work in good lighting when testing pH.

- ✔ **Lab immersion thermometer:** An important piece of equipment at the intermediate level, this thermometer is absolutely necessary for the mashing procedures in all-grain brewing.

- ✔ **Grain mill:** Unless you want to continue to rely on other people to grind your grain for you (and often charge you for the service) or whack an enormous amount of grain yourself with a rolling pin, you want to invest in a good grain mill. Don't say I didn't warn you.

- ✔ **Kitchen or postal scale:** A good scale is absolutely necessary at this brewing level. You may opt to buy a scale at a culinary specialty store. Check out Table 2-2 for pricing information.

- ✔ **Gypsum:** Along with calcium carbonate and calcium chloride, you may need gypsum to adjust the pH of your water. You can use gypsum to simulate the gypsum-laden water of Burton-on-Trent, but it only lowers pH when mashed with grain. For more information on the unique brewing water of Burton-on-Trent, see Chapter 7.

- ✔ **Calcium carbonate:** Calcium carbonate raises pH. You can also use it to simulate the water sources of classic stouts and porters.

- ✔ **Calcium chloride:** You can use calcium chloride in place of gypsum to lower pH without increasing the sulfate level in the water. It also works in place of salt (sodium chloride) to add chlorides without increasing the sodium content of the water.

With the addition of all these new and larger pieces of equipment to your collection, your kitchen is likely to become a lot more cluttered on brewing day. And in order to get a large-volume brewpot up to a rolling boil, you're also probably going to want increased burner output and heating capacity.

Figure 2-5:
Testing pH
is an
important
part of the
advanced
brewing
process.

Chillin' out

Because the advanced level of homebrewing involves *full-wort boils* (boiling the entire batch of wort at once), it's imperative that you're able to cool 5 gallons of wort down quickly — cold water baths in your kitchen sink just don't cut it anymore.

Although the immersion-type wort chiller listed in Table 2-3 is a dandy (and highly recommended) piece of equipment, the gadget-freak homebrew geek can find another, more efficient wort-chilling device. It's called a *counter-flow* wort chiller, and it's more like the chillers commercial breweries use. At the homebrewing level, a counter-flow chiller consists of a copper tube (much like the immersion-type wort chiller) inserted into a rubber hose. While the hot wort runs through the copper tubing in one direction, cold water runs through the hose in the other direction. This process cools the wort very rapidly while allowing the brewer to recapture the hot water flowing out the end of the hose for future use.

For these reasons (and others), many advanced brewers have moved their brewing operations into their basements, garages, and utility rooms (and some of their spouses have moved to new addresses). Although this expansion idea has merit, never overlook the safety considerations of such a move — have you ever tried to explain homebrewing procedures to an insurance claims adjuster?

Chapter 3

Creating Your Own Department of Sanitation

In This Chapter

▶ Understanding the importance of cleanliness

▶ Keeping those beer-swilling fungi and bacteria at bay

▶ Determining the best cleaning agents for your equipment

▶ Cleaning and sanitizing your equipment

So you have all your brewing equipment, and now you're ready to brew, right? Not so fast, rookie.

Anyone who intends to become a proficient brewer of good beer must properly clean and sanitize all brewing equipment first. You can find out about sanitation techniques in several different ways. You can read about sanitizing, ask other brewers sanitation questions, and experiment with sanitizers on your own. Or — I guarantee — you can find out about them by accident. Contaminating a batch of beer out of carelessness is a painful lesson to endure. The only fate worse than throwing out 5 gallons of bad beer is drinking 5 gallons of bad beer (hiccup) — especially after you've spent your time and effort bottling it all. In this chapter, I explore the different levels of cleanliness required by brewing and give you information on the products and practices that can help you meet those standards. I also discuss the nasty little vermin these practices help you fight.

No Dirty Words: Sanitation Lingo

Scrupulously clean brewing equipment and a pristine brewing environment are the keys to making good beer. And by clean, I don't mean just soap-and-water clean. In homebrewing, serious sanitation is necessary.

Take a closer look at a few important words used in this chapter. *Clean,* as it pertains to homebrewing, means that you've removed all dust, dirt, scum, stains, and other visible contaminants from your brewing equipment and bottles to the best of your ability. After the visible contaminants are history, you need to *sanitize* your equipment and bottles; sanitation is the elimination of invisible contaminants (bacteria and other microorganisms) that can ruin your brew. Clean requires a little elbow grease; sanitized requires chemicals.

Never assume that clean equipment is sanitized, and never assume sanitized equipment is clean. For the good of your beer, practice good cleaning and sanitizing techniques — in that order.

A third and equally important word is *sterilize*. Sterilization is another method of germ-killing accomplished with very high temperatures (over 200 degrees Fahrenheit). Boiling your wort for at least an hour is an effective way of sterilizing the ingredients in your beer. After your wort cools, however, air-borne, water-borne, and human-borne germs can easily recontaminate it. For this reason, clean and sanitized equipment is imperative. From the boiling point forward, you need to treat your wort like a person without an immune system — safeguarded from the bacterial world.

Battling Bacteria (and Fungi)

Nothing is more important to your production of clean, drinkable, and enjoyable beer than utilizing proper sanitizing procedures prior to your brewing. You must sanitize or sterilize anything and everything that will come into contact with your beer at any time.

"What's the big deal?" you may ask. Well, millions of hungry *microbes* just love to make meals of freshly brewed beer. These microbes are in your home, on your body, and even in the air you breathe (cough, wheeze). Bacteria and fungi are the forms of microbes that you need to be wary of — they're both opportunistic, and if you let them have their way with your brew, they do so (always with negative results). Beer that bacteria has contaminated smells and tastes awful.

Ironically, certain bacteria and fungi work for the betterment of beer, but only under strict control. Because the classification *fungi* consists of mold spores and wild yeast, beer yeast actually falls into the fungus category. However, beer yeasts are of the friendly, laboratory-controlled variety. A couple of strains of bacteria also show up in beer (intentionally), but mostly in specific Belgian specialty beers that are still fermented in microbe–harboring, oak fermentation vessels.

Fungi and bacteria thrive in very warm temperatures — up to 120 degrees Fahrenheit. The activity of these microbes does tend to decrease as the temperature drops, which is why cooling down your hot wort as quickly as possible is imperative (as further described in Chapter 10). The cooler, the better.

No pathos for pathogens

Because freshly brewed beer is warm and sweet, it's the perfect breeding ground for microbiological opportunists. However, none of the bacteria that grow in beer are even remotely as harmful as the bacteria found in raw eggs, fish, or uncooked meat that cause people to become deathly ill. The germs that breed in beer are just free-loading little buggers that make your beer taste bad. Beer germs can't kill you, but throwing out a batch of brew just may.

So, how can you get rid of these little beer-ruining pests? Well, in truth, you can't really get rid of them completely; the idea is to keep them away from your beer (or at least minimize their effect). I provide the following helpful tips to assist you in deterring these foes:

- ✔ Keep your brewery (kitchen, laundry room, basement, or wherever you make your beer) as clean and dust-free as possible.

- ✔ Quarantine all furry, four-legged family pets in another part of the house while you brew or bottle your beer.

- ✔ Consider every cough and sneeze a threat to your beer.

- ✔ Finally, treat your equipment well. Clean and sanitize it properly prior to brewing, rinse it well, and dry it off after every use and before storing it away. Keep your equipment stored in a dust- and mildew-free location if at all possible. You may even want to go as far as sealing all your equipment in large-capacity garbage bags between brewing sessions.

Soaps for Suds: Cleansers and Sanitizers

The variety of chemicals that you can use to clean and sanitize your home-brewing equipment includes iodine-based products, chlorine-based products, *caustics* (which can burn your skin), ammonia, and a couple of environmentally safe cleansers that contain oxygen-based *percarbonates*. The following bits of information are some pros and cons to the use of these various chemicals:

- ✔ **Ammonia** is good for cleaning bottles in a dilution of 1 cup of ammonia to 5 gallons of water — if you can stand the pungent odor. If you use ammonia for sanitizing, be sure to give your equipment a thorough hot-water rinse. Also, make sure to avoid prolonged exposure to ammonia fumes, and wear gloves if you have sensitive skin. Goggles are also a good idea.

- ✔ **Chlorine** is an ingredient in simple household bleach, which is very effective and cost-efficient for cleaning homebrewing equipment. One ounce of bleach per gallon of water is sufficient, which makes a gallon of generic bleach an incredibly good deal. Be sure to buy unscented bleach and to rinse all equipment thoroughly with hot water. An exception: Chlorine bleach can corrode stainless steel brewing equipment, so avoid using bleach for these items if you can. If bleach is your only option, see Chapter 14 for more on this issue.

  Never mix ammonia with chlorine bleach; this combination releases toxic chlorine gas.

- ✔ **Iodine-based sanitizers** are popular in the medical field and the restaurant and commercial brewing industries as a disinfectant. You can apply iodine's disinfectant properties to homebrewing, but note that it stains plastics as well as human skin. Although iodine-based products may vary in strength, the typical dilution ratio is 1 ounce of iodine per 5 gallons of water. Iodine-based products are also FDA-approved as no-rinse sanitizers.

- ✔ **Lye** is a caustic that you want to use only to remove the most stubborn stains and obstinate organic material from bottles or glass carboys. Technically, caustics are cleansers and not sanitizers. However, most small concentrations of caustic material dissolve and kill almost any bacteria and organic buildup. If you use lye, make sure that you always wear protective gear, such as goggles and rubber gloves.

- ✔ **Percarbonates** accomplish their cleaning activity with oxygen molecules; they produce oxygen bubbles and help to loosen soils. Because of this unique cleaning method, sanitizers that work with percarbonates, such as One Step, don't require rinsing.

- ✔ **Sodium metabisulphite** is another food-grade sanitizer that doesn't require rinsing. A 4-ounce-to-1-gallon dilution is a standard mixture, but at about $2 per 4 ounces, a 5-gallon solution runs you ten bucks!

- ✔ **TSP** (trisodium phosphate) is a safe and effective nonsudsing powdered cleanser good for cleaning beer bottles, glass carboys, and even glasses used for beer drinking. TSP is not a sanitizer, however, and thorough rinsing is imperative. Also, because TSP is a skin and eye irritant, always wear protective gear when you use this cleanser.

Several brand-name sanitizers, including B-T-F Iodophor, Star San, Saniclean, One Step, PBW (Powdered Brewery Wash) and B-Brite, along with generic sodium metabisulphite, are available through homebrew supply stores. TSP, ammonia, and chlorine bleach can be purchased at your local grocery and/or hardware stores. The capacity of these products to sanitize homebrewing equipment is directly proportionate to the way in which you use them; in other words, if you don't follow instructions, don't blame the manufacturer for a blown batch of beer.

Dilution rates and contact time are important variables to consider when cleaning and sanitizing. Read all product instructions before using.

For my money, ordinary unscented household bleach is still the best bet.

Cleaning Up Your Act: Equipment Cleaning Practices

The most effective methods of sanitizing involve soaking rather than intensive scrubbing. For this purpose, the best place to handle sanitizing procedures is a utility basin or large-capacity sink. (A bathtub can do in a pinch, but bathtubs often harbor tons of bacteria, soap residues, and, occasionally, small children. Remove all these potential contaminants prior to use — especially the wee ones.) Remember that chlorine can wreak havoc on stainless steel; if you're sanitizing with bleach, make sure your bleach and basin are compatible.

Never use any abrasives or materials that can scratch your plastic or metal equipment, because pits and scratches are excellent hiding places for those wily bacteria. Using a very soft sponge that you've devoted to cleaning only homebrew equipment is a good idea.

Okay, so now that you're ready to begin sanitizing, follow these instructions:

1. **Place the items you want to sanitize in the plugged utility basin and begin drawing cold water into the basin.**

   Because chlorine is volatile, don't use hot water with bleach; the heat of the water causes the chlorine gas to leave the water much more quickly.

   If you're sanitizing the fermenter, carboy, or bottling bucket, you need to fill only those items rather than the whole basin or sink. You can place smaller items in the sanitizing solution within these larger items. However, for bottles, you need to fill the entire sink.

2. **As the water runs, add cleansing/sanitizing chemicals according to package directions, or pour in 1 ounce of unscented household bleach per gallon of water.**

3. **Completely immerse all the items you want to sanitize in the sanitizing solution.**

   Don't forget to include the fermenter lid, which you have to force into the fermenter sideways. Always allow 30 minutes for all bottles and equipment to soak.

4. **After 30 minutes, remove your equipment and thoroughly rinse the various pieces in hot water.**

5. **Sanitize the spigots on the fermenter and bottling bucket by draining the sanitizing solution through each spigot.**

6. **Allow everything to air dry.**

   The fermenter lid, placed upside down on a clean surface, is a good place to dry the smaller sanitized items.

In spite of all your hard work, you may still occasionally end up with a batch of contaminated beer — how and by what you may never know. That's why attention to detail is so important.

Bottle Cleanliness Is a Virtue

When you're absolutely sure that your brew is bottle-ready (you can verify this decision with a hydrometer reading — see Chapter 2), you need to clean and sanitize your bottles. You can clean your bottles pretty much at your convenience if you store them properly, but sanitizing your bottles too far ahead of time may lead to bacterial recontamination.

Using a dishwasher with a dry cycle is a convenient way of cleaning bottles (be sure you load the bottles into the dishwasher upside down). This practice does *not* relieve you from your bottle-sanitizing duties.

To sanitize your bottles, follow these steps:

1. **Fill the entire basin or sink with water and sanitizer (per package instructions).**

   Of course, exactly how much water you need to add depends on the capacity of the utility basin or sink — and don't forget to adjust the volume of sanitizing chemical to the volume of water (I give you some guidelines in the "Soaps for Suds" section, but always read the label on your particular sanitizer). You need enough water to immerse at least 54 12-ounce bottles. Again, add cleansing/sanitizing chemicals according to package directions, or pour in the proper amount of unscented household bleach (1 ounce per gallon of water).

2. **As you immerse the bottles, make sure the sanitizing solution fills each one, with no pockets of air left in them.**

3. **Allow the bottles to soak for 30 minutes (or according to the sanitizer's package directions).**

4. **After 30 minutes, affix the bottle rinser to the faucet (you may have to use an adapter) and turn on the hot water.**

Don't worry about water spraying everywhere; the bottle rinser is designed to hold back the water pressure until you slip a bottle over the opening and apply downward pressure.

5. **Clean the bottles one by one with the bottle brush while the sanitizing solution is still in them.**

6. **Drain the sanitizing solution from each bottle, rinse each bottle twice with the bottle rinser, and allow the bottles to air-dry.**

One stumble into several dozen free-standing bottles can make for a doozy of a breakable mess. Put your cleaned bottles back into 6-pack holders or cardboard cases to prevent accidental catastrophes.

Don't forget that you also need to sanitize your bottle caps before using them. Boil them for 10 minutes in a small pot of water on your stove top. If you're using the oxygen-barrier type of bottle cap, however, you should soak them in a percarbonate or iodine-based solution for the same amount of time. Boiling this type of cap reduces its ability to absorb oxygen.

Part II
It's in There: The Nuts and Bolts of Beer

The 5th Wave   By Rich Tennant

SUCCESSFUL BEER-MAKING ESSENTIALS

Barley | Hops | Malt

Water | Yeast | Drinking Buddy

In this part . . .

Four basic building blocks make beer — barley (malt), hops, yeast, and water. I devote one chapter in this part to each one of these important primary ingredients. I add another two chapters to discuss all the miscellaneous additives and flavorings that aren't primary ingredients in beer.

Chapter 4

Malt: A Tale of Two Sources (Grain and Extract)

In This Chapter

▶ Defining malt: Beer's biggest building block

▶ Malting and mashing

▶ Distinguishing between base grains, adjunct grains, and specialty grains

▶ Extracting malt

▶ Comparing and contrasting malt extracts

The word *malt* generally refers to the natural maltose sugars derived from certain grains (mainly barley) that eventually become beer. At the commercial brewing level, as well as the advanced homebrewing level, brewers produce beer through procedures that create and capture the malt sugars from the grain. At the beginner and intermediate levels of homebrewing, however, a commercially produced malt syrup that homebrewers can easily use to make beer at home eliminates the need for these procedures.

In this chapter, I look at the different types of grains used in brewing as well as the processes the grain undergoes to become brew-ready. I also explore the shortcuts available in the form of malt extract and compare and contrast its two forms: dry and liquid.

Going with Grain

Of the four main ingredients used to make beer (barley, hops, yeast, and water), barley — really, grain in general — makes the biggest contribution. It's responsible for giving beer its color, its underlying flavor, its sweetness, its body, its head of foam, and its *mouthfeel* (or the textural qualities of beer on your palate and in your throat — *viscosity*, or thickness; carbonation; alcohol warmth; and so on). Grains also contribute the natural sugars that feed the yeast, which in turn converts the sugars into alcohol and carbon dioxide during fermentation.

For as long as humans have been making beer, they've experimented with all different kinds of *cereal grains* for beermaking purposes. Wherever grains grew uncultivated, the indigenous peoples made a beer-like beverage from them: wheat in Mesopotamia, barley in Egypt, millet in Africa, rice in Asia, and corn in the Americas.

Cereal grains are the same ones that are puffed, popped, pulverized, and poured into the colorful boxes of breakfast cereal that line your grocer's shelves: corn flakes, Rice Krispies, Wheat Chex, oatmeal. Name any cereal grain, and you can bet someone has tried to put it in beer. One grain that isn't very popular at the breakfast table is the one that works best for making beer: barley. (It works pretty well in soup, too.)

Barley grows in two major strains: *6-row* barley and *2-row* barley. These names refer to the number of rows of barley kernels visible when you look down from the top of the stalk. 2-row barley generally goes into Ales, and 6-row barley generally goes into Lagers (but these aren't hard-and-fast rules).

Malting

Before you can brew with barley, it must undergo a process known as *malting*. The malting process, simply put, simulates the grain's natural germination cycle. (Who says it's not nice to fool Mother Nature?) Under closely monitored conditions, malting companies wet the barley kernels and allow them to sprout. As the seedlings begin sprouting, the starchy insides of the kernels (or *endosperm*) begin to change. This modification causes the hard, starchy endosperm to begin to break down into natural malt sugars (*maltose*) that brewers later liquefy, during the mashing process. (See the "Mashing" section in this chapter for details on this process.) One of the most important features of this process is the production of the enzymes brewers later use in the mashing process. And the maltose sugars, along with proteins and dextrins, contribute the aforementioned color, flavor, sweetness, body, mouthfeel, and foam in the beer.

Only after the barley has undergone the malting process does it become *malt*, or *barleymalt*.

Malted barley is an incredibly complete and convenient package, seemingly designed exclusively for brewing beer. Each grain kernel contains *carbohydrates* (which eventually convert to sugar), *enzymes* (which do the actual converting), *proteins* (which provide yeast nutrition, mouthfeel, and head stability), and a *husk* (which, when multiplied by thousands, acts as the perfect natural filter bed through which you can drain the unfermented beer).

Very few commercial brewers — usually only the huge beer factories — do their own malting. Professional malting companies (also called *maltsters*) malt most of the grain for the brewing industry (including smaller commercial brewers and homebrew supply shops).

Mashing

In order to make beer from the malted grain, the starch within the kernels of malt must be made soluble. This liquefying process takes place during the mashing procedures in a vessel called a *mash tun*. The mashing process is where the natural enzymes found in grain break down the grain's starches; hot water then dissolves the starches so they leech out of the cracked grain. After you've rinsed all the malt sugars from the grain, you transfer the syrupy-sweet malt tea, called *wort,* over to the brew kettle, where you boil it. (For more on mashing, see Chapter 12.) Homebrewers who make their beer with malt extract can avoid the mashing process altogether.

Wort (rhymes with dirt) is the German word for unfermented beer. Some brewers also call wort *green beer* (and not just on St. Patrick's Day).

Mixing it up with other grains

Although barley is the best base grain for brewing, it's by no means your only option. You can enhance the flavor of barleymalt in beer with specialty grains or substitute the barley with adjunct grains. The following list details the characteristics of these different types of grains:

- **Base malted grain** is the main source of fermentable sugars and the body and flavor of the beer. Base grain must undergo modification during malting; make sure it's fully mashed before brewing with it. Most commercial beer recipes and many all-grain homebrew recipes call for more than one type of base grain.

- **Specialty grains** allow the brewer to add all kinds of colors, flavors, and textures to beer, therefore providing a variety of visual, aromatic, and taste enhancements. Also, specialty grains may contribute dextrins and head-retaining and body-building proteins (the beer's body, not yours). These grains create complexity in beer (and perplexity in the beer critic). Most specialty grains don't require mashing because they don't add significant amounts of fermentable sugars to the wort. Simply put, without the use of specialty grains, very few distinctive beer styles would exist.

  In a 5-gallon batch, which typically starts with about 10 pounds of grain, you don't need much specialty grain to lend a noticeable effect. Depending on the grain type, quantities of as little as ¼ of a pound are detectable in the finished beer.

- **Adjunct grains** are unmalted cereal grains that still add fermentable sugars to the wort (as well as some underlying flavor). Adjunct grains, such as corn and rice, are popular for fiscal reasons; they're used in place of the more expensive barleymalt. They're also used to dilute flavor and make lighter-bodied beers.

Corn and rice aren't malted like barley, so brewers must cook them in a cereal cooker to gelatinize the starchy interior of the grain in order for the brewer to extract their sugars. *Gelatinization* is a softening of the hard grain kernel. Although corn and rice aren't popular with homebrewers, those who do use these grains must also gelatinize them by cooking them on the stove-top before adding them to the mash.

For more specific information on particular grain types, consult the appendix.

A few specialty grain types aren't malted but still undergo mashing procedures (because throwing these unmalted specialty grains in with the rest of the malted grains in the mash tun is the only logical time and place to add them to the beer). These unmalted specialty grains include roasted barley, raw wheat, and raw oats, among others, and are used for flavoring and texture purposes, not for adding fermentable sugars. Intermediate and advanced homebrewers can easily add uniqueness to their brews by simply adding specialty grains to their mashing vessel.

Manipulating grain: Kilning and milling

In addition to these grains, you can also manipulate malted barley in a variety of ways to create unique specialty malts. *Kilning,* or roasting the grain to various degrees, is one way of achieving this variety. Depending on the degree of roasting, specialty grains imbue beer with a broad palette of earth-toned colors, and their flavor contributions range from caramelly to chocolatey to roasty to smoky. *Milling* is the process of cracking the grain husk to allow access to the natural sugars contained within the kernel (also called cracking).

Don't mill highly kilned grains such as roasted barley and black malt. Because they're quite brittle, they have a tendency to crumble during the milling process, creating a fine, dark grain powder that adds harshness to your beer.

Homebrew recipes usually call out specialty grains by the pound or in increments of a pound. In the absence of a kitchen or postal scale, you can measure specialty grains with relative accuracy by using a measuring cup.

For conversion purposes, 1 cup of milled grain equals approximately ¼ pound, ergo, 4 cups equal 1 pound.

To add-junk or not to add-junk?

Although enhancing a beer's malt character with specialty grain is perfectly acceptable, many purists (this author included) shy away from substituting barleymalt with adjunct grain. One way to enhance the barley character of a beer is by adding rye to the recipe, which gives the beer a distinctive rye flavor. The most obvious examples of brewers substituting barley with adjuncts occur at the big corporate brewhouses, where they replace the rich malt character of barley with lighter and cheaper adjunct grains like corn and rice (much to the delight of millions of oblivious beer drinkers).

Enjoying the Ease of Extracts

Fortunately for homebrewers (particularly novices), they can make beer much more easily, without having to deal with grains. (It sounds too good to be true, doesn't it?) The same companies that malt the raw grain for the brewing industry have also figured out a way to make a product homebrewers can rehydrate to reproduce the wort you get by mashing malted grain. These companies market the product as *malt extract,* and it's been nothing less than a boon to the homebrewing industry (some professional brewers use it, too).

The Pacific Coast Brewing Company in Oakland, California, has won several medals at the Great American Beer Festival for its malt-extract-based beers.

Malt extract (also called *malt syrup*) is a premade, premeasured beer concentrate. Malt extract starts out as wort produced from grain that is then dehydrated to the point that it contains as little as 20 percent water content. Basically, all you need to do is add malt extract to water and boil it. I may be oversimplifying the process just a tad, but all-inclusive malt extract kits are just about that easy. The hardest part of the brewing process is often deciding which kit to buy — check out the appendix for brand names. (I give plenty of extract-based beer recipes in Part IV.) For more on brewing with a kit, take a look at Chapter 10.

These concentrated malt extracts usually come premeasured (in pounds or kilograms) in cans or heavy-duty plastic bags. The typical can of malt extract weighs 3.3 or 6.6 pounds, and these extracts are available in most of the recognized beer styles. Malt extract can imbue your homebrew with all the malt flavor, sweetness, body, and mouthfeel you'd get if you made it from grain.

TECHNICAL STUFF

Lovibonds to love and SRMs, EBCs, and HCUs 4 U 2 C

All of the various maltsters who malt the grain for the American brewing industry produce it in much the same way. One of the industry standards they follow is the production of kilned grains according to a color scale called the *Lovibond scale*. Actually, the Lovibond method of color measurement can be applied to wort, malt extract, and beer as well, but these qualities all trace their roots back to the malt-house.

Because you can more easily *see* differences in color depth than *describe* them accurately, the Lovibond scale designates a specific number to each specific color depth. Each of the specialty grains on the upcoming list has its own degree on the Lovibond scale (though Lovibond can be abbreviated as L, most packages and recipes just use the number without the *L*). Here are those numbers, including some base malts for comparison:

- Pale Lager   1.6
- Pale Ale   1.8
- Vienna   3
- Munich (light)   10
- Munich (dark)   20
- Crystal   20–120

- Chocolate   350
- Black Patent   500+
- Roasted barley   500+

A more updated color scale for beer is the American standard of color measurement — the *SRM* (Standard Reference Method) scale. It closely approximates the older Lovibond scale, with the main difference being that the SRM scale is much more accurate because it relies on a *spectrophotometer* (an instrument used to measure the absorbance of light — and no, you don't need to buy one) to do the measuring. The Lovibond scale, on the other hand, relies on the human eye to discern color depths compared to tinted glass filters.

And just to further complicate matters, homebrewers have their own color scale called *HCU*, or Homebrew Color Units. This crude method of establishing beer color relies on a simple formula: Take the weight in pounds of each type of grain used, multiply each by its corresponding degrees Lovibond, add all of these multiplied numbers together, and divide by the total number of gallons in the batch of beer. Honestly, I don't know anyone who uses this method, but you can't say I didn't tell you about it.

TIP

For full body and flavor, use two 3.3-pound cans to make one full batch of beer (5 gallons), or no less than 1 pound of extract per gallon of water (1 pound of extract per gallon of water results in a beer with a specific gravity of 1.040; 6.6 pounds in a 5-gallon batch results in a specific gravity of 1.052).

BEER NUT

The rather odd (by U.S. standards) measure of 3.3 pounds was set by the British, who pioneered the malt-extract-producing industry. The majority of kits initially sold in the U.S. were from the U.K., where 3.3 pounds is 1.5 kilograms (the standard can size).

Thick as a brix

Malt extract manufacturers use heat and/or vacuum power to remove moisture from the wort, which concentrates the wort into an extract. How much water they remove determines the extract's *viscosity,* and the percentage of remaining solids determines the *brix.* The brix scale provides a number that correlates to the amount of sugar (solids) found in a 100-pound sample. Most malt extracts range between 70 and 80 brix.

From an economic standpoint, it makes more sense to buy the most concentrated extract available — those with the highest brix rating. To make this point clearer, 3½ pounds of 80 brix extract contain as much fermentable sugar as 4 pounds of 70 brix extract. Unfortunately, not all malt extract manufacturers disclose this information on the product labels, so you may have to ask your retailer.

Also, be aware that extracts with high brix ratings may be unsuitable for making pale beers because the extra heat needed to concentrate the wort usually results in darker and more caramelly malt extracts.

Kits are all-inclusive setups that include a *prehopped* malt extract (an extract that already has the hop bitterness added to it) and a packet of yeast to match the style of beer listed on the can's exterior. These kits come in a variety of colors and flavors and are clearly labeled according to the style of beer they produce. I recommend these kits for all first-time homebrewers. Be aware, however, that not all extracts are the same quality. Cheaper malt extracts often add sugar (read the labels). For better-tasting brews, pay a little extra and buy top-quality *all-malt* extracts — you'll be glad you did.

Also, don't follow any directions provided with cans of extract that recommend adding sugar to the brew. Just follow the brewing guidelines in Chapter 10.

Graduating to other malty methods

Although homebrew kits specify the particular beer styles they're ideal for, they can also be somewhat confining in this respect. Homebrewers who rely on the kit-maker to reproduce true beer styles may decide at some point to take more personal control of the situation. Graduating into the realm of extract brewing without a kit requires the brewer to separately buy and add whatever ingredients don't come with the can of extract: The hops, yeast, and whatever specialty grains the recipe calls for. (I cover the details on how to work with these various ingredients in Chapter 11.)

When a homebrewer has enough confidence to take this leap on his own, he's maltriculated (okay, graduated) to the intermediate level of homebrewing.

I always encourage intermediate homebrewers to start with the palest base extract available because they're the most neutral-tasting and allow the most flexibility. You can always add dark color and additional flavor to a beer by using specialty grains.

Comparing liquid versus dry malt extract

Malt extract comes in two distinct forms. One is *liquid,* which is quite thick and viscous, and the other is *dry,* which is a rather sticky powder. These two forms share similarities that far outnumber their differences. Actually, the main distinction between liquid and dry extracts is that dry malt extract (*DME* in homebrewer lingo) has been spray-dried to remove up to 99 percent of its moisture content.

Convenience is also a benefit of working with DME: Though it can get sticky if it contacts water, steam, or humid air, it's nowhere near as messy as liquid extract. You can effortlessly and accurately measure DME with little cleanup required. The storage factor can also come into play. Just like bread, liquid extract can grow mold when exposed to air, so you need to use opened cans as soon as possible. DME, because of its minuscule moisture content, can simply be refrigerated in self-sealing plastic bags. Dry extract is also a great convenience to those who practice the yeast-propagating techniques I discuss in Chapters 6 and 12.

Unopened cans of liquid extract have a fairly long shelf-life. They may be usable for up to two to four years, but as with most consumables, the fresher they are, the better for your beer (and don't even think of using malt extract from a can that's bulging at the seams). Six to eight months is the generally accepted window of freshness. Dry malt extract has a much longer shelf-life; if you keep it sealed and refrigerated, DME can last almost indefinitely.

I need to point out that, for all its usefulness, DME has its disadvantages. It's not packaged according to any particular style; it's just sold in light, amber, dark, and wheat variations. You also pay for its convenience; because of the extra processing required to produce it, DME is more expensive than liquid extract. Of course, you're also getting more bang for your buck (because of the lower water content in DME), which brings up another good point: Because of the difference in water content, using dry extract in place of liquid extract affects your gravity readings in a side-by-side, pound-for-pound comparison. This difference adds up to about one specific gravity degree per pound, with the DME having a greater yield than liquid extract. Woo-hoo!

Chapter 5

Hop Heaven

In This Chapter

▶ Understanding hops' contributions to beer

▶ Discovering where hops come from

▶ Using hops for bittering, flavoring, and aromatizing

▶ Making hop substitutions

*I*f malts represent the sugar in beer (as I discuss in Chapter 4), hops surely represent the spice. As a matter of fact, you use hops in beer in much the same way that you use spices in cooking. The divine mission of hops is to accent the flavor of beer and, most importantly, contrast the sweetness of the malt. This spiciness isn't all hops have to contribute, however.

Hops contribute five qualities to beer:

- **Bitterness** offsets the cloyingly sweet flavor of malt

- **A zesty, spicy flavoring** accents the malt character in beer

- **A pungent floral/herbal aroma**

- **Bacterial inhibitors**

- **Natural clarifying agents**

In this chapter, I discuss the plant origins of hops and the various ways these plants become the products you see on the shelves at the homebrew shop. I also look at the world's hop-growing regions and explain how to decipher hopping instructions in brewing recipes. Finally, I give you some tips on keeping your hops fresh and making hop substitutions or replacements.

Seeing the Hop Flower up Close

For the uninitiated, the hop cones used in the brewing process grow on vines that may reach upwards of 25 feet on commercial hop farms. Hop plants are hardy perennial plants that are quite prolific under ideal conditions, and each may produce up to 2 pounds of dried hop cones per season. Figure 5-1 shows you what hops look like.

Figure 5-1:
Hops are vining plants with conelike flowers.

Humulus Lupulus (also known as *hops*) is one of a small number of species distantly related to the *cannabis* plant; hemp, the nettle, and the elm are also distant cousins to cannabis.

Closer inspection of a mature hop cone, shown in Figure 5-2, reveals that it's mostly vegetative material (leaves and stems and whatnot), but at the base of each little leaf is a cluster of minute yellow sacs about the size of pinheads. These sacs are the waxy *lupulin glands* that contain the bitter acids, resins, and essential oils that contribute bittering, flavoring, and aromatic qualities to beer. Only when boiled extensively do these tiny glands erupt and deliver their precious contents.

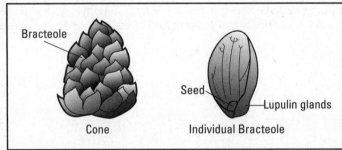

Figure 5-2:
A close-up of the hop cone reveals the lupulin glands.

The various methods of processing and packaging hops have made delivering hop character to your homebrew easier; you can choose between whole leaf hops, hop pellets, hop plugs, and hop extracts.

Isomerization takes place when the hops' lupulin glands dissolve and release their acids and resins into the wort. Through boiling, the alpha acids are converted to soluble iso-alpha acids, which are the main source of hop bitterness. Complete isomerization in boiling wort may take up to an hour.

Traditionally speaking, brewers handpicked hops from the vine and air-dried them in bulk before tossing them whole into the brewkettle. Today, however, hops are processed and sold in four different forms, which I describe in the following list (and show in Figure 5-3).

- **Whole-leaf hops:** As they did in the old days, farmers pick, dry, and bale the hops exactly as they come off the vine. A downside is that whole-leaf hops rarely come in oxygen-free packaging, leading to oxidation and staleness (which you can delay if you store your hops properly in dark, cool, and dry conditions).

- **Pellets:** Hop processors create pellets by pulverizing hop flowers and compacting them into small pellets about the size of a pencil eraser. Ounce-for-ounce, these pellets take up only a quarter of the space of whole leaf hops, but the process that pulverizes the hops also ruptures the hop lupulin glands. On the plus side, the ruptured lupulin glands allow the acids and resins to isomerize more quickly. Also, compressed hop pellets make packing and storing more efficient, and the hop is rendered more stable. To guard against oxidation, the best way to package pelletized hops is in nitrogen or in oxygen-barrier bags. If packaged and stored properly, pellets deteriorate at only one-tenth the rate of whole hops (see the "Freshness is fundamental" section in this chapter for more information).

- **Plugs:** This form of hops is more modern and seems to represent the best of both worlds. Plugs are small hop chips formed by compressing whole-leaf hops. Plugs combine the freshness of whole hops with the convenience of pellets, though the gentler processing of plugs leaves more lupulin glands intact. Also, plugs typically come in 2- to 5-ounce quantities — way more than enough for a single 5-gallon batch of beer.

  Brewing industry insiders also call hop plugs *type-100 hoplets*. Developers initially created hoplets with commercial dry-hopping in mind (see the "Dry hopping" sidebar in this chapter); plugs fit neatly through the bungholes (the opening through which the kegs are filled) in kegs and casks. They're not very good for playing checkers, though.

- **Hop extract:** Just as with malt extract, you can make your job easier by buying a highly concentrated liquid product that keeps the important components and characteristics of hops intact. Although you typically find these extracts in the large breweries, some extracts are available to homebrewers (particularly the hop oils).

You can find three basic prepackaged hop extract products. One is a concentrated bittering and flavoring agent that you can easily isomerize. The second is Late Hop Essence, which adds spicy and floral hop flavors to the beer, and the third (commonly known as *hop oil*) is strictly for aroma adjustments in post-fermentation beer.

Initially, processors used steam distillation and chemical extraction to capture these hop products, but the steaming process negatively affected their flavor and brewers became concerned about residual chemicals left in the product. More recently, a newer CO_2 extraction process extracts oils and alpha acids with none of the previous problems.

Whether you use extracts, essences, or oils, you add them in small amounts (usually measured in increments of teaspoons). These seemingly small amounts can have a big effect on the finished product, because the human senses can perceive quantities in *parts per million*. Therefore, a 2-ounce bottle of hop oil is sufficient to treat 30 gallons of beer (six batches of homebrew)!

Figure 5-3:
Some of the different ways that brewers process hops.

Hop pellets   Hop plug   Whole-leaf hops

Dry hopping

Dry hopping is adding hops (in any form) to the beer after primary fermentation for an added touch of hop aroma. Because they're compact, hop plugs are better for dry hopping than whole hops; however, hop pellets are usually best because they're compact and because their smashed lupulin glands make the aromatic oils more easily accessible to the beer.

You find two schools of thought as to whether you can dry hop without contaminating your beer. One side says the hops are unboiled and may potentially contaminate your brew; the other side (the one I agree with) says the alcohol in the fermented beer is antiseptic enough to keep any

bacteria at bay. As a safeguard, you may want to try steaming the hops in a strainer for about 5 minutes before adding them to the beer.

If you want to dry hop your beer, you should do so during secondary fermentation (see Chapter 11 for more info on secondary fermentation). In any case, whatever you put into the secondary fermenter needs to be strained out of the brew on bottling day. The best way to avoid sucking up hops or anything else from your secondary fermenter is to attach a *sanitized* plastic or stainless steel scrubber that you would ordinarily use for washing dishes to the end of your racking cane.

Hopping with Variety

More than 50 recognized hop varieties exist, and most of them grow in one of the six well-known hop growing regions throughout the world (see Table 5-1). Many of these varieties bear names that hint at their origins.

Table 5-1	Major Hop Zones
Hop Growing Region	*Regional Hop Variety*
Hallertau District, northern Bavaria, Germany	Hallertauer
Zatec, Bohemia, Czech Republic	Saaz
Victoria, Australia	Pride of Ringwood
County Kent, England	East Kent Goldings
Pacific Northwest, United States (Idaho, Oregon, Washington)	Mount Hood
British Columbia, Canada	Olympic

Outside of the regions listed in Table 5-1, hops also grow in parts of Belgium, France, Poland, Slovenia, New Zealand, and my backyard, but these regions aren't nearly as distinguished as those shown in the table.

Regardless of their place of origin, the vast majority of cultivated hop varieties are *hybrids* of original wild varieties, crossbred to capitalize on specific genetic qualities such as high yields and resistance to disease. An amazing amount of effort has gone into such hop cultivation, especially considering that you use hops rather sparingly in the brewing process (only a few ounces are needed for a 5-gallon batch of homebrew).

You may be asking yourself, "So if I use hops in such a minimal fashion, why do so many regions grow so many varieties?" Well, the answer is quite simple. Each hop variety offers different nuances in bittering intensity, flavor, and aroma. The differences between them are often so subtle that even the most experienced brewers and beer judges are hard-pressed to recognize their individual attributes in a given beer — especially when you consider that brewers often use blends of different hops in a single batch of beer.

Each hop variety is more or less bitter (like lovers scorned). But instead of measuring hop bitterness in the number of forlorn letters sent and pleading phone calls made, brewers use a scientific scale to determine hops' *percent alpha acid content*. Alpha acid content is the component within the lupulin gland that correlates to bitterness, and brewers are very aware of these percentages when they formulate recipes so that they can estimate the hops' bittering potential in the beer. They also acquaint themselves with each hop variety's unique flavoring and aromatic properties so they know how and when to use them. See the "Bittering potential is important too" section in this chapter for more information.

✔ Hops that are used for their bittering potential are *bittering hops* or *kettle hops.*

✔ Hops that are used for flavoring (but not necessarily bittering) are *flavoring hops* or *late-kettle hops.*

✔ Hops that are used for their aromatic contributions are *aroma hops* or *finishing hops.*

✔ Hops that are held in school gymnasiums are *sock hops.*

Hey, this ain't rocket science.

How and when you use the hops determines the effect that they have on the finished brew. The longer you boil the hops, the more bitterness dissolves into the wort (up to a point). Boiling hops for five minutes to a half an hour imbues the beer with far less bitterness than the hops could potentially add, but you get some hop flavor. Adding hops very late in the boil and boiling them for less than five minutes provides the beer with aromatics and little else.

Many homebrew recipes tell you not only which hop varieties to use and in what quantities but also how long to boil them to get bittering, flavoring, or aromatizing characteristics from them. In a homebrew recipe (including the recipes in this book), you may see something like the following instruction: 1.5 oz. Galena (60 mins.), 1 oz. Kent Goldings (15 mins.), and 0.5 Cascade (5 mins.). This notation tells you that you want to boil an ounce and a half of Galena hops for 1 hour (for bittering), add an ounce of Kent Goldings hops in the last 15 minutes of the boil (for flavoring), and add just a half-ounce of Cascade hops in the last 5 minutes of the boil (for aroma).

You don't want to boil aroma hops for more than 5 to 10 minutes because the aromatic oils are very volatile and vaporize fairly quickly. The longer you boil these hops, the more their aroma diminishes.

First wort hopping is yet another method of imbuing your beer with hop flavor. Unfortunately, this method, which requires the brewer to add hops to the brew during the sparging/lautering phase of mashing, is only useful to brewers who produce their beer entirely from grain (see Chapter 12 for more information).

Noble hops: Brewing royalty

Noble hops are distinguished old-world varieties, most of which have been cultivated for centuries. They have relatively low alpha acid contents but are popular for their aromatic and flavoring characteristics. Among the noble varieties are Hallertauer, Hersbrucker, Spalt, and Tettnanger in Germany; Saaz from Bohemia in the Czech Republic; and Styrian from the former Yugoslavia.

European Noble varieties are typically more expensive than the same varieties grown in North America, so many homebrew supply shops and catalogs may not feature them (but commercial beer labels often boast of their use).

Selecting the Best Hops

Homemakers who want everything they cook or bake to come out tasting just right tend to fuss about the finer details of their recipes. Having the right ingredients isn't enough — they have to be fresh, too.

And so it is with beer. It's important to use the right hops for your brew — especially if you are duplicating a recipe, but it's even more important to use the freshest hops you can. If you use old or stale hops, you could be brewing up a recipe for disaster.

Freshness is fundamental

The freshness of hops is vital to the outcome of the beer. And, of course, in order for them to stay fresh, you need to store your hops properly. This means that you need to keep them packed in nitrogen- or oxygen-barrier bags and refrigerated (or, preferably, frozen) for long-term storage. But first things first: You must know how to identify the fresh hops from the stale hops.

The first indicator of a hop's freshness is its color. Fresh hops that are whole or in plug form usually have a light (almost lime) green color; fresh pelletized hops are typically a darker shade of green (a few hop varieties, such as Goldings, have a yellowish cast) and may have a shiny exterior due to the dried hop resins. Hops that look brown, dried out, and curled are probably pretty old; if the tiny lupulin glands are orange instead of yellow, the hops are *oxidized* (stale) — get rid of 'em.

Check hops for aroma, too. Fresh hops have a fresh and piquant aroma that you may describe as piney, floral, spicy, herbal, and even citrusy. Any hops that have a pungent odor reminiscent of Parmesan or Romano cheese are likely to be old and oxidized — throw them away. Any off flavors and aromas evident before you use the hops will surely manifest in your beer.

Hop varieties are also graded according to their *stability,* which refers to how well they keep in storage. The freshness scale assigns a rating (very good, good, fair, or poor) based on the percentage of the hop bitterness that remains after a six-month storage period at 70 degrees Fahrenheit (21 degrees Celsius). (You can find out about individual hop stability ratings in the appendix.) Unless you buy your hops in large quantities, however, you don't really need to concern yourself with their stability. Just make sure that you buy them fresh, store them right, and use them soon.

Bittering potential is important too

After freshness, bittering potential is the next most important consideration in your choice of hops. At harvest time, farmers measure hops for their alpha acid content. You express the alpha acid content as a percentage of the acid's weight relative to the weight of the whole hop flower. For example, the 2006 Northdown crop from the U.K. has an alpha acid content of 7 percent, which means that 1 pound of these hops contains 0.070 pounds of bittering acids. This information appears on hop packaging as 7.0 AAU, which means *alpha acid units.*

Each hop variety has a different acid content than another, and brewers need to take this discrepancy into consideration. Alpha acid contents also vary slightly from one growing season to the next, depending on the elements, and from one place of origin to another. In this way, hops are to brewers what varietal grapes are to winemakers.

Rumor has it brewers in the post-war Soviet Union resorted to bittering their beer with ox bile when hop shipments became impossible to obtain. To your health, Komrade!

Utilizing the utilization factor

Homebrewers need to be aware of the *utilization factor,* particularly when brewing high-gravity beers. Utilization refers to the amount of bitterness (alpha acid) extracted from the hops during the boiling phase. Both boiling time and beer gravity (density) affect utilization.

The longer you boil the hops, the more bitterness you extract from the lupulin glands and dissolve into the wort. This rule is only true up to a point, however; by the time you boil your hops for 90 minutes, all available bitterness should be extracted.

Higher-gravity worts use hops less efficiently; the density of the wort keeps the alpha acids from easily dissolving into the liquid. This tendency is especially apparent in wort gravities of 1.050 and higher. Most recipes already take this utilization factor into account, but if you're taking a low-gravity recipe (1.050 or lower) and increasing its malt content, you need to calculate the *Gravity Adjustment* (GA) factor when figuring the appropriate hop increase in order to keep your beer flavor in balance.

Don't worry, the following is a sample formula that can help you find the GA when necessary: GA= wort gravity – 1.050, ÷ 0.2. For example, if your wort gravity is 1.070, your calculation should look something like this: GA= 1.070 – 1.050 = .020; .020 ÷ 0.2 = 0.10. This means you have to use 10 percent more hops to achieve the same amount of bittering in a beer with a 1.070 gravity as a beer with a 1.050 gravity. See — still not rocket science.

Calculating AAUs

Many homebrew recipes call for a certain hop variety by name or require a certain number of alpha acid units (*AAUs*). These suggested varieties aren't always available to all homebrewers, so you may have to make hop substitutions by figuring AAUs. This equation is simple, assuming you or your supplier knows the alpha acid content of the hops that you plan to use.

Here's how you can plug in the numbers: Say that a recipe calls for 3 ounces of Northern Brewer hops with 7.5 percent alpha acid; this means that the recipe requires 22.5 AAUs (3 ounces × 7.5 percent alpha acid). To achieve bittering purposes only, you should be able to use 2 ounces of Chinook hops (for example) with an alpha acid content of 11.25 percent (2 ounces × 11.25 = 22.5 AAUs).

Note: I say "for bittering purposes only" because Chinook hops and Northern Brewer hops differ in taste.

Be sure to consider your recipe batch size; 22.5 AAUs called for in a 10-gallon batch would be twice as bitter if used in a 5-gallon batch!

Despite being an imperfect science, calculating AAUs is much easier for homebrewers to deal with than IBUs (International Bitterness Units). The difference is that AAUs measure how much alpha acid a recipe calls for; IBUs actually measure bitterness in beer.

The formula for figuring IBUs in beer is rather complex. A Bitterness Unit is equal to 1 milligram of isomerized alpha acid in 1 liter of beer (okay, maybe this really *is* rocket science).

One more system for figuring bittering units in homebrew recipes is Homebrew Bitterness Units, or HBUs. The HBU system is virtually identical to the AAU system. You calculate HBUs by multiplying the alpha acid percentage of a given hop by the number of ounces of that hop the recipe requires. For example, if a recipe calls for a total of 24 HBUs, you need 3 ounces of hops with 8 percent alpha acid, or 6 ounces of hops with 4 percent alpha acid (or any other ounce/percentage combination whose product is 24).

The lists in Table 5-2 provide the most popular beer styles and their recommended approximate HBU levels.

Table 5-2		HBUs by Beer Styles	
Ales	*HBU*	*Lagers*	*HBU*
Altbier	10–20	Bock	8–12
Barley Wine	15–40	Pilsener	8–13
Kölsch	8–15	Doppelbock	10–15
English Brown Ale	5–10	Munich Dunkel	7–11
American Brown Ale	10–20	Münchner-Style Helles	7–13
Pale Ale	10–17	Dortmunder/European-Style Export	8–12
India Pale Ale	13–20	Rauchbier	7–10
Porter	8–12	Vienna/Märzenbier	8–12
Classic Irish-Style Dry Stout	8–15		
Sweet Stout	5–10		
Stout (imperial)	15–40		
Berliner Weisse	2–3		
Weizen/Weissbier	4–7		

Taking Note of Top Hops

The North American microbrewing industry is developing a reputation for its experimentation with new and experimental hop varieties. Of course, North American homebrewers are quick to take note and follow suit.

The following is a list of the more widely used bittering and aromatic hops (though not all of these varieties are new and experimental). For individual hop characteristics, see the appendix.

Bittering hops	**Aromatic hops**
Centennial	Amarillo
Challenger	Cascade
Chinook	Crystal

Bittering hops	Aromatic hops
Columbus	East Kent Goldings
Cluster	Fuggles
Galena	Glacier
Magnum	Hallertauer
Newport	Liberty
Northern Brewer	Mount Hood
Nugget	Progress
Perle	Saaz
Target	Santiam
Warrior	Tettnanger
	Willamette

TIP

Using replacement hops

Most beer recipes allow you a fair amount of latitude in choosing hop varieties because certain hops have limited availability. Occasionally recipes may include an alternative variety to replace a first-choice variety. Often, the replacement hops are American-grown varieties used in place of the harder-to-get, more expensive European varieties. For the record, American hops are cheaper than European hops because the U.S. has more consistent growing seasons, not because the hops are inferior. The following table shows you which American hops are good replacements for traditional European types (based on their similar bittering potential, flavoring, and aromatic qualities). You can find out more about hop varieties and descriptions in the appendix.

European	American
Hallertauer	Mount Hood, Liberty
Fuggles	Willamette (pronounced wil-*lam*-mit, dammit!)
Northern Brewer	Aurora (Super Styrian), Perle

Chapter 6

Yeast and Fermentation

In This Chapter

▶ Understanding the basics of yeast

▶ Exploring fermentation

▶ Propagating yeast

▶ Figuring alcohol content

Yeast is one of the four primary ingredients in beer (the other three are barley, hops, and water). Although yeast is an ingredient that the average beer consumer rarely contemplates, brewers often consider it the most important ingredient. As a matter of fact, yeast can have a greater influence and effect on the finished beer than any other single ingredient.

Brewers categorize and classify beer styles by the type of yeast used to ferment them; therefore, they choose a yeast according to the style of beer they want to make. In this chapter, I discuss the nuts and bolts of yeast and its role in fermentation, as well as give you the lowdown on the myriad of options you have when choosing a yeast for your brew. I also provide some tips on figuring alcohol content and deliver a bit of bad news for those of you hoping to brew a nonalcoholic batch.

There's a Fungus among Us

Yeast is a member of the fungus family. It's a living single-celled organism and one of the simplest forms of life. Because it has cell-splitting capabilities, it's also *self-reproducing*. Yeast is the one ingredient responsible for carrying out the fermentation process in brewing.

Fermentation, simply put, is the natural conversion of sugar to alcohol. Yeast has a voracious appetite for sweet liquids. And, in exchange for a good, sweet meal, yeast produces equal amounts of ethanol (ethyl alcohol) and carbon dioxide. Yes, the alcohol in your beer is similar to that which is added to gasoline, except car ethanol is made from corn (yikes, adjunct gas!)

Yeast genus and genius

For all the biology fans out there, here's the scoop on yeast. You can classify beer yeast into two categories, or species, of the genus Saccharomyces: Saccharomyces cerevisiae and Saccharomyces uvarum. (Bread yeast is also a part of this genus, but that's just a crummy factoid.)

✔ *Saccharomyces cerevisiae* (*S. cerevisiae*) is commonly known as *Ale yeast* and contains many substrains. It's a *top-fermenting* strain, meaning it floats on the top of the beer. Virtually all Ale yeast works best in fairly warm temperatures (60 to 70 degrees Fahrenheit).

✔ *Saccharomyces uvarum* (*S. uvarum*) is a *bottom-fermenting* strain (meaning it sinks to the bottom of the fermentation vessel at the end of fermentation) and is better known as *Lager yeast*. Brewers developed Lager yeast to ferment beer in cooler temperatures, and it works best between 38 and 50 degrees Fahrenheit. This strain is sometimes referred to as *S. carlsbergensis,* for the Danish brewery where brewers isolated and developed it in 1883.

Yeast not only ferments beer, but it also ferments wine and any other naturally alcoholic beverage. Because yeast produces carbon dioxide, it's also what causes bread dough to rise.

The temperature at which beer ferments can have a great effect on the finished product. The top-fermenting Ale yeast strains can complete their gluttonous feast in as little as three days. This quick, warm fermentation has a tendency to give the resulting beer a rich and complex aroma and flavor profile. As a direct result of the marriage of yeast type and temperature, ales tend to be fruity and estery, often full of buttery or butterscotchy notes. *Estery* is a word used to describe a beer that possesses aromas reminiscent of flowers or fruits. Some yeast strains generate more esters than others.

Lager yeast actually developed a gradual genetic acclimation to its surroundings over hundreds of years. But because the cool temperatures at which Lager yeast feeds result in sluggishness, Lager yeast needs lengthier fermentation periods to complete its job. On the up side, however, the benefit of such long and labored fermentation is the absence of fruitiness and buttery character found in Ales. Lagers are therefore cleaner, smoother beers.

The word *lager* comes from the German *lagern,* which means *to store.* Because summertime fermentations often resulted in sour beer, brewers knew better than to brew beyond late spring. To keep up their stores of beer, Bavarian brewers began brewing bigger-bodied beers in March and storing them in Alpine caves throughout the warm summer months. Over time, the yeast actually performed better under these cool conditions.

The Magic of Fermentation

Fermentation is, indeed, magical and mystical. A simple yeast cell consumes sugar (in liquid form) and in turn excretes alcohol and carbon dioxide in addition to hundreds of flavor compounds. As part of the growth process, a single cell reproduces by cloning itself — splitting into two separate cells. Multiply this chain of events by billions, and you have fermentation.

It's cyclical

Before yeast can begin eating and multiplying, it must do its aerobics — taking in as much of the oxygen from the wort as possible. Similar to oxygen-breathing life forms, yeast needs oxygen to complete its metabolic processes. After the yeast cells consume all or most of the oxygen in the wort, they remain in suspension (float around in the liquid) for maximum contact with the liquid sugars. After the yeast consumes all or most of the sugars, it begins to *flocculate,* or clump together and fall out of suspension. At this point, the yeast has lost energy and is preparing for a state of dormancy.

You can clearly separate the fermentation cycle into three phases:

- ✔ **Yeast growth phase:** This is the initial phase when the yeast cells absorb the oxygen in the wort in preparation for their feast.

- ✔ **Fermentation:** This is the main event — the yeasts are devouring the sugars in the wort and producing alcohol and CO_2. Dividing yeast cells double the total number of yeast cells in the wort every day.

- ✔ **Sedimentation:** This is the anticlimactic close of the fermentation cycle; with the wort now devoid of oxygen and short on fermentable sugar, the yeast begins to flocculate and settle to the bottom of the fermenter.

Peak fermentation is known as *high kraeusen* (pronounced *kroy*-zen). High kraeusen usually occurs between days three and five of fermentation, assuming that the yeast got off to a good start.

Factoring in fermentation variables

How well fermentation takes place and how long it lasts depends on many variables, including temperature, the amount of oxygen in the wort, the amount of yeast *pitched* (added), the *viability* (health) of the yeast pitched, and the amount of available fermentable sugars in the wort.

✔ **Fermentation temperature,** of course, should be within the recommended ranges of the yeast according to species. Ale yeast works best in temperatures between 60 and 70 degrees Fahrenheit. Lager yeast performs best when temperatures are between 38 and 50 degrees Fahrenheit.

Fermentation temperatures that are too low slow down the fermentation or even stop it cold. Extreme temperatures on the high end cause an increase in fermentation activity and an increased risk of bacterial contamination. High fermentation temperatures (above 75 degrees Fahrenheit) often result in off flavors and production of an alcohol other than ethyl alcohol.

✔ **Proper oxygen levels in wort** enable the yeast to grow. You need to properly aerate your wort prior to pitching the yeast. You can aerate by sloshing the cooled wort around in the fermenter or with an oxygenating device called a *beer stone* (see Chapter 27 for more information on beer stones).

✔ **The amount of yeast pitched** is important primarily because of lag time. *Lag time* is the length of time between the pitching of yeast into the wort and the time that active fermentation begins to take place (for healthy fermentations, lag time shouldn't exceed 24 hours). Lag time is affected by the *pitching rate* (the number of cells added to the wort).

If the yeast volume is slow to multiply to desired quantities, any mutant yeast cells or bacteria present can easily take over and ruin a batch of beer. You can avoid this problem by pitching the proper amount of yeast (overpitching is always better than underpitching). I recommend 1 cup of *yeast slurry* (a high concentration of yeast cells in solution) per 5-gallon batch. See the section "Propagating yeast" in this chapter to find out more about how to increase your yeast quantities.

One bacterial cell per 1,000 yeast cells constitutes a serious contamination and may result in a blown batch of beer.

✔ **Yeast viability** is rarely a problem with fresh yeast products purchased new. Viability comes into question when you use an old, out-of-date yeast product or attempt to revive old, tired yeast from the bottom of a bottle-conditioned commercial beer (such as a well-aged Belgian Trappist Ale).

✔ **The amount of available fermentable sugars** has a direct effect on the quality and length of fermentation. The more food you give the yeast cells, the longer they continue to eat — up to a point. At around 8 or 9 percent alcohol, fermentation becomes self-destructive to yeast. In that concentration of alcohol, most beer yeast can no longer continue fermenting; it falls into a stupor and eventually quits working. Reminds me of some people I know.

When brewers set out to create a beer with an alcohol content greater than 8 or 9 percent, they bring in more alcohol-tolerant yeast types such as Mead or champagne yeast to finish the job.

Liquid yeast versus dry yeast: A foamenting debate

You've decided on a yeast type, so now you're ready to brew, right? Not so fast — you still have to choose what *form* of that yeast you're going to use. Yeast for the homebrewer comes in both a dry form and a liquid form. Because of its convenience, I highly recommend dry yeast at the beginner level. Dry yeast comes in granular form in small foil packets. You simply tear these packets open and rehydrate the yeast in water before pitching it into fresh wort. However, because of dry yeast's lack of stylistic variety, I encourage you to progress to liquid yeast cultures as soon as you're comfortable with the handling procedures outlined in this chapter.

How dry 1 am. . .

The small packets (or do you say *sachets?*) of dried yeast that come with malt extract kits are sufficient to ferment a 5-gallon batch of homebrew. Dry yeast is freeze-dried, so it should last a long time (but refrigerate all yeast to maintain optimum freshness). And best of all, it's the cheapest option.

For the best results with dry yeast, always rehydrate the dormant cells by pouring them into a cup of warm water (as I explain in Chapter 10). This gentle wake-up call prepares the yeast for the upcoming fermentation. Be sure to sanitize the vessel in which you rehydrate the yeast.

Of all the brands of dried yeast on the market, Nottingham Ale yeast, Windsor Ale yeast, and Safale and Saflager are some of the best. They're so good, in fact, that some commercial brewers even use them.

In the early days of homebrewing, dry yeasts weren't entirely sterile; mutant yeast and bacteria sometimes mingled with the good yeast in the packets. You could only hope that the good yeast cells far outnumbered the bad. Also, dry yeast often consumed a greater percentage of available sugar in the wort, which resulted in lower terminal gravities and drier beers (it's almost as if they were drinking up for lost time). Now I'm happy to report that these problems are largely a thing of the past. However, dry yeast comes in relatively generic packets simply labeled "Ale" or "Lager" with no further classification. This can be somewhat limiting to homebrewers wanting to reproduce some of the more obscure beer styles, such as traditional German Kolschbiers or Belgian Lambics.

Saying that dry yeast is more than capable of making good, drinkable beer is like saying a 1971 Ford Pinto is more than adequate for getting you to work in the morning. But with pure liquid yeast strains now available to the home-brewer in a wide variety of beer styles, why settle for reliable transportation when you can drive a *real* car? Check out Table 6-1 for some pros and cons of using dry yeast.

Table 6-1	Dry Yeast Qualities
Dry Yeast Positives	*Dry Yeast Negatives*
Less expensive	Limited with regards to beer style
Easily stored	May create drier beers (depends on brand)
Easy to use	Packets not always freshness-dated
Always ready to use	
Easier to pitch amount necessary	

Liquid assets

Brewing supply companies produce pure liquid yeast cultures in a sterile environment; these come with limited guarantees for good brewing results. Luckily, they culture the yeast according to individual beer styles. A small handful of companies are now producing sterile liquid yeast cultures for both the homebrewing and microbrewing industries. Many of these cultures were obtained from their traditional sources, such as Trappist abbey breweries and prestigious brewing institutes in Europe. Check out Table 6-2 for a comparison of the positives and negatives of using liquid yeast cultures.

To give you an idea of the wide range of individual yeast strains available, Wyeast Labs (the original and best-known producer of liquid yeast cultures) produces 17 different Ale cultures, 12 different Lager cultures, 5 different Lambic cultures, 14 different Belgian Ale cultures, and 10 different wine, sake, Mead, and Cider cultures.

Table 6-2	Liquid Yeast Qualities
Liquid Yeast Positives	*Liquid Yeast Negatives*
Pure yeast strains	More expensive than dry yeast
Wide variety of styles	Must prepare foil pouches in advance
True to style profiles	Must propagate before pitching into high gravity brews

Smack packs

You may come across Activator packs (typically referred to as *smack packs),* or liquid yeast cultures sold in foil packets. These packets contain both a small amount of pure yeast culture and a smaller, sealed plastic packet filled with a small amount of sterile liquid medium and malt nutrient. This packaging keeps the yeast from feeding until you're ready.

The responsibility of feeding the nutrient mixture to the yeast is yours. While holding the foil pouch firmly on a flat surface with one hand, locate the inner packet and pop it with the heel of the other hand. The little packet is pretty squirmy, so popping it may take a couple of tries. After the inner packet has burst, shake the foil pouch briskly to fully mix the yeast and nutrient.

Depending on how old the foil packet is (check the freshness date stamp), the packet may take between one and five days to expand. Allow the pouch to plump up before you repitch the yeast into a sterile container for propagating. Always read and follow the directions printed on the back of these foil packets.

Propagating yeast

Whether you prefer to work with vials or foil pouches, you may find that they don't provide you with the proper volume of yeast for pitching into a 5-gallon batch (depending on your beer's original gravity). Both types require you to *propagate* (increase by natural reproduction) the yeast by feeding it more sugar and nutrient in a separate container.

By adding more fermentable sugar in liquid form, you're encouraging your yeast to eat heartily, be fruitful, and multiply. Eventually, over the span of a few days, you'll have the proper volume of yeast to pitch into a 5-gallon batch of beer.

These procedures apply to liquid cultures only, not freeze-dried yeast.

High-gravity worts (those with gravities of 1.056 or higher) have a greater need for yeast. For every gravity increase of 0.008 above 1.048, double the yeast volume.

Propagating can take place in any glass vessel that you can seal with a rubber stopper, such as a mason jar, an old wine carafe, or an expensive glass flask. The bottom line is that you must thoroughly sanitize the propagating container and seal it with an airlock, just as you would any other fermentation vessel.

You can create the perfect sterile holding tank with a large 22-ounce or quart-size beer bottle. The small rubber stopper that fits the hole in the primary fermenter lid will also fit the bottle's opening.

Waiting in the bullpen

Since the introduction of smack packs, another useful product has made homebrewers' lives even easier. *Ready-to-Pitch* (RTP) yeast doesn't even require propagation. Each yeast vial contains an estimated 75 to 150 billion viable yeast cells, which is plenty for the average 5-gallon batch of brew.

RTP yeast consists of fresh, pure cultures that combine the superior quality of liquid yeast with the ease and convenience of dry yeast. Always follow the package directions, but generally speaking, all you have to do is warm and resuspend the yeast slurry and add it to your fermenter when your wort is at an appropriate pitching temperature.

Here's how to put your sterile holding tank to good use:

1. **Sanitize your bottle as you would any other piece of homebrewing equipment, along with a rubber stopper and an airlock.**

    (See Chapter 3 for more about sanitizing.)

2. **Mix ½ cup of pale dry malt extract with 2 cups of water and boil.**

3. **When the extract and water mixture has cooled, pour the wort into the bottle, add the yeast culture, and give it a good shake to introduce some oxygen into the wort.**

    If you use a funnel, make sure it's sanitized, too!

4. **Seal the bottle with the stopper and airlock.**

Lager yeast tends to reproduce more slowly than Ale yeast, even at proper temperatures. Therefore, higher pitching rates are necessary in order to achieve the same concentration of yeast cells in the fermenting beer. The general rule is to pitch double the amount of Lager yeast, or 2 cups of yeast slurry per 5-gallon batch.

You need to maintain a fairly high temperature (75 degrees Fahrenheit) for the first 24 hours of the incubation period to encourage rapid yeast growth. The best time to pitch the yeast into your wort is while you can see visible, active fermentation taking place; definitely pitch the yeast before it sediments out of suspension. For batches of beer larger than 5 gallons or with gravities greater than 1.056, you can easily increase the yeast volume by propagating your culture a second or third time, using the same procedures outlined above.

Every time you transfer the yeast to a new vessel, you increase the risk of contamination. Always practice immaculate sanitation when it comes to yeast handling.

Yeast energizers and nutrients

As if all the different yeast choices discussed earlier in this chapter weren't enough, you can also find energizers and nutrients for beer yeast. These vitamins and minerals are dietary supplements for yeast, designed to accelerate cell growth.

These products, which you can easily obtain through your regular homebrew supplier, are fairly inexpensive (but not always necessary). You only need to use energizers and nutrients for high-gravity worts (those over 1.056) or fermentable beverages with less than 60 percent malt content, such as Cider or Mead, because your malt and (to a lesser extent) brewing water contain most of the essential nutrients necessary for yeast nutrition.

Considering Alcohol Content

You can brew beer at home without caring one whit about its alcohol content, but I think you'd be in a very small minority. All the homebrewers I know are very interested in knowing how much alcohol is in their brew, whether it's on the high side or the low side. And they also make a concerted effort to target specific alcohol levels in their beer.

The same can be said for millions of non-homebrewers who simply want to know how much alcohol they're consuming when they drink commercially made beers. This section helps you understand how alcohol levels in beer are measured and how that information is expressed to the consumer.

ABV versus ABW

You can express alcohol content in beer in two ways. Both are scientifically accurate, but one can be somewhat misleading when compared to the other. What I'm talking about here is the measurement of *alcohol by volume* and *alcohol by weight*.

The more common method of listing alcohol content in beer is by actual percentage of volume, which is the law in the U.K. and Europe. In the U.S., some corporate brewers list the alcohol by weight. Darn Yankees gotta be different.

Hydrometers used by homebrewers always register alcohol by volume, and they say so right on the paper insert (see Chapter 2 for information on hydrometers).

By standard measure, a pint of water weighs 1 pound (actually a fraction of an ounce more). A pint of alcohol, on the other hand, weighs only .79 pounds. Because alcohol weighs less than water (and beer, and most other liquids), the weight of alcohol appears to be lower in weight comparisons. Rather deceptive, don't you think?

To make the point clearer, imagine the container of beer as a carton of ten masonry bricks. If you take out one brick and fill the open space with a foam block of equal size, the foam block still takes up 10 percent of the space in the carton, but it weighs considerably less than the brick it replaced.

So, a beer with an alcohol content of 3.2 percent by weight actually contains 4.05 percent by volume; a beer that is 4 percent alcohol by weight actually contains 5 percent by volume. To figure it out yourself, convert an ABW reading to an ABV by multiplying the ABW by 1.25. To convert an ABV reading to ABW, multiply the ABV by 0.79. Are you having fun yet?

Just remember that figures for weight are *lower* than figures for volume.

N/A (nonalcoholic) beer is n/a (not achievable)

Brewers who want to produce a nonalcoholic brew at home are going to be sorely disappointed. In order to make a beer without alcohol, you need a lot of money to pay for the equipment or a lot of extra steps that are hardly worth the time or effort.

As illustrated in this chapter, yeast is one of the four primary ingredients in beer. It's not only the catalyst for fermentation, but it also adds all kinds of aromas and flavors to beer and is a major influence on the beer's texture and mouthfeel. Therefore, just not adding yeast to the beer in not a viable solution to making nonalcoholic beer. Unfermented beer is very thick, sweet, and not at all thirst-quenching.

Commercial brewers are able to produce nonalcoholic beers in a number of ways, all of which require equipment and technology far beyond the resources of homebrewers. All things considered, it's a lot cheaper and easier to buy nonalcoholic beer at your local store.

Chapter 7

On the Water Front

In This Chapter

▶ Identifying water's role in good homebrew

▶ Examining the elements that affect water

▶ Debating the use of bottled water

Water is just one of the four primary ingredients used to make beer, but considering that it constitutes up to 95 percent of a beer's total ingredient profile, water can certainly have a tremendous influence on the finished product. Fortunately, today's brewers can alter and adjust the chemical make-up of a given water source to suit their brewing needs.

The various minerals and salts found in water used for brewing can accentuate beer flavors or contribute undesirable flavor components. In many cases, water chemistry is key in the flavor profile of a classic beer style.

Having said that, however, most of you will never apply the information in this chapter to your brewing habits. Why? Because in spite of the somewhat ominous statement made above, you can still make good beer with average tap water. Thousands of homebrewers are proving it every day. A very general rule says, "If your water tastes good, so will your beer." A caveat is important here, though: This general rule pertains solely to extract-based homebrews.

The importance of certain aspects of water composition — namely *pH balance* (see the "pHundamentals of pH balance" section in this chapter) — becomes much more important when homebrewers begin mashing their own grains. And water chemical profiles are really only important to the small percentage of homebrewers who are determined to imitate the water found in famous brewing cities around the world.

H₂OH: Understanding How Water Chemistry Affects Your Homebrew

At the homebrewing level, water is perhaps the most overlooked ingredient in the beer recipe, and understandably so. The subject of water chemistry can get pretty complicated, and the majority of homebrewers just don't want to immerse themselves in something so deep. Although water purity is genuinely important for making good beer, your need for concern ranges from not-all-that-important at the beginner homebrewing level (see extract brewing in Chapter 10) to immensely important at the advanced homebrewing level (see all-grain brewing in Chapter 12). This assumes, of course, that your current water source is perfectly drinkable.

At any skill level, make sure that you keep the following things in mind:

✔ If your water is from a private underground well, it may be high in iron and other minerals that may affect your beer's taste.

✔ If your water is softened, it may be high in sodium.

✔ If your water is supplied by a municipal water department, it may have a high chlorine content. Other than chlorine, the *filtering* (the primary method of removing elements and impurities from water) performed at municipal water sources usually produces water that is sufficiently pure for brewing.

High iron, sodium, and chlorine contents in your brewing water are not desirable. If these minerals are present in your brewing water, you may want to consider buying bottled water for your brewing needs.

If you're interested in finding out the chemical profile of your municipal water, call your local public works department and request an analysis of their water — this information is usually provided free-of-charge. However, if you use a private water source, such as a well, you may have to hire an independent company to perform a water analysis for you. In addition to comparing your water analysis to that of famous brewing cities in Europe (see the nearby sidebar), you can be the first on your block to have one!

Something Is in the Water

What is it about crystal-clear water that's so inviting — to drink, to swim in, to brew with? Ah, but this subject matter is murkier than it seems. And as a homebrewer, you can't dilute the reality that even crystal clear water harbors things you need to know about. In the following section I plumb the depths of these topics. My advice to you is to pay attention and just go with the flow.

Water world

Compare your water analysis with the water profiles of some of Europe's great brewing cities.

	Burton	Munich	London	Dortmund	Plzen
Calcium	294	75	50	225	7
Carbonate	200	180	160	180	15
Chloride	36	60	60	60	5
Magnesium	24	18	20	40	2
Sodium	24	2	100	60	2
Sulfate	800	120	80	120	5

pHundamentals of pH balance

pH is an abbreviation for *potential of hydrogen* or *power of hydrogen,* depending on whom you ask. *pH balance* refers to the acidity and alkalinity level in various liquids; you measure this balance on a 14-point pH scale. A rating of 1–6 on this scale is *acidic,* and a rating of 8–14 is *alkaline.* A pH of 7 is *neutral,* or *balanced.*

For beginners, the pH balance in brewing water is, for the most part, irrelevant. When brewers progress to mashing procedures, however, monitoring pH levels in mashing water is absolutely critical. At the more advanced levels of homebrewing, you may need to add either gypsum or calcium carbonate to the water to achieve the desired pH level when a given water source is either acidic or alkaline. (See the "Mineral ions" section in this chapter for information on the effects of gypsum and calcium carbonate on brewing water.) For pH measuring and adjustment procedures, see Chapter 12.

Speaking in very general terms, brewers prefer slightly acidic water over alkaline water; a pH level of 5.5 is usually ideal. Slightly alkaline water is acceptable for brewing dark beers, however, because dark malt's acidity strikes a natural balance with the alkaline profile of the water.

Antibacterial agents

Chlorine — the one element municipal water treatment stations add to water — is something that beginner brewers need to be particularly aware of. Chlorine is added to water as an antibacterial agent. Even in minute dilutions (measured in parts per million), chlorine kills bacteria, and it can kill your beer, too — in terms of flavor, that is. Don't worry about the fluoride added to some municipal water supplies; as far as I know, it has no negative effect on the beer.

Chlorinated water used for brewing may create *chlorophenols* in your beer. Chlorophenols are unpleasant-smelling and -tasting compounds that are reminiscent of burnt plastic and cheap vinyl furniture. (How's that for mental imagery?) You can avoid this problem in a few different ways, depending on the time, money, and energy you have to spend.

- ✔ Buy and attach a carbon filter to the faucet you draw your brewing water from. Carbon filters are very effective at removing chlorine. On the down side, this method can be expensive.

- ✔ Buy bottled water from a bottled water delivery company or by the gallon at your local supermarket. This method can save you time (especially if you get your water delivered to your door), but it also can prove inconvenient if you have to drag jugs of water home from the store. (See the following section for more information about buying bottled water.)

- ✔ Preboil all the water you need for your beer. Boiling causes the chlorine to melt into a gas and float up and out of the water, evaporating in the steam. This method is effective, but it can be a time- and energy-consuming practice.

- ✔ Buy a bunch of hydrogen and oxygen atoms, some molecule glue, and start your own water factory. This method can land you in a padded room.

Not all water sources get the chlorine treatment. Some rural water supplies are contaminated with *enterobacteria* (otherwise known as *wort spoilers*). Consider having a water analysis company determine whether your water is contaminated with this foe. If there are enterobacteria in your water, keep your water heater set at 160 degrees Fahrenheit or higher and, for sanitizing purposes, rinse your equipment with hot water only.

Hard facts, fluid concepts

Many people have a tendency to see water as being merely soft or hard, but water chemistry is just not that simple. Soft water is very low in mineral content, and hard water has a very high mineral content. What *is* pretty simple, though, is the generalization that soft water is preferable to hard water because adding minerals to the water (if needed) is a lot easier than removing them.

Of course, if you have hard water, you must determine whether you have *temporary hardness* or *permanent hardness*. Temporary hardness refers to the presence of soluble bicarbonates of calcium and magnesium that *precipitate* out when you boil the water. Precipitation occurs when mineral ions are attracted to one another, bond together, and then fall out of solution as sediment (see the section "Mineral ions" later in this chapter). Permanent hardness refers to water hardness after you've boiled the water and all the nonprecipitating minerals are still there. Your water can be temporarily hard, permanently hard, or both at once — prior to boiling, that is.

Mineral ions

In simple terms, *mineral ions* are components of mineral salts that dissolve in water. And because ions have either a positive or negative charge, they're electrically attracted to the ingredients used to make beer (malt, hops, and so on). The effects of these mineral ions can range from enhancing protein coagulation (which helps to clarify beer) to accentuating the flavor of the malt.

Some mineral salts — namely calcium carbonate and magnesium carbonate — are responsible for leaving the telltale white scale on the sides of pots of boiling water.

At least seven principal ions exert a substantial influence on the beer-making process. The following list provides a brief description of these ions and their influences (the term ppm means *parts per millions*):

- **Calcium:** Lowers pH and assists enzyme action during mashing.

- **Carbonate:** Halts enzyme action and promotes harsh flavor derived from hops.

- **Chloride:** At high levels (250+ ppm) may enhance the sweetness of beer.

- **Bicarbonate:** Halts enzyme action and promotes harsh flavor derived from hops.

- **Magnesium:** Lowers pH and is an important yeast nutrient at 10 to 20 ppm.

- **Sodium:** Has no chemical effect and may impart roundness (fill out beer flavor). At too high a concentration, sodium can also give a salty flavor.

- **Sulfate:** Has no chemical effect and may impart harsh dryness when used with sodium.

Yet brewers sometimes use other mineral salts to adjust the pH level of their mashing water (see the "pHundamentals of pH balance" section in this chapter) or increase the ion profile of their brewing water. These include

- **Calcium carbonate:** More commonly known as *chalk,* calcium carbonate raises pH; 1 teaspoon in 5 gallons of liquid adds 60 ppm of carbonate and 36 ppm of calcium.

- **Calcium sulfate:** More commonly known as *gypsum,* calcium sulfate lowers pH; 1 teaspoon in 5 gallons of water adds 140 ppm of sulfate and 60 ppm of calcium.

- **Magnesium sulfate:** More commonly known as *Epsom salt,* magnesium sulfate lowers pH; 1 teaspoon in 5 gallons of water adds 100 ppm of sulfate and 25 ppm of magnesium.

- **Sodium chloride:** More commonly known as *table salt,* sodium chloride has no effect on pH; 1 teaspoon in 5 gallons of water adds 170 ppm of chloride and 110 ppm of sodium.

Trace metals

Also considered secondary ions, trace metals don't have a significant impact on beer flavor unless they're present in large quantities; then these trace metals can ruin a brew altogether. Copper, iron, lead, manganese, and zinc are some trace metals that may be found in a natural water source.

Although most of these trace metals are generally undesirable in brewing water, a few are actually beneficial in very small amounts. Manganese, copper, and zinc, for example, are valuable nutrients for yeast-cell development. Iron, on the other hand, can have an extremely detrimental effect on beer flavor, and lead can be toxic to yeast (not to mention humans) in high quantities. You can remove all of these metals from the water by filtration or distillation, or you can simply adjust their concentrations by diluting with filtered or distilled water.

Buying Brew-Friendly Bottled Water

If you choose to buy your water, you may be tempted to buy *distilled* water because it's the purest form available. But distilled water is also completely devoid of some of the important natural elements beneficial to beer.

Distilled water is made by boiling water, recapturing the steam, and cooling it back down to liquid form. This steam distillation method leaves all natural elements, chemicals, and impurities behind.

I try to strike a compromise. I like to use about 2 to 2½ gallons of municipal water straight from the kitchen faucet for the boiling in the brew kettle (most, if not all, of the chlorine is gassed out). Then, to cool and dilute the wort in the fermenter (just prior to pitching the yeast), I use up to 3 gallons of store-bought distilled water that I've refrigerated. See Chapter 10 for more details on these processes.

Wetting your appetite

No doubt, you've heard ads for beer that tout "from the land of sky-blue waters" or "brewed with pure, Rocky Mountain spring water." Breweries like to boast about the purity of the water that they use to brew their beer.

Some of the classic world styles of beer became classics because of the water used to make the beer. The famed Pilsener beers of Bohemia, such as Pilsener Urquell, are considered premier examples. These crisp, hoppy Lagers are made with extremely soft water that the brewers pump from the aquifers below the brewery. By contrast, the legendary British ales of Burton-on-Trent, such as Bass Ale, are made with particularly hard water. Considering these examples (among others), it's obvious that water can play a big role in beer flavor.

But any water, regardless of its source, can be manipulated to match the profile of another source. For example, brewers wanting to emulate the beers from Burton-on-Trent simply add certain minerals called *Burton salts* to the brewing water in a process known as *Burtonizing*.

Chapter 8

Adjuncts and Flavorings

In This Chapter

▶ Adding to your brew with adjuncts

▶ Savoring flavorings

▶ Spicing up your beer with herbs and spices

Anyone paying even the slightest bit of attention to the current beer market knows that brewers now put a lot of unusual ingredients into their beers — ingredients that may make the beer purist choke on her Old Frothy. Fruits, herbs, sugars, spices, and who knows what else show up in commercial beers almost as frequently as bubbles.

This trend hasn't always been the case, though experimentation is far from the cutting edge. Beer makers over the ages have used some odd ingredients in their beers from time to time. But homebrewers, with their innate desire to experiment and push the limits, just seem to take the concept to another level.

These unusual ingredients, whatever they may be, aren't limited to the role of flavorings, although flavoring is often their primary purpose. Brewers also utilize a variety of *adjunct* ingredients (any fermentable ingredients other than malted grains) to jack up alcohol levels, to thin out or fill out a beer's mouthfeel, or even to enhance the beer's foaminess. Adjuncts aren't the same as *adjunct grains* (cereal grains such as rice and corn used to make beer in general), which I discuss in Chapter 4. For the purposes of this chapter, the adjuncts I focus on are nongrain sugars that you can use in smaller portions to add certain flavors or fermentable ingredients to the beer-making process.

Keep in mind that the line between adjuncts and flavorings is often blurry (along with everything else after a few tasty homebrews). Adjuncts are used with the express intent of contributing fermentable sugars, but they can also add flavor; flavorings are used with the express intent of adding flavors, but they may also add fermentable sugars.

You won't find any hard-and-fast rules about how to use adjuncts and flavorings in your brews — you're limited only by your own imagination. Given the vast amount of experimentation in the world of homebrew, though, some adjuncts and flavorings just go better with certain beer styles than others (like smoke character in Porter, for example). In this chapter, I give you the lowdown on adjuncts and flavorings and how to use them. I also explore the rising popularity of using herbs and spices in homebrewing.

Adjuncts: Sugar, Sugar . . . Aw, Honey, Honey

Adjunct sugars are often called *kettle adjuncts* because you add them directly to the wort in the brew kettle instead of treating them in a separate vessel like adjunct grain. These kettle adjuncts are available in many different forms. Some are sweeter than others, and some ferment more easily than others. The following list describes some of these sugars:

- **Fructose:** Found in fruits and, to a lesser extent, malted grain. The sweetening power of fructose is more than 1½ times that of refined white sugar (which is also known as *sucrose*, or table sugar).

- **Dextrose:** Also a refined white sugar derived from *hydrolyzed* cornstarch (starch that has reacted with water and changed into glucose). Dextrose is highly fermentable and popular for priming (see Chapter 13 for more about dextrose and priming).

- **Glucose:** Derived from starch (on a molecular level, glucose and dextrose are identical) and many fruits. Glucose has only 50 percent of the sweetening power of ordinary table sugar.

- **Sucrose:** A compound of one molecule each of glucose and fructose; sucrose is found in sugar cane, sugar beets, sorghum, and malted grain. Table sugar is about 99.5 percent sucrose.

- **Lactose:** Found in milk. Beer yeast can't ferment lactose, so whatever lactose you add to your beer will remain there. Lactose is common in infant formula and various confections — not to mention Sweet Stout.

Most often, you find these sugars in processed form (such as refined white sugar), but you can also use some of them in their natural form, as is the case with honey and pure maple syrups. Again, the primary objective in using adjunct sugars is to add fermentable ingredients to the beer (which results in increased alcohol levels), and the secondary objective is to imbue the beer with unique flavor. The following is a list of optional adjuncts that contain various sugars:

- **Honey:** Honey is made from the nectar of flowers and processed with enzymes secreted by the honeybee. The two main ingredients in honey are glucose and fructose, with traces of sucrose and maltose — say that three times fast! Honey is highly fermentable and can add delicate sweetness and aroma to your brew, depending on the type of honey you choose. The quality and flavor of honey can vary greatly from one variety to the next (literally thousands of varieties are on the market), but light honeys, such as alfalfa and clover, work well in beer because their flavor is less aggressive. Because it's so fully fermentable, using honey also results in thinner-bodied beers. For this same reason, using honey also results in more alcohol per pound of honey added to the beer (compared to the same quantity of malt extract). Check out Chapter 19 for more information about honey.

✔ **Rice syrup or corn syrup:** Both rice and corn syrup are very neutral in flavor. Using high percentages of these processed syrups (relative to the rest of the ingredients) results in pale-colored, lighter-bodied, lighter-flavored beers, such as North American Light Lagers. These syrups are also effective in raising alcohol levels in dark beers without appreciably affecting the beers' flavor profiles. *Note:* Use only brewer's grade rice or corn syrup. Both of these syrups are highly fermentable and result in higher alcohol levels per pound of syrup added (compared to the same quantity of malt extract). Also note that rice syrup is available in a powdered form known as *rice syrup solids*.

✔ **Sorghum syrup:** Pure white sorghum syrup is especially handy for creating low-gluten or gluten-free beers (see Chapter 21 for more information on gluten-free brewing), but you can also use this syrup like rice or corn syrup for making lighter-bodied and -colored brews.

✔ **Maple syrup:** Natural maple syrup is mostly sucrose with some *invert sugar* (a mixture of certain forms of glucose and fructose. See the sidebar "Making invert sugar syrup" for more information.) The more natural the syrup, the better (pure maple syrup must weigh no less than 11 pounds per gallon). Depending on the quality, which is based on the percentage of maple sugar in the syrup, maple flavor may be very assertive in the beer. Maple syrup, depending on the sugar content, is about 65 percent fermentable, which means the yeast eats about 65 percent of whatever amount you add to your beer.

✔ **Brown sugar:** Brown sugar is derived from unrefined or partially refined sugar (cane or beet), and flavored with molasses. It's usually available in light and dark brown choices. The darker brown the sugar, the more residual flavor it leaves in the beer.

✔ **Molasses:** Molasses syrup is produced during the refining of white sugar from sorghum or from the juice of sun-ripened cane. Be sure to buy unsulfured molasses (sulfur fumes used in the sugar-making process are retained in molasses and must be commercially extracted). Usually, molasses is available in three colors/flavors — light, dark, and blackstrap — based on its degree of caramelization and concentration.

Light molasses results from the first boiling of the cane, and dark molasses is the product of a second boiling. Blackstrap molasses, produced from a third boiling, is a waste product in the sugar industry, but it's great for Stouts and other dark beers.

- ✔ **Treacle:** Often incorrectly defined as molasses in the King's English, treacle is a brown-colored syrup also known as *refiner's syrup*. Although it's derived in much the same way as molasses, it often comes clarified and decolorized, so it's not as dark and aggressive in flavor as molasses. Treacle isn't an equal substitute for molasses, but it still makes an interesting adjunct sugar for beer-making purposes.

- ✔ **Belgian candi sugar:** Chunky, caramelized sugar in crystals and granular form are popular in Belgian Strong Ales and Trappist beer varieties; they usually come in golden to dark amber varieties. Candi sugar enhances a beer's flavor and alcohol levels. More recently, candi syrup has become available to homebrewers. Pound for pound, the syrup gives more color and caramelized flavor than the sugar crystals. Belgian candi sugar is a good source of sucrose.

- ✔ **Turbinado sugar:** Also known as raw sugar, turbinado sugar is a partially refined, coarse, beige-colored crystal that still contains some of the molasses from the original sugar. Depending on the source, turbinado sugar may contain impurities. Homebrewers who can get their hands on this stuff like to experiment with it in high-gravity Ales such as English Old Ales or Barley Wines. Check your local ethnic grocery store for turbinado sugar. It's also another good source of sucrose.

- ✔ **Demarara sugar:** Demarara sugar is very close in character to turbinado sugar but with a darker color and more pronounced molasses flavor. Readily fermentable, it's excellent for dark Ales.

You should add these naturally occurring sugars sparingly to your brew, and they shouldn't constitute a large percentage of the total fermentable ingredients in your recipe. One pound or less per 5-gallon batch is a typical amount. Make sure you stay away from using refined white sugars (sugar made from cane or beets) in brewing. White sugars used in quantities of more than 20 percent of total fermentable ingredients result in a noticeable cidery smell and taste. Also, white sugars are so highly fermentable that your beer will have a measurable increase in alcohol while suffering a measurable decrease in body and mouthfeel. Dextrose (corn sugar) is the only granular white sugar that you should use for priming beer at bottling time (see Chapter 13 to find out more about dextrose and bottling).

Flavoring Your Brew with Flavorings

Beyond adding adjunct sugars to your brew, an unlimited number of flavorings exist that you can add to beer. Some may contain sugars that result in added gravity and alcohol, but I cover most of those flavorings in previous sections in this chapter. In this section, I focus on those ingredients that are primarily used to add unique flavors to beer.

Making invert sugar syrup

A handful of beer styles — primarily those from England and Belgium — regularly use added sugar in their recipes. Because using large amounts of refined sugar can create a cidery tang in beer, brewers can safely make and use invert sugar to reduce the sugar's acidic effect on their beer's flavor. Here's how:

Ingredients:

- ✔ 8 pounds of white cane/beet sugar

- ✔ 2 pints of water

- ✔ 1 tablespoon (or 3 teaspoons) of citric acid

Directions:

1. Mix all ingredients in a large pot and heat to boiling (the mixture will foam and then turn a clear, golden color).

2. Cool and then dilute in water to reach a total volume of 1 gallon.

One pint of this liquid invert sugar equals 1 pound of granular sugar.

Add too much of this sugar to your beer, and you can still get a cidery taste. I recommend that invert syrup make up less than 20 percent of your total fermentable ingredients.

The goal when using these flavorings is to complement the underlying beer flavor, not to create a whole new one. Whenever possible, make sure you add these ingredients directly to the brewpot to take advantage of the disinfecting action of the boiling wort and to meld the flavors into the brew. (I note the exceptions to this "add to the brewpot" rule in the next section.)

Funky flavorings: The exotic and the esoteric

The following is a list of flavorings that are commonly used in the homebrewing world:

- ✔ **Chocolate:** Beer made with real chocolate is an *esoteric* (old-but-not-out-of-date) brew that brewers make only occasionally (most brewers create chocolate character in their beers by using chocolate malt, which has nothing to do with the cocoa bean). Use only unsweetened baker's chocolate (found in the baking goods aisle of your local supermarket), not milk chocolate or sweetened chocolate. One or two 1-ounce squares in a 5-gallon batch are sufficient. Or you can use cocoa powder (the same stuff used in baking) or the powdery chocolate substances popular for chocolate-milk making. Try chocolate (sparingly) in a medium-bodied spiced Ale. Gives a whole new meaning to the term chocoholic, doesn't it?

- **Spruce essence:** Spruce beer was an early American favorite. Using the new spring growth (the needles) of the spruce tree was the old fashioned method. Today, you can buy spruce essence through your homebrew supplier, but this stuff is pretty potent. Two to five teaspoons give your beer a refreshing spruce taste. Pretend you're a patriot and spruce up your favorite Ale.

- **Licorice:** Drinkers often experience a licorice flavor in dark beers even when it hasn't been specifically added to the brew. Brewers who like this flavor can add all they want to their own beer by using unsweetened brewer's licorice sticks, which you can find at your homebrew supply shop. But be careful not to overuse licorice — a little goes a long way. One or two inches are sufficient for a 5-gallon batch. Licorice is especially good for Porters, Stouts, and Schwarzbiers.

- **Fruit flavorings:** Some fruit flavorings are available without added sugar. You use these liquid flavorings in the same way you use fruit juices or extracts, except that unsweetened fruit flavorings don't require fermentation time. Of these flavorings, the most common flavors are blueberry, cherry, raspberry, peach, and apricot — check with your local homebrew supply shop. Doses depend on the fruit, the brand, your personal taste, and so on. Fruit flavorings are much easier to work with than real fruit; they're widely available and never out of season. To preserve as much fruit character as possible, some producers even suggest adding the flavoring to the beer at bottling time. These flavorings work well in virtually all beer styles, but the darker the beer, the more flavoring you need to compete with the flavors of the underlying beer.

- **Oak chips/oak extract:** Brewers wanting to emulate the oaky character of traditional India Pale Ales or their favorite oak-aged Belgian beers can try using oak chips. Because oak adds tannin to beer, you never want to boil the chips. (*Tannin* is derived from organic compounds such as cereal grain husks, oak bark, grape skins, and the rinds of shelled nuts. Tannin is a sharp, astringent [bitter] flavor; if you've ever accidentally eaten some of the red rind found inside a pecan, you know how unpleasant tasting tannin can be.) The best way to use oak chips is to steam them for 15 minutes (to sanitize them) before adding them to the secondary fermenter. You can find oak chips in regular and toasted form (hold the butter). Oak flavor is also available in extract form.

- **Lactose:** Lactose powder has a very limited use in the homebrewing world — it's primarily used to add sweetness and body to beer without the risk of cidery flavors or higher alcohol levels. Beer yeast can't ferment lactose, so the lactose retains virtually all of its sweetness. Lactose is a prerequisite for making London-Style Sweet Stout (also called Cream Stout or Milk Stout for obvious reasons). Six to twelve ounces per 5-gallon batch gets the job done.

✔ **Smoke:** Rauchbier (Smoked Beer) is another esoteric brew. Fans of German Rauchbier — and even Scottish Ales — can emulate their favorite smoky brews by using liquid smoke extract. Add a tablespoon or two per 5-gallon batch at the very end of the boil, depending on your tolerance for smoke aroma and flavor. Well-stocked grocery stores carry this extract because cooks often use it for making homemade barbecue sauces. Avoid buying cheaper brands that contain vinegar or preservatives. The drawback to this method is that most liquid smoke extracts give off the aroma and flavor characteristics typically associated with barbecued meats, like hickory, mesquite, and so on.

You can also imbue smoke flavor in a more natural way by using smoked malts. You can buy these malts at homebrew supply shops or create them at home on a barbecue grill (see Chapter 26 for more information on creating your own smoked malts).

✔ **Vanilla:** Homebrewers can choose between working with pure vanilla extract and using the purist's vanilla bean, though neither is terribly common in beer making. Commercial brewers who produce this unusual flavor of brew usually reserve it for a once-a-year specialty Spiced Ale or Christmas beer.

✔ **Orange peel:** Due to the growing popularity of Belgian Witbier, dried orange peel is now available at most good homebrew supply stores. Choose between sweet orange or bitter (Curaçao) orange variety. A couple of ounces per 5-gallon batch are a typical amount.

✔ **Fruit liqueurs:** Certain fruit liqueurs can be used for flavoring beer, but because they contain large amounts of refined sugar, they're best as priming agents (see Chapter 13 to read more about priming with liqueurs).

Herbs and spice and everything nice

At some point in your blossoming brewing career, you're likely to grow the same wild hair that every other homebrewer has grown. One day you'll be contemplating your next brew over an odoriferous plate of Italian food when out of nowhere it'll hit you: — "Hmmm, I wonder what garlic beer tastes like?" You may laugh, but somebody actually made a garlic beer (unfortunately for those of us who tasted it). In fact, in the world of homebrew, you're hard-pressed to find a stone left unturned.

Herb and spice beer is the category that really challenges the conventional ideas of beer, although what seemed alien a half a dozen years ago is now reaching the mainstream. Coriander seems to be the *herb du jour* (or is it a spice — I'm not sure). Allspice is on the rise, and ginger is making a comeback; cinnamon and cloves are passé.

Your spice rack at home presents an (almost) unlimited variety of choices for your next brew, but don't make the same mistake many brewers before you have made. Just because you like the taste of cumin and lemongrass doesn't mean adding such a combination to your brew makes a great beer. Before forging ahead, you need to reflect a bit on your idea. Try to imagine the taste of the beer you have in mind. Is it something you want to drink two cases of? If so, move cautiously, remembering that using too little of an ingredient is better than using too much.

Give your beer flavoring idea a taste test: Try brewing a little "tea" of the herb or spice you have in mind and strain it into a commercial beer similar to the style you intend to make. You may also want to jot down your tasting notes to help fine-tune your final recipe.

You can introduce herbs and spices two ways in the beermaking process:

- ✔ **Add them directly to the brewpot.**
- ✔ **Put them in the secondary fermenter.** (See Chapter 11 for more on secondary fermentation.)

If you go the brewpot route, wait until the last 15 minutes of the boil. Allowing certain herbs or spices (such as cinnamon bark) to boil in the wort for long periods of time can sometimes create an astringency or harshness similar to the result of boiling grain.

If you hold out until the secondary fermentation stage, you need to sanitize the ingredients. Hold the bleach — this is a job for distilled alcohol. Whatever consumable spirits (whisky, vodka, gin, and so on) you may have in your home can get the job done. Allow the herb or spice of choice to soak in ½ cup of whatever booze you choose for about a week prior to putting the herb or spice in the secondary fermenter; what you do with the spiced liquor is your business. Actually, dumping the entire herb/spice liquor concoction into the secondary fermenter is okay, too.

To make the ingredient-soaking process easier, try fashioning a small filter or pouch out of an unused coffee filter or fresh tea bag you've emptied of its contents; close with a twist-tie or string.

Fresh and whole herbs and spices are better than those that are old, stale, chopped, or powdered.

Spices

A wide variety of spices are available for you to use to enhance the flavor of your brews. The following is a short list of some of the most popular spices in the homebrewing world — the tried-and-true choices:

✔ **Allspice:** Allspice is one of the more interesting spices to use; within the single small berry is a natural mixture of flavors reminiscent of cinnamon, clove, nutmeg, and juniper berries. Brewers often use allspice in seasonal pumpkin beers.

✔ **Anise:** The star anise variety is most common. This spice gives beer a subtle licorice undertone.

✔ **Cardamom:** The plump seeds of the cardamom family appear in culinary applications as diverse as coffee flavoring, barbecue sauces, and curry powder. Used judiciously, cardamom lends beer a unique and subtle spicy flavor.

✔ **Caraway:** You rarely use this seed on its own, but it's a natural complementary flavoring for anyone attempting to make a flavorful rye beer.

✔ **Cinnamon:** Cinnamon seems to be the go-to spice for pastries and other confections. Cinnamon works well in big-bodied beers made for wintertime consumption. Make sure you use cinnamon bark rather than powder because you can easily remove the sticks from the brew; cinnamon powder (unless filtered out) remains in the beer and may create a harsh flavor and an unpleasant lingering mouthfeel.

✔ **Cloves:** Clove-like aromas and tastes occur naturally in some beer styles — most notably the Bavarian Weizenbiers and some Belgian Ales. Homebrewers can introduce this clove character by using whole cloves — in small quantities. Many people perceive cloves to have a strong *phenolic* or medicinal character.

✔ **Coriander:** Coriander is the seed of the same plant from which cilantro is derived. The lemony coriander is a key ingredient in a traditional Belgian Witbier, but it also works well in many beer styles.

✔ **Gingerroot:** The flavor of raw gingerroot (also known as just *ginger*) is intense and spicy-hot or sharp in anything but small quantities or dilutions. The actual flavor — most closely associated with ginger ale (soda) — actually works quite well in beer and Mead. The key is to use grated gingerroot rather than ginger powder. Use gingerly; 1 ounce in a 5-gallon batch of beer is plenty noticeable.

The original ginger ale really was Ale. The concoction was a standard beer in colonial America because the colonists used ginger and other spices in the absence of hops to offset the malty sweetness of beer.

✔ **Juniper berries:** Because juniper berries are used to make gin, you can use them to give your brew the same aroma and flavor as gin — if you happen to like gin.

✔ **Vanilla bean:** Although high-quality vanilla extract is easier to work with, the oil of the vanilla bean can also lend a pleasant mouthfeel to your brew while it gives a rich aroma and flavor. For best results, use *macerated* (crushed) vanilla beans during secondary fermentation only.

Herbs

The following herbs are also worth trying in your homebrew:

- **Sweet gale:** This herb is an aromatic seasoning that many Belgian brewers use to add a lightly sweet flavor. Use sparingly.

- **Heather tips:** Dried heather tips were popular in Scotland to balance malty sweetness before the advent of hop usage. You can find a Heather Ale currently available in the United States by the brand name Fraoch.

- **Mint:** Mint isn't normally high on the list of brewing herbs, but I can personally attest that it can work in certain beer styles if handled properly — a Mint Stout stands out in my memory. You're probably familiar with peppermint and spearmint, but some lesser known mint varieties, such as apple mint, are less assertive and equally refreshing.

Many other popular cooking herbs can also successfully flavor beer; basil, oregano, and rosemary come to mind. Be bold, be brave, be intrepid, and be ready to drink two cases of whatever it is you dream up!

Chapter 9

Making Your Brew Bionic: Additives, Preservatives, Finings, and Clarifiers

In This Chapter

▶ Exploring additives and preservatives

▶ Using clarifying agents

▶ Working with acidifying agents

*W*elcome to the chapter that concentrates on all the nonessential minor ingredients sometimes found in beer. The various elements discussed in this chapter have little or nothing to do with beer flavor and aren't absolutely necessary for making good beer. However, you can use all of the elements defined here to *polish* your homebrew (in other words, to manipulate your beer in various ways that may affect the quality and perception of the finished product).

It's important to note the distinction between quality and the perception of quality. *Quality* is an objective term; homebrew is either well made or it isn't. *Perception of quality,* on the other hand, is subjective. The clarifying agents outlined in this chapter, for example, help you produce crystal-clear beer. Most drinkers *perceive* transparent beer as being better than cloudy or hazy beer, but, in fact, a beer's clarity has little bearing on its quality. A perfectly clear beer isn't necessarily well made, and a cloudy beer may be incredibly well made. (Just something to keep in mind.)

To Add and Preserve

You can use a wide variety of other ingredients to affect the outcome of your finished beer. These optional ingredients fall loosely into the additives and preservatives category. *Additives,* generally speaking, affect the interactions among the basic ingredients (malt, hops, yeast, and water) — how they behave throughout the mashing, boiling, cooling, and fermentation phases of homebrewing. *Preservatives,* generally speaking, preserve the character of the beer you create. None of these products are absolutely necessary for making good beer, but they can be helpful. The following list provides some of these options:

- **Amylase enzyme:** This enzyme breaks down malt, barley, and adjunct starches into soluble dextrins and small quantities of fermentable sugars and therefore reduces chill haze in the finished beer. (*Chill haze* is a temporary cloudiness that forms in beer when you refrigerate it; it's caused by the combination and *precipitation* [solids forming in and dropping out of solution] of protein matter and *tannin* [a bitter compound derived from organic matter — in this case, grain] molecules during secondary fermentation. Chill haze usually appears around 36 degrees Fahrenheit and disappears around 64 degrees Fahrenheit.) Although you typically use it in all-grain beers, you can add amylase enzyme to any high-gravity wort because it's also effective at sustaining active fermentation. Add 1 teaspoon per 5-gallon batch.

- **Burton salts:** *Burton salts* is a generic name for a blend of natural minerals that emulates the brewing water in the English brewing city of Burton-on-Trent. Burton salts increase the hardness of brewing water (see Chapter 7 for more information on water hardness) and also help prevent chill haze.

- **Foam control:** *Foam control* inhibits the formation of foam during primary fermentation, which means that your brew hangs on to the head-forming compounds during the brewing process. Thus, the addition of foam control results in denser heads when you pour the finished beer for consumption. You can add foam control to the wort at the same time that you add the yeast. One teaspoon per 5-gallon batch is all you need.

- **Heading compound:** This compound improves head retention in the finished beer and increases foam stability. One teaspoon dissolved in a half cup of water is sufficient for a 5-gallon batch. This compound is available in both liquid and powdered form; the liquid form is more expensive, but it's also easier to work with than the powdered form. The average homebrew shouldn't need the assistance of artificial heading compounds unless it has a very, very low original gravity or a very low malt content.

The difference between foam control and heading compound is that foam control suppresses natural foaming during fermentation and preserves it for pouring; the heading compound artificially increases foaming in the beer.

The most popular heading compound is *polypropylene glycol alginate*, which is derived from seaweed.

✔ **Malto-dextrin:** Dextrins are the (beer) body-building components of malted grain; the more dextrins in the beer, the fuller the mouthfeel. Malto-dextrin powder is a convenient shortcut to creating body and mouthfeel in low-gravity beers.

✔ **Yeast energizer:** As the name suggests, this additive energizes old and tired yeast and is helpful for reviving stuck or slow fermentations. Dissolve a teaspoon of energizer in a cup of boiling water, cool, and add directly to the fermenter. To avoid having to open a sealed fermenter, try anticipating the need for yeast energizer (such as in beers with original gravities over 1.056) and add the energizer directly to the cooled wort as you pitch your yeast (or to the secondary fermenter as you rack the beer over to it). See Chapter 6 for more information on yeast energizers.

✔ **Yeast nutrient:** Typically, this type of product consists of di-ammonium phosphate and nitrogen. This yeast fertilizer provides the yeast with a balanced diet and is perfect for yeast starters and low-malt-content worts. You can find more on yeast nutrient in Chapter 6.

A Little Clarification, Please

Regardless of whether you work with malt extracts or grains, whole hops or pellets, dry yeast or liquid cultures, a number of organic compounds are floating around in your brew: proteins, starches, oils, resins, yeast cells basically, particulate matter of all shapes and sizes. Given time, most of this stuff eventually settles out of your beer naturally. Time, however, isn't a friend to beer. This urgency is why brewers often resort to the use of *clarifying agents* to impel this floating matter to clump up and fall to the bottom of the fermenter. All clarifying agents can be considered preservatives since they remove organic particles from the beer that might otherwise cause your beer to eventually develop off flavors and aromas.

Generally speaking, what little particulate matter remains suspended in your brew doesn't initially affect the taste or aroma of your beer in an adverse way; it mostly affects the visual presentation. Whether you want a clear beer for competition purposes or for personal preference, clarifying agents can help clear up your beer.

Note: Beer filtration is an expensive option that's open to you nonetheless; I discuss this procedure in Chapter 23.

Some of the clarifying agents in the following list are organic or mineral in composition and have been used for eons (not to be confused with mineral ions). A couple of these agents, such as Irish moss and isinglass, are called *finings.* Finings do the same job as the other clarifiers — the rest are just technologically advanced products of our modern era.

- **Bentonite:** *Bentonite* is a nonorganic material combined with a form of powdered clay. Bentonite is more closely associated with winemaking, but it also works well in beer. Just mix this material with water (according to package directions) and add to the secondary fermenter a week prior to bottling.

- **Gelatin:** Gelatin is derived from collagen in pork and cattle skin and bones. It's a colorless, tasteless, and odorless water-soluble protein that attracts negatively charged proteins and yeast. Gelatin works best when you rehydrate it, pour it into cool beer, and give it 5 to 7 days to accomplish its task after primary fermentation is complete.

  Use 1 teaspoon per 5-gallon batch of beer. Dissolve the gelatin in 1 cup of cool water and slowly heat over a low flame for about 15 minutes; do *not* let it boil. Add the mixture to the fermenter immediately after it has cooled.

- **Irish moss:** Also known as *carrageen* (and *copper finings* in the U.K.), Irish moss is actually a form of brown seaweed. Because this substance is a *kettle-coagulant* (meaning it works in the brew kettle), you want to add it to the brew during the boil. Doing so causes a lot of the protein in the wort to coagulate as it cools. Irish moss comes in flaked and powdered form.

  Because Irish moss requires a rehydration period in order to be effective, add ½ tablespoon of it to the wort in the last 15 minutes of the boil (this amount is sufficient for a 5-gallon batch).

- **Isinglass:** Derived from the swim bladders of sturgeons, isinglass is perhaps the most unusual of the fining family of clarifiers; however, it's also highly effective. *Isinglass* (also known as *white finings*) attracts negatively charged proteins and yeast, causing them to settle out of the beer. You use isinglass in the same way you use gelatin, but isinglass may be a little harder to dissolve in water (follow package instructions). This naturally gelatinous substance comes in powdered form, and 1 teaspoon of this powder treats a 5-gallon batch.

Because isinglass finings have a charge opposite that of the other finings, you can use them in combination with some of the other finings or clarifiers to improve beer clarification. By contrast, if you use two similarly charged finings simultaneously, they interfere with each other's activity and actually impede beer clarification.

✔ **Polyvinylpolypyrrolidone (PVPP):** *PVPP* is actually made up of minute beads of plastic that are statically charged, which allows them to attract particulate matter to themselves like electrostatic glue. Rehydrate the PVPP in hot tap water for about an hour before stirring it gently into the finished beer in the last few days of secondary fermentation. Another positive quality of PVPP is that it's very effective at combating chill haze. Use ¼ ounce per 5-gallon batch.

You don't need to be concerned about having powdered plastic in your brew. The largest consumer of PVPP is the pharmaceutical industry, which uses it to produce capsule-type drugs.

✔ **Silica gel:** *Silica gel* is a hard, granulated form of hydrated silica that works by absorption. Each particle is a hollow silica honeycomb with pores just large enough to let haze-forming proteins in. As each particle adsorbs the protein, the particle falls out of solution and forms a firm sediment on the bottom of the fermentation vessel.

Silica gel is a lot like PVPP without the rehydration; stir silica gel into the secondary fermenter a few days before bottling or kegging. Use ½ ounce per 5-gallon batch of beer.

✔ **Sparkolloid:** Sparkolloid is a brand-name blend of polysaccharides and diatomaceous earth. It's popular in the winemaking industry, but you can also adapt it to the clarification of beer. Heat 1 gram of Sparkolloid per gallon of beer in water and then add it (hot or cooled) to your beer as you transfer the brew from the primary fermenter to the secondary fermenter.

✔ **Super Kleer KC Finings:** *KC finings* are an excellent all-purpose fining agent that contains kieselsol and chitosan (derived from shellfish). Add to secondary fermenter for clarifying within 12 to 48 hours.

✔ **Whirlfloc:** A blend of Irish moss and purified Carrageen that helps precipitate haze-causing proteins and beta glucans. Add one tablet (per 5 gallons of brew) in the last 15 minutes of the boil.

The famous beechwood-aged beers made by Anheuser-Busch supposedly gain clarity from aging over large chips of beechwood. Kids — don't try this at home.

The Acid Test

Brewers can introduce a number of different acids to beer at various stages in the brewing process; each acid has its own purpose (additive, preservative, or clarifier), and they should all be readily available at well-stocked homebrew stores.

The following is a list of those acids and general descriptions of how they can aid you in the beer making process. Exactly how you use these acids depends on your needs (always follow package directions). For questions regarding pH balance, see Chapter 7.

- **Ascorbic:** *Ascorbic acid* is an antioxidant, which qualifies it as a preservative. Ascorbic acid protects beer from the off aromas and tastes associated with oxidation. This acid is also known as vitamin C. Use ½ teaspoon per 5-gallon batch (overuse lends a citrus flavor to your beer). Add to beer at bottling time.

- **Citric:** *Citric acid* protects against haze, increases the acidity of brewing water by lowering the pH, and aids in the fermentation process. You can also find it premixed in a product called Acid Blend, which is a convenient mix of citric, malic, and tartaric acids.

- **Lactic:** *Lactic acid* is a mild acid used to *acidify* (lower the pH of) the mash or sparge water. (See Chapter 12 for more on mashing and sparging.) Lactic acid gives Berliner Weisse beer its characteristic tartness. When you use lactic acid, add 1 teaspoon per 5-gallon batch just prior to bottling.

- **Malic:** *Malic acid* increases the tartness in beer. Like citric acid, you can find malic acid premixed in Acid Blend.

- **Phosphoric:** You can use *phosphoric acid* in weak dilutions (approximately 1 part phosphoric acid per 10 parts water) to acidify mash water.

- **Tartaric:** *Tartaric acid* increases the tartness in beer and is also an ingredient in Acid Blend.

Part III
Ready, Set, Brew!

In this part . . .

This is where you actually make the beer, following step-by-step procedures. Chapters 10 through 12 cover the beginning, intermediate, and advanced levels of home-brewing, and Chapters 13 and 14 illustrate the options you have to package your brew once it's done fermenting.

Chapter 10

Beginner Brewing Directions

In This Chapter

▶ Discussing the pros and cons of brewing with a kit
▶ Brewing step by step
▶ Reading hydrometers

My philosophy is that beginning brewers have to start somewhere (profound, huh?), and that somewhere needs to be with an all-inclusive homebrewing kit. A *kit* is simply a package you buy from a homebrew supply store that includes all the ingredients (pre-hopped malt extract and a packet of yeast) that you need to brew a particular style of beer. The kits I'm referring to here are ingredient kits only (as discussed in Chapter 4), mind you; they don't include any equipment.

But brewing beer from a kit also has a possible downside, depending on your perspective. At the beginner homebrewing level, you the brewer have little personal control over most of the beer-making process. (Practicing proper sanitation is the glaring exception to this rule — see Chapter 3.) When you use a kit, much of the thinking and the work have been done for you. (I like to compare homebrewing at the beginner level to making soup from a can. Cold, fizzy soup. Darn tasty soup.) Don't get me wrong — this extra guidance is good for those of you just starting out in the world of homebrewing who want to work with a net the first few times through the process.

And so, in exchange for its simplicity, brewing at the novice level has its limitations. Making brewing easy means keeping it simple, and keeping it simple means not using unusual ingredients or lengthy procedures. Because you've relied on the malt extract producer to provide all the ingredients in one tidy kit, many of the world beer styles can't be faithfully duplicated at the beginner level of homebrewing. Instead, what you find at the beginner level in the beer recipe chapters in this book (see Part IV) are time- and effort-saving hints and shortcuts for making a beer that comes reasonably close to the intended beer style.

The two biggest pluses to brewing at this level are the speed at which you can produce beer and the rapid rate at which you can conquer the learning curve associated with it. The more quickly and cheaply you can produce beer, the more you can make. The more you make, the more efficient you become and, presumably, the more you comprehend about the nuts-and-bolts of brewing. You can master several aspects of homebrewing (sanitation, racking, observing fermentation, and bottling) at the beginner level. Thus, another simple rule at the beginner level: The more you brew, the better your beer gets. It's a delicious circle.

Gathering the Tools You Need

Before you start the brewing process, make sure you have all your homebrewing equipment (see Chapter 2), you've properly sanitized it (see Chapter 3), and it's in place and ready to use. Here's a quick equipment checklist for you:

- **Airlock**
- **Brewpot with lid**
- **Brew spoon**
- **Coffee cup or small bowl** (for proofing the yeast)
- **Fermentation bucket with lid**
- **Rubber stopper** (to attach to the airlock)
- **Hydrometer** (the hydrometer cylinder isn't necessary at this time)

Now you just need a couple of simple household items to complete the ensemble. Gather together a long-handled spoon or rubber spatula (for scraping the gooey malt extract from the cans), hot pads (to hold onto hot pots and pans), and a small saucepan (to heat up the cans of extract). Speaking of which, be sure to have your homebrew kits on hand — your beer will be awfully watery-tasting without them!

I recommend either two 3.3-pound cans of pre-hopped malt extract (plus yeast), or one 6.6-pound can. This is the appropriate amount for the average 5-gallon batch of beer. The style of beer or brand of malt extract is your choice, but I give you suggestions in the appendix.

Brewing Your First Batch

Enough of the preliminary stuff. Here's where the rubber meets the road — it's time to get brewing! This section walks you through the step-by-step process of brewing at home. Just follow along and you can make great beer in no time.

The following numbered list covers 24 steps that walk you all the way through the brewing process. Twenty-four steps may sound pretty intense, but I assure you they're easy, quick, and painless steps (unless you consider turning on a burner to be exhausting work). Besides, when you're done, you've brewed your first beer!

1. **Fill your brewpot about ⅔ full with clean tap water or bottled water and then place it on the largest burner of your stove.**

   Use bottled water if your home's water source is loaded with chlorine, iron, or high concentrations of other trace metals. (See Chapter 7 to find out more about the importance of good water.)

   The exact volume of water isn't terribly important during this step, because you add cold water to the fermenter later to bring the total to 5 gallons.

2. **Set the burner on medium-high.**

3. **Remove the plastic lids from the kits and set the yeast packets aside.**

4. **Strip the paper labels off the two cans of extract and place the cans in a smaller pot or saucepan filled halfway with tap water. Place the pot or saucepan on another burner near the brewpot.**

   The water's purity isn't important here because you don't use this water in the beer.

5. **Set the second burner on medium.**

6. **Using hot pads, flip the cans in the warming water every couple of minutes.**

7. **As the water in the brewpot begins to boil, turn off the burner under the smaller pot (containing the cans), remove the cans from the water, and remove the lids from the cans.**

8. **Using a long-handled spoon or rubber spatula, scrape as much of the warmed extract as possible from the cans into the water in the brewpot.**

9. **Immediately stir the extract/water solution and continue to stir until the extract completely dissolves in the water.**

This malt extract/water mixture is now officially called *wort*.

If you don't stir the wort immediately, you risk scorching the extract on the bottom of the brewpot.

10. **Top off the brewpot with more clean tap or bottled water, keeping your water level a reasonable distance — about 2 inches — from the top of the pot to avoid boilovers.**

11. **Bring the wort to a boil (turn up the burner if necessary).**

12. **Boil the wort for about an hour, stirring the pot every couple of minutes to avoid scorching and boilovers.**

Never put the lid on the brewpot during the boiling phase! Stove-top boilovers occur regularly when a brewpot's lid is on. Boilovers aren't only a sticky, gooey mess, but they're also a waste of good beer!

13. **Turn off the burner and place the lid on the brewpot.**

14. **Put a stopper in the nearest sink drain, put the covered brewpot in the sink, and fill the sink with very cold water.**

Fill the sink completely (or up to the liquid level in the brewpot if the sink is deeper than the brewpot).

15. **After 5 minutes, drain the sink and refill it with very cold water — repeat as many times as you need until the brewpot is cool to the touch.**

16. **While the brewpot is cooling in the sink, draw at least 6 ounces of lukewarm tap water into a sanitized cup or bowl.**

17. **Open the yeast packets and pour the dried yeast into the cup or bowl of water.**

Called *proofing*, this process is a gentle but effective way to wake up the dormant yeast and ready it for the fermentation to follow.

18. **When the brewpot is relatively cool to the touch, remove the brewpot lid and carefully pour the wort into the fermentation bucket.**

Make sure the spigot is closed!

19. **Top off the fermenter to the 5-gallon mark with cold, clean water, pouring it vigorously into the bucket.**

This splashing not only mixes the wort with the additional water, it also aerates the wort well.

The yeast needs oxygen in order to get off to a good healthy start in the fermentation phase. Because boiled water is virtually devoid of oxygen, you need to put some oxygen back in by aerating the wort. Failure to aerate may result in sluggish and sometimes incomplete fermentations.

20. **Take a hydrometer reading.**

    See the section "Brewing day reading" in this chapter for specific information about this process.

21. **After you take the hydrometer reading and remove the hydrometer, pour the hydrated yeast from the cup or bowl into the fermenter and give it a good brisk stir with your brew spoon.**

22. **Cover the fermenter with its lid and thoroughly seal it.**

23. **Put the fermenter in a cool, dark location, such as a basement, a crawl space, or an interior closet.**

    Don't put the fermenter in direct sunlight or where there's a daily fluctuation in temperatures, such as your garage. This temperature fluctuation can mess with your beer's fermentation cycle.

24. **After the fermenter is in a good place, fill the airlock halfway with water and replace the cap; attach the rubber stopper and position it snugly in the fermenter lid.**

    Check to make sure that the fermenter and airlock are sealed airtight by pushing down gently on the fermenter lid. This gentle pressure causes the float piece in the airlock to rise; if it doesn't, you have a breach in the seal. Recheck the lid and airlock for leaks.

    Fermentation should begin within the first 24 hours and last anywhere from 7 to 10 days. This wait can be nerve-wracking for first-timers, but patience is rewarded with great beer.

How quickly the beer begins to ferment and how long the fermentation lasts depends on the amount of yeast, the health of the yeast, the temperature at which the beer is fermenting, and whether or not the wort was properly aerated. Healthy yeast, mild temperatures (65 to 70 degrees Fahrenheit), and an abundance of oxygen in the wort make for a good, quick ferment. Old, dormant yeast, cold temperatures, and under-oxygenated wort cause fermentations to start slowly, go on interminably, or even quit altogether.

After your beer has been in the fermenter for about a week or so, check the bubbling action in the airlock. If visible fermentation is still taking place (as evidenced by the escaping bubbles), continue to check the bubbling on a daily basis. When the float piece within the airlock appears to be still and the time between bubbles is a minute or more, your beer is ready for bottling. Before you begin the bottling procedures, however, you need to take a second gravity reading to make sure that the fermentation is complete (see the section "Prebottling reading" in this chapter for specifics on how to do this).

Bottling beer before it's done fermenting may result in exploding bottles. Chapter 13 gives you the lowdown on this nasty mishap and how to avoid it.

Taking Hydrometer Readings

I cover the purpose of a hydrometer and how to use one in homebrewing extensively in Chapter 2. The following information shows you specifically how to take hydrometer readings on brewing and bottling days. If you have any lingering questions on this subject, please check out Chapter 2.

Brewing day reading

You want to take the first hydrometer reading on brewing day (see Step 20 in the "Brewing Your First Batch" section of this chapter). To take a good reading, do the following:

1. **Lower the sanitized hydrometer directly into the cooled and diluted wort inside the fermenter.**

   As you lower the hydrometer into the wort in the fermenter, give the hydrometer a quick spin with your thumb and index finger; this movement dislodges any bubbles clinging to the hydrometer that may cause you to get an incorrect reading.

2. **Record the numbers at the liquid surface on the hydrometer scales.**

   You need this information on bottling day to decide whether fermentation is complete and to figure out the alcohol content in your beer. The gravity of your malt extract and water mixture will determine the numbers you'll see on the scales. Typically, 6 or so pounds of malt extract diluted in 5 gallons of water appear on the hydrometer's O.G. scale as 1.048, and the alcohol potential (as noted on the hydrometer's alcohol potential scale) is around 6 percent.

Prebottling reading

When you think your beer is ready for bottling (based on the bubbling action in the airlock), it's time to take another hydrometer reading. When compared to the first (brewing day) reading, this reading helps you decide whether or not your beer is actually ready to be bottled.

1. **With your hydrometer test cylinder in hand, take a sample of beer from the spigot of the fermenter.**

   Be sure to fill the cylinder to within 1 inch of the opening, leaving room for liquid displacement of the immersed hydrometer.

2. **Immerse the hydrometer in the beer, record the numbers at the liquid surface of the hydrometer, and compare with those numbers recorded on brewing day.**

   Remember that the average healthy yeast consumes at least 65 percent of the available sugars in the wort. If the final gravity reading on your fermented beer isn't 35 percent or less of the original gravity, too much natural sugar may be left in your beer.

Here's a sample equation: If your beer has an original gravity of 1.048, subtract 1 so that you have 0.048; then multiply .048 by 0.35, which results in 0.017. Now add the 1 back in. If the final gravity of your beer is higher than 1.017, you want to delay bottling a few more days.

Calculating alcohol content percentage

Shown here is a sample equation to help you figure out how much alcohol has been produced in your beer during fermentation. If you find this all a bit confusing, I suggest you check out the sidebar "Of liquid density and hydrometers" in Chapter 2.

Here's a sample figuring for your first batch of beer. If you use about 6 pounds of liquid malt extract for your brew, your original gravity (or *O.G.* in homebrew lingo) is in the neighborhood of 1.048. If your yeast is good and hungry, your final gravity *(F.G.)* a week or so later (after fermentation) will be about 1.012. Because a *ten-forty eight* (also acceptable homebrewer lingo for the 1.048 gravity) represents an alcohol potential of 6 percent, and a *ten-twelve* (the 1.012 gravity) represents an alcohol potential of 2 percent, the yeast produced 4 percent alcohol in your brew. (Subtract the final alcohol potential from the original alcohol potential to derive the alcohol content percentage.)

Chapter 11

Intermediate Brewing Directions

In This Chapter

▶ Increasing your control over the brewing process

▶ Amping up your ingredients

▶ Conditioning your hair, er, I mean your beer

*T*his chapter picks up where Chapter 10 leaves off, encouraging you, the budding homebrewer, to get more personally involved in the brewing processes and become less dependent on the malt extract producer. This increased involvement means that you choose and add a variety of ingredients to create your brew, as well as perform other, more involved brewing procedures.

Before attempting any procedures outlined in this chapter, I strongly recommend that you first read Beginning Brewing Directions in Chapter 10. If you already have, well, then, read on!

Taking Control of Your Beer

The basic differences between beginner and intermediate homebrewing can be easily — but not completely — summed up in a few lines. Intermediate brewers can

> ✔ **Use specialty grains (to add more color and flavor in your beer).**
>
> ✔ **Choose and add hops (as opposed to using hopped extract).**
>
> ✔ **Use liquid yeast cultures (instead of freeze-dried yeast).**
>
> ✔ **Perform secondary fermentation procedures.**

The combination of ingredient changes and new procedures can make a world of difference in the quality of your homebrew. And you don't even have to apply these changes all at once.

Try to make your ingredient changes one at a time in successive batches of beer. This staggered experimentation allows you to appreciate how each process makes an incremental improvement in your beer.

Beer, as I discuss in Part II, basically consists of four simple ingredients: malt (or barley), hops, yeast, and water. Brewers can use various combinations of these ingredients to produce a vast array of beer styles. But regardless of how many variations of these basic beer-making ingredients you use, you can scientifically dissect all beer styles into three simple variables: color, bitterness, and gravity. These variables are defined by the ingredients that go into the brewpot: The *color* is defined by the grain (or malt extract), the *bitterness* by the hops, and the *gravity* by the grain- or malt-extract-to-water ratio. A fourth variable, responsible for defining the Ale, Lager, or Mixed-Style classifications, is the *yeast strain* used to ferment the beer.

If you haven't already found a source of good brewing water, by all means, do so now. (See Chapter 7 to find out more about how to choose your water.)

Fooling Around with Ingredients

Your first step away from being a novice brewer is to take effective but simple measures toward improving your beer. The first of these measures has to do with adding more and better ingredients. (The second deals with conditioning your brew differently. See the section "Conditioning for Better Beer" in this chapter for more information.)

Whenever you buy homebrewing ingredients, make sure you store them properly if you aren't going to use them immediately. You need to refrigerate all grains, hops, and yeast packets (freeze the hops if you plan to store them long-term). Never allow any of your ingredients to lie around in a warm environment or in direct sunlight, even if they ask you nicely. Think of beer ingredients as food products and think of how most food products decay over time — especially in warmer environments.

Grain and strain

Specialty grains are typically those that are *kilned* (roasted) to various degrees of roastedness after they're *malted* (see Chapter 4 for more on malting) — and some aren't malted at all (specialty malts come already malted and kilned, so you don't need to concern yourself with these processes). Such grains don't substitute for malt extract; they improve it by adding a variety of visual, aromatic, and taste enhancements as well as head-retaining and body-building proteins and dextrins (see Chapter 4 for more information on the function of specialty grains in beer making).

You can add all kinds of colors, flavors, and textures to your beer by adding specialty grains to the brewpot — but don't add them directly! Specialty grains, like all other grains in the brewing business, are never boiled; you should *steep* them at subboiling temperatures (160 to 170 degrees Fahrenheit) just long enough for them to yield their goods. Twenty minutes to a half hour is sufficient.

Boiling grain can lead to a number of problems in your beer, not the least of which is the harsh, astringent, tannin-like taste and mouthfeel that can ruin a whole batch of beer.

I suggest you crack your specialty grain, steep it in a separate pot, and then strain it into the wort in the brewpot. Or, steep it in the brewpot before you add the extract. And make sure you use a grain bag that acts like a big tea bag to allow the hot water to leech all the colors and flavors out of the grain.

With the exception of the most highly roasted grains, you always want to crack, or *mill*, your specialty grains prior to the steeping procedures to maximize the flavoring potential of the grain. You have the added choice of buying the grain already cracked or cracking it yourself at home. For the sake of freshness, you really want to crack your own grain. If you choose not to buy a grain mill, you can still find inventive ways to mill your grain. Try putting the grain into a self-sealing plastic bag and using a rolling pin to crush it (even a baseball bat can do the job). The idea is just to crack the hard outer grain husk, not to mill the grain into flour — don't even think about using your coffee grinder to do this job.

As an intermediate brewer with the ability to add color and flavor to your beer by using specialty grains, you no longer need to buy amber or dark extracts to make amber or dark beers. In fact, after you're comfortable using specialty grains, you're better off deriving these colors and flavors from grain anyway; the taste difference is appreciable.

Another great characteristic of specialty grains is that you don't need to add a whole lot of them in order to influence the flavor of your beer. The amount of specialty grains that most malt extract-based recipes call for rarely exceeds 2 pounds. More often than not, at least half of the total amount of specialty grain consists of *crystal malt* (also called *caramel malt*) — often considered an extract brewer's best friend. Crystal malt is kind of an all-purpose specialty grain because it can add color, mouthfeel, mild sweetness, and caramelly grain flavor to beer all at once.

Hop to it

You can continue to exert your beery autonomy by making your own choices in hop varieties and adding them as you see fit. Remember that about 50 different hop varieties grow around the world, and new or experimental cultivars pop up regularly. Each hop variety offers different nuances in flavors, aromas, and bittering intensity (see Chapter 5 and the appendix for more on hops).

The typical 5-gallon batch of medium gravity beer (1.040 to 1.050) rarely requires more than 3 or 4 ounces of hops to achieve the desired bittering, flavoring, and aromatic profile. Of course, this estimation depends on the type of hops you use (and their corresponding alpha acid contents) as well as the style of the beer you intend to make.

You can add hops to the brewpot at any time; brewers typically add hops at one-hour, half-hour, and quarter-hour increments (homebrew recipes typically specify which increments to use). What you want to get out of the hops determines when you want to introduce them into the boil. Adding smaller quantities at various intervals imbues your beer with a more complex aromatic, flavoring, and bittering profile than if you add a whole bunch all at once. The following are very general guidelines for hop usage:

✔ You want to boil bittering hops for at least 60 minutes.

✔ You want to boil flavoring hops for 10 to 30 minutes.

✔ You want to add finishing (aromatic) hops in the last 5 minutes of the boil.

Regardless of whether the hops are pellets or whole leaves, you have the choice of dropping them into the kettle loosely or putting them into a disposable or reusable hop bag. If you choose to throw the hops loosely into the kettle, you need to strain the wort on its way into the fermenter. A hop bag, on the other hand, works in much the same way as a tea bag: It allows the hops to steep in the boiling wort without requiring you to strain them later. Just use a strainer, tongs, or your brew spoon to remove the hop bag at the end of the boil and toss its contents on the compost pile.

Hops and house pets can be a fatal combination. If certain dogs ingest discarded hops, they may develop a condition called *malignant hyperthermia,* which manifests itself as heavy panting and a rapid heartbeat. Keep Fido — and all pets, for that matter — away from your hop supply (new or used).

Check out Chapter 5 and the appendix for more information about hops.

Yeasty beasties

Yeast is another one of the ingredients that you can change and improve, and it's also the fourth variable in the beer-making process (after gravity, color, and bitterness). Yeast is largely responsible for how the finished beer turns out. The time, effort, and high-quality ingredients you put into your brew are all for naught if your yeast ruins everything.

Liquid yeast cultures may not come with guarantees of purity, but they measurably increase the quality of your beer. And you can't dispute that the stylistic variety that's available in liquid yeast cultures is lacking in the world of dry yeast.

A small downside to using liquid yeast products that aren't ready-to-pitch is that you may need several days to increase the yeast quantity to the proper pitching rate. So if you use liquid yeast, you may need to plan your brewing itinerary in advance (if you plan to brew on Saturday, you better start preparing your yeast by Thursday). Always read and follow the directions on the liquid yeast products you purchase. (See Chapter 6 for more information on liquid yeast cultures and their preparation.)

Conditioning for Better Beer

As I mention earlier in this chapter, using different ingredients is only one way that intermediate homebrewers set themselves apart from the beginners. The other way is by using different methods of conditioning.

Conditioning means allowing your beer additional time to mature, mellow, clarify, and carbonate.

Secondary fermentation

Secondary or *two-stage fermentation* is all about conditioning your beer. When you brewed at the beginner level, you put the fresh wort in the primary fermenter, let the yeast do its thing, and then you bottled the beer. The beer had about two weeks to condition in the bottle before you started sucking it down. You did the right thing (within the limitations of your equipment and expertise), but now you can do more.

At the beginner level, taking the freshly fermented beer out of the primary fermenter was necessary not just because the initial fermentation was over, but also because all those little yeasties, fresh from a gluttonous feast, were about to start decomposing. That's right, enzymes in the sugar-starved yeast begin to break down the yeast cells. This horrific event is called yeast *autolysis*. Autolysis can impart a sulfury, rubbery stench and flavor to your beer. So leaving your fresh, young beer sitting on that bulging layer of self-destructing yeast dregs is akin to allowing your child to wallow with pigs in the mud — and you don't want to smell either one of them when they're done. Racking your beer over to a secondary fermentation vessel effectively leaves most of the sedimented yeast and other organic matter behind.

So if bottling the beer after one week worked before, why can't it now? It still can, but now that you're introducing more ingredients into the brewpot, the added flavors and textures in your beer need more time to blend together. By allowing the beer to undergo a secondary fermentation, you promote a mellowing process that makes a noticeable improvement in your beer.

Considering the advantages of secondary fermentation

Allowing your beer to age in a secondary fermenter before you bottle it also reduces *yeast bite,* the harsh flavor and mouthfeel associated with having excessive yeast sediment in the bottle.

Because the yeast has eaten most of the consumable sugars in the wort during primary fermentation, secondary fermentation yields very little yeast activity and rarely produces a measurable amount of alcohol. This second fermentation period is just an opportunity for all the beer's ingredients to acclimate to one another and establish a good, friendly (and tasty) relationship.

The secondary fermenter represents a world of new possibilities for your brew. You can add many different additives and flavorings to the secondary fermenter that may have a huge effect on the finished beer. (See Chapters 8 and 9 for ideas on what to add at the secondary fermentation stage.)

The two-stage aspect of secondary fermentation also allows you to perform some real beer-improving feats:

- ✔ **Dry hop:** You can impart more hop aroma to your beer by simply adding ¼ ounce to 2 ounces of hops (in pellet, plug, or whole leaf form) to the secondary fermenter and then draining your beer over them. You can do the same thing with spices, too. Chapter 5 has more information on this process.

- ✔ **Make true Lagers:** In order to make genuine Lager beers, you must age the beer in the secondary fermenter for at least a few weeks at very cold temperatures (32 to 40 degrees Fahrenheit) for proper flavor development. (Check out Chapter 26 for ideas on how to set up a lagering cellar.)

- ✔ **Clarify your brew:** You can add various clarifying agents to the secondary fermenter to speed up the process of clarification. Typical finings and clarifiers include isinglass, gelatin, Sparkalloid, and PVPP. Chapter 9 gives you more information about finings and clarifiers.

One final vote in support of secondary fermentation: By using this procedure, you can not only quit worrying about unfinished primary fermentations (and exploding bottles), but you can also actually cut the primary ferment short by a day or two if that helps you rack the beer over to the secondary fermenter at a more convenient time. This shortcut is possible *only* after the peak fermentation activity subsides (usually by the fifth or sixth day of a normal, healthy fermentation).

TIP

Propagation preparation

In anticipation of future brews, consider maximizing your time and consolidating your efforts on behalf of imminent yeast propagations. In plain English, that means instead of making one small batch of sterile wort for propagating yeast for a single batch of beer, try to make a lot of wort and divide it into several bottles. You can store these bottles of sterile wort for long periods of time to be used for future yeast propagations.

Start with a half-dozen or so cleaned and sanitized bottles (you choose the size — larger is better) with an appropriate number of sanitized bottle caps. Prepare a medium gravity wort (1.040–1.050) by using pale malt extract — enough to fill all your bottles two-thirds full. Boil and cool the wort, pour it into the bottles using a sanitized funnel, and cap the bottles.

In order to ensure that the wort is completely sterile, you must boil the capped bottles (this is a crude form of pasteurization). To do so, place the bottles in a deep pot and fill the pot with tap water so that the water in the pot rises to the liquid level inside the bottles. Place the pot on the stove and bring the water to a boil; turn off the heat immediately (be very careful during this process; bottles have been known to burst!). To avoid any possibility of thermal shock, allow the bottles to cool down with the water in the pot — this may take a while, so be patient. After the bottles have cooled, dry them and store them in the refrigerator. When you need to propagate your next liquid yeast culture, you have good, sterile wort ready and waiting.

Jumping into secondary fermentation

Secondary fermentation always needs to take place in either glass or stainless steel vessels. A 5-gallon glass carboy is the most popular secondary fermentation vessel, though a few homebrewers prefer to age their beer in stainless steel soda kegs. However, I don't recommend secondary fermentation in plastic vessels. Even the food-grade plastics used to make homebrewing equipment are penetrable by certain gasses (such as oxygen) over an extended period of time.

Remember that no phase of homebrewing is exempt from cleaning and sanitizing. When you add another fermentation phase, you must disinfect all the equipment that goes along with it. In addition to the use of a good sanitizing agent, you want to use a carboy brush to make sure you scrub the entire inner surface of the carboy. Rinse the carboy well with hot water and allow it to air-dry. Be sure to have an appropriately sized, sanitized rubber stopper to seal the carboy, as well as an airlock. Don't forget to sanitize all other equipment, especially the plastic hosing, before you use it. If necessary, review the sanitation methods I discuss in Chapter 3.

If you decide to use additives or flavorings and they're liquids (or can be dissolved in water), you can simply pour them into the carboy prior to adding the beer (which takes care of mixing). If your additive or flavoring is bulky or leafy, you want to place it in a hop bag or some kind of filter for easy removal.

This bag saves you some work, because you have to strain whatever you put into the secondary fermenter out of the brew on bottling day.

Speaking of bottling, the procedure is delayed another week or two while the beer is mellowing in the carboy. A secondary fermentation isn't really worth the effort unless you allow it to last at least one week. Two to three weeks is the norm, and a month or more may be needed for Barley Wines, Imperial Stouts, and other complex and high-gravity beers and Meads.

Before transferring your beer from the primary fermenter to the secondary fermenter, you want to be sure that the initial, vigorous fermentation (also called *high kraeusen*) is complete. You can do this check simply by watching the bubbles in the airlock; if they appear at half-minute or longer intervals, you can proceed with the following racking procedures.

1. **Place your primary fermenter on a table or sturdy work surface and position the empty carboy on the floor directly below the fermenter.**

2. **Connect one end of the plastic hose to the spigot on the primary fermenter and put the other end inside the carboy.**

   Be sure that you space the two vessels so that the dangling plastic hose reaches the bottom of the carboy — this practice prevents aerating the beer as you drain it. You may want to prop the carboy up on beer bottle cases, a step stool, or large books (basically, anything that can withstand the weight of a carboy full of beer).

   If you invest in a carbon dioxide kegging system, you can fill your carboy with CO_2 (because it's heavier than air) before you rack the beer into it. This practice helps limit oxidation of the beer. Just let the CO_2 flow into the carboy at 1 to 2 *psi* (pounds per square inch). (See Chapter 14 for more about kegging.)

3. **Fill the carboy with beer to within an inch or two of the opening.**

   In some cases, you may have to stop the flow of beer before it finishes draining out of the primary fermenter; in other cases, you may have to top the carboy off with clean water that you've boiled and cooled down. What little water you may need to add doesn't affect the beer's gravity.

   Speaking of gravity, you don't need to take a hydrometer reading when you rack the beer from the primary to the secondary fermenter, but if you do you can get an idea of how your brew is progressing and how long you need to consider leaving it in the carboy. Getting a beer sample from the hose into the hydrometer test cylinder can be tricky and may lead to a big mess if you're not careful. The key is to control the flow of beer with the spigot on the primary fermenter. Just remember to practice good sanitation and avoid aerating your beer.

4. **Place the appropriate rubber stopper in the neck of the carboy, fill your airlock halfway with water, and place it in the hole in the rubber stopper.**

TIP

Mastering the art of siphoning

The use of a carboy in homebrewing requires you to practice your siphoning techniques, because carboys don't come equipped with spigots. To perform such siphoning, you need a curved racking tube (or *cane*) and your plastic hosing. (I discuss racking tubes and other necessary equipment in Chapter 2.)

The most effective siphoning occurs when the opening of the siphon hose is lower than the bottom of the vessel you're siphoning the beer out of (the lower the better). If you keep large air bubbles out of the siphon hose, you also increase the siphoning efficiency; air bubbles can actually slow or stop liquid flow. They can also oxidize the beer.

You can use a handful of ways to start a siphon, but not all of them are appropriate for homebrewing. For speed and simplicity, sucking on one end of the siphon hose sure gets a flow going, but it also opens the door to all kinds of contamination possibilities. Some brewers feel that a good gargle and rinse with whiskey or vodka prior to sucking on the hose is a good

temporary cure for this problem. Personally, I think it's in bad taste (and so was that pun).

A better idea is to add a false end to the siphon hose that can be removed as soon as the beer begins flowing. A stiff straw, a piece of copper tubing, or a short piece of small-diameter hosing can be fitted snugly inside the siphon hose. After starting the flow of beer by sucking the false end, you can remove it and allow the flow to continue. One brewer I know uses the cylindrical part of a turkey baster to accomplish this. With the baster's bulb off and the thin end held tightly inside the siphon hose, one good inhale and the beer is flowing. (And no fowled beer!)

Another, more widely accepted practice is to fill the plastic hosing with water just prior to fitting it onto the racking tube. After you connect the tube and hose (with the tube resting in the carboy), just drop the open end of the hose into the bottling bucket and the beer automatically starts to flow. This method may take a few tries before you get the system down. But what are a few beer stains on the floor in pursuit of a healthy libation?

5. **Store the filled carboy in a cool, dark place for a couple of weeks.**

6. **Padlock the door to the room where you've stashed the carboy and position a sentinel at the threshold. You're just 14 days away from some of the best beer you've ever tasted.**

When you're ready to bottle your well-conditioned brew you'll have no choice but to use siphoning procedures to drain the carboy, since carboys don't have spigots for convenience. Lucky for you, I've provided all the helpful information you need in the "Mastering the art of siphoning" sidebar.

Tertiary fermentation

Tertiary or *three-stage fermentation* is really no different from two-stage fermentation in its objective and procedure. Brewers don't typically need to rack a beer over to a third fermentation vessel, but it may be useful under certain conditions:

- ✔ If, after a prolonged secondary fermentation, you have a considerable build-up of yeast sedimentation on the bottom of the carboy, tertiary fermentation can help you avoid the yeast autolysis problem mentioned earlier in this chapter. This situation is only likely to happen in very high-gravity Barley Wines, Russian Imperial Stouts, or other similar beer styles. (Part IV gives you some insight on beer-style descriptions and parameters.)

- ✔ If your beer has been sitting on real fruit in the secondary fermenter, you may consider a brief tertiary fermentation. Racking the beer off the decomposing fruit before you bottle it may go a long way toward melding the fruit flavors into the beer as well as reducing the pectin haze that the fruit often creates. (*Pectin* is a carbohydrate that occurs naturally in ripe fruit. Because of its thickening properties, it can solidify to a gel that, diluted in your beer, can create a hazy appearance — called *pectin haze* — in the beer.)

Keep in mind that every time you handle your brew, you increase the odds of contamination. Always practice good sanitation techniques.

Intermediate homebrewing basics at a glance

This flowchart shows you, in a nutshell, the steps you need to take to brew at the intermediate level. Enjoy!

Chapter 12

Homebrewing Directions for the Serious Beer Geek

In This Chapter

▶ Discovering mashing procedures

▶ Comparing partial and full mashing

▶ Starting from scratch with all-grain brewing

▶ Increasing batch size

▶ Harvesting yeast

*Y*ou've made it — you're now at the advanced stage of the homebrewing process! You're pumped, you're psyched — you're ready to take the ultimate step in homebrewing. The first and biggest step between the intermediate and advanced levels of homebrewing takes you from relying on prepared extracts to making beer from scratch out of grain. The process integral to this step is *mashing* — and, no, the process has nothing to do with boiling spuds.

After you master the mashing procedures that I outline in this chapter, you've pretty much joined the ranks of the professional brewers. And even though you're still making beer in relatively small amounts, you are, for the most part, unlimited as to where your talent, knowledge, and ability can take you.

Many homebrewers have gone on to new careers in the brewing industry; some have even opened up their own microbreweries and brewpubs.

After mastering the science of producing beer from grain, many advanced brewers (in their never-ending quest to achieve bigger and better brews) concentrate on the bigger picture (and pitcher). Five gallons of beer is no longer worth the time and effort of brewing for these guys; 10 and 15 gallons a crack — now that's brewing! You may want to consider these possibilities for yourself.

As I discuss in Chapter 11, after you graduate to another level of homebrewing you must acquaint yourself with new procedures and new equipment — see the section about advanced homebrewing equipment in Chapter 2.

In the first part of this chapter, I mention general brewing procedures. I cover exactly how to perform these procedures later in this chapter. Also, be aware that your comprehension of this chapter relies on knowledge you gain by reading the two preceding chapters — make sure that you check them out first.

Yes, We Have No Potatoes: Mashing Procedures

Put your potato peeler away; the kind of mashing I'm talking about is the process by which you manipulate your grain to create and capture the natural grain sugars that feed the yeast during fermentation. At the beginner and intermediate levels of homebrewing, you can cut corners by buying commercially made malt extract (concentrated wort). By using mashing procedures, however, you make your own wort directly from grain.

How is *mashing* different from *steeping* specialty grains? As I discuss in Chapter 11, you steep specialty grains primarily for coloring and flavoring your beer, not for their contribution of fermentable sugars (which you get by mashing). In the absence of malt extract, you need base grains to produce the malt sugars that feed the yeast during fermentation. (As the name implies, *base grain* is the foundation on which the beer is built.) The production of these sugars from the grains takes place during the mashing procedures.

The mashing process utilizes the naturally occurring enzymes in pale malts to convert the starch to sugars. The malt sugars then become food for the yeast during fermentation.

What do these enzymes actually do? Well, you can think of a starch molecule as a bunch of sugar molecules arranged like beads on a string. These enzymes cut the bonds (or strings) between the sugar molecules (the beads). This process, called *conversion,* frees up the sugars so that the yeast can utilize them. Conversion occurs when enzymatic action in the mash tun or vessel converts the starches in grain to soluble sugars that the yeast can consume.

Three important variables

You should consider the following three important variables in mashing:

✔ **Temperature:** In terms of the mashing temperature's effect on the finished beer, higher temperatures (153 to 158 degrees Fahrenheit) create a less fermentable wort, and, conversely, lower temperatures (148 to 153 degrees Fahrenheit) produce a more fermentable wort. This knowledge enables you to exercise more control over the flavor and mouthfeel of the finished beer. A more fermentable wort results in more alcohol and less body in the beer. A less fermentable wort results in less alcohol but more body and mouthfeel.

If you really must know, high mashing temperatures promote the action of *alpha-amylase,* which produces less fermentable sugars than does the *beta-amylase* promoted by lower mashing temperatures. Both alpha- and beta-amylase are already present in malted grain.

✔ **pH:** As I discuss in Chapter 7, *pH* is the measurement of the acidity or the alkalinity of the mash. The pH of the mash needs to be between 5.0 and 5.5 for the enzymes to work best. (I cover exactly how to adjust the pH in the section "Easing into Mashing with a Partial Mash" later in this chapter.)

✔ **Time:** Time is the last variable; you must give the enzymes sufficient time to work. Theoretically, 10 to 20 minutes is sufficient, but you generally want to give yourself some leeway — 60 to 90 minutes — to ensure complete conversion.

Don't worry — you don't need to know how the mashing process works for it to work predictably every time. Just make sure that the temperature, pH, and time are in order. After all, you don't need to know the workings of internal-combustion engines just to drive a car!

Gimme some water: Simplified water treatment for mashing

I'm going to let you in on something: I'm making assumptions about you at this point. I'm assuming that you've already brewed a few batches of beer and you have a supply of good, clean, chlorine-free water with which to brew. Fair enough? Now if you're going to start grain brewing (mashing), you need to take a few more water variables into account:

✔ **The hardness of your brewing water:** By *hardness,* I mean the amount of minerals dissolved in the water. If you have a difficult time creating a lather with soap, you can probably safely say that your water is hard (or that you need to find better soap).

Hard water isn't necessarily a bad thing. Brewers specifically use hard waters to create certain beer styles, such as Pale Ales, Dortmunder Exports, and some dark beers. Excessive hardness, however, can be detrimental to your brew.

One easy way to remove temporary hardness is to boil the water for 30 to 60 minutes and let it cool. (Boiling also offers the benefit of removing chlorine.) After it cools and settles, siphon the water off of any precipitated sediment. This process generally removes chalky (calcium carbonate) hardness. See Chapter 7 for more information on water hardness.

✔ **The pH of your mash water:** To prepare mash correctly, you need a mash-water pH of 5.7 to 6.3 (lower for pale beers and higher for dark beers) because the acidity level of the mash will automatically increase when the *grist* (grain) is added to the wort. How much it increases depends on how much dark grain is added; dark grain is naturally more acidic. Check the pH of your water — if it's higher than 6.5, you need to add gypsum and boil as you would to decrease temporary hardness (which I describe in the preceding Tip paragraph). Because you may use any one of so many different types of water, this process is not a cure-all, but it tends to work well in practice for most types of water. Check out Chapter 7 for more on manipulating water pH with additives.

Remember that the pH level is what's most important for mashing procedures to work correctly — the mash must be between 5.0 and 5.5 pH. The actual mineral content is important, but not as important as the pH.

✔ **The temperature of the mash:** After mixing crushed malt with water, you can generally expect a 10 degree Fahrenheit or so drop in temperature. This change means that, for a mash temperature of 150 to 158 degrees Fahrenheit, your mash water must be 160 to 168 degrees Fahrenheit. (Coincidentally, this temperature range is the ideal *sparge* or rinse water temperature.)

And then there were three: Mashing types

You have three basic types of mashing procedures. All three procedures are in use in the commercial brewing industry, and you can use any of them at the homebrewing level. The following list describes these procedures:

✔ **Infusion:** This procedure is the most basic form of mashing (and also the easiest). You just mix the crushed malt with water and stabilize the temperature at 150 to 158 degrees Fahrenheit. You then measure and adjust the pH to 5.0 to 5.5 and hold the mixture at that temperature level for 60 to 90 minutes. Infusion mashing requires that you use *fully modified* (or Pale Ale) malts. This mashing method is primarily found in use in Great Britain and most American craft breweries for making Ales. (See the Infusion Mashing Procedure Flow Chart in Figure 12-1.)

The *modification* of the grain mentioned in the preceding paragraph occurs at the malting stage (see Chapter 4 for more on malting). You can purchase your grain according to your desired level of modification — for example, 2-row English pale malts are typically more highly modified than others (see Chapter 4 and the appendix).

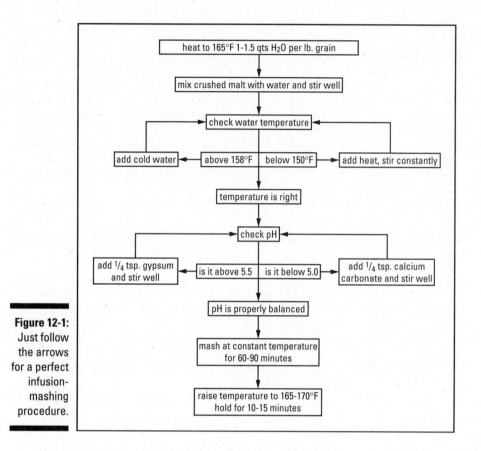

Figure 12-1:
Just follow
the arrows
for a perfect
infusion-
mashing
procedure.

✔ **Step infusion (or multistep infusion):** This mashing method is like infusion mashing but gives you even more control over the process. Mix the water and crushed malt as you do in regular infusion mashing, adjust the temperature to 122 to 131 degrees Fahrenheit, and hold at that temperature for 15 to 30 minutes; you then boost the temperature to the starch conversion range (150 to 158 degrees Fahrenheit). This process is a *protein rest*. Providing a protein rest enables other enzymes present to break down large proteins in the malt to smaller proteins. These smaller proteins contribute to body and head retention. Generally, a protein rest is necessary only for less-modified malts, such as Lager malts.

The main advantage to the step-infusion mashing technique is control. Generally, you apply heat or add boiling water to bring the mash through the temperature rests. By judiciously applying heat, you can control temperatures more precisely.

Cereal killers: Cereal grain mashing

Many major industrial breweries, such as Anheuser-Busch, Coors, and Miller, use raw (unmalted) cereal grains to lighten the flavor, body, and color of their beers — typically, light Lagers. They first must boil the unmalted grain (as with a decoction mash) to make the grains' starch available to the enzymes. The brewers then return the boiled grains to the mash for conversion. Adjunct grains may include rice, corn, rye, and oats.

For homebrewing purposes, however, buying "flaked" adjunct grains is much easier and less time-consuming; these grains are pregelatinized (precooked) (see Chapter 4 for more on these grains). In this form, you can simply mash them with the rest of your base and specialty grains, using one of the three methods mentioned in this chapter.

✔ **Decoction:** This procedure is the most complicated and time-consuming method of mashing. The basic procedure is similar to that of a step mash in that the mash progresses through various temperature ranges. You take the mash through these temperatures by pulling off the thickest part of the mash — grains and all — and boiling it in a separate vessel. You then return this thick mash to the main mash to bring the entire mixture to the next temperature rest. You can perform up to three decoctions and temperature rests.

The main advantage to decoction mashing is that the boiling helps to impart a rich, malty character to certain beer styles, such as Bocks, Märzens, and Weizens.

Very few homebrewers use the decoction method of mashing, because decoction mashing requires extra time, effort, and expertise. Unless you're trying to make truly authentic versions of these three beer styles, this method is usually not worthwhile. For these reasons, I don't cover decoction mashing any further in this book.

The aftermash or mash-out

After you have completed conversion in your mash, you need to finalize the mashing process by doing a mash-*out*. Regardless of which mashing method you use, raise the mash temperature to 160 to 170 degrees Fahrenheit for about 15 minutes after starch conversion is complete. (If water pH and temperature are right, complete conversion should occur after 60 minutes.) You want to do so for the following two reasons:

✔ When you rinse the sugars from the grains, the thick and syrupy wort flows faster at these high temperatures. (See the "Lautering" and "Sparging" sections in this chapter.)

Parti-gyle brewing

Due to the nature of first- and second-run wort, you can quite conceivably create two different brews from the same initial mash by utilizing *parti-gyle brewing.* A recipe with a very high grain-to-water ratio can conceivably produce a high-gravity first-run wort (such as a Barley Wine or Old Ale) and still provide enough residual sugar in the second runnings for a low-gravity beer (such as a Mild or a Bitter). To avoid any dilution of the first-run wort and to minimize dilution of the second-run wort, don't increase

the beer volume of either brew to full batch size (5 gallons or otherwise) — leave them as two smaller partial batches. Parti-gyle brewing methods obviously require two separate fermentation vessels as well.

The general rule says that the first third of the wort contains half the sugars. Because a 50/50 split of the wort would leave the second-run wort too weak, I recommend that you shoot for a 30/70 split.

✔ These temperatures also destroy the enzymes in the mash after the enzymes accomplish their task. This enzyme destruction preserves the degree of fermentability of the wort, which you purposely set with your mashing temperatures.

Lautering

Now for the question that you've been dying to ask: "After I create all these liquefied sugars, how do I separate them from the grains?" Transfer the mash into a *lauter tun,* a vessel with some sort of strainer or *false bottom* arrangement and a tap for draining the wort away from the grain. (See Chapter 2 for more information about lauter tuns.)

After transferring the mash to the lauter tun, carefully draw off the sweet, syrupy liquid called *first runnings*. First runnings have a very high specific gravity because they have a high concentration of sugars. *Second runnings* (the residual wort rinsed from the grain during sparging) have a rather low gravity because they're heavily diluted by the sparge water. First and second runnings achieve a more moderate starting gravity for your beer when you combine, boil, and reduce them in the brewpot. (See the sidebar "Parti-gyle brewing" later in this chapter.)

Unfortunately, these first runnings contain a lot of solid matter (grain husks, finely ground malt, and so on). To make a stable beer, you must eliminate most of this solid matter. How do you achieve this task? Just draw off the first runnings and *recirculate* them, or pour them back over the top of the grain in the lauter tun. Recirculation relies on the grain husks to filter, and thus clarify, the wort. Recirculate the wort through your grain bed only until the wort begins to run clear. After you clarify the runoff this way, you can drain it into the brew pot and rinse (or *sparge*) the grains.

Excessive recirculation of the first runnings may result in wort oxidation and other off flavors that show up in the finished beer. Chapter 24 gives you tips to combat such troubles.

Sparging

Sparging is rinsing the grain bed with hot water. Why do you need to sparge? Because the grain bed still retains a lot of liquid sugar after you collect the first runnings. You therefore need to percolate treated water (pH of 5.0 to 5.5, temperature of 165 to 170 degrees Fahrenheit) through the grain bed. (I address the topic of water pH in Chapter 7.) You then collect the second runnings just as you do the first runnings (but you don't need to recirculate them).

Sparging is an important part of the mashing procedure because the process enables you to maximize the grain yield by capturing most of the fermentable sugars from the grain. (You get the most wort for your money.) You need to be aware, however, that oversparging can negatively affect your brew's taste; see Chapter 24 for troubleshooting advice. When the sparge water you're pouring through the grain bed begins to run clear, you need to stop sparging. (Two quarts of water per pound of grain in the recipe is the general rule.)

Easing into Mashing with a Partial Mash

The concept of partial mashing is to substitute some — but not all — of the malt extract with pale malt to provide the fermentable material. You generally continue to use specialty grains (crystal malt, roasted malts, and so on) in the same quantities as you do in extract-based recipes (which appear in Chapter 10).

Why do a partial mash rather than an all-grain batch (which I discuss in the next section)? Partial mashing is a great way to familiarize yourself with the mashing procedures for the following reasons:

- The smaller quantities of grain and water are easier to handle.
- You don't need a large brewpot. (The brewpot left over from your beginner homebrewing days is fine.)
- You don't need a lauter tun. (A kitchen colander or strainer is sufficient.)
- The entire process is less time-consuming and is generally easier if your beer is not completely dependent on the mashing process.

To perform the following partial-mash procedures, here's what you need:

- A bottling bucket or similar bucket (to hold wort).
- An 8- to 20-quart pot (in which to mash) — your brewpot is sufficient for this purpose. Larger is better.

✔ A strainer or colander.

✔ A 2- to 10-quart stock pot (for holding sparge water). Larger is better.

✔ Some pH papers (you should always have plenty on hand because you may need to check the wort several times) or a pH meter.

✔ A set of teaspoons.

✔ Gypsum (calcium sulfate). You should always have at least a teaspoon on hand, but you may end up not needing any at all.

✔ Calcium carbonate (food-grade chalk). You should keep at least a teaspoon of this on hand as well, but you may not need any at all.

✔ A lab immersion thermometer.

✔ A grain mill (if you aren't using preground malt).

✔ A postal or kitchen scale (to weigh the malt).

✔ Pale malt base grain. (For a beginner's mash, 2-row Pale Ale malt is preferable because it's fully modified and thus easier to work with.)

✔ Other specialty grains as specified in your Ale recipe.

Here's a step-by-step run-through of a partial mash:

1. **Add 1⅓ quarts of treated water per pound of grain (based on the recipe you're using) to your brewpot.**

   See the nearby sidebar "Adjusting pH levels" to prepare your water.

2. **Heat your water to 160 to 168 degrees Fahrenheit.**

   This range is the *strike* temperature.

3. **Add your crushed malt to the water and mix well.**

   A reminder about the correct crushing of your grain: As you crush the malt, don't grind it too finely — this only creates problems later. Just try to crack the husk of the malt to expose the white, starchy interior. (This step may take some careful adjustment of the mill to get it just right.) Try to keep as much of the husk intact as possible.

4. **Check the temperature of the mash (holding the thermometer in the center of the mash for a more accurate reading).**

   Thermometers generally need about 10 to 20 seconds to register correctly.

   The temperature should now be 150 to 158 Fahrenheit.

5. **If the temperature is too low, apply heat while stirring constantly; if the temperature is too high, add small amounts of cold water to bring the temperature lower than 158 degrees Fahrenheit.**

Adjusting pH levels

How can you adjust the pH? If the pH is too high, add half a teaspoon of gypsum and stir well. Check the pH again, as I describe in Steps 6 and 7 of the nearby list. Repeat these steps until the pH level is between 5.0 and 5.5. At any rate, don't add more than 2 teaspoons of gypsum to the mash. Natural materials in the malt resist changes in pH, so adding larger amounts of minerals doesn't really change the pH. What if the pH level is lower than 5.0? You simply add calcium carbonate in the same way that you add gypsum if the mash pH level is too high. (But never add more than 2 teaspoons of any mineral; if you are unable to reach a desired pH level by using 2 teaspoons of mineral additive, you're just wasting money while negatively affecting the taste of your beer.)

Watch for wort scorching, and don't exceed 158 degrees Fahrenheit; higher temperatures destroy the enzymes. If you do overshoot 158 degrees, add small quantities of cold water to bring the temperature back down as quickly as possible.

6. **After the temperature stabilizes, use a teaspoon to draw up some of the liquid that's on top of the grains and then let the liquid cool to room temperature so that you can check the pH.**

7. **Following the instructions provided with the pH papers, dip the paper into the mash sample contained in the teaspoon, read the pH, and record the level in your notes (or simply use your pH meter).**

   Discard all used strips and wort samples.

   Is the pH between 5.0 and 5.5? If so, you're home free!

8. **If the pH level and temperature are correct, cover the mash and hold the temperature at 150 to 158 degrees Fahrenheit for 60 minutes.**

   Remember, if the pH level is *not* between 5.0 and 5.5, you *must* adjust it to this range. The enzymes need this pH range to work correctly and produce a well-made beer.

   Check the temperature of the mash every 20 minutes. You may need to adjust the temperature back into the 150 to 158 degree Fahrenheit range by heating and stirring constantly.

   During the last 45 minutes of the mash, you need to start preparing your sparge water.

9. **In a separate pot, heat two quarts of water per pound of grain (as called for in your recipe) to 160 to 170 degrees Fahrenheit.**

   You use this water to rinse the grains. If you're using water with a pH level higher than 7.0, you need to lower the pH to between 5.7 and 6.5. (Check the pH after every mineral addition.)

First Wort Hopping

First Wort Hopping (FWH) is an old yet recently rediscovered process for adding hop character to your brew. At the beginning of the sparging process, you add hops to the brew kettle where you collect the first runnings. The idea is that the hops steep in the collecting wort (which usually runs out of the lauter tun at temperatures ranging from 150 to 170 degrees Fahrenheit, depending on your setup) for the duration of the sparge; this steeping produces a complexity of hop bitterness and aroma that you can't get by using any other method.

One study among professional brewers determined that using FWH resulted in a more refined hop aroma, a more uniform bitterness (no harshness), and a more harmonious beer overall (compared to an identical beer produced without FWH).

Your best bet is to use only low alpha finishing hops for FWH and to use at least 30 percent of the total amount of hops used in the boil. This FWH addition should therefore be taken from the hops intended for finishing additions. How's that for an odd reversal of hop additions?

10. **After starch conversion (after 60 minutes), raise the temperature of the mash to 160 to 170 degrees Fahrenheit and hold for 10 to 15 minutes.**

    This stage is the *mash-out.* After the mash-out, you need to strain out the liquid (wort) and rinse the grains. This process is *lautering and sparging.*

11. **Pour or ladle the mash into the strainer suspended over your bottling bucket and let the sweet wort drain out of the grains.**

    This process may take a few minutes.

    Don't squeeze or press the grains to hasten the draining of the wort. Just let gravity do the work naturally.

12. **Next, put the strainer full of grain over your brewpot and recirculate the cloudy wort in your bottling bucket back through the grains in the strainer.**

    The grain filters out most of the minute solid particles in the wort.

    Now it's time to sparge.

13. **Pour the hot (165 to 170 degree Fahrenheit) sparge water over the grains to rinse away the sugars trapped in the grain.**

14. **After you pour out all the sparge water, let the grains that are still in the strainer drain for 5 to 10 minutes into the brewpot.**

You're done! Just add the malt extract to the brewpot and brew as you normally would an all-extract batch (see Chapter 10). Now you deserve a beer!

Going All Out with All-Grain Brewing

Are you ready to brew beer from scratch? This procedure is the ultimate in control for a brewer. All-grain brewing gives you complete control over the entire malt flavor and source of fermentable material for your beer — something not possible if you use malt extracts.

The main difference between partial mashing and all-grain brewing is size — more grains, more water, bigger brewpot, and so on are all necessary in all-grain brewing. I describe the three pieces of equipment you need to go from partial mashing to all-grain brewing in the following list:

- **A large brewpot:** This item needs to be at least 7 gallons in capacity because you're collecting the entire volume of wort. Boiling the entire batch volume is a *full wort boil* (6 to 7 gallons of wort boil down to the typical 5-gallon batch size).

- **A wort chiller:** Because you're boiling 6 to 7 gallons of wort, you really need an effective way to chill the wort to pitching temperature (approximately 70 degrees Fahrenheit) within 30 to 45 minutes. Cold-water baths in the sink just don't cut it anymore.

- **A lauter tun:** This item is really a big, glorified strainer. Generally, this vessel can hold 8 to 14 pounds of mash (crushed grain and water). It has a false bottom with holes or slots that enable you to drain the sweet wort from the grain.

Check out Chapter 26 for money-saving tips on how to make your own equipment.

Other than these changes in size and equipment, the mashing, runoff, and sparging procedures are just about the same.

Note: If you haven't done any partial mashing yet, refer first to the section "Easing into Mashing with a Partial Mash" earlier in this chapter for terms and concepts. (You have to walk before you can run.) In this section, I discuss in detail only the differences between the two processes.

Here's a step-by-step run-through of an all-grain infusion mash; just follow these steps:

1. **Heat 1⅓ quarts of treated water for every pound of grain in the recipe to 160 to 170 degrees Fahrenheit.**

    See the section "Gimme some water: Simplified water treatment for mashing" earlier in this chapter for details.

2. **Mix in crushed malt and stir well.**

    This process is *mashing in* (sometimes called the *dough-in*).

3. **Check the temperature (150 to 158 degrees Fahrenheit) and the pH (5.0 to 5.5) of the mash and adjust as necessary to reach these levels.**

4. **Hold the mash at this temperature for 60 to 90 minutes to achieve total starch conversion.**

   You may need to reheat mash to keep it in the correct temperature range.

5. **In the meantime, prepare 2 quarts of treated sparge water per pound of grain.**

   See Step 9 in the "Easing into Mashing with a Partial Mash" section for instructions on treating sparge water.

6. **After starch conversion, raise the temperature of the mash to 160 to 170 degrees Fahrenheit and hold for 10 to 15 minutes.**

   This step is the mash-out.

7. **Carefully ladle or pour the mash into your lauter tun.**

8. **Into a sauce pan, very slowly draw off 1 or 2 quarts of the wort from the spigot or hose at the bottom of the lauter tun and then take the sweet wort (first runnings) and pour (or *recirculate*) it over the top of the grain bed.**

   Continue until few or no solid particles appear in the runoff. This task may take 1 or 2 gallons of wort to accomplish.

   Try to keep splashing and frothing of the wort to a minimum. You can do so by always using a piece of hose connected to the spigot on your lauter tun. Never let the wort just waterfall into the saucepan as you recirculate or sparge, because doing so can cause aeration of the wort, which can result in off flavors and aromas (and a beer that goes stale more quickly).

9. **After the first runnings clear up, start letting the wort drain slowly into your brewpot.**

   This process should take 10 to 15 minutes. Use a long length of plastic hose to let the wort drain gently into the bottom of the brewpot — and make sure you avoid aerating the wort.

   If the wort runs off too fast, the grains may compact down on themselves. If that happens, you get what's called a *stuck runoff,* which is one huge pain in the mash! You can't drain any more wort from the mash. The only solution is to stir the entire mash and start the runoff again.

10. **Carefully watch the level of the wort above the grains and, after the level is about ½ inch above the top of the grain bed, begin to add your sparge water, which should be 160 to 170 degrees Fahrenheit.**

    To add the sparge water, pour about 2 to 4 quarts at a time periodically over the grain. (Don't overfill the lauter tun.)

11. **Continue to add the sparge water and run off the resulting wort over the course of the next 45 to 60 minutes.**

    Slower is better in this process.

    Always keep some sparge water above the top of the grain bed. Don't let the grain bed run dry! After you use all the sparge water, you then — and *only* then — let the grain bed run dry.

    If you run off and sparge too fast, not only can you get a stuck runoff, but you may not extract enough sugar from the grains, which can result in lower-than-expected original gravities.

12. **After you've added all the sparge water, just let all the liquid in the lauter tun drain into the brewpot and then close the tap and clean out the grain in the lauter tun.**

    You should collect 6 to 7 gallons of wort. The grain left in the lauter tun makes great garden mulch or hog slop.

    At this point, you may want to consider first wort hopping procedures (see the "First Wort Hopping" sidebar)

    Carefully put the brewpot on the stove — remember that you have 6 to 7 gallons of hot wort in there. This amount of wort weighs more than 50 pounds.

13. **Bring the wort up to a boil and boil for 60 to 90 minutes to reduce the volume of the wort to 5 to 5½ gallons; add hops and other ingredients per the recipe.**

    You may need to experiment with the actual boil time to boil off just the right amount of water to get 5 to 5½ gallons of wort. This variation occurs because everyone's stove or heating apparatus is different.

14. **Fifteen minutes before the end of the boil, put your rinsed immersion wort chiller into the brewpot and bring the wort back up to a boil.**

    This step effectively sterilizes the chiller (see Figure 12-2). (If you're using a counter-flow-type wort chiller, don't immerse it in the wort.) See Chapter 2 for more information on wort chillers.

15. **Add 1 teaspoon of Irish Moss to the wort.**

    This clarifying agent helps clear the finished wort. (See Chapter 9 for more on clarifiers.)

16. **Finish boiling the wort and, after the boiling is done, hook up the wort chiller to your sink and cover the brew pot.**

17. **Run cold water through the chiller to cool the wort to lower than 80 degrees Fahrenheit.**

    You're probably going to need to move your hot and heavy brewpot to a location nearer your faucet and sink — do so carefully.

    The preferred method is to chill your wort to the same approximate temperature as your yeast culture — typically, room temperature.

The water exiting the wort chiller is *very hot* (180 degrees Fahrenheit and hotter)! Be very careful, because this water can easily scald you.

18. **Siphon or pour the cooled wort into a sanitized fermenter.**

    As you do so, try to introduce as much air into the cooled wort as possible to aerate it for the necessary yeast growth. You can do so by pouring the wort vigorously into the fermenter and by rapidly stirring the wort with your brewing spoon.

19. **Pitch your yeast (just pour it into the wort) and attach the airlock (just like with any other type of brew).**

20. **Have a beer.**

Congratulations! You're now an all-grain brewer.

Figure 12-2: An immersion wort chiller, shown here in a brewpot, works like a reverse radiator.

Cold water inflow

Hose clamps

Hot water outflow

Copper tubing

Brewpot

Increasing Your Batch Size

Many homebrewers, after mastering the mashing techniques of all-grain brewing, find themselves in need of yet another challenge. Of course, in addition to experiencing the thrill and satisfaction of achieving a formidable goal, most homebrewers are also primarily interested in serving a common need — making more beer!

Do's and don'ts for all-grain brewing

Brewing can get pretty hectic with all that equipment sitting around and ingredients everywhere. The following list may help make your brewing experience go a bit more smoothly. *Note:* A fitting complement to reading this list may be to have a cold one from your last batch before beginning this batch.

The following list describes a few things you need to do:

- Sanitize and sterilize everything that comes in contact with your beer!

- Treat the mash for the correct mash pH.

- Grind the malt correctly.

- Stir the mash well.

- Use a wort chiller.

- Use ready-to-pitch liquid yeast cultures.

- Aerate the cooled wort well.

- Use secondary fermentation techniques.

The following list describes several things *not* to do:

- Allow the beer to become contaminated.

- Overgrind the malt.

- Boil the grain.

- Mash or sparge with alkaline water.

- Oversparge the grain.

- Add too many minerals to your mash.

- Scorch the mash.

- Aerate hot wort.

- Pitch yeast into hot wort.

- Aerate fermented wort.

- Let the fermented beer sit on the yeast too long.

- Get too serious — it's still a hobby!

That the mashing procedures I outline in this chapter require more knowledge, effort, and, perhaps most important, time than other brewing procedures do is obvious. Because of time considerations, many all-grain brewers try to maximize their brewing sessions by brewing a greater volume of beer at one time. All things considered, this practice makes perfectly good sense.

Formulating the recipes for these increased batch sizes is no big deal. Increases in ingredients correspond to increases in the number of gallons you want to brew — the ratios don't change. To brew larger volumes of beer, however, you need equipment capable of handling those larger volumes: a bigger brewpot, a bigger lauter tun, and a larger fermenter (or more fermenters). Other considerations include a burner or heating element capable of bringing larger volumes of liquid to a boil (and adequate venting of such equipment), greater volumes of yeast slurry for fermenting bigger batches of beer, and lots of available bottles or kegs for packaging and storing your bodacious brews.

At this point in the brewery expansion, the kitchen becomes, for most people, obsolete. Handy and inventive brewers like to move their operations into a large laundry room, the basement, or a garage.

And on goes the argument about whether a beer geek really *is* committed or really *should be.*

Harvest Time: Reusing Your Yeast

After brewers progress to greater levels of brewery output, as I mention in the preceding section, yeast again becomes an issue. Because larger batches of beer require greater volumes of yeast slurry to achieve correct pitching rates, you must factor cost and effort into the brewing requirements.

Buying more packages or test tubes of sterile yeast culture for each batch that you brew may be an intelligent option but certainly isn't frugal. Yeast propagation is a smart option but may require multistep propagation procedures to achieve the desired pitching rates.

At this time, you may want to consider the possibilities of collecting yeast from a healthy fermentation to repitch in your subsequent brews. After primary fermentation is complete, *harvesting* the yeast from the fermenter is a simple matter. Here's all you need to do:

1. **Prepare a sanitary jar with stopper and airlock per the starter culture instructions in Chapters 11 and 26.**

   You use this vessel for collecting and storing the yeast.

2. **Drain the fermented beer from your primary fermenter into a bottling bucket, carboy, keg, or whatever you normally use.**

3. **Remove the siphon tube and put the cover back on the primary fermenter.**

4. **Sanitize a ladle or spoon and dig yeast off the bottom of the fermenter; then pour the yeast into the jar and seal it with the airlock.**

   Try to collect 4 to 8 ounces of yeast slurry/sediment.

5. **Put the jar in the refrigerator if you're not planning on using it right away.**

   You may store the yeast this way for a week or two, maximum.

6. **To reuse the yeast after refrigeration, take the jar out of the fridge and let it warm to room temperature.**

7. **Swirl the slurry and pitch it into the cooled wort of your next batch.**

Before reusing the yeast, taste a sample of the brew you took it from. (Hydrometer reading samples are great for this task.) If the beer tastes contaminated, the yeast slurry is also contaminated. Reusing the yeast from an imperfect batch of beer makes no sense. I don't recommend reusing yeast more than two or three times either, but let your taste of the subsequent beer be your guide and don't ever become lax on the rules of sanitation.

Chapter 13

Bottling Your Brew

In This Chapter

▶ Choosing your bottles

▶ Bottling wisdom

▶ Putting the bubbles in your brew

▶ Priming procedures

▶ Choosing your caps

Bottling homebrew isn't a difficult procedure, but brewers often deride it as one that's tedious at worst and boring at best. But for millions of people who brew their beer at home, bottling represents the only option for packaging their finished brew.

The key to breaking the tedium is to get your system down to a science — and to drink a brew while you're bottling one. (Kind of like whistling while you work, except that you're sucking brew and not blowing air.) The more you go through the bottling steps, the more familiar they become, and then you can begin to anticipate your next move. Having all the necessary equipment sanitized and ready to go before you begin any of the bottling procedures is especially handy.

Picking Out Bottles

Using good, sound, safe bottles is an important part of the bottling process. Your beer may start out as a world-class brew, but if the bottles aren't worthy, you can end up with leakers, exploders, and sticky messes. When you're buying bottles, don't skimp.

Bottles come in all sizes and shapes, but before I delve into the various choices, I want to give you a few very important suggestions. Your homebrew bottles

   ✔ **Should be the thick, returnable type (no cheap throwaways).** The thick, returnable-type bottles can withstand repeated uses; cheap throwaways mean thin glass and easy breakage.

✔ **Should be made of colored glass (the darker the better).** Light damages beer; tinted glass protects against light damage.

✔ **Shouldn't have a twist-off opening.** Bottle caps can't seal across the threads on twist-off bottles.

✔ **Should be of uniform size.** Although uniform bottles aren't a requirement, having all your beer in bottles of the same size and shape makes capping and storing much easier.

Even within these parameters, you still have a fairly wide choice in usable bottles; however, availability may become an issue. You can easily purchase brand-new 12- and 22-ounce bottles through homebrew supply shops, but the cost is sometimes prohibitive — if not for the bottles themselves, for the cost of having them shipped across the country if you don't have a local supplier.

Check with your local microbrewers (if you have any); you may be able to buy bottles directly from them.

The American brewing industry continues to package beer — albeit in limited markets — in a variety of 7-, 12-, 16-, and 22-ounce and quart-size returnable bottles; check with your local beer retailer. A few European brewers package their export beer in reusable bottles; the popular 17-ounce Weizenbier bottles are a good option.

Using larger bottles is a way to expedite the bottling process as well as free you from its drudgery. The more beer the bottles can hold, the fewer bottles you need. For instance, to bottle an entire 5-gallon batch of beer in 7-ounce nip bottles, you need to clean, fill, and cap more than 90 of them. If you use 22-ounce bottles, on the other hand, you need only 30 of them.

Homebrewers should also be aware that homebrewing competitions place strict limitations on the size and color of bottles allowed in competition. For more information on homebrew competitions, check out Chapter 25.

Ready, Set, Bottle!

Before you start any bottling procedures, take a hydrometer reading of the beer in the fermenter to verify that fermentation is sufficiently complete. Just steal a little beer out of the spigot to fill the hydrometer cylinder to within an inch of the top (but no more). (See Chapter 2 for complete directions on taking hydrometer readings.)

After you take your hydrometer reading, *don't* pour the beer from the cylinder back in with the rest of the beer — if you do so, you risk contaminating your beer. But don't throw the sample down the sink, either. It may be uncarbonated, but it's still good beer — drink it! You may be surprised to find out how good it already tastes.

After you've made certain that the beer is done fermenting, retrieved the bottling equipment, and quarantined the family pets, you're ready to start the bottling process. As always, setup starts with sanitizing all the necessary equipment, which includes the following:

- ✔ **A bottling bucket**
- ✔ **A racking cane** (if bottling from a vessel without an attached spigot)
- ✔ **A plastic hose**
- ✔ **A bottling tube** (with spring-action or gravity-pressure valve)
- ✔ **Bottles** (enough to hold 640 ounces of beer)
- ✔ **Bottle caps** (enough to cap all your bottles, plus some extras — just in case); see "Crowning Achievements" later in this chapter for more on caps

You need to sanitize all of these items before bottling, so you also need a sanitizing agent; for more information on sanitizing and sanitizing agents, see Chapter 3. You also need the following:

- ✔ **A bottle brush**
- ✔ **A bottle rinser**
- ✔ **A bottle capper**
- ✔ **Two small saucepans**
- ✔ **Dextrose (corn sugar) for priming** — ¾ **cup;** see "A Primer on Priming" later in this chapter
- ✔ **A beer to drink**

Now, here are the steps for the bottling brigade:

1. **Fill your utility tub or other designated sanitizing basin with enough cold water to cover your submerged bottles, adding bleach or another sanitizing agent according to the package directions.**

2. **Submerge as many bottles as you need to contain your full batch of 5 gallons of beer.**

   Make sure your bottles are scum-free before dunking them in the sanitizing solution. Any bottle with dried or living crud in the bottom needs to be scrubbed separately with a cleanser such as trisodium phosphate (TSP) before you sanitize it.

   You can fill and submerge the bottles in less than half the time if you place a drinking straw in the bottles; the straw enables the air within the bottle to escape through the straw instead of slowly bubbling through the opening (your bottling tube with the valve detached suffices here).

3. **Allow your bottles to soak for at least half an hour (or the time necessary according to package directions).**

4. **Crack open your bottle of beer.**

5. **While the bottles soak, dissolve ¾ cup of dextrose in a pint or so of water in one of the saucepans, cover the solution, and place it on a burner over low heat.**

6. **Put your bottle caps into your other saucepan, fill the pan with enough water to cover all the caps, and place the pan on another burner over low heat.**

Put enough bottle caps for as many bottles as you have soaking plus a few extra; having too many sterilized caps ready for bottling is better than not having enough.

7. **Allow both pans to come to a boil, remove them from the heat, and allow them to cool.**

8. **After the bottles soak for half an hour, connect the bottle rinser to the faucet over the sanitizing tub.**

9. **With one hand over the opening (so that you don't get squirted), turn on the hot water.**

After the initial spray, the bottle washer holds back the water pressure until a bottle is lowered over the stem and pushed down.

10. **Start cleaning the bottles one-by-one with the bottle brush, and then drain the sanitizer, rinse your bottles with the bottle rinser, and allow them to air dry.**

Continue this step until all bottles are clean.

Visually check each bottle for cleanliness rather than just assume that they're all clean.

Four dozen free-standing bottles make one heck of a breakable domino effect. Always put your cleaned bottles back into six-pack holders or cardboard cases to avoid an aggravating and easily avoidable accident.

11. **Take a sip of beer.**

12. **Drain the utility tub of the bottle-cleaning water.**

13. **Place the bottling bucket in the tub and fill it with water and the sanitizing agent of your choice.**

14. **Place the bottling hose, bottling tube, and hydrometer cylinder into the bottling bucket and allow them to soak for half an hour (or according to sanitizing agent directions).**

15. **While the bottling equipment soaks, retrieve the still-covered fermenter from its resting place and place it on a sturdy table, counter, or work surface about 3 or 4 feet off the ground.**

At this point, you need to set up your bottling station, making sure that you have the priming sugar mixture (still in the saucepan), bottle caps, bottle capper, bottles, and hydrometer with cylinder on hand.

If you're bottling your brew directly from the primary fermenter, you want to have already taken a hydrometer reading to confirm completion of fermentation. If you're bottling from your secondary fermenter (glass carboy), incomplete fermentation isn't a concern, and you can take a hydrometer reading (to determine final gravity and alcohol content) as the beer drains into the bottling bucket.

16. **After half an hour, drain the sanitizing solution from the bottling bucket through the spigot on the bottom and, after the bucket is empty, thoroughly rinse the remaining pieces of equipment (hose, bottling tube), along with the bottles and caps, and bring them to your bottling station.**

17. **Take a sip of beer.**

18. **Place the bottling bucket on the floor directly below the fermenter and connect the plastic hosing to the spigot on the fermenter, allowing the other end of the hosing to hang inside the bottling bucket.**

    If you're initiating the bottling procedures from your glass carboy, you can't rely on the convenience of a spigot to drain out the beer. You need to use your racking cane and siphon the brew. Chapter 11 explains siphoning procedures in more detail.

19. **Pour the dextrose and water mixture into the bottling bucket.**

    The dissolved corn sugar mixes with the beer as the beer drains from the fermenter into the bottling bucket. After you've bottled the beer, this sugar becomes another source of food for the few yeast cells still remaining in the liquid. As the yeast consumes the sugar, it produces the beer's carbonation within the bottle. Eventually, the yeast again falls dormant and creates a thin layer of sediment on the bottom of each bottle.

    If, by chance, you bottle a batch of beer that isn't fully fermented or you somehow add too much dextrose at bottling time, you may find out first-hand what a mess exploding bottles can make. Excess sugar (whether added corn sugar or leftover maltose from an unfinished fermentation) overfeeds the yeast in an enclosed bottle. With nowhere for the pressure to go, the glass gives before the bottle cap. Kaboom! Mess! Do not overprime. (Use no more than ¾ cup of dextrose in 5 gallons of beer.) See the "A Primer on Priming" section in this chapter for more advice on priming.

20. **Open the spigot on the fermenter and allow all the beer to run into the bottling bucket.**

    Don't try to salvage every last drop from the fermenter by tilting it as the beer drains down the spigot. The spigot is purposely positioned about an inch above the bottom of the fermenter so that all the spent yeast and miscellaneous fallout remains behind.

21. **After the last of the beer drains, close the spigot, remove the hose, and rinse it.**

    Avoid splashing or aerating your beer as you bottle it. Any oxidation that the beer picks up now can be tasted later. Yuck.

22. **Carefully place the bottling bucket up where the fermenter was, connect the rinsed hose to the spigot on the bottling bucket, and attach the bottling tube to the other end of the hose.**

23. **Arrange all your bottles on the floor directly below the bottling bucket (keeping them all in cardboard carriers or cases to avoid potential breakage and spillage).**

24. **Open the spigot on the bottling bucket and begin to fill all the bottles.**

    Gently push the bottling tube down on the bottom of each bottle to start the flow of beer. The bottle may take a short while to fill, but the process always seems to accelerate as the beer nears the top. Usually, a bit of foam rushes to the top of the bottle; don't worry! As soon as you withdraw the bottling tube, the liquid level in the bottle falls.

25. **Remove the tube from each bottle after foam or liquid reaches the top of the bottle.**

    Figure 13-1 shows you how full you want your bottles to be.

    After you remove the bottling tube from the bottle, the level of the beer falls to about an inch or so below the opening. Homebrewers have differing opinions as to how much airspace (or *ullage*) is necessary. Some say the smaller the airspace, the less oxidation that can occur. Others claim that if you don't have correct ullage, the beer can't carbonate properly. Rather than jump into the fray, I say if it looks like the space in bottles of beer from commercial breweries, go with it!

Figure 13-1: Correct bottle fill level.

Approximately 1 inch

Fill line

26. **After you completely drain the bottling bucket, close the spigot, remove the hose, toss it inside the bottling bucket, and set everything aside to be cleaned after all the bottling procedures are complete.**

27. **Place all the bottles on your tabletop or work surface; place a cap on each bottle, position your bottles in the capper (one at a time), and pull down on the capper handle or levers slowly and evenly.**

    You may want to do this task as soon as each bottle is full as insurance against everything that can go wrong when full bottles of your precious brew are sitting around open.

    Both bench- or two-handle-style cappers come with small magnets in the capper head designed to hold and align the cap as you start crimping. I don't trust the magnet to hold the caps in alignment and prefer to seat them on the bottles by hand.

    Occasionally, a cap may crimp incorrectly. If you suspect that a cap didn't seal right, tilt the bottle sideways and check for leakage. If you find you have a leaker, yank the cap and replace it. (You boiled extras — right?)

28. **Your homebrew needs to undergo a two-week conditioning phase, so store your liquid lucre in a cool, dark location (such as the same place that you kept the fermenter).**

    This phase is where the remaining yeast cells chow down on the dextrose and carbonate your beer.

    Putting your brew in the fridge isn't a good idea — at least for the first two weeks — because the very cold temperatures stunt the yeast's carbonating activity.

29. **You must thoroughly rinse your brewing equipment in hot water and store it in a place that's relatively dust- and mildew-free. You may even want to go that extra step and seal all your equipment inside a large-capacity garbage bag.**

    This step may be the most important one of all, not so much for the brew just made but for the next one. Consider this step an insurance policy on your next batch of beer. Boring but worthwhile, like most insurance policies.

30. **Finish drinking your beer (if you haven't already).**

After two weeks pass, check to see whether the bottles have clarified (the yeasty cloudiness has settled out). Chill a bottle or two for taste-testing. Like any commercial beer, you need to decant homebrew before drinking, not only to release the carbonation and the beer's aromatics but also to pour a clear beer. Drinking homebrew out of the bottle stirs up the sediment, creating a hazy beer. (See Chapter 22 for more information on proper decanting practices.)

Swingtime

If you're looking to save a few bucks on bottle-capping equipment and a little time on bottling procedures, you may want to consider packaging your brew in the swing-top bottles known as *Grolsch bottles*. These bottles aren't only unique in style, they also provide you the advantage of not needing to commit to drinking a full bottle at one sitting because they're self-sealing.

You do face some negatives with swing-top bottles, however. Unless you know someone who drinks a lot of Grolsch (or similarly packaged products) and wants to part with the empty bottles, the cost for two cases of these bottles can be considerable. This type of bottle also requires a little more attention at sanitation time. You need to remove the rubber gasket and clean the plastic (or ceramic) top thoroughly. Be aware that the gaskets can wear out and occasionally need to be replaced after repeated uses.

Finally, for those of you who want to send your homebrew to competitions, stay away from bottling your beer in swing-top bottles; these bottles aren't accepted at major competitions in the U.S.

Tanks a Lot! Bottling Kegged Beer

If you invest in a CO_2 system for kegging your beer, you may appreciate the ways you can use a CO_2 system for certain bottling applications, too. To get the lowdown on CO_2 kegging systems for homebrewing, check out Chapter 14.

For all its convenience and time- and effort-saving simplicity, kegging homebrew does have some limitations. What happens if you want to take a sample of your beer over to friend's home on poker night? What happens if you want to send a beer out to a homebrew competition in another state? You probably don't want to lug your kegging system over to your buddy's house, and having your kegged beer evaluated at faraway competitions is out of the question. Or is it?

Carbon-aid: Sharing kegged beer in plastic bottles

One enterprising company has created a simple little device called The Carbonater valve coupling. This plastic thingamajig is designed like a ball-lock fitting on a soda keg, and it's threaded so that you it can screw it onto plastic soda bottles. You can dispense some of your kegged beer into a plastic soda bottle, seal the bottle with The Carbonater cap, and pressurize the soda bottle to maintain the carbonation in the beer. Of course, you have to remove The Carbonater cap each time you want to pour beer from the bottle.

Currently, The Carbonater is available only in the ball-lock style. Owners of kegs with pin-lock fittings are out of luck, at least for the time being.

A couple of things to keep in mind when using The Carbonater: Carbonated beer in a pressurized plastic bottle isn't the ideal situation, nor should it be. Homebrew isn't meant to be stored in soda bottles for long periods of time. The Carbonater bottling method simply enables you to dispense and transport smaller quantities of beer from your keg. And because you use The Carbonater with plastic bottles, close attention to gas pressure is important; 40 psi is the maximum recommended pressure for standard plastic soda bottles.

One last caveat: Soda bottles — pressurized or not — are never accepted at homebrew competitions.

The Carbonater also enables you to carbonate water or any other beverage in your home for a spritzy, refreshing drink.

Counterintelligence: Flowing from keg to bottle for competition

If you want to send samples of your kegged beer to far-flung homebrew competitions, you can bottle your kegged beer in one of two ways:

- ✔ Fill your bottles by using your kegging system's beverage dispensing hose.
- ✔ Fill your bottles by using a *counterpressure bottle filler,* hooked up to your kegging system.

The first method is suspect because the beer not only loses carbonation during the transfer but also risks picking up oxidation or contamination along the way. The second method is far more sound and proper for a competition-worthy beer.

A *counterpressure bottle filler* is an apparatus that first backfills the bottle with CO_2, thus purging the bottle of air, and then maintains pressure within the bottle while the beer is flowing in through the filler tube. Counterpressure bottle filling eliminates both the loss of carbonation and the threat of oxidation and contamination. A typical counterpressure bottle filler setup includes a gas line, a beer line, a filler tube, and shutoff valves. Figure 13-2 shows how to use a counterpressure filler. For more detail, refer to package directions.

Figure 13-2:
Typical
counterpres
sure bottle
filler setup.

Beer line — Valves

Gas line

Filler tube

A Primer on Priming

As you may know, yeast is responsible for producing the natural carbonation in beer and other fermentable beverages (see Chapter 6 for more on yeast and fermentation). And, because carbon dioxide escapes from the fermenter, you may be wondering how you can put the carbonation back into your beer. The answer is a simple little trick called priming.

Priming means adding more fermentable sugar to the beer just prior to bottling it. The small number of yeast cells that remain in the solution when you bottle your brew gladly see to it that they eat the sugars you add and thus provide the desired carbonation within the bottle. Of course, this process doesn't happen overnight. You need to allow another one to two weeks before your beer is properly carbonated and ready to drink.

Getting ready to prime

When you choose a priming sugar for beer, you need to consider two things: the *quantity* and the *fermentability* of the priming ingredient you're going to use. The first factor is dependent on the second factor.

As I mention earlier, the idea of priming is to put more fermentable sugar into the beer so that the yeast can create the needed carbonation within the bottle. But consider the consequences of giving the yeast too little or too much sugar to eat: Too little priming sugar can result in an under-carbonated beer, but too much sugar may cause your bottles to explode! Don't panic — I discuss proper priming quantities in the "Deciding which and how much primer to use" section in this chapter.

Two important points regarding beer priming: First, not all beer styles contain the same level of carbonation. A Berliner Weisse, for example, is far more effervescent than, say, a Scotch Ale. At a competitive level, you may want to take this discrepancy into consideration; otherwise, you may just want to use the standard measure of priming sugar detailed in the next section. The second important point is that high-gravity beers you intend to condition in the bottle over longer periods of time are likely to build up increasing carbonation levels as they age. If you plan on storing a particularly big Barley Wine away for several months, you may want to cut back on the amount of priming sugar you add at bottling time.

Another consideration for those who brew high-gravity beers and age them a long time: If your beer has been aging for a month or longer, what yeast is left in it is probably old and fatigued. With your yeast's declining viability in mind, you probably want to add some fresh yeast to the beer along with the priming agent at bottling time. Using generic dry yeast is perfectly acceptable here.

Deciding which and how much primer to use

Different sugar sources (refined sugar, honey, molasses, and so on) have different levels of fermentability, which means that the more fermentable sugar a priming mixture has, the less of the mixture you need. Conversely, you need more of a priming mixture with less fermentable sugar. You can potentially use any one of the adjunct sugars mentioned in Chapter 8 for priming purposes. Note that because you use them in such small quantities, priming sugars have virtually no effect on the beer's taste.

To keep the priming process simple, I recommend using dextrose (corn sugar). Dextrose is highly fermentable, widely available, easy to work with, and inexpensive.

Regardless of what form of priming sugar you use to prime your beer, always dissolve and dilute it in boiling water first, and allow the priming mixture to cool before adding it to the beer. The amount of water used to boil the sugar in is of little concern — 1 or 2 cups are typical.

In the average 5-gallon batch of beer, ¾ of a cup (*not* ¾ of a pound!) of dextrose is the maximum recommended amount for priming. Using more than this may result in exploding bottles but is more likely to result in over-carbonated beer and *gushers* — bottles that act like miniature volcanoes when your buddies pry the caps off. Hmmm, sounds like a good prank, come to think of it.

Exploring alternative primers

Although dextrose (corn sugar) is the cheapest and most convenient priming agent available to homebrewers, you do have other options when you're ready to carbonate your beer. Read on. . .

Dry malt extract: The purists' choice

Brewing purists may cringe at the thought of adding a refined white sugar to homebrew, so they often use a more-unadulterated alternative. *Dry malt extract,* or DME, is a second choice for priming beer. But, as I point out in Chapter 4, DME is only about 70 percent fermentable. Therefore, you need to use more DME than dextrose (which is about 99 percent fermentable). If you take the purists' route, make sure you increase your priming volume to 1 1/4 cups of dry malt extract per 5-gallon batch of beer.

Not only do you need to use more DME than dextrose, but you also need to allow more time for the carbonation within the bottle to build up. Yeast can consume and convert the simple dextrose sugars into carbon dioxide much more quickly than it can the more complex maltose sugars found in malt extract.

Fruit liqueurs: The exotic choice

As a really progressive homebrewer, yet another priming ingredient exists that not only carbonates your beer but also imbues it with various fruit flavors: fruit liqueurs. Most liqueurs are a great alternative priming agent for the following reasons:

- **Liqueurs contain a fair amount of sugar.** One 750 milliliter bottle contains just about enough sugar to prime a 5-gallon batch of beer. Because the actual sugar content of any liqueur depends on the company that made it (although it more likely has too little sugar than too much), you may want to add another ounce or two of dextrose to be sure.

- **Fruit liqueurs are available in a variety of flavors.** My local liquor store stocks cherry, blueberry, blackberry, peach, strawberry, raspberry, orange, and even black currant liqueur.

- **Fruit syrups used in liqueurs are usually of high quality.** Fruit liqueurs offer rich and consistent fruit flavor and aroma.

For keggers only

If you intend to keg your beer, you may choose to prime before you keg it or not to prime it at all. The use of kegs and compressed carbon dioxide gas cylinders allows you to carbonate beer without the use of priming sugars (see Chapter 14 for more about the kegging process).

If you choose to prime your kegged beer, you can afford to be a little more relaxed about overpriming than if you bottled your beer — kegs come with pressure relief valves to vent excessive pressure. No exploding kegs!

✔ **Liqueurs are already antiseptic.** Because they contain alcohol contents of up to 40 percent, no further treatment is necessary before adding them to your beer. (Don't worry about the added alcohol; the total content in your beer isn't likely to rise more than 1 or 2 percent, at most.)

Use only translucent liqueurs — never cream liqueurs. Cream liqueurs add an unappealing milky haze to your beer (yech!).

Crowning Achievements

Although I typically refer to bottle caps, keep in mind that many brewers call caps *crowns*. Caps or crowns — whatever you call them, they're one of the most useful but inexpensive tools available to you, the homebrewer.

By and large, a bottle cap is a bottle cap is a bottle cap. They're plentiful, inexpensive, come in a limited variety of colors, and are usually sold by the batch (60 pieces — includes extras) or by the gross (144 pieces). Bottle caps are metal on the outside with a plastic seal on the inside. That plastic gasket is what makes one kind of bottle cap special (see the "Rare air" sidebar in this chapter). You need to sanitize all bottle caps before using them. To do so, simply boil them in water or soak them in your sanitizing agent of choice.

Because bottle caps are expendable (you use them once and then discard them), such a one-time-use piece of equipment is actually more like an ingredient — you need to replenish it for each batch of beer you brew and bottle. And because you may choose to bottle your beer in self-sealing, swing-top bottles, you may have no need for bottle caps at all (you find more on swing-top bottles in the "Swingtime" sidebar earlier in this chapter).

Rare air

The SmartCap Pure Seal is a brand of bottle cap that has an inner seal that actually absorbs oxygen within the sealed bottle. These caps are moisture-activated (which means you need to store the caps in a humidity-free location). Unlike all other plain bottle caps, you should never boil or soak these special caps prior to using them.

These oxygen-absorbing caps are especially important to homebrewers who create high-gravity beers with long shelf-lives; the SmartCap guards against the oxidation (absorption of oxygen by the beer) that usually affects aging beers. Instead of oxygen being absorbed by your beer, it's absorbed by the cap. These caps generally cost about 50 percent more than regular caps, but considering the bottom line, they're worth it.

Shortly after the oxygen-absorbing caps were introduced to the homebrewing market, skeptical and inquisitive members of a homebrew club staged an unscientific experiment using these caps. They bottled a batch of hoppy pale Ale using both the Pure Seal cap and regular bottle caps. Labeled simply beer "A" and beer "B," other club members then evaluated the aroma and taste of both beers and commented on their freshness levels. By a notable margin, club members preferred the beer capped with the newfangled crowns.

Chapter 14

Kegging: Bottling's Big Brother

In This Chapter

▶ Cleaning your keg

▶ Kegging your beer

▶ Dispensing your brew

As I mention in Chapter 13, homebrewers seem to universally agree that bottling is the worst part of homebrewing. The cleaning, storing, sanitizing, and capping of bottles is very tedious and time-consuming. If you can't stand bottling, kegging your brew is a viable option if you have a little disposable income.

In this chapter, I give you some advice on how to make decisions that answer the questions you face when you decide to keg your own beer: "What type of keg do I need (and what equipment goes along with it)?"; "How do I sanitize it properly?"; and "How do I tap it like a pro?" (See Chapter 13 for information about how to bottle your kegged beer when you want to transport small amounts.)

Roll Out the Barrel: Buying Your Kegging Equipment

Buying kegging equipment isn't easy; that's why I'm here — to simplify your decision. The system I recommend for homebrewers is a 5-gallon soda keg system, because it's easier to clean, fill, handle, and obtain than commercial beer kegs. Using commercial beer kegs requires special tools and equipment, and they're almost impossible to clean properly without more expensive equipment.

Any kegging system, even on the homebrewing level, is going to require somewhat costly specialized equipment, such as a CO_2 tank with regulators and hoses. These items can take a bite out of your wallet even if you buy them used. On the positive side, a CO_2 setup is multifunctional; you can use it for filtering and force-carbonating your beer, among other things (see Chapter 27 and the "Making bubbles: Carbonating procedures" section in this chapter).

Here's what you need for the kegging procedures outlined in this chapter:

✔ **One or more stainless steel soda kegs:** A new keg can cost as much as $100, although a used one may be as little as $25. Whatever route you choose, be sure your kegs seal properly and hold pressure.

Soda keg fittings come in two types — *ball* or *pin lock* — and either type is acceptable. These names relate to the configuration of the valve connection that allows pressurized gas to flow into (but not out of) the valve until you depress it (kind of like the valve on a bicycle or car tire). Pin lock configuration tends to be a bit more expensive.

✔ **A pressurized carbon dioxide tank:** This tank will run you $75 to $125, and it costs another $15 to $20 each time you refill it.

✔ **A carbon dioxide tank regulator (preferably a dual gauge):** This item isn't cheap either — it sets you back $75 to $90.

Tank regulators are available in single gauge and dual gauge types. The single gauge only tells you the pressure of the gas flowing through the gas line; the dual gauge is better because it tells you the line pressure as well as the gas pressure remaining in the tank.

✔ **Appropriate quick-disconnect fittings (for ball or pin lock):** Get one fitting for the gas inflow and one for the liquid outflow. They're reasonably priced at $6 to $8 each.

✔ **A carbon dioxide hose line (gas inflow line):** It's not a bad deal at about $1 per foot.

✔ **A beer dispenser line with a tap faucet (liquid outflow line):** This is another item with a fairly cheap price: $5 to $10.

✔ **A sanitizing agent:** I recommend Iodophor or another iodine-based sanitizer, which costs $2 to $10 depending on the container size.

Although ordinary household bleach is fine for sanitizing most other homebrew equipment, stainless steel is an exception. Chlorine can actually eat away the surface of stainless steel at high concentrations or over an extended period of time, especially at low pH levels. If you must use bleach out of desperation, use only 1 ounce per 5 gallons and limit contact time with the keg to 30 minutes. Consider yourself warned.

✔ **A screwdriver and adjustable wrench:** You may have these items lying around your house.

✔ **A carboy brush or similar cleaning brush:** Again, you may already have an appropriate brush.

Figure 14-1 shows you what your soda keg system looks like when you're all set up and ready to keg.

Figure 14-1:
The typical soda keg setup for home-brewers, including a 5-gallon keg, CO_2 tank, dual CO_2 gauges, and dispensing hoses and fittings.

Getting Your Keg Up and Flowing

After you've made your decisions and your purchases, the first thing you want to do is thoroughly clean and sanitize your kegging equipment. I cover the information on how to do this in the following section. When you have a beer ready to keg, all you need to do is follow the easy directions I provide a bit later in this chapter.

Clean 'em out and fill 'em up: Sanitizing and racking procedures

When it comes to storing your beer in kegs, the cleaning and sanitizing of your equipment is important (just as it is with any other aspect of homebrewing). Unlike bottles, however, kegs pose a slightly different problem: Because kegs have many parts, it's more difficult to make sure that all the parts are equally clean and sanitized. This means you need to disassemble your keg in preparation for the cleaning and sanitizing procedures. After you've properly disinfected and reassembled it, filling it with your brew is a snap. The following steps walk you through sanitizing your keg.

1. **After obtaining all the necessary system parts, hook up the regulator to the CO_2 cylinder.**

   Make sure you use the gasket that comes with the regulator. This gasket must be in place between the regulator fitting and the CO_2 tank to prevent gas leakage. (Too bad humans don't come with gaskets.)

2. **Vent any pressure from the keg by depressing the relief valve on top of the keg.**

If your keg doesn't have a relief valve, you can depress the gas in valve (at the top of the keg) with the tip of a screwdriver.

Always vent your keg of pressure before you open or disassemble it.

3. **Open the large lid on top of the keg and clean the inside with water and a carboy brush. Visually inspect the inside to make sure it's clean.**

If the keg is dirty or has beer or soda residue in it, you can clean it with some *trisodium phosphate* (TSP) — never use ordinary household soap. Rinse well with water. Remember that TSP is a cleanser, not a sanitizer.

4. **If you own a used keg, you may want to replace the five gaskets to get rid of the soda pop smell.**

Alternatively, you can remove the gaskets and soak them in ethyl or grain alcohol (be sure you rinse the alcohol away very thoroughly). See Figure 14-2 for the locations of the gaskets you may need to clean or replace. If it's a new keg, proceed to Step 5; if you're dealing with used gaskets, the following checklist can help you find and clean them:

Figure 14-2: Locations of the five rubber gaskets on a typical soda keg.

- The first gasket is easy to find — it's around the lid. Remove it, clean the lid thoroughly, and replace the gasket.

- Another two gaskets are around the outside of the tank plugs (the in/out fittings). Carefully remove these gaskets and either clean or replace them. Make sure to refit the plugs onto your keg.

- The last two gaskets are hidden on the dip tubes; you can find them by using an adjustable wrench to loosen and remove the tank plugs one at a time (don't strip the plugs). Be careful not to lose any of the small pieces (including the gaskets) inside the tank plugs.

  Removing these plugs one at a time is important because the tank plugs aren't interchangeable — each is a different size and/or shape. Be sure not to mix up the dip tubes (found under the tank plugs) either. The fluid out tube is as long as the tank is deep, and the gas in tube is about ½ inch long.

- Thoroughly clean the tank plugs (inside and out) of any soda pop syrup or beer residue with a small brush and warm water (four out of five brewers recommend using an old toothbrush).

- Remove the dip tubes by pushing them up from the inside with your hands (don't use pliers because they can damage the tubes).

- Now you can remove the two gaskets around the dip tubes and clean or replace them.

- Clean the inside and outsides of the two dip tubes (don't mix them up). Reassemble the keg and apply 10 *psi (pounds per square inch)* of carbon dioxide to see whether it still holds pressure. If the keg doesn't hold pressure, check to make sure you reassembled the keg properly and tightened all the fittings.

You want to disassemble and clean the keg on a regularly scheduled basis — every third brew or so.

5. **After the keg is clean, fill it with 1 to 2 ounces of Iodophor sanitizer (or according to the directions for the sanitizer of your choice) in 5 gallons of cool water to sanitize it.**

   Leave the sanitizer in the keg for at least 15 minutes.

   Don't forget to depress the out valve to allow Iodophor to flow up into the long dip tube. You should also turn the keg upside down or on its side for 15 minutes so that you sanitize the top, too.

6. **After at least 15 minutes, drain the solution from the keg.**

   Pour some of the sanitizing solution in a bucket so that you can soak the lid in it while you rinse and fill the keg.

7. **Rinse the inside of the keg and drain all excess water.**

   Be sure you run some water through the out dip tube: Put the lid on the keg, apply CO_2 pressure, and dispense the water as if you're tapping a beer.

If there is any question about the cleanliness of your water, I suggest pre-boiling it before using it to rinse your kegs.

8. **Rinse and replace the keg lid. Pressurize the keg to 10 psi and release the CO₂.**

   This step purges air from the keg.

9. **Sanitize your siphon hose and siphon the finished beer into the keg through its lid hole.**

   If you're keeping track of your beer's gravity and alcohol content, this is the time to take another hydrometer reading with your sanitized hydrometer cylinder. (See Chapter 2 for more information on taking hydrometer readings.)

10. **Rinse the sanitized lid and then seal the keg.**

    Don't forget to properly seat the gasket.

11. **Apply 10 psi to the keg and vent.**

    Repeat this step five times to ensure that the atmosphere inside the keg is almost pure CO_2.

    If the kegs aren't kept under 5 to 10 pounds of pressure, the gaskets may not seal completely. Be sure your keg is under pressure while you're storing beer in it.

Making bubbles: Carbonating procedures

Okay, so you've filled the keg. Now how do you carbonate it? This section describes the method in minute detail.

Force carbonating is exactly what it sounds like — you're forcing CO_2 into the beer by pressurizing the keg to a certain psi level (see Figure 14-3).

The advantage of force-carbonating is that the beer has little sediment (especially if you allowed the beer to age in a carboy for two to three weeks). The beer is also ready to drink in a day or two. The following steps show you how to force-carbonate your brew:

1. **Chill your beer to 60 degrees Fahrenheit or cooler and take the precise temperature of the beer.**

   (Check out Chapter 27 for the lowdown on stick-on type thermometers.)

2. **Next, hook up the CO₂ line to the "CO₂ in" plug on the keg.**

3. **Find the temperature of your beer at the left of the gas volume table in Figure 14-3 and then follow the top row of the table to the right to find the volumes of CO₂ to which you want to carbonate your beer. Follow the column that you choose down to the pressure (psi) indicated.**

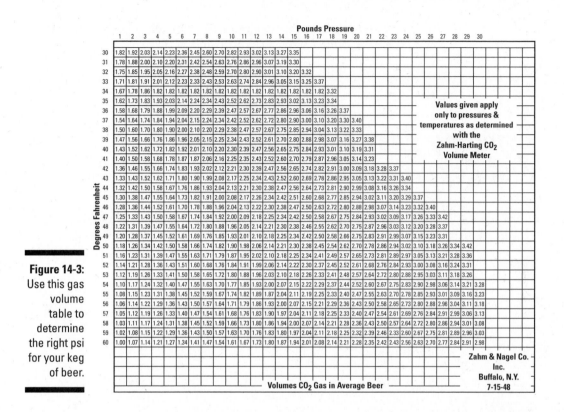

Figure 14-3:
Use this gas volume table to determine the right psi for your keg of beer.

Check out the nearby "Pump up the volume" sidebar for more on volume.

4. **Open the CO_2 tank and set your regulator to the pressure you got from the gas volume table.**

5. **Vent the keg and put the black disconnect onto the out valve of the keg.**

   If you hear gas bubbling through the beer, congratulations: You did this step correctly.

6. **Shake the keg to force the CO_2 into the beer. Do this for 5 minutes, disconnect the CO_2 from the keg, and then shut off the gas.**

   Repeat Steps 5 and 6 as often as you can over the next 24 hours or so. Make sure you always keep the temperature-to-pressure ratio the same. If the temperature or the pressure changes, the amount of CO_2 dissolved into the beer changes. When you can't hear any gas going into the solution, you know your beer is at the desired level of carbonation.

   Always disconnect the gas line from the keg before you shut off the CO_2 tank valve. Without pressure in the line, the beer may back up into the regulator. Remember that CO_2 is a pressurized gas; observe all necessary safety precautions. Consult your gas supplier for further information.

7. **After your beer reaches the desired CO_2 level, allow the keg to settle for a couple of hours before dispensing.**

The CO_2 needs a few days to thoroughly dissolve into the beer, but your brew is drinkable at this time.

Enjoying Your Brew: Tapping and Lapping Procedures

Here you go — your beer is kegged and ready to drink; all you need to do is grab your favorite beer glass and plop into your easy chair. Actually, you have to hook up the keg and start the flow of CO_2 first, but homebrew enjoyment doesn't get much easier than this.

After the beer is carbonated:

1. **Open the gas cylinder and set the regulator to 5 to 8 psi.**
2. **Vent the keg and hook up the gas and the dispense lines.**
3. **Tap and enjoy.**

Always tap your beer with the tap head wide open (depress the valve completely). Opening the tap only halfway causes foaming. Also, if the beer still foams too much (even when the tap head is wide open), turn the dispensing pressure down a pound or two by adjusting the line pressure on the gas gauge.

When you're done dispensing beer for the day, repressurize the keg to the original carbonating pressure (if you force-carbonated) or to 10 psi (if you primed it) to maintain the proper CO_2 level in the beer.

Pump up the volume

How much is a *volume?* Two volumes of CO_2 are the equivalent of two 5-gallon containers' worth of CO_2 compressed into a single 5-gallon container (the average beer has 2.4 to 2.7 volumes of CO_2).

How many volumes of CO_2 do you need to put into your beer? The answer depends greatly on the particular beer style, but here are some general guidelines to follow: British-style Ales = 1.75 to 2.5 volumes, American and European Lagers = 2.25 to 2.75 volumes, and highly carbonated beers (Weizen, Fruit beers, and Belgian Ales) = 2.75 to 3.25 volumes. Clearly, force carbonating gives you much more control over your beer's carbonation than simple priming techniques.

Part IV
Homebrew Recipes

The 5th Wave   By Rich Tennant

"This time, let's keep the eye of newt out of the wort."

In this part . . .

This is the fun part of the book — the part where you get to put all your knowledge to work and try brewing some real beer. The recipes in this part were hand-chosen for their popularity, usability, and great taste. Note that many of them are award winners from various AHA competitions; these recipes are marked with little ribbons next to their names and are extra-tasty examples of homebrew. Note, too, that I have included some of my own recipes for you to sample. Have fun and enjoy!

Please note that several beer styles aren't represented by recipes in this book. This is due to the fact that reproducing these styles requires ingredients, equipment, and/or procedures beyond the scope of this book.

Most beer styles are represented by recipes at two levels of difficulty: intermediate and advanced. Beginner recipes, because they're identical in procedure and only vary by malt extract brand name, are limited to tips or suggestions on how to mimic more difficult procedures.

Also note:

- ✔ The number/letter designations next to each style represent its place on the hierarchical listing on this book's Cheat Sheet. If you check out that listing, you can easily tell where each beer fits into the scheme of things.

- ✔ All recipes in this section are designed for 5-gallon batches.

- ✔ Original and final gravities are measured in the Specific Gravity scale.

- ✔ All measurements are given in pounds, ounces, tablespoons, and teaspoons. See the Cheat Sheet for some basic conversions.

- ✔ L = Lovibond (color scale).

Chapter 15

Ale Recipes

. . . .

In This Chapter

▶ E.S.B.

▶ Irish Red Ale

▶ Strong Ale

▶ American Ale

▶ Brown Ale

▶ Porter

▶ Stout

▶ India Pale Ale

▶ Wit

▶ Belgian Ale

▶ Old Ale

▶ Belgian Strong Ale

▶ Barley Wine

. . . .

*A*les, by traditional definition, are beers fermented with top-fermenting yeast at warm temperatures for relatively short periods of time. Ales are primarily associated with England and Ireland, but you can find them in a wide variety of styles in most brewing nations such as Australia, Belgium, Canada, and the United States.

This chapter provides beer recipes for most of the beer styles that are Ale varieties. *Note:* Not all of the Ale beer styles and substyles listed on the AHA hierarchical list (on the Cheat Sheet) are included in this chapter. Because certain beer styles are very difficult to produce at the homebrewing level without highly advanced information, equipment, ingredients, and techniques, I've omitted some of them from this chapter (trust me, this is for your benefit!). Instead, I've placed my emphasis on popular beer styles. Also note that, although I've compiled these recipes, I didn't create all of them and have little control over how much or how little information they provide. As a general guideline, all water treatments in intermediate recipes are assumed to be added to the brewpot unless otherwise noted; water treatments in advanced recipes are assumed to be added to the mash water.

Extra Special/Strong Bitter (E.S.B.) (8-c)

The history of this style of beer is rather hazy because it probably developed over a long period of time and was influenced by a number of factors. To begin with, the pale malt needed to brew Pale Ale was developed only as recently as the 1700s — most of the barley malt used prior to this time was a brown malt (because of the kilning procedures) that resulted in darker beers. Secondly, hop character is very important to the English-style Pale Ale that drinkers recognize today, but hops were not in widespread use in England until the mid-16th century. Furthermore, the English people made a clear distinction between unhopped Ale and any beer made with hops; these beers were called *bitters*.

Think of strong bitters as a higher-gravity version of best bitters (traditionally the brewer's finest product). In England today, ESB is a brand unique to Fullers; Americans have co-opted the name to describe a malty, bitter, reddish, standard-strength English-type ale. Hopping can be English or a combination of English and American.

The parameters of the style are fairly loose, allowing for a generous range of color and a fair fluctuation in gravities. Two things are certain about Pale Ales: They exhibit fruity esters in the nose and a big hop presence in both the flavor and the aroma. In fact, hops are the key to developing a good Pale Ale. The Classic English Pale Ale should use a hop from England known as Kent Goldings, but other aromatic varieties are perfectly acceptable. Pale Ales are often *dry-hopped*, which is a method of imbuing the beer with a fresh hop aroma (without the bitterness) by adding hops directly to the beer while it's in the aging tank or barrel instead of during the boiling process. See Chapters 5 and 11 for more information on dry hopping.

Flavor profile: Golden to deep amber. Lots of fruity esters can be expected. High hop bitterness, flavor, and aroma dominate low to medium maltiness. Toastiness and low levels of diacetyl are okay. Medium bodied.

OG/FG:	1.048–1.060+ / 1.010–1.016
ABV:	4.6–6.2
IBUs:	30–50+
SRM:	6–18

Commercial examples: Fuller's ESB, England; Marston's Pedigree, England

Beginner suggestions

Start with 6 to 7 pounds of pale hopped extract and steep between 1 and 1.5 pounds of 40-L crystal malt; strain into the wort. In the last 10 minutes of the boil, toss in between 0.5 and 1 ounce of a traditional English hop (Fuggles, Kent Goldings) for additional hop character. Prime with a lower dose of corn sugar (½ cup) to reduce carbonation levels.

(Intermediate)
Brewer: Marty Nachel

1-4-U, 2-4-ME S.B.

Malt extract:	6 pounds Munton and Fison pale extract	**Misc. fermentable ingredients:**	1 cup brown sugar
Specialty grain:	1 pound 40-L crystal malt	**Fining agent/ clarifier:**	1 teaspoon Irish moss
	0.5 pound Victory malt	**Primary:**	8 days at 65 degrees Fahrenheit
Bittering hops:	2 ounces Kent Goldings (60 mins.)	**Secondary:**	10 days at 65 degrees Fahrenheit
Flavoring hops:	1 ounce Kent Goldings (15 mins.)		
Yeast:	Wyeast #1968		

Typical/unusual procedures used: You may need to rouse this yeast by agitating the primary fermenter every other day.

(Advanced)
Brewer: Andy Leith

Bridge House Bitter

Award won: 1st Place, AHA Nationals

Base grain:	9 pounds Pale Ale malt	**Yeast:**	Wyeast #1084
Specialty grain:	8 ounces 60-L crystal malt	**Primary:**	4 days at 65 degrees Fahrenheit
Bittering hops:	1.75 ounces Willamette (90 mins.)	**Secondary:**	10 days at 65 degrees Fahrenheit
	0.5 ounce Cascade (90 mins.)		
Finishing hops:	1 ounce Kent Goldings (2 mins.)		

Typical/unusual procedures used: Perform a step infusion mash for 30 minutes at 125 degrees Fahrenheit, and for 90 minutes at 154 degrees Fahrenheit.

Irish Red Ale (9-d)

Traditional Irish Ales are easy-drinking, but full-flavored, malt-accented brews. One of the first Irish brands to hit the American market was George Killian Lett's Irish Ale. Unfortunately, when the Coors Brewing Company bought the label and began to produce it in the United States, it lost most of its original character — in fact, it isn't even brewed as an Ale anymore. Due to its popularity, though, numerous Red beers are produced throughout the U.S. in an effort to capitalize on the success of Killian's.

Flavor profile: Irish Red Ales are amber to deep copper/red in color (thus their name). This style's caramel malt flavor and sweetness sometimes has a buttered-toast or toffee quality. Irish Ales often exhibit a light taste of roasted malt, which lends a characteristic dryness to the finish. And not a shamrock in sight. . . .

OG/FG:	1.044–1.060 / 1.010–1.014
ABV:	4.0–6.0%
IBUs:	17–28
SRM:	9–18

Commercial examples: Smithwick's Irish Ale, Ireland; Kilgubbin Irish Ale, Chicago

Beginner suggestions

You can use either pale extract or amber hopped extract — both finish within the generous color range for this style. If you choose the pale extract, try getting a little *kettle caramelization* by vigorously boiling the wort an extra half hour or more.

Why'd You Kilkenny?

(Intermediate)
Brewer: Marty Nachel

Malt extract:	6.6 pounds North-western Gold extract	**Flavoring hops:**	1 ounce Fuggles (20 mins.)
Specialty grain:	1 pound 60-L crystal malt	**Finishing hops:**	0.5 ounce Kent Goldings (5 mins.)
	⅛ pound roast malt	**Yeast:**	Wyeast #1084
Bittering hops:	0.5 ounce Fuggles (60 mins.)	**Primary:**	6 days at 65 degrees Fahrenheit
	0.5 ounce Fuggles (40 mins.)	**Secondary:**	12 days at 65 degrees Fahrenheit

Hooligan's Red

(Advanced)
Brewer: Steve Kamp

Base grain:	18.5 pounds British pale 2-row malt	**Yeast:**	Wyeast #1084
Specialty grain:	1 pound 20-L crystal malt	**Primary:**	(not given)
	0.25 pound black patent malt	**Secondary:**	(not given)
Bittering hops:	1 ounce Northern Brewer (60 mins.)		

Typical/unusual procedures used:
Perform a single step infusion mash. Boil for 60 minutes.

Strong Scotch Ale (9-e)

Strong Scotch Ale is — surprise! — the Scottish equivalent of English Old Ale. The main differences are that Strong Scotch Ales are less aggressively hopped, which contributes to this rounder, maltier character. Low levels of carbonation are also an important characteristic of the style and help maintain a certain softness on the palate.

Strong Scotch Ale (or Scots Ale) is known as a *wee heavy* and, like most Scottish Ales, is categorized by a *Shilling designation*, which corresponds to the higher gravities of these Ales. Strong Scotch Ales usually start at around 90 Shilling and can go as high as 120 Shilling. Scotch ales are ordered by their Shilling designation in Highland pubs.

Strong Scotch Ales share the same flavor characteristics as lighter Scottish Ales but to an exaggerated degree. Strong Scotch Ales are typically overwhelmingly malty — almost to the point of being cloyingly sweet — and the low hopping rates do little to cut the intense maltiness. Regrettably, the lack of protective hop resins in this beer style also tends to diminish its shelf life, leaving only the alcohol to fend off the inevitable stale off flavors. Strong Scotch Ale is often roused during the fermentation process to keep the yeast active. This practice results in relatively low final gravities and alcohol potentials as high as 8 percent by volume. The use of peat-smoked malt is one of the traits of the finest Scotch whiskies, one that's often shared between Strong Scotch Ale and Scotch whisky.

Flavor profile: Deep copper to dark brown. Hop flavor and aroma are very low. Overwhelmingly malty, but clean alcohol flavor balances the malt character. Hop bitterness is low, and diacetyl is medium to high. Full-bodied. Faint smoky character is okay.

OG/FG:	1.070–1.130 / 1.018–1.030+
ABV:	6.5–10.0
IBUs:	17–35
SRM:	14–25

Commercial examples: Orkney Skull Splitter, Scotland; Traquair House, Scotland

Beginner suggestions

Strong Scotch Ales require a fair amount of fermentable material — try starting with at least 7 pounds of extract. You don't age Strong Scotch Ales as long as English Old Ales, and they're much maltier. Try progressing to a liquid yeast culture that's not as attenuate (doesn't eat as much of the malt sugar) as dry yeasts. Try adding a small dose of liquid smoke extract (1 to 2 teaspoons) to emulate the smokiness of the style.

A Peek Under the Kilt Ale

(Intermediate)
Brewer: Jim Campbell

Award won: 1st Place, AHA Nationals

Malt extract:
6 pounds light extract
3.3 pounds amber extract
1 pound light DME

Specialty grain:
2 pounds crystal malt
0.5 pound Munich malt
0.5 pound flaked barley
0.5 pound wheat malt
0.25 pound roasted barley

Bittering hops:
0.75 ounce Chinook (75 mins.)
1 ounce Hallertauer (75 mins.)

Flavoring hops:
1 ounce Cascade (30 mins.)
1 ounce Kent Goldings (10 mins.)

Finishing hops:
1 ounce Cascade (5 mins.)

Yeast: Wyeast #1056

Water treatment:
0.5 teaspoon gypsum
0.5 teaspoon salt
0.5 teaspoon ascorbic acid

Fining agent/ clarifier:
0.5 teaspoon Irish moss

Primary: 38 days at 65 degrees Fahrenheit

Secondary: (not given)

Scotch Ale

(Advanced)
Brewer: Jerry Bockmore

Award won: 1st Place, AHA Nationals

Base grain:
3.5 pounds Mild Ale malt
3 pounds Klages malt
3 pounds Pale Ale malt

Specialty grain:
2 pounds British crystal malt
2 ounces chocolate malt
2 ounces black patent malt

Bittering hops:
1 ounce Chinook (60 mins.)
0.5 ounce Kent Goldings (60 mins.)

Flavoring hops:
1 ounce Kent Goldings (10 mins.)

Yeast: Wyeast #1028

Misc. fermentable ingredients:
1 pound dark brown sugar
1 teaspoon gypsum

Water treatment:
1 teaspoon Burton salts

Primary: 3 weeks at 65 degrees Fahrenheit

Secondary: (not given)

Typical/unusual procedures used:
Perform a single step infusion mash at 154 degrees Fahrenheit for 1 hour.

American Pale Ale (10-a)

Americans have been brewing Ale since the first wave of colonists reached the shores of the New World in the 1600s. Despite the onslaught of Lager-brewing in the mid-1800s and the subsequent dominance of this country's beer market by bottom-fermenting breweries, American-Ale brewing has persevered. With the recent upsurge in small-batch brewing, American Ales are now leading the microbrewing renaissance.

American-style Ale is characterized by a copper color and medium maltiness. It's lighter in color and body compared to its English counterpart, but American Pale Ales are rather aggressively bittered with American-grown hop varieties from the Pacific Northwest.

Flavor profile: Pale to deep amber to copper. These beers offer medium hop flavor and aroma and are fruity and estery. Expect low to medium maltiness and high hop bitterness, with a bit of diacetyl and low caramel flavor. Medium-bodied.

OG/FG:	1.045–1.060 / 1.010–1.015
ABV:	4.5–6.0
IBUs:	30–45+
SRM:	5–14

Commercial examples: Sierra Nevada Pale Ale, California; Great Lakes Burning River Pale Ale, Ohio

Beginner suggestions

Try making this beer by using two 3.3-pound cans of pale, unhopped extract. You can add hop character by boiling 2 ounces of Northern Brewer hops for 1 hour and 1 ounce of Cascade hops in the last 5 minutes of the boil for the classic American Pale Ale character.

Give Me Liberty, or. . . Else

(Intermediate)
Brewer: Marty Nachel

Malt extract:	6 pounds Northwestern light
Specialty grain:	2 pounds 40-L crystal malt
Bittering hops:	1 ounce Northern Brewer (60 mins.)
Flavoring hops:	1 ounce Northern Brewer (30 mins.) 1 ounce Spalt (15 mins.)
Finishing hops:	1 ounce Cascade (5 mins.)
Dry hop:	1 ounce Cascade
Yeast:	Wyeast #2112
Primary:	7 days at 65 degrees Fahrenheit
Secondary:	21 days at 65 degrees Fahrenheit

The Dad's Beer

(Advanced)
Brewer: Dick Van Dyke

Award won: 2nd Best of Show, Central Illinois Homebrew Competition

Base grain:	7 pounds 2-row malt
Specialty grain:	1 pound 10-L crystal malt 1 pound Munich malt 1 pound wheat malt 0.5 pound CaraPils malt
Bittering hops:	1 ounce Galena (12 AAU) (60 mins.) 1 ounce Perle (8 AAU) (60 mins.) 1 ounce Cascade (5.7 AAU) (45 mins.)
Flavoring hops:	3 ounces Cascade (4.9 AAU) (30 mins.)
Finishing hops:	0.25 ounce Cascade (5.7 AAU) (5 mins.) 0.25 ounce Cascade (4.9 AAU) (5 mins.)
Yeast:	Windsor Dry Ale
Fining agent/ clarifier:	1 teaspoon Irish moss at 10 minutes left in the boil
Primary:	3 days at 64 degrees Fahrenheit
Secondary:	7 days at 64 degrees Fahrenheit

American Amber Ale (10-b)

Amber-colored Ales are similar to Pale Ales in terms of the brewing process; their basic difference is in their colors. The grains you use to impart the deeper hue in Amber Ales tend to give the beer a toasty character and a more complex malt palate. Amber Ales are most often malt-accented, but they can also have an aggressive hop character.

Flavor profile: Similar to American Pale Ale, but because of the addition of toasted grain or dark crystal malts, the amber ales are likely to be slightly darker and have a more pronounced toasty and malty aroma and flavor. Noticeable to assertive hop flavor and aroma aren't unusual. Medium-bodied.

OG/FG:	1.045–1.060 / 1.010–1.015
ABV:	4.5–6.0
IBUs:	25–40+
SRM:	10–17

Commercial examples: Boont Amber Ale, California; North Coast Red Seal Ale, California

Beginner suggestions

You can use either pale extract or amber hopped extract — both finish within the generous color range for this style. If you choose the pale extract, try getting a little *kettle caramelization* by vigorously boiling the wort an extra half hour or more. Try adding 1 ounce of Cascade hops to the wort with 10 minutes left in the boil.

(Intermediate)
Brewer: Northwestern Extract Co.

Dudley Brewright Amber Ale

Malt extract:	6.6 pounds amber extract
Specialty grain:	0.75 pound 60-L crystal malt
Bittering hops:	1 ounce Fuggles (60 mins.)
	0.5 ounce Fuggles (40 mins.)
Flavoring hops:	1 ounce Fuggles (20 mins.)
Finishing hops:	1 ounce Cascades (5 mins.)
Yeast:	Glenbrew Ale (dry)
Primary:	10 days (temperature not given)

(Advanced)
Brewer: Marty Nachel

Amber Waves

Malt extract:	1 pound amber DME
Base grain:	10 pounds 2-row malt
Specialty grain:	1 pound 60-L crystal malt
	0.5 pound Victory malt
Bittering hops:	2 ounces Willamette (60 mins.)
Flavoring hops:	0.5 ounce Cascade (20 mins.)
Finishing hops:	0.5 ounce Cascade (5 mins.)
Yeast:	Wyeast #1056
Primary:	7 days at 65 degrees Fahrenheit
Secondary:	14 days at 65 degrees Fahrenheit

Typical/unusual procedures used: Mash for 90 minutes at 152 degrees Fahrenheit. Mash out 10 minutes at 170 degrees Fahrenheit. Sparge with 170-degree Fahrenheit water.

American Brown Ale (10-c)

As Americans are often inclined to do, American brewers have taken a foreign beer style and adapted it to local tastes. The American rendition of Brown Ale maintains similar color and gravity profiles but is dry rather than sweet and has far more hop character in the aroma and flavor.

Flavor profile: Medium to dark brown. Unlike English Brown Ales, American Browns have a relatively high degree of hop bitterness, flavor, and aroma. Medium maltiness with chocolate accents along with caramel and nutty flavors and low diacetyl. Medium-bodied.

OG/FG:	1.045–1.060 / 1.010–1.016
ABV:	4.3–6.2
IBUs:	20–40+
SRM:	18–35

Commercial examples: Brooklyn Brown Ale, New York; Lost Coast Downtown Brown, California

Beginner suggestions

Choose your hopped Brown Ale kit from among a number of brands that produce them. Try adding an extra dose of hop character by adding 1 ounce of Cascade hops to the brewpot in the last 10 minutes of the boil.

Cedar Mountain Brown Ale

(Intermediate)
Brewer: Jim Dilldine

Award won: 2nd Place, AHA Nationals

Malt extract:	6.6 pounds Northwestern light	**Flavoring hops:**	0.5 ounce Fuggles (3.8 AAU) (10 mins.)
	1 pound William's Australian dark DME		0.5 ounce Cascade (4.6 AAU) (10 mins.)
Specialty grain:	6 ounces chocolate malt	**Finishing hops:**	0.5 ounce Cascade (4.6 AAU) (2 mins.)
	6 ounces roasted barley	**Yeast:**	Wyeast #1007
	6 ounces 80-L crystal malt	**Fining agent/ clarifier:**	1 teaspoon Irish moss
Bittering hops:	1 ounce Fuggles (3.8 AAU) (60 mins.)	**Primary:**	7 days at 65 degrees Fahrenheit
	1 ounce Northern Brewer (7.9 AAU) (60 mins.)	**Secondary:**	7 days at 65 degrees Fahrenheit

Southeast Texas Northern Brown Ale

(Advanced)
Brewer: Steve Daniel

Award won: 2nd Place, AHA Nationals

Base grain:	9 pounds pale malt	**Yeast:**	Worthington White Shield cultured from bottle
Specialty grain:	2 pounds crystal malt		
Bittering hops:	1 ounce Perle (60 mins.)	**Primary:**	14 days at 70 degrees Fahrenheit
Flavoring hops:	0.5 ounce Hallertauer (30 mins.)	**Secondary:**	(not given)
Finishing hops:	0.5 ounce Hallertauer (5 mins.)		

Northern English Brown Ale (11-c)

Brown Ale is a close relative to Pale Ale. Aside from the obvious color difference, Brown Ales are also slightly maltier than the Pale Ales. Brown Ales are also less aggressively hopped because the water you use for brewing traditional Brown Ale is chalky, and this hardness in the water tends to accentuate the hop's bitter qualities.

Brown Ales are relatively low-gravity beers that yield low alcohol content after quick fermentations. You use chocolate malt to impart the brown color and chocolatey palate. Some brewers add small quantities of molasses or brown sugar to lend other flavor and aroma nuances to the beer. The nose may also hint of fruit, nuts, and toffeelike aromas.

Flavor profile: Deep copper to brown. Hop flavor and aroma are low, with fruity esters lingering behind. Sweet and malty with hints of chocolate; low bitterness and diacetyl. Medium-bodied.

OG/FG:	1.040–1.052 / 1.008–1.013
ABV:	4.2–5.4
IBUs:	20–30
SRM:	12–22

Commercial examples: Newcastle Brown Ale, England; Samuel Smith Nut Brown Ale, England

Beginner suggestions

Start with 5 pounds of amber hopped malt extract and add 1 cup of dark brown sugar for added color and complexity.

Buxton Brown of Derbyshire County

(Intermediate)
Brewer: Marty Nachel

Malt extract:	6 pounds liquid malt extract	**Yeast:**	Wyeast #1028
Specialty grain:	1 pound 40 L crystal malt	**Misc. fermentable ingredients:**	0.5 pound light brown sugar
	0.25 chocolate malt	**Primary:**	7 days at 65 degrees Fahrenheit
Bittering hops:	1 ounce Fuggles (60 mins.)	**Secondary:**	9 days at 60 degrees Fahrenheit
Flavoring hops:	0.5 ounce Fuggles (20 mins)		

Ol' Brown Bear Brown Ale

(Advanced)
Brewer: Todd Ashman
Brewmaster at Fifty Fifty Brewing Co., Truckee, CA

Award won: 2nd Place, California Small Brewers Association

Base grain:	7.5 pounds Marris Otter	**Misc. non-fermentable ingredients:**	4 ounces dextrin powder
Specialty grain:	1.25 pounds Caramel 60	**Fining agent/ clarifier:**	1 teaspoon Irish moss
	6 ounces chocolate malt		
Bittering hops:	1 ounce Fuggles (60 mins.)	**Primary:**	8 days at 65 degrees Fahrenheit
Flavoring hops:	0.5 ounce Fuggles (30 mins.)	**Secondary:**	2 weeks at 65 degrees Fahrenheit
Finishing hops:	1 ounce Kent Goldings (5 mins.)		
Yeast:	Wyeast #1098		
Misc. fermentable ingredients:	1 pound dark brown sugar		

Typical/unusual procedures used:
Perform a single infusion mash at 156 degrees Fahrenheit; hold for 90 minutes. Sparge with 170-degree Fahrenheit water.

Brown Porter (12-a)

The Porter name is borrowed from a group of people known to consume large quantities of this beer: the porters at London's Victoria Station. Originally, it didn't exist as a single style. The porters had a habit of ordering portions of several beers mixed into the same drinking glass. This concoction came to be known as *entire.* One enterprising brewer capitalized on this habit by marketing a beer that closely approximated this blend of brews, and he used the name Porter to identify it.

The brown malt used to make Porter beer was kilned over a wood fire, which gave the malt, as well as the resulting beer, a distinctive smoky flavor and aroma. Although Porters are no longer brewed with wood-kilned malts, today's Porters may still suggest a hint of smokiness in the nose or on the palate. Today, two basic styles of Porter are available: Brown and Robust (covered in the next section). Generally speaking, American microbrewers favor the Robust style of Porter, although the Brown Porter remains the forte of the British brewers.

Brown Porter is a meeker version of its big brother. Body and color are lighter, though still maintaining a minimized dark-grain flavor and hue. Both the malty sweetness and hop bitterness are downplayed, which lowers the resulting alcohol to between 4 and 6 percent and makes this brew a little closer to a *session beer* (a beer conducive to consumption in large volumes).

Flavor profile: Medium to dark brown. Fruity esters are acceptable, and hop flavor and aroma are nonexistent to medium. No roast barley or strong burnt character is expected. Low to medium malt sweetness, with medium hop bitterness and low diacetyl. Light- to medium-bodied.

OG/FG:	1.040–1.052 / 1.008–1.014
ABV:	4.0–5.4
IBUs:	18–25
SRM:	20–30

Commercial examples: Samuel Smith Taddy Porter, England; Young's London Porter, England

Beginner suggestions

Try producing the color and flavor in your Porter by adding specialty grains (dark caramel, chocolate malt, black malt, roasted barley) to your pale malt extract rather than just buying a dark malt extract — the result is more satisfying.

(Intermediate)
Brewer: Dennis Kinvig

Coal Porter

Award won: 1st Place, AHA Nationals

Malt extract:	3.3 pounds Brewmaker Mild hopped extract	**Dry hop:**	0.25 ounce Cascade
			0.5 ounce Hallertauer
	3.3 pounds Munton and Fison amber	**Yeast:**	Wyeast #1028
Specialty grain:	1.66 pounds caramel malt	**Misc. fermentable ingredients:**	6 ounces barley syrup
	5 ounces chocolate malt	**Water treatment:**	0.5 teaspoon noniodized salt
Bittering hops:	0.5 ounce Northern Brewer (8 AAU) (35 mins.)	**Primary:**	12 days at 65 degrees Fahrenheit
Finishing hops:	0.25 ounce Northern Brewer (8 AAU) (2 mins.)	**Secondary:**	(not given)

(Advanced)
Brewer: Paddy Giffen

Entirely Yours

Award won: 1st Place, AHA Nationals

Base grain:	5 pounds British pale malt	**Flavoring hops:**	0.75 ounce Chinook (30 mins.)
	4 pounds Klages malt		0.75 ounce Cascade (30 mins.)
	1.5 pounds Vienna malt	**Dry hop:**	1 ounce Cascade (in primary fermenter)
Specialty grain:	1 pound 90-L crystal malt	**Yeast:**	Wyeast #1028
	1 pound chocolate malt	**Primary:**	7 days at 65 degrees Fahrenheit
	0.5 pound CaraPils malt	**Secondary:**	6 weeks at 65 degrees Fahrenheit
	0.25 pound black patent malt		
Bittering hops:	0.25 ounce Northern Brewer (60 mins.)		
	0.25 ounce Perle (60 mins.)		

Typical/unusual procedures used:
Perform a single step infusion mash at 158 degrees Fahrenheit for 1 hour.

Robust Porter (12-6)

Robust Porter is a cousin of Stout. This beer is very dark — typically opaque. It often takes on a reddish appearance in the presence of light. Dark-grain aromas dominate the nose. Robust Porter is medium- to full-bodied with an alcohol content that ranges between 5 and 7 percent. The most noticeable characteristic is the dark-grain flavors derived from the chocolate malt and/or black malts in the grist. Hop bitterness combined with mild grain astringency balance the sweetness of the crystal malt. (Check out the previous section on Brown Porter for more on Porter beer.)

Flavor profile: Opaque black. Fruity esters are okay. Hop flavor and aroma are nonexistent to medium. No roast barley character — just the sharp bitterness of black malt with a hint of burnt charcoal-like flavor. Medium to full bodied and malty sweet with low diacetyl in the background. Hop bitterness is medium to high.

OG/FG:	1.048–1.065 / 1.012–1.016
ABV:	4.8–6.0
IBUs:	25–50+
SRM:	22–35+

Commercial examples: Edmund Fitzgerald Porter, Ohio; Anchor Porter, California

Beginner suggestions

Try producing the color and flavor in your Porter by using specialty grains (dark caramel, chocolate malt, black malt, roasted barley) rather than buying a dark malt extract — the result is more satisfying. Toss an inch or two of brewer's licorice into the brewpot for added complexity.

Pugnacious Porter

(Intermediate)
Brewer: Marty Nachel

Award won: 1st Place, Wisconsin State Fair

Malt extract:	3.3 pounds John Bull dark	**Finishing hops:**	0.5 ounce Fuggles
	4 pounds amber DME	**Misc. flavoring ingredients:**	2-inch licorice stick
Specialty grain:	1 pound 90-L crystal malt	**Yeast:**	Wyeast #1028
	0.75 pound chocolate malt	**Primary:**	7 days at 65 degrees Fahrenheit
Bittering hops:	2 ounces Northern Brewer	**Secondary:**	16 days at 65 degrees Fahrenheit
Flavoring hops:	1 ounce Fuggles		

TransPorter

(Advanced)
Brewer: Marty Nachel

Base grain:	8 pounds pale malt	**Finishing hops:**	0.5 ounce Fuggles (5 mins.)
Specialty grain:	1 pound Special "B" 221 L crystal malt	**Yeast:**	Wyeast #1318
	0.5 pound black malt	**Misc. fermentable ingredients:**	8 ounces blackstrap molasses
	0.25 pound roast malt	**Primary:**	7 days at 65 degrees Fahrenheit
Bittering hops:	1 ounce Northern Brewer (60 mins.)	**Secondary:**	12 days at 55 degrees Fahrenheit
	0.5 ounce Fuggles (30 mins.)		
Flavoring hops:	0.5 ounce Fuggles (15 mins.)		

Typical/unusual procedures used:
Perform a simple infusion mash (90 minutes at 152 degrees Fahrenheit).

Baltic Porter (12-c)

English-style Porter was traditionally brewed in countries bordering the Baltic Sea, but that style was greatly influenced by Russian Imperial Stouts. Thus, a Baltic Porter may also be referred to as an Imperial Porter.

A Baltic Porter often has the malt flavors reminiscent of an English Brown Porter and the restrained roast of a Schwarzbier with a higher OG and alcohol content than either. It's a very complex beer with multilayered flavors. Silky smoothness in the mouthfeel is a hallmark of the style.

Flavor profile: Baltic Porter offers a rich, malty sweetness with a complex blend of deep malt, dried fruit esters, alcohol, and a prominent yet smooth roasted flavor that stops short of burnt. It's mouth-filling and very smooth; it starts sweet, but darker malt flavors quickly dominate and persist through finish. The malt character can have a caramel, toffee, nutty, molasses, and/or licorice complexity, and you may taste a hint of roast coffee or licorice in the finish. Medium-low to medium bitterness from malt and hops just to provide balance.

OG/FG:	1.060–1.090 / 1.016–1.024
ABV:	5.5–9.5 (7.0 to 8.5 is most typical)
IBUs:	20–40
SRM:	17–30

Commercial examples: Sinebrychoff Porter, Finland; Utenos Porter, Lithuania

Beginner suggestions

In order to achieve the minimum OG, you'd need to start with at least 8 pounds of dark malt extract. Try producing the color and flavor in your porter by using specialty grains (dark caramel, chocolate malt, black malt, roasted barley) rather than buying a dark malt extract — the result is more satisfying. Toss an inch of brewer's licorice or a couple of ounces of blackstrap molasses into the brewpot for added complexity.

Brass Baltics Imperial Porter

(Intermediate)
Brewer: Marty Nachel

Malt extract:	6.6 pounds Northwestern Gold	**Misc. flavoring ingredients:**	½ cup Lyle's Black Treacle
	6 pounds light dry malt extract		6 ounces lactose
Specialty grain:	1 pound 40-L crystal malt		6 ounces malto-dextrin powder
	1 pound 120-l crystal malt	**Yeast:**	Wyeast #1338 (European)
	0.5 pound chocolate malt	**Primary:**	12 days at 60 degrees Fahrenheit
Bittering hops:	1.5 ounces Northern Brewer (60 mins.)	**Secondary:**	3 weeks at 60 degrees Fahrenheit
Flavoring hops:	1 ounce Hallertau (30 mins.)		

Klasinski Baltic

(Advanced)
Brewer: Tom Dennis

Award won: 2nd Place, 2006 B.U.Z.Z. Boneyard Brew-Off

Base grain:	14.25 pounds pale 2-row malt	**Flavoring hops:**	0.75 ounce Hallertau (60) mins.)
Specialty grain:	0.75 pound CaraMunich 60	**Finishing hops:**	0.5 Saaz (20 mins.)
	0.75 pound chocolate malt	**Yeast:**	Wyeast #2308 Munich lager
	0.5 pound 20-L crystal malt	**Primary:**	3 weeks at 55 degrees Fahrenheit
	0.5 pound 80-L crystal malt	**Secondary:**	7 weeks at 35 degrees Fahrenheit
	0.25 pound black patent malt		
Bittering hops:	1 ounce Northern Brewer (60 mins.)		

Typical/unusual procedures used:
Perform an infusion mash at 153 degrees Fahrenheit for 60 minutes. Boil for 60 minutes. Use a 1.5-liter yeast starter.

Dry Stout (13-a)

Stout is a hearty, top-fermented beer strongly associated with the British Isles and Ireland; it's known for its opaque-black appearance and roasty flavors. The world of homebrew now boasts six different styles of Stout.

The term *Stout,* as it applies to beer, was first attached to the Porter style. A bigger-bodied, more-robust Porter was aptly described as being a Stout Porter. Exactly when a clear distinction was made between Stout Porters and the separate Stout style that brewers recognize today is uncertain. Stout appears to have come into its own in the early 1800s, following the invention of a device for roasting barley and creating black malts — two of the hallmark ingredients for making Stout.

Guinness Stout is probably the standard-bearer for the Stout style throughout the world, but it's more correctly known as a Classic Dry Stout, or Irish-style Stout. The Classic Irish-style Dry Stout is the lightest and driest of the Stout styles, as well as the least alcoholic. The Classic Irish-style Dry Stout is defined by the roastiness of the unmalted roasted barley and the charred flavor of the black malt in the recipe.

Flavor profile: Opaque black. No hop flavor or aroma. Roasted barley character is expected. Slight malt sweetness or a caramel malt character is okay. Medium to high hop bitterness with a slight acidity or sourness is possible. A very low diacetyl level is okay. Medium bodied.

OG/FG:	1.036–1.050 / 1.007–1.011
ABV:	4.0–5.0
IBUs:	30–45
SRM:	25–40

Commercial examples: Guinness Stout, Ireland; Murphy's Stout, Ireland

Beginner suggestions

Try producing the color and flavor in your stout by using specialty grains (dark caramel, chocolate malt, black malt, roasted barley) rather than buying a dark malt extract — the result is more satisfying.

St. James Gate Stout

(Intermediate)
Brewer: Northwestern Extract Co.

Malt extract:	6.6 pounds amber extract	**Bittering hops:**	2 ounces Fuggles (60 mins.)
Specialty grain:	0.5 pound black malt	**Finishing hops:**	1 ounce Willamette (10 mins.)
	0.5 pound 40-L crystal malt	**Yeast:**	Wyeast #1084
	0.25 pound roasted barley	**Primary:**	(not given)
		Secondary:	(not given)

New Years Day

(Advanced)
Brewer: Paddy Giffen

Award won: 3rd Place, AHA Nationals

Base grain:	5 pounds British pale malt	**Flavoring hops:**	1 ounce Cascade (30 mins.)
	4 pounds Klages malt		0.25 ounce Chinook (30 mins.)
	1 pound Vienna malt	**Dry hop:**	1 ounce Cascade (in primary fermenter)
	0.5 pound wheat malt		
Specialty grain:	1.5 pounds roasted barley	**Yeast:**	Wyeast #1056
	1 pound CaraPils malt	**Primary:**	7 days at 60 degrees Fahrenheit
	0.5 pound 90-L crystal malt	**Secondary:**	14 days at 60 degrees Fahrenheit
	4 ounces black patent malt		
	4 ounces chocolate malt		
Bittering hops:	0.25 ounces Chinook (90 mins.)		
	0.25 ounces Northern Brewer (60 mins.)		

Typical/unusual procedures used:
Perform a single step infusion at 158 degrees Fahrenheit for 1 hour.

Sweet Stout (13-b)

Sweet Stout (alternatively known as London-style or Cream Stout) is the English counterpoint to the Classic Irish-style Dry Stout. Although you find many similarities between the two, the principal difference is how you achieve their roasted character. The Classic Irish-style Dry Stout is defined by the roastiness of the unmalted roasted barley and black malt, although the London-style Sweet Stout often uses chocolate malt in its place. With regards to the obvious contrast between these Stouts' sweet and dry character, the Sweet Stout has a creamier texture, a slightly higher gravity, and sweetness across the palate resulting from the use of milk sugar (lactose), which beer yeast can't ferment. In rare instances, this style is also referred to as Milk Stout.

Flavor profile: Opaque black. No hop flavor or aroma. Sweet maltiness and caramel flavors are evident, and the roasted barley character is mild. Hop bitterness is low. Low diacetyl is okay. Medium- to full-bodied.

OG/FG:	1.042–1.056 / 1.010–1.023
ABV:	4.0–6.0
IBUs:	25–40
SRM:	30–40+

Commercial examples: Watney's Cream Stout, England; Mackeson XXX Stout, England

Beginner suggestions

The key ingredient in a Sweet Stout is lactose powder. Add 8 to 12 ounces of this unfermentable sugar to your brewpot for a taste of sweet success.

(Intermediate)
Brewer: Marty Nachel

Macke's Son Stout

Award won: 1st Place, B.O.S.S. 5th Annual Homebrew Competition

Malt extract: 6 pounds Northwestern light

Specialty grain: 1 pound roasted barley

1 pound Belgian Special "B" 221-L crystal malt

0.25 pound black malt

Bittering hops: 2 ounces Northern Brewer

Flavoring hops: 1 ounce Fuggles

Yeast: Wyeast #1084

Misc. fermentable ingredients: 12 ounces dark molasses

Misc. flavoring ingredients: 1 pound lactose powder

Primary: 7 days at 60 degrees Fahrenheit

Secondary: 14 days at 65 degrees Fahrenheit

(Advanced)
Brewers: Brian and Linda North

D & J Stout

Award won: 1st Place, B.O.S.S. Challenge

Base grain: 4 pounds English Lager malt

3 pounds English Pale Ale malt

Specialty grain: 1 pound 90-L crystal malt

1 pound 35-L toasted malt

1 pound roasted barley

Bittering hops: 1 ounce Kent Goldings (60 mins.)

Flavoring hops: 1 ounce Bramling Cross (30 mins.)

Yeast: Wyeast #1056

Water treatment: 0.5 teaspoon calcium carbonate

Primary: 14 days at 60 degrees Fahrenheit

Secondary: 9 weeks at 55 degrees Fahrenheit

Tertiary: 3 weeks at 45 degrees Fahrenheit

Typical/unusual procedures used:
Mash at 152 degrees Fahrenheit for 1 hour and 45 minutes; mash out at 168 degrees Fahrenheit for 15 minutes. Sparge with 170-degree Fahrenheit water.

Foreign-Style Stout (13-d)

After the Classic Irish-style Dry Stout, the next most popular Stout style in the world is the somewhat xenophobically named Foreign-Style Stout. This style is more or less a free-form style of Stout that doesn't necessarily fit into the Classic Irish-style Dry or London-style Sweet Stout categories discussed in the previous sections.

Flavor profile: Opaque black. Low fruity esters are okay; no hop aroma or flavor expected. A slight malt sweetness is okay, as is a slight acidity or sourness. Very low diacetyl is acceptable. Medium- to full-bodied.

OG/FG:	1.056–1.075 / 1.010–1.018
ABV:	5.5–8.0
IBUs:	30–70
SRM:	30–40+

Commercial examples: Dragon Stout, Jamaica; Tooth's Sheaf Stout, Australia

Beginner suggestions

Try producing the color and flavor in your Stout by using specialty grains (dark caramel, chocolate malt, black malt, roasted barley) rather than buying a dark malt extract — the result is more satisfying.

Yulebrew '92

(Intermediate)
Brewer: Marty Nachel

Award won: 1st Place, Headhunters Mid-Winter Homebrew Competition

Malt extract:	6.6 pounds John Bull dark extract	**Flavoring hops:**	1 ounce Fuggles (20 mins.)
Specialty grain:	1.5 pounds 40-L crystal malt	**Yeast:**	Edme Dry Ale
	0.5 pound roasted barley	**Misc. fermentable ingredients:**	1 cup light-brown sugar
	0.25 pound chocolate malt	**Primary:**	8 days at 60 degrees Fahrenheit
	0.25 pound black patent malt	**Secondary:**	14 days at 60 degrees Fahrenheit
Bittering hops:	2 ounces Bullion (60 mins.)		

New Stout 11

(Advanced)
Brewers: David and Melinda Brockington

Award won: 1st Place, AHA Nationals

Base grain:	9 pounds English pale malt	**Yeast:**	Wyeast #1084
Specialty grain:	3 pounds roasted barley	**Primary:**	15 days at 65 degrees Fahrenheit
	0.5 pound 40-L crystal malt	**Secondary:**	(not given)
	0.5 pound black patent malt	**Typical/unusual procedures used:**	Perform a single step infusion mash at 155 degrees Fahrenheit for 1 hour.
Bittering hops:	2 ounces Kent Goldings (60 mins.)		

Imperial Stout (13-f)

Another Stout style, rarer than most, is strongly associated with pre-Bolshevik Russia. British brewers found favor among the Czarist rulers of Russia, particularly for their brand of Stout. Unfortunately, the English-made Stout didn't travel well to St. Petersburg and other points east. To compensate for the short shelf life of their beer, the British brewers did as they'd done for the India Pale Ale being shipped to Bombay and Calcutta: raise the gravity and increase the hop content. (Because these Ales were designed to condition on the high seas, couldn't the same be done for Stout?) Sure enough, the Russian rulers deeply admired this complex high-alcohol brew. The style has since come to be known as Russian Stout, Imperial Stout, or the combined Russian Imperial Stout.

Flavor profile: Dark copper to very black. High level of fruity esters. Hop bitterness flavor and aroma medium to high. Rich and complex maltiness with a chewy texture; roasty, fruity, and bittersweet. Full-bodied with evident alcohol strength.

OG/FG:	1.075–1.095+ / 1.018–1.030+
ABV:	8.0–12.0+
IBUs:	50–90+
SRM:	30–40+

Commercial examples: Samuel Smith's Imperial Stout, England; North Coast Old Rasputin, Califonia

Beginner suggestions

Imperial Stouts need a lot of fermentable material as well as a lot of dark grain complexity. Start with at least 9 pounds of extract, and try achieving the color and character of this style by using specialty grains (dark crystal malt, chocolate malt, black malt, and roasted barley). Brewer's licorice and unsulfured dark molasses can also add fermentable sugars and complexity.

Fountainhead Black Magic

(Intermediate)
Brewer: Rande Reed

Award won: 1st Place, AHA Nationals

Malt extract:	6.6 pounds Munton and Fison Old Ale kit	**Specialty grain:**	12 ounces black patent malt
	5 pounds Munton and Fison light DME		12 ounces roasted barley
			12 ounces 40-L caramel malt

Bittering hops:	3 ounces Nugget (60 mins.)	***Primary:***	7 weeks at 70 degrees Fahrenheit
Flavoring hops:	1 ounce Nugget (10 mins.)	***Secondary:***	6 weeks at 70 degrees Fahrenheit
Yeast:	Red Star Dry Champagne		

(Advanced)

Rose's Russian Imperial Stout

Brewer: Dick Van Dyke

Award won: 1st Place, AHA Nationals

Malt extract:	6.6 pounds Northwestern dark	***Flavoring hops:***	1 ounce Kent Goldings (4.7 AAU) (30 mins.)
Base grain:	5 pounds English 6-row malt		0.75 ounce Cascade (4.9 AAU) (30 mins.)
Specialty grain:	2 pounds 90-L crystal malt	***Finishing hops:***	1 ounce Kent Goldings (4.7 AAU) (10 mins.)
	1 pound black patent malt		1 ounce Fuggles (3.4 AAU) (10 mins.)
	1 pound chocolate malt	***Yeast:***	2 packages Red Star Dry Champagne
	1 pound Munich malt	***Misc. fermentable ingredients:***	1 cup unsulfured dark molasses
	0.75 pound roasted barley	***Misc. flavoring ingredients:***	1-inch licorice stick
	0.25 pound wheat malt	***Fining agent/ clarifier:***	1 teaspoon Irish moss
Bittering hops:	5.5 ounces Eroica (10.6 AAU) (60 mins.)	***Primary:***	3 days at 65 degrees Fahrenheit
	1 ounce Chinook (11.3 AAU) (60 mins.)	***Secondary:***	6 days at 63 degrees Fahrenheit
	1 ounce Kent Goldings (4.7 AAU) (45 mins.)	***Tertiary:***	28 days at 63 degrees Fahrenheit
	1 ounce Cascade (4.9 AAU) (45 mins.)		
	1 ounce Fuggles (4.5 AAU) (45 mins.)		
	1 ounce Chinook (11.3 AAU) (45 mins.)		

Typical/unusual procedures used:
Perform a step infusion: protein rest for 30 minutes at 128 degrees Fahrenheit; 1 hour at 150 degrees Fahrenheit; and 30 minutes at 155 degrees Fahrenheit. After conversion, heat to 168 degrees Fahrenheit and hold for 5 minutes.

English India Pale Ale (IPA) (14-a)

One particular substyle of English-style Pale Ale is known as India Pale Ale, or IPA for short. The beer gets its name from Britain's colonial presence in India during the 1800s. British royal subjects living in India demanded to have their favorite Ales shipped to them at their outposts, but the month-long journey on the open sea proved devastating to the average cask of beer. A British brewer named Hodgson recognized this problem and decided to brew an Ale of greater strength to withstand the rigors of oceanic transit. The antiseptic properties of the increased alcohol volume, coupled with a high concentration of hop acids, assured the colonialists of a palatable product at journey's end. They also realized a surprising dividend on receipt of the beer: The gentle rocking motion of the ship on the waters caused the beer within the casks to pick up some of the oaky character, much like barrel-aged wine. Some brewers today maintain that link with the past by employing oak barrels for the aging process. Some believe that the IPA style was actually defined before the Pale Ale style itself!

Flavor profile: Golden to light copper. Very fruity and estery. Medium maltiness with high hop bitterness and low diacetyl. Hop flavor and aroma are medium to high. Alcoholic strength is often evident. Medium-bodied.

OG/FG:	1.050–1.075 / 1.010–1.018
ABV:	5.0–7.5
IBUs:	40–60
SRM:	8–14

Commercial example: Samuel Smith's India Ale, England; Fuller's IPA, England

Beginner suggestions

IPAs are essentially higher-gravity Pale Ales with higher hopping ratios. Follow the recommendations given for Classic English Pale Ale but add another pound of extract and, at the 20-minute and 5-minute marks in the boil, increase the hop quantities to full ounces rather than half-ounces. Some brewers emulate the style by imbuing their IPAs with a woody flavor — try steeping 6 ounces of oak chips in the wort in the last 15 minutes of the boil. When you're comfortable with the idea, consider dry-hopping your IPA by tossing an ounce of English hops into your secondary fermenter.

Exchequer Pale Ale

(Intermediate)
Brewer: Marty Nachel

Malt extract: 6.6 pounds Northwestern extract

Specialty grain: 1 pound 40-L crystal malt

⅛ pound roast malt

Bittering hops: 1.5 ounces Northern Brewers (60 mins.)

Finishing hops: 1 ounce Kent Goldings (10 mins.)

Dry hop: 1 ounce Fuggles

Yeast: Wyeast #1098

Misc. flavoring ingredients: 8 ounces malto-dextrin powder

Primary: 1 week at 65 degrees Fahrenheit

Secondary: 2 weeks at 65 degrees Fahrenheit

Typical/unusual procedures used: Add 1 ounce of Fuggles hops and malto-dextrin powder to secondary fermenter.

Brewmistress I.P.A.

(Advanced)
Brewer: Dick Van Dyke

Award won: 1st Place, Taste of the Great Lakes

Base grain: 7 pounds 2-row English malt

2 pounds 2-row American malt (Klages)

Specialty grain: 1 pound 90-L crystal malt

0.5 pound 40-L crystal malt

1 pound Munich malt

0.5 pound flaked barley

Bittering hops: 2 ounces Chinook (11.3 AAU) (60 mins.)

Flavoring hops: 1 ounce Fuggles (3.4 AAU) (20 mins.)

Finishing hops: 1 ounce Kent Goldings (4.5 AAU) (5 mins.)

Yeast: Windsor Dry Ale

Water treatment: 1 ounce gypsum and ½ teaspoon noniodized popcorn salt in mash, 1 ounce gypsum in the boil

Primary: 2 days at 60 degrees Fahrenheit

Secondary: 8 days at 60 degrees Fahrenheit

Typical/unusual procedures used: Preboil all mashing and brewing water. Perform a step infusion mash at 122 degrees Fahrenheit for 40 minutes, 148 degrees Fahrenheit for 60 minutes, and 152 degrees Fahrenheit for 55 minutes.

American India Pale Ale (IPA) (14-b)

American craft brewers — and American craft-beer drinkers — have fully embraced the IPA style to the point where they have virtually made it their own. The motto for these IPA devotees seems to be hops, hops, and more hops — American hops, of course! (See the previous section for more about the IPA style.)

Flavor profile: Golden to deep amber. Very fruity and estery. Medium maltiness with high hop bitterness and low diacetyl. Hop flavor and aroma are medium to high, accentuating the fruity, citrusy, and piney qualities of American hops. Alcoholic strength is often evident. Medium-bodied.

OG/FG:	1.056–1.075 / 1.010–1.018
ABV:	5.5–7.5
IBUs:	40–60+
SRM:	6–15

Commercial example: Goose Island I.P.A., Illinois; Alpha King, Indiana

Beginner suggestions

IPAs are essentially higher-gravity Pale Ales with higher hopping ratios. Follow the recommendations given for Classic English Pale Ale but add another pound of extract and, at the 20-minute and 5-minute marks in the boil, increase the hop quantities to full ounces rather than half-ounces. When you're comfortable with the idea, consider dry-hopping your IPA by tossing an ounce of American hops into your secondary fermenter.

Indiana Pale Ale

(Intermediate)
Brewer: Marty Nachel

Malt extract:	6.6 pounds North-western extract
	1 pound Northwestern light DME
Specialty grain:	1.5 pounds 40-L crystal malt
	1 pound biscuit malt
Bittering hops:	1.5 ounces Northern Brewers (60 mins.)
Finishing hops:	1 ounce Cascades (10 mins.)

Dry hop:	1 ounce Amarillo
Yeast:	Wyeast #1056
Primary:	1 week at 65 degrees Fahrenheit
Secondary:	2 weeks at 65 degrees Fahrenheit

Typical/unusual procedures used:
Add 1 ounce Amarillo hops to secondary fermenter.

Veronica's Nectar I.P.A.

(Advanced)
Brewer: Joe Formanek

Award won: 2nd Place, 2003 AHA Nationals

Base grain:	6 pounds DMC pale 2-row
	5 pounds Mid American pale 2-row
Specialty grain:	1 pound Cargill Special Pale
	1 pound Weyermann Wheat
	0.5 pound DMC aromatic malt
	0.5 pound DMC biscuit malt
	0.5 pound DMC CaraPils
Bittering hops:	2 ounces Centennial (60 mins.)
Finishing hops:	1 ounce Centennial (10 mins.)
	1 ounce Willamette (10 mins.)
	1 ounce Cascade (10 mins.)

	1 ounce Northern Brewer (10 mins.)
	1 ounce homegrown hops (Cascade/Liberty blend) (10 mins.)
Dry hop:	1 ounce Centennial
	1 ounce Willamette
	0.5 ounce Northern Brewer
Clarifier:	1 teaspoon Irish Moss (rehydrated)
Yeast:	WLP002 English Ale
Water treatment:	Carbon-filtered tap water
Primary:	14 days at 65 degrees Fahrenheit
Secondary:	16 days at 65 degrees Fahrenheit

Typical/unusual procedures used:
Perform a single infusion mash at 155 degrees Fahrenheit. Boil for 75 minutes.

Imperial India Pale Ale (IPA) (14-c)

Taking IPA to a whole 'nother level, this recent American innovation reflects the trend of American craft brewers pushing the envelope to satisfy the need of hop aficionados for increasingly intense products. Imperial IPAs are obviously bigger than a standard IPA in both alcohol strength and overall hop level (bittering and finish), though they don't quite approach the level of Barley Wine. They're definitely a showcase for hops, however.

The adjective *Imperial* is arbitrary and simply implies a stronger version of an IPA, calling to mind the Russian imperial version of Stout.

Flavor profile: Golden amber to reddish copper; dry-hopped versions may be a bit hazy. Very fruity and estery. Medium maltiness with high hop bitterness and low diacetyl. Biscuity and toasty malt flavors may be experienced. Hop flavor and aroma are medium to high, accentuating the fruity, citrusy, and piney qualities of American hops. Alcoholic strength is often evident. Medium-bodied.

OG/FG:	1.075–1.090+ / 1.012-1.020
ABV:	7.5–10.0+
IBUs:	60–100+
SRM:	8–15

Commercial example: Stone Ruination I.P.A., California; Three Floyd's Dreadnaught, Indiana

Beginner suggestions

Imperial IPAs are essentially very high-gravity India Pale Ales with huge hopping ratios and corresponding alcohol levels. Follow the recommendations given for American IPA but add another pound or two of extract and increase the hop quantities by at least a third. If you don't dry hop your IPA with at least 2 ounces of American hops, it'll fall short of the imperial expectation. All of the increased malt, hops, and alcohol benefit from additional aging; I suggest adding another week or so to the secondary fermentation.

Goliath Imperial Pale Ale

(Intermediate)
Brewer: Steve Kamp

Malt extract:	14 pounds light dry malt extract
Specialty grain:	1 pound 40-L crystal malt
	0.5 pound wheat malt
	0.25 pound rye malt
Bittering hops:	1 ounce Cascade (first wort hopped)
	2 ounces Northern Brewer (60 mins.)
	1 ounce Fuggles (60 mins.)

	2 ounces Cluster (45 mins.)
Flavoring hops:	1.5 ounces Fuggles (30 mins.)
Finishing hops:	2 ounces Cascade (15 mins.)
Dry hop:	2 ounces Amarillo Gold
Yeast:	Nottingham dry
Primary:	(not given)
Secondary:	(not given)

Hannah's Ambrosia Imperial I.P.A.

(Advanced)
Brewer: Joe Formanek

Award won: 1st Place, Northwest Regional, 1st round AHA Nationals

Base grain:	15 pounds Simpson's Maris Otter pale 2-row
Specialty grain:	2 pounds Cargill special pale malt
	1 pound Weyermann wheat
	0.5 pound DMC aromatic malt
	0.5 pound DMC biscuit malt
	0.5 pound DMC CaraPils malt
Bittering hops:	4 ounces Centennial (60 mins.)
Flavoring hops:	2 ounces Centennial (10 mins.)
	2 ounces Willamette (10 mins.)
	2 ounces Cascade (10 mins.)

	1 ounce homegrown hops (Cascade/liberty blend) (10 mins.)
Dry hop:	1 ounce Centennial
	1 oz Willamette
Yeast:	WLP002 English Ale
Clarifier:	1 teaspoon Irish Moss (rehydrated)
Water treatment:	Carbon-filtered tap water
Primary:	7 days at 65 degrees Fahrenheit.
Secondary:	16 days at 65 degrees Fahrenheit.

Typical/unusual procedures used:
Perform a single infusion mash at 155 degrees Fahrenheit for 45 minutes. Boil for 60 minutes.

White (Wit) (16-a)

This Belgian style of beer is now quite popular in the United States. (The U.S. is one of the few countries that brew White beer, or Witbier, outside of Belgium.) Belgium is a linguistically divided nation, a situation that can cause additional misunderstanding of this style of beer. In the French-speaking provinces, people call this brew Biere Blanche, and in the Flemish-speaking regions, the same beer is known as Witbier. Both names refer to the white appearance of the beer. It's not actually white, but it's very pale yellow and often cloudy with sediment, which helps create its white cast. Both the paleness and the cloudiness can be partly attributed to the high percentage (45 percent) of unmalted wheat that goes into the beer. The balance of the grist is pale barley malt.

This style comes from the Brabant town of Hoegaarden, which is known for its wheat-based beers. What sets Witbier apart from the other Wheat Beers of the region is the inclusion of unconventional beer ingredients, such as the rind of the bitter Curaçao orange, the lemony coriander seed, and another secret spice believed to be Grain of Paradise (also known as alligator seed). The beer is generally hopped with the English Kent hop. After a relatively short and cool fermentation, the beer gets another dose of yeast before being bottled for additional conditioning.

Flavor profile: Hazy pale yellow. Hop flavor and aroma are desirable, but bitterness should be only low to medium. Low to medium fruity esters are typical. Low to medium body. Mild, sweet malt and spicy character early, finishing on the dry side. Low diacetyl levels are okay.

OG/FG:	1.044–1.052 / 1.008–1.012
ABV:	4.5–5.5
IBUs:	10–20
SRM:	2–4

Commercial examples: Hoegaarden Witbier, Belgium; Unibroue Blanche de Chambly, Canada

Beginner suggestions

Starting with a base of the palest malt extract you can find, you can easily emulate Witbier's most identifiable flavor character by adding dried orange peel and crushed coriander to the boiling wort. Using wheat malt and this style's specific yeast strain are your next most important moves.

Jealous Wit

(Intermediate)
Brewer: Northwestern Extract Co.

Malt extract:	6.6 pounds Northwestern Weizen	**Misc. fermentable ingredients:**	3 pounds clove honey
Bittering hops:	2 ounces Cascades (5.5 AAU) (50 mins.)	**Misc. flavoring ingredients:**	0.5 ounce crushed coriander seed (in secondary fermenter)
Flavoring hops:	0.5 ounce Styrian Goldings (5.3 AAU) (20 mins.)		0.25 ounce orange peel (in secondary fermenter)
Finishing hops:	1 ounce Northern Brewer (7.5 AAU) (10 mins.)	**Fining agent/ clarifier:**	1.5 tablespoons Irish moss
Dry hop:	0.5 ounce Cascades	**Primary:**	(not given)
Yeast:	Wyeast #3944	**Secondary:**	(not given)

Wit or Witout You

(Advanced)
Brewer: Marty Nachel

Base grain:	7 pounds Belgian Pilsener malt	**Misc. flavoring ingredients:**	1 ounce dried Curacao orange peel
	1 pound wheat malt		1 ounce coriander seeds
Specialty grain:	0.5 pound Belgian aromatic malt	**Primary:**	7 days at 75 degrees Fahrenheit
	0.5 pound Belgian CaraVienne malt	**Secondary:**	12 days at 40 degrees Fahrenheit
	0.5 pound unmalted wheat		
Bittering hops:	0.5 ounce Styrian Goldings (60 mins.)		
Flavoring hops:	0.5 ounce Styrian Goldings (30 mins.)		
Yeast:	Wyeast #3944		

Typical/unusual procedures used:
Perform a protein rest at 128 degrees Fahrenheit for 15 minutes; an intermediate rest at 145 degrees Fahrenheit for 15 minutes; and a saccharification rest at 152 degrees Fahrenheit for 60 minutes. Sparge with 168-degree Fahrenheit water. Add half of the orange peel and crushed coriander seeds to the brewpot; add remaining amounts to the secondary fermenter.

Belgian Pale Ale (16-6)

This group of beers is somewhat indistinct. Belgian brewers produce a staggering variety of top-fermented beers, and not all of them fit neatly into specialized categories. The Belgian Pale Ale category serves as a catchall for low- to medium-gravity Ales that don't match any other preexisting Belgian styles.

Flavor profile: Golden to deep amber. Hop character is subdued, and so is the malt. Light- to medium-bodied. Mild fruity esters and flavors and a bit of a caramel or roasted malt flavor should be noticeable. A slight acidity may be experienced but no diacetyl.

OG/FG:	1.048–1.054 / 1.010–1.014
ABV:	4–5.5
IBUs:	20–30
SRM:	8–14

Commercial examples: Chimay, Belgium; Ommegang Rare Vos, New York

Beginner suggestions

As with most Belgian beers, yeast is the single most important ingredient to achieve this style. Progressing to the use of style-specific yeast strains is the best way to replicate these styles.

Belgian Abbey

(Intermediate)
Brewer: Northwestern Extract Co.

Malt extract: 9.3 pounds Northwestern Gold

Specialty grain: 10 ounces CaraMunich malt

Bittering hops: 2 ounces Mount Hood (60 mins.)

Finishing hops: 0.5 ounce Hersbrucker (5 mins.)

Yeast: Wyeast #1098

Wyeast #1214

Primary: 2 weeks (temperature not given)

Secondary: 4 weeks (temperature not given)

Typical/unusual procedures used: Pitch the first yeast in the primary fermenter and the second yeast in the secondary fermenter.

Cream City Abbey Ale

(Advanced)
Brewer: Robert Burko

Award won: 2nd Place, AHA Nationals

Base grain: 7 pounds 2-row malt

Specialty grain: 3 pounds Munich malt

0.75 pound chocolate malt

Bittering hops: 1.5 ounces Saaz (60 mins.)

Finishing hops: 1 ounce Willamette (2 mins.)

Yeast: Chimay yeast cultured from bottle

Misc. fermentable ingredients: 0.5 pound brown sugar

Misc. flavoring ingredients: 5 ounces molasses

Primary: 14 days at 68 degrees Fahrenheit

Secondary: (not given)

Dubbel (18-6)

The word *Trappist,* which often precedes the name of this Belgian Dubbel, doesn't so much denote a type of beer as it does a type of brewery. A Trappist beer is brewed at one of only six Trappist abbey breweries that exist in Europe (five in Belgium and one in the Netherlands). Any secular brewer who markets an imitation of one of these breweries' products must use the term *abbey beer.*

Although the beers made by these Cistercian monks vary in style, they all feature high gravities, warm fermentations, top fermenting yeasts, and bottle-conditioning. Some of these monastic brewers add candi sugar to the brew during the boiling process, resulting in rather high-octane libations. The high fermentation temperatures produce a full range of fruity and estery aromas and flavors.

Some abbeys produce Ales in three graduated strengths. The mild Single is just for the monks' personal consumption; the dark Dubbel is a stronger version of the Single; and the golden Tripel is the most potent (which leads me to wonder what a Home Run would taste like).

Because much of the Trappist beers' characters are a result of the yeast, brewers must obtain these strains to replicate the style correctly.

Flavor profile: Dark amber to brown. The aroma is a combination of sweet, malty, and nutty, with low levels of fruity esters in the background. Medium- to full-bodied, with mild bitterness and very low diacetyl.

OG/FG:	1.062–1.075 / 1.010–1.018
ABV:	6.0–7.5
IBUs:	15–25
SRM:	10–14

Commercial examples: Affligem, Belgium; LaTrappe, Belgium

Beginner suggestions

Start with at least 6.5 pounds of extract to achieve the correct body and strength of the style. Consider using Belgian Candi sugar or Belgian specialty malts (such as 221-L special "B" crystal malt) to add flavor and complexity. Yeast is an important part of the Dubbel profile — try progressing to liquid yeast strains as soon as you feel confident enough.

(Intermediate)
Brewer: Marty Nachel

Dubbel Trubbel

Malt extract:	7 pounds liquid malt extract
Specialty grain:	1 pound Special "B" 221 L crystal malt
	0.5 pound Belgian CaraVienne malt
	0.5 pound biscuit malt
Bittering hops:	1 ounce Styrian Goldings (60 mins.)
Flavoring hops:	0.5 ounce Saaz (40 mins.)
Yeast:	Wyeast #1214
Misc. fermentable ingredients:	1 pound brown sugar
Primary:	7 days at 65 degrees Fahrenheit
Secondary:	12 days at 55 degrees Fahrenheit

(Advanced)
Brewer: Jamie Wika

Ain't Monkin' Around Dubbel

Base grain:	8.25 pounds Belgian Pilsener malt
Specialty grain:	0.33 pound Belgian aromatic malt
	0.33 pound Belgian Special "B" malt
	0.25 pound Belgian CaraVienne malt
	0.10 pound Belgian CaraMunich malt
Bittering hops:	0.5 ounce Styrian Goldings (90 mins.)
	0.5 ounce Styrian Goldings (60 mins.)
Flavoring hops:	0.33 ounce Hallertauer (30 mins.)
Finishing hops:	0.33 ounce Saaz (5 mins.)
Yeast:	Yeast Culture Kit #A-25
Misc. fermentable ingredients:	1 pound brown sugar
Fining agent/ clarifier:	1 teaspoon Irish moss (20 mins.)
Primary:	10 days at 75 degrees Fahrenheit
Secondary:	3 days at 40 degrees Fahrenheit

Typical/unusual procedures used:
Perform a protein rest at 128 degrees Fahrenheit for 15 minutes; an intermediate rest at 145 degrees Fahrenheit for 15 minutes; and a saccharification rest at 152 degrees Fahrenheit for 60 minutes. Sparge with 168-degree Fahrenheit water.

Tripel (18-c)

The word *Trappist,* which often precedes the name of this Belgian Tripel, doesn't so much denote a type of beer as it does a type of brewery. A Trappist beer is brewed at one of only six Trappist Abbey breweries that exist in Europe (five in Belgium and one in the Netherlands). Any secular brewer who markets an imitation of one of these breweries' products must use the term *Abbey beer.*

Although the beers made by these Cistercian monks vary in style, they all feature high gravities, warm fermentations, top fermenting yeasts, and bottle-conditioning. Some of these monastic brewers add candi sugar to the brew during the boiling process, resulting in rather high-octane libations. The high fermentation temperatures produce a full range of fruity and estery aromas and flavors.

Some abbeys produce Ales in three graduated strengths. The mild Single is just for the monks' personal consumption; the dark Dubbel is a stronger version of the single; and the golden Tripel is the most potent. The elusive Quadrupel is the rarest of them all — so rare that this is the only mention of this style in this book.

Because much of the Trappist beers' characters are a result of the yeast, brewers must obtain these strains to replicate the style correctly.

Flavor profile: Light, pale gold. Light malty and hoppy aroma. Banana esters and flavors are expected. The hop/malt balance is neutral, but the finish may be sweet. Medium to full body. Alcohol content is high but shouldn't be tasted. Spicy and phenolic flavors may be evident.

OG/FG:	1.075–1.085 / 1.010–1.016
ABV:	7.5–9.0
IBUs:	25–38
SRM:	4.5–6

Commercial examples: Unibroue La Fin du Monde, Canada; New Belgium Trippel, Colorado

Beginner suggestions

Start with at least 8 pounds of pale malt extract to achieve the correct color, body, and strength of the style. Consider using Belgian candi sugar to add flavor, complexity, and alcohol content. Yeast is an important part of the Tripel profile — try progressing to liquid yeast strains as soon as you feel confident enough.

Tripel Play

(Intermediate)
Brewer: Marty Nachel

Malt extract:	7 pounds liquid malt extract
Specialty grain:	0.5 pound Belgian aromatic malt
	0.5 pound Belgian CaraVienne malt
Bittering hops:	1 ounce Hallertau (60 mins.)
Flavoring hops:	0.5 ounce Saaz (40 mins.)
Yeast:	Wyeast #1214
Misc. fermentable ingredients:	0.5 pound invert sugar
	0.5 pound light honey

Fining agent/ clarifier:	1 teaspoon Irish moss
Primary:	7 days at 65 degrees Fahrenheit
Secondary:	12 days at 55 degrees Fahrenheit

Typical/unusual procedures used: See the sidebar "Making invert sugar syrup" in Chapter 8.

Do-Well Trappist Tripel

(Advanced)
Brewer: Rich Larsen

Award won: 1st Place, Dixie Cup

Base grain:	12.5 pounds Belgian Pils
Specialty grain:	0.5 pound flaked barley
Bittering hops:	1.25 ounces Styrian Goldings (5.2 AAU)
Flavoring hops:	1.25 ounces Saaz (3.6 AAU)
Yeast:	Cultured from bottle of Witkap Pater Single

Misc. fermentable ingredients:	1.25 pounds homemade invert sugar
Primary:	(not given)
Secondary:	(not given)

Typical/unusual procedures used: See the sidebar "Making invert sugar syrup" in Chapter 8.

Belgian Golden Strong Ale (18-d)

As is true of other Belgian Ale categories, the Belgian Golden Strong Ale category functions as a catchall — in this case, for lighter-colored high-gravity Ales that don't fit in with any other Belgian styles.

Flavor profile: Pale yellow to medium gold. Medium-bodied and fairly alcoholic. Low hop flavor and aroma belie the potential for high hop bitterness. Very malty but with an acidic edge.

OG/FG:	1.070–1.095 / 1.010–1.016
ABV:	7.5–10.0
IBUs:	25–35
SRM:	4–6

Commercial examples: Duvel, Belgium; Delirium Tremens, Belgium

Beginner suggestions

These stronger Ales require more fermentable material for the yeasts to eat; I suggest starting with at least 8 pounds of malt extract. And, as with most Belgian beers, yeast is the single most important ingredient for achieving this style. Progressing to the use of style-specific yeast strains is the best way to replicate these styles.

Belgian Abbey

(Intermediate)
Brewer: Northwestern Extract Co.

Malt extract:	9.3 pounds Northwestern Gold	**Finishing hops:**	0.5 ounce Hersbrucker (5 mins.)
Specialty grain:	10 ounces CaraMunich malt	**Yeast:**	Wyeast #1214
Bittering hops:	2 ounces Mount Hood (60 mins.)	**Primary:**	(not given)
		Secondary:	(not given)

(Advanced)
Brewer: Brian Bliss

Ester the Molester

Award won: 1st Place, AHA Nationals

Malt extract:	3.3 pounds amber extract	**Dry hop:**	0.5 ounce Saaz
	2 pounds amber DME	**Yeast:**	Whitbread Ale
	1.3 pounds light DME	**Misc. fermentable ingredients:**	2 pounds turbinado sugar, 0.6 pound dextrose
Base grain:	9 pounds Pale Ale malt		
Specialty grain:	0.5 pound CaraMunich malt	**Primary:**	6 weeks at 65 degrees Fahrenheit
	0.5 pound aromatic malt	**Secondary:**	(not given)
	0.25 pound Special "B" 221-L malt		
Bittering hops:	3 ounces Kent Goldings (5.2 AAU) (70 mins.)		
	2 ounces Fuggles (4.2 AAU) (70 mins.)		
	1 ounce Northern Brewer (7.5 AAU) (70 mins.)		
	0.5 ounce Hallertauer (4.5 AAU) (70 mins.)		

Typical/unusual procedures used: Mash at 152 degrees Fahrenheit for 45 minutes. Heat the fermenter with an electric blanket to 90 to 100 degrees Fahrenheit for 12 hours after fermentation begins.

Belgian Dark Strong Ale (18-e)

As is true of other Belgian Ale categories, the Belgian Dark Strong Ale category functions as a catchall — in this case, for darker-colored high-gravity Ales that don't fit in with any other Belgian styles.

Flavor profile: Deep amber to coppery brown. Medium-bodied and fairly alcoholic. Low hop flavor and aroma belie the potential for high hop bitterness. Very malty but with an acidic edge.

OG/FG:	1.075–1.110 / 1.010–1.024
ABV:	8.0–12.0+
IBUs:	15–25
SRM:	12–20

Commercial examples: Abbaye de Rocs Grand Cru, Belgium; Chimay Grande Reserve, Belgium

Beginner suggestions

These stronger Ales require more fermentable material for the yeasts to eat; I suggest starting with at least 8 pounds of amber malt extract. Try adding 1 pound of dark Belgian candi sugar. And as with most Belgian beers, yeast is the single most important ingredient for achieving this style. Progressing to the use of style-specific yeast strains is the best way to replicate these styles.

Flabby Abbey Not-So-Grande Reserve

(Intermediate)
Brewer: Marty Nachel

Malt extract:	9 pounds Northwestern Gold	**Finishing hops:**	1 ounce Kent Goldings (15 mins.)
Specialty grain:	1.5 pounds Special "B" 221-L crystal malt	**Misc. fermentable ingredients:**	1 pound dark candi sugar
	1 pound 40-L crystal malt	**Yeast:**	Wyeast #1214
	0.25 pound chocolate malt	**Primary:**	8 days at 65 degrees Fahrenheit
Bittering hops:	2 ounces Fuggles (60 mins.)	**Secondary:**	14 days at 65 degrees Fahrenheit

Brune Dream

(Advanced)
Brewer: Tom Dennis

Award won: 3rd Place, 2007 Dayton Beerfest

Base grain:	12 pounds pale malt	**Yeast:**	WLP 500
Specialty grain:	2 pounds Vienna malt	**Misc. fermentable ingredients:**	1 pound corn sugar (dextrose)
	1 pound Munich malt	**Primary:**	2 weeks at 75 degrees Fahrenheit
	1 pound CaraMunich malt	**Secondary:**	2 weeks at 70 degrees Fahrenheit
	¾ pound CaraPils malt		
	¼ pound biscuit malt		
	1 ounce chocolate malt		
Bittering hops:	2.5 ounces Hallertau (60 mins.)		
Flavoring hops:	.75 ounce Hallertau (10 mins.)		
Finishing hops:	.75 ounce Hallertau (3 mins.)		

Typical/unusual procedures used: Mash at 152 degrees Fahrenheit for 60 minutes. Mash out at 170 degrees Fahrenheit for 10 minutes. Sparge with 170-degree Fahrenheit water. Boil for 90 minutes.

Old Ale (19-a)

English Strong Ale was the standard drinking-man's beer in the 1600s and 1700s. Lack of refrigeration and clean storage conditions called for a beer of considerable gravity and strength to prevail against bacterial contamination. Because these beers were particularly robust, high hopping rates were necessary to offset the cloying nature of the malt. The resulting beer had natural hop-preservative resins and a high alcohol content to stave off any contamination that was likely to occur during the long aging process. This extended aging period is the reason these brews are called Old Ales.

Old Ales are full-bodied brews with a nutty, grainy malt character balanced by a fair amount of hop bitterness. Vigorous fermentations give the beer a noticeable fruity, estery nose resulting in a robust, complex, and slightly *vinous* (winelike) beer overall.

Flavor profile: Light to deep amber. Fruitiness and esters are high; hop flavor and aroma can be assertive. Medium- to full-bodied. Very malty, with a fair amount of diacetyl evident. Alcoholic strength is noticeable.

OG/FG:	1.060–1.090+ / 1.015–1.022+
ABV:	6.0–9.0+
IBUs:	30–60+
SRM:	10–22+

Commercial examples: Gale's Prize Old Ale, England; Theakston's Old Peculier, England

Beginner suggestions

Old Ales require a fair amount of fermentable material in the recipe — try starting with 7 pounds of amber extract. Long, warm fermentations produce an abundance of fruity and alcoholic aroma, flavor, and mouthfeel. Two to three ounces of English bittering hops are necessary to maintain flavor balance.

Jack the Sipper

(Intermediate)
Brewer: Marty Nachel

Malt extract:	6 pounds English pale extract	**Flavoring hops:**	1 ounce Fuggles (30 mins.)
	2 pounds pale DME	**Finishing hops:**	1 ounce Fuggles (10 mins.)
Specialty grain:	1 pound 40-L crystal malt	**Yeast:**	Wyeast #1028
	0.25 pound chocolate malt	**Misc. flavoring ingredients:**	6 ounces light molasses
	0.25 pound roasted barley	**Primary:**	8 days at 65 degrees Fahrenheit
Bittering hops:	2 ounces Northern Brewer (60 mins.)	**Secondary:**	14 days at 65 degrees Fahrenheit

Old Alt Ale

(Advanced)
Brewer: Dick Van Dyke

Award won: 1st Place, B.O.S.S. Challenge

Malt extract:	6.6 pounds Northwestern amber	**Flavoring hops:**	2.5 ounces Hallertauer (30 mins.)
Base grain:	1 pound 2-row pale malt		2 ounces Hallertauer (20 mins.)
	2 pounds Munich malt	**Finishing hops:**	1 ounce Hallertauer (5 mins.)
Specialty grain:	0.5 pound CaraPils malt	**Yeast:**	2 14-gram packages of Whitbread Dry Lager
	0.25 pound wheat malt		
Bittering hops:	1 ounce Chinook (60 mins.)	**Primary:**	4 days at 62 degrees Fahrenheit
	1 ounce Perle (60 mins.)	**Secondary:**	8 days at 62 degrees Fahrenheit
	2 ounces Cascade (40 mins.)		

English-Style Barley Wine (19-b)

The term *Barley Wine* sounds more like something you make from grapes, and yet its name mentions a grain. What's up with that? Well, the name implies a beverage made from barley but that has the strength and character of wine; you soon see that the name is apropos.

Barley Wine is a classic English style of old Ale. With its huge body, almost-overwhelming malty flavor, and the kick of a mule, Barley Wine isn't for the weak-kneed. These complex and alcoholic brews pack a one-two punch of flavor and strength because of the high level of fermentable sugars, or *gravity*. Barley Wine has more than twice the strength of a European Pilsener. The resulting alcohol content is around 8.5 to 12 percent by volume. Needless to say, these potent potables aren't intended for summer consumption. In fact, brewers usually produce Barley Wine in limited quantities, often earmarked for holiday celebrations. And because of its alcoholic strength and high terminal gravities, you can store Barley Wine for future consumption.

The color range for Barley Wine is forgiving, usually starting out around copper and working its way into the deep ambers. The nose is pungent — an olfactory cornucopia of fruits and malt aromas, ethanol, and hop bouquet. Correctly balancing the bold, malty character of this style requires copious amounts of hop bittering, further intimidating the novice beer drinker. The finish is always long, complex, and warming in the throat.

Flavor profile: Copper to medium brown and medium to full-bodied. Barley Wines are usually malty sweet, fruity, and estery, with medium to high bitterness levels. Hop aroma and taste can be anywhere from low to high. Expect to taste the alcohol. Low to medium diacetyl is acceptable.

OG/FG:	1.080–1.120+ / 1.018–1.030+
ABV:	8.0–12.0+
IBUs:	35–70
SRM:	8–22

Commercial examples: Young's Old Nick, England; Thomas Hardy's Ale, England

Beginner suggestions

Successful Barley Wines are big and bold beers. Use at least 9 pounds of extract to achieve the correct body and strength. Remember to aerate the wort sufficiently before pitching the yeast and to pitch enough healthy yeast to ferment the beer completely. Full fermentation should take at least three weeks.

Boobs Barley Wine

(Intermediate)
Brewer: Chuck Boyce

Award won: 2nd Place, AHA Nationals

Malt extract:	12 pounds light malt extract	**Finishing hops:**	1.5 ounces Cascade (2 mins.)
Specialty grain:	3 pounds Klages malt	**Yeast:**	Wyeast #1056
	0.5 pound dextrin malt	**Primary:**	4 weeks at 75 degrees Fahrenheit
	0.5 pound crystal malt	**Secondary:**	2 weeks at 65 degrees Fahrenheit
Bittering hops:	9 ounces Bullion (90 mins.)		
Flavoring hops:	1.5 ounces Fuggles (15 mins.)		

MLC (Moe, Larry, and Curly) Barley Wine

(Advanced)
Brewers: Rich Larsen, Bob Ward, Jamie Wika

Award Won: 1st Place, B.O.S.S. Challenge

Malt extract:	3 pounds Northwestern Light Extract	**Misc. fermentable ingredients:**	1.5 pounds turbinado sugar
Base grain:	13 pounds Hugh Baird Pale Ale malt	**Primary:**	(not given)
Bittering hops:	1.25 ounces Target (10.7 AAU)	**Secondary:**	(not given)
Flavoring hops:	1.5 ounces Challenger (7.3 AAU)		
Finishing hops:	1 ounces Northdown (6.4 AAU)		
Yeast:	Yeast Culture Kit Barley Wine		
	Wyeast #1728 Scotch Ale in secondary		

Typical/unusual procedures used: Pitch a second dose of yeast while racking the beer into the secondary fermenter.

Fun Label Ideas

American IPA

INDIANA PALE ALE

We know of no other beer that is made from **grainier** grain, **hoppier** hops, or **wetter** water.

Schwipps Brewery, Wilbur, IN

"From the Crossroads of America"

Not-so-Grande Reserve • • Belgian Dark Strong Beer •

Flabby Abbey Ale

10% A.B.V.

"The big bodied brew for big bodied people"

Nachel Brewery
Oakland Park, Illinois

Chapter 16

Lager Recipes

In This Chapter

▶ American Lager

▶ Bohemian Pilsener

▶ Märzen/Oktoberfest

▶ German Dark Lager

▶ German Light Lager

▶ Bock beers

*L*agers are beers fermented with bottom-fermenting yeast at cool temperatures for relatively long periods of time. They're primarily associated with northern and eastern European countries such as Germany, Denmark, the Netherlands, and Czechoslovakia but are produced in a wide variety of styles in most brewing nations, including France, Belgium, the U.K., Ireland, Russia, the Nordic and Baltic countries, China, Japan, other Asian nations, Australia, New Zealand, most South American countries, Canada, Mexico, and the United States. Whew!

This chapter provides beer recipes for most of the beer styles considered Lager varieties. *Note:* Not all of the Lager beer styles and substyles listed on the AHA hierarchical list (on the Cheat Sheet) are discussed in this chapter. Because some beer styles are hard to produce at the homebrewing level without highly advanced ingredients, equipment, information, and techniques, I decided to spare you from them. Also note that, although I've compiled all of these recipes, I didn't author all of them and have little control over how much or how little information they provide. As a general guideline, all water treatments in intermediate recipes are assumed to be added to the brewpot unless otherwise noted; water treatments in advanced recipes are assumed to be added to the mash water.

American Premium Lager (1-c)

The pale American-style Premium Lager represents the most-produced beer style in the United States, as well as in other countries such as Australia, Canada, Japan, and Mexico that have followed in the footsteps of the American industrial brewers.

American-style Premium Lagers, despite their categorical name, are still rather one-dimensional beers compared to those made in Europe and else-where. The reasons for this condition are largely the cheaper ingredients used to make them and the treatment of beer in America as a beverage designed for mass consumption. American craft brewers, on the other hand, are producing Premium Lagers that are more deserving of the name.

Flavor profile: Very pale to golden. No fruitiness, esters, or diacetyl. Low malt aroma and flavor are okay. Low hop flavor or aroma is okay, but low to medium bitterness is expected. Effervescent. Light-bodied.

OG/FG:	1.046–1.056 / 1.008–1.012
ABV:	4.7–6.0
IBUs:	15–25
SRM:	2–6

Commercial examples: Leinenkugel's, Wisconsin; Brooklyn Lager, New York

Beginner suggestions

Start with 5 pounds of the palest extract you can find and add 0.5 pound of brewer's rice syrup. Use a high-quality Lager yeast (preferably liquid) and allow a long, cool fermentation and aging period.

Gullywasher

(Intermediate)
Brewer: Marty Nachel

Malt extract:	5 pounds Alexander's pale extract	**Misc. fermentable ingredients:**	1 pound brewer's rice syrup
Specialty grain:	1 pound 10-L crystal malt	**Fining agent/ clarifier:**	2 teaspoons Irish moss
Bittering hops:	1 ounce Northern Brewer (60 mins.)	**Primary:**	6 days at 60 degrees Fahrenheit
Flavoring hops:	1 ounce Perle (20 mins.)	**Secondary:**	21 days at 50 degrees Fahrenheit
Finishing hops:	0.5 ounce Saaz (5 mins.)		
Yeast:	Wyeast #2035		

Butt-Scratcher

(Advanced)
Brewer: Steve Daniel

Award won: 1st Place, AHA Nationals

Base grain:	4 pounds 2-row malt	**Primary:**	21 days at 50 degrees Fahrenheit
	3 pounds 6-row malt	**Secondary:**	30 days at 32 degrees Fahrenheit
Specialty grain:	1 pound rice		
Bittering hops:	1.5 ounces Hallertauer (60 mins.)	**Typical/unusual procedures used:** Precook the rice prior to mash. Mash all grains at 151 degrees Fahrenheit for 60 minutes.	
	1 ounce Cascade (10 mins.)		
Yeast:	Wyeast #2308		

Münchner-Style Helles (1-d)

German Light Lagers aren't low-calorie beers; they're just pale-colored. The original pale Lager beer was brewed in Munich in 1928. In that year, the famous Paulaner Brewery introduced a *Helles* (pale) Lager, which was therefore known as Münchner-style Helles. This style is meant to be an everyday libation, and it's quaffed by the liter throughout Bavaria.

Münchner-style Helles, sometimes called *Continental Lager,* is pale yellow to brilliant gold in color and light- to medium-bodied. The accent is on the maltiness, with just enough hop bitterness extracted from noble hop varieties to balance the malt. The downplayed hop character is the principal difference between pale Lager and Pilsener and one to look out for in buying American microbrews.

Flavor profile: Pale to golden. No fruitiness or esters; hop flavor and aroma are okay. Medium malty sweetness. Low bitterness and no diacetyl are expected. Medium-bodied.

OG/FG:	1.045–1.051 / 1.008–1.012
ABV:	4.7–5.4
IBUs:	16–22
SRM:	3–5

Commercial examples: Spaten, Germany; Augustinerbrau, Germany

Beginner suggestions

Start with 6 pounds of the palest hopped malt available. Steep 1 pound of 20-L crystal malt in 1 gallon of water and strain into the wort in the brewpot. Use a high-quality Lager yeast (preferably liquid). I highly recommend a long, cool fermentation.

Meltdown Lager

Award won: 1st Place, AHA Nationals

Malt extract:	5.5 pounds Munton and Fison pale DME	**Finishing hops:**	1 ounce Saaz (2 mins.)
		Yeast:	Wyeast #2124
Specialty grain:	0.5 pound crystal malt	**Water treatment:**	⅜ teaspoon gypsum
	0.5 pound dextrin malt	**Primary:**	4 days at 45 degrees Fahrenheit
Bittering hops:	0.5 ounce Hallertauer (60 mins.)	**Secondary:**	28 days at 35 degrees Fahrenheit
Flavoring hops:	0.5 ounce Hallertauer (30 mins.)		

Helles

(Advanced)
Brewer: Dave Miller

Award won: 2nd Place, AHA Nationals

Base grain:	5.75 pounds 2-row Lager malt	**Primary:**	3 weeks at 50 degrees Fahrenheit
Specialty grain:	1 pound CaraPils malt	**Secondary:**	7 days at 50 degrees Fahrenheit
	0.25 pound Munich malt		
Bittering hops:	1.75 ounces Hallertauer (75 mins.)		
	1.75 ounces Hallertauer (45 mins.)		
Yeast:	Wyeast #2007		
Water treatment:	lactic acid (enough to acidify water to pH 5.7)		

Typical/unusual procedures used: Mash the grains with a protein rest for 30 minutes at 130 degrees Fahrenheit and a starch rest for 60 minutes at 150 degrees Fahrenheit; mash out for 5 minutes at 168 degrees Fahrenheit. Sparge with 5 gallons of water at 165 degrees Fahrenheit.

Dortmunder/European-Style Export (1-e)

Dortmunder beer gets its name from the city of Dortmund, which is one of the most prolific beer brewing cities in the world. Although the Dortmunder style of Lager beer is very popular in central Germany, it's not very well known elsewhere, which may explain its large blue-collar customer base of miners and steelworkers. Additionally, Dortmunder beer gets kind of lost between the world-famous Pilsener beers and the revered pale Lagers from Munich. Typically, Dortmunder beer is fuller-bodied than Pilsener, somewhat dry compared to a Münchner-Style Helles, and slightly higher in alcohol than both.

The European-style Export tag was attached to this style after a few of Dortmunder's larger brewers began exporting their local beers to the international market.

Flavor profile: Pale to golden. No fruitiness, esters, or diacetyl are acceptable. Very low hop flavor and aroma are okay. Medium bitterness balances medium malty sweetness. Alcohol warmth is sometimes evident. Medium body.

OG/FG:	1.048–1.056 / 1.010–1.015
ABV:	4.8–6.0
IBUs:	23–30
SRM:	4–6

Commercial examples: D.A.B., Germany; Berghoff Beer, Wisconsin

Beginner suggestions

Start with 6 pounds of the palest hopped extract available. Add 0.5 ounce of Hallertauer or Tettnanger hops in the last 5 minutes of the boil. Use a high-quality Lager yeast (preferably liquid). A long, cool fermentation is highly desirable.

3-D (Duisberg, Dortmund, Düsseldorf) Export

(Intermediate)
Brewer: Marty Nachel

Award won: 1st Place, AHA Nationals

Malt extract:	6 pounds pale German extract	**Finishing hops:**	0.5 ounce Hallertauer (10 mins.)
Specialty grain:	1 pound 10-L crystal malt	**Yeast:**	Wyeast #2042
Bittering hops:	1.5 ounces Perle (60 mins.)	**Fining agent/ clarifier:**	2 teaspoons Irish moss
Flavoring hops:	0.5 ounce Tettnanger (20 mins.)	**Primary:**	7 days at 60 degrees Fahrenheit
		Secondary:	21 days at 50 degrees Fahrenheit

Grain-n-Beerit

(Advanced)
Brewer: Norman Dickenson

Award won: 1st Place, AHA Nationals

Base grain:	8.5 pounds 2-row pale malt	**Finishing hops:**	0.25 ounce Perle (10 mins.)
	1 pound Munich malt	**Yeast:**	Wyeast #2206
Specialty grain:	0.5 pound Vienna malt	**Primary:**	10 days at 52 degrees Fahrenheit
	0.5 pound dextrin malt	**Secondary:**	(not given)
Bittering hops:	0.5 ounce Perle (60 mins.)		
	0.66 ounce Saaz (60 mins.)		
Flavoring hops:	1 ounce Tettnanger (30 mins.)		

Typical/unusual procedures used: Mash the grains at 149 degrees Fahrenheit for 50 minutes; raise the temperature to 168 degrees Fahrenheit for 10 minutes.

Bohemian-Style Pilsener (2-6)

Pilsener beer developed in Plzen, Bohemia, in the mid-1800s. Today, Pilsener is the world's most popular style of beer and, more than any other, is what most Americans think of if the subject turns to beer. Small wonder. Most major breweries in the world produce something akin to this style. Unfortunately, most pay little tribute to the original.

The original brand of Pilsener beer — still the standard-bearer in the industry — hails from the town of Plzen, which is now part of the Czech Republic. The name of that brand — Pilsner Urquell — even makes note of the fact that it's the original; *Urquell* means "original source." The Pilsener name (in all its many forms: Pils, Pilsner, Pilsener, Plzensky) derives from this Bohemian town, where the brewery was built in 1842. The golden-colored, bottom-fermented beer brewed there quickly became popular in Europe and, eventually, throughout the world.

The style is pale, malty, and well-hopped. The aroma has the unmistakable kiss of the Saaz hop from the Zatec region near Plzen. Caramel notes are often observed, as is a hint of diacetyl rounding out the sweetness and mouthfeel. One key ingredient in a real Pilsener beer is the extremely soft water, similar to that pumped from the aquifers under the Urquell Brewery.

Flavor profile: Pale to golden. No fruitiness or esters; low to medium hop flavor and aroma are expected. Low to medium maltiness is evident in aroma and flavor, with caramel notes in background. Medium to high bitterness with low diacetyl is okay. Light- to medium-bodied.

OG/FG:	1.044–1.056 / 1.013–1.017
ABV:	4.2–5.4
IBUs:	35–45
SRM:	3.5–6

Commercial examples: Pilsner Urquell, Czech Republic; Czechvar Pilsner, Czech Republic

Beginner suggestions

Start with 6 pounds of the palest hopped malt extract available. Steep 1 pound of 20-L crystal malt in 1 gallon of water and strain into the wort. Add 1 ounce of Saaz hops in the last 5 minutes of the boil. Use a high-quality Lager yeast (preferably liquid). I highly recommend a long, cool fermentation.

Yellow Dogs Pilsener

(Intermediate)
Brewer: Matthew Holland

Award won: 1st Place, AHA Nationals

Malt extract:	6 pounds William's American light extract	**Dry hop:**	1 ounce Saaz
	1 pound William's Australian light extract	**Yeast:**	Wyeast #2124
Bittering hops:	0.5 Chinook (11.5 AAU) (60 mins.)	**Fining agent/ clarifier:**	1½ teaspoons Irish moss
Flavoring hops:	1 ounce Saaz (15 mins.)	**Primary:**	14 days at 54 degrees Fahrenheit
Finishing hops:	1 ounce Saaz (5 mins.)	**Secondary:**	(not given)

Bitter Pill (s)

(Advanced)
Brewer: Marty Nachel

Base grain:	8 pounds Pilsener malt	**Primary:**	6 days at 55 degrees Fahrenheit
Specialty grain:	0.5 pound CaraVienne malt	**Secondary:**	16 days at 45 degrees Fahrenheit
Bittering hops:	1 ounce Saaz (60 mins.)		
Flavoring hops:	0.5 ounce Saaz (45 mins.)		
Finishing hops:	0.5 ounce Saaz (20 mins.)		
Yeast:	Wyeast #2278		
Fining agent/ clarifier:	1 teaspoon Irish moss		

Typical/unusual procedures used:
Perform a protein rest at 128 degrees Fahrenheit for 15 minutes; an intermediate rest at 145 degrees Fahrenheit for 15 minutes; and a saccharification rest at 152 degrees Fahrenheit for 60 minutes Sparge with 168-degree Fahrenheit water.

Märzen/Oktoberfest (3-6)

Märzen, Oktoberfest, and Vienna beers are pretty much of the same pedigree — they're all bottom-fermented, malty, and medium- to full-bodied.

Oktoberfest beer, as an individual style, is an offshoot of another, larger Lager style known as Märzen or Märzenbier. This fairly heavy, malty style of beer is brewed in the spring and named for the month of March (März). It was often the last batch of beer brewed before the warm summer months, during which brewing was ill-advised (back before the invention of refrigeration, of course). This higher-gravity beer was then stored in Alpine caves and consumed throughout the summer. Whatever beer was left in storage at harvest time, also the beginning of the new brewing season, was hauled out and joyously consumed.

A party atmosphere was already present in the Oktoberfest celebration, but it took on a more reverent slant in 1810. In late September of that year, Bavaria's Crown Prince married Theresa Von Sachsen-Hildburghausen. This very public event just happened to coincide with the rollout of the excess Märzenbier. The good people of Munich so enjoyed the state celebration that they agreed to commemorate the nuptial feast and its pageantry on an annual basis. The breweries of Munich were certainly not against the idea — more than a million people attend the event every year, which takes place on the *Theresienwiese* (Theresa's meadow), named for the royal bride.

Today, Munich's Oktoberfest begins on a Saturday in mid-September with the Lord Mayor's proclamation *"O'zapft is!"* ("It's tapped!") as he taps the ceremonial first keg of beer. The festival then lasts 16 days and ends on the first Sunday in October.

Flavor profile: Amber to coppery orange. No fruitiness, esters, or diacetyl are evident. Low hop flavor and aroma are okay. The malty sweetness boasts of a toasty malt aroma and flavor. Low to medium bitterness is just enough to keep the malty character from becoming cloying. Medium-bodied.

OG/FG:	1.050–1.056 / 1.012–1.016
ABV:	4.8–5.7
IBUs:	20–28
SRM:	7–14

Commercial examples: Wurzburger Oktoberfest, Germany; Capital Oktoberfest, Wisconsin

Beginner suggestions

Oktoberfest/Märzenbiers are malt-accented beers. Start with at least 6 pounds of pale extract and steep 1.5 pounds of 20-L crystal malt and 0.5 pound toasted malt in water and then strain into wort. Use a high-quality Lager yeast (preferably liquid) and allow a long, cool fermentation.

Dominion Day Oktoberfest

(Intermediate)
Brewer: John Janowiak

Award won: 1st Place, AHA Nationals

Malt extract:	6.6 pounds Bierkeller extract	**Finishing hops:**	0.75 ounce Tettnanger (1 min.)
	1 pound amber DME	**Yeast:**	Wyeast #2206
Specialty grain:	0.5 pound 10-L crystal malt	**Primary:**	11 days at 50 degrees Fahrenheit
	0.5 cup chocolate malt	**Secondary:**	10 days at 45 degrees Fahrenheit
Bittering hops:	1 ounce Cascade (60 mins.)	**Tertiary:**	15 days at 35 degrees Fahrenheit
Flavoring hops:	1 ounce Hallertauer (30 mins.)		

(Unnamed)

(Advanced)
Brewers: Dennis and Cindy Arvidson

Award won: 1st Place, AHA Nationals

Base grain:	5 pounds 2-row malt	**Water treatment:**	1 gram calcium chloride each in mash and sparge water
	3 pounds Munich malt		
	0.75 pound home-roasted 2-row malt	**Primary:**	40 days at 38 degrees Fahrenheit
	0.5 pound wheat malt	**Secondary:**	30 days at 38 degrees Fahrenheit
	0.33 pound Scottish malt		
Bittering hops:	1 ounce Styrian Goldings (120 mins.)		
	1 ounce Saaz (120 mins.)		
Yeast:	Wyeast #2308		

Typical/unusual procedures used: Mash the grain at 156 degrees Fahrenheit for 90 minutes.

American Dark Lager (4-a)

The production of American Dark Lagers was in steep decline for most of the 1950s, 1960s, and 1970s. The relatively newer, lighter-bodied pale Lager beers had become the national standard in beer drinking, and dark beers in general fell out of favor among American beer drinkers. Thus, the few dark lagers still being made became dark in color more than in style or substance. The addition of very small percentages of highly kilned malts enabled brewers to achieve a maximum of beer color with a minimum effect on beer taste. In other words, the beer looked dark (in relative comparison to pale Lager) but didn't taste dark.

Flavor profile: Deep copper to dark brown. No fruitiness or esters. Low hop flavor or aroma is okay; so is low bitterness. Low malt aroma or flavor is okay. Very low diacetyl is okay — really, it is! Effervescent. Light- to medium-bodied.

OG/FG:	1.044–1.056 / 1.008–1.012
ABV:	4.2–6.0
IBUs:	8–20
SRM:	14–22

Commercial examples: Shiner Bock, Texas; Berghoff Dark, Wisconsin

Beginner suggestions

Start with 5 pounds of the palest extract you can find and add 0.5 pound of brewer's rice syrup and 0.25 pound of chocolate malt. Use a high-quality Lager yeast (preferably liquid) and allow a long, cool fermentation and aging period.

Dark Vader Lager

(Intermediate)
Brewer: Marty Nachel

Malt extract: 6 pounds pale Lager extract

Specialty grain: 1 pound 40-L crystal malt

0.33 ounce chocolate malt

Bittering hops: 1.5 ounces Perle (60 mins.)

Flavoring hops: 1 ounce Mount Hood (20 mins.)

Yeast: Wyeast #2035

Fining agent/ clarifier: 2 ounces Irish moss

Primary: 7 days at 60 degrees Fahrenheit

Secondary: 24 days at 45 degrees Fahrenheit

League City Dark

(Advanced)
Brewer: Steve Daniel

Award won: 2nd Place, AHA Nationals

Base grain: 4 pounds domestic 6-row malt

3 pounds Harrington 2-row malt

Specialty grain: 1 pound rice

2 ounces chocolate malt

1 pound dark crystal malt

Bittering hops: 1 ounce Cascade (6.7 AAU) (90 mins.)

Yeast: Wyeast #2308

Primary: 14 days at 50 degrees Fahrenheit

Secondary: 30 days at 32 degrees Fahrenheit

Typical/unusual procedures used:
Preboil the rice. Mash the grains at 151 degrees Fahrenheit for 60 minutes.

Munich Dunkel (4-6)

What most drinkers know as German Dark beer is basically a Lager beer that has an additional roasted malt thrown in to add complexity to the aroma and palate. These dark versions of the Munich Pale Lager (Münchner-style Helles) style tend to be somewhat sweeter and only marginally heavier on the palate; most of this style's reputation as being heavy and strong is exaggerated. (Confusion reigns because any and every malt beverage with a color that remotely resembles the amber band in the color spectrum is now branded a dark beer.)

Ironically, *all* the original Münchner-made beers were fairly dark until the introduction of Helles Lager earlier this century. Because of its widespread popularity, most Bavarian brewers began making Helles Lager, thus making the Dunkel style even less popular.

Flavor profile: Copper to dark brown. No fruitiness or esters should be experienced. Nutty, roasty, chocolatey, and malty characteristics may be noticeable in the aroma and flavor. Low hop flavor and aroma are typical, as is medium bitterness. Low diacetyl is acceptable. Medium-bodied.

OG/FG:	1.048–1.056 / 1.010–1.016
ABV:	4.5–5.6
IBUs:	18–28
SRM:	14–28

Commercial examples: Hopf Dunkles, Germany; E K U Rubin, Germany

Beginner suggestions

Try starting with at least 6 pounds of pale extract and add the dark color and flavor by using 0.5 pound chocolate malt. The longer and cooler the fermentation, the more Lager-like the end result is. (Ferment a minimum of 1 week at 50 degrees Fahrenheit for the primary and 3 weeks at 40 degrees Fahrenheit for the secondary.)

(Intermediate)
Brewer: Ross Herrold

Lady of the Morning

Award won: 1st Place, AHA Nationals

Malt extract:	4 pounds Alexander's pale extract	**Finishing hops:**	1 ounce Hallertauer (1 min.)
	2 pounds dark malt extract	**Yeast:**	Wyeast #2007
Specialty grain:	0.5 pound crystal malt	**Water treatment:**	Preboil and prechill all brewing water
Bittering hops:	1 ounce Hallertauer (60 mins.)	**Primary:**	7 weeks at 50 degrees Fahrenheit
	0.5 ounce Cascade (60 mins.)	**Secondary:**	6 weeks at 30 to 40 degrees Fahrenheit
Flavoring hops:	1 ounce Hallertauer (30 mins.)		
	0.5 ounce Cascade (30 mins.)		

(Advanced)
Brewer: Stu Tallman

Stu Brew

Award won: 1st Place, AHA Nationals

Base grain:	7.5 pounds pale Lager malt	**Yeast:**	Wyeast #2206
	2 pounds Munich malt	**Primary:**	21 days at 50 degrees Fahrenheit
	2 pounds 40-L crystal malt	**Secondary:**	21 days at 37 degrees Fahrenheit
Bittering hops:	1.25 ounces Saaz (90 mins.)	**Typical/unusual procedures used:**	Perform a three-step infusion mash.

German-Style Helles Bock/Maibock (5-a)

German-style Helles Bock is a pale version of Traditional Bock. The profile is similar except for the omission of the chocolate grain, which in essence removes the chocolate flavors and most of the dark color. Maibock is a style brewed for consumption in the month of May (Mai). It's basically a Helles Bock with a more pronounced hop character in the aroma and on the palate. Some brands are even dry hopped for added bouquet.

Flavor profile: Pale to amber. No hop aroma, fruitiness, or esters. The malty, sweet character predominates in aroma and flavor. Unlike the Traditional Bock, it has no toasted chocolate-malt character. Low bitterness, low hop flavor, and low diacetyl are okay. Medium-bodied.

OG/FG:	1.064–1.072 / 1.011–1.018
ABV:	6.3–7.4
IBUs:	23–35+
SRM:	6–11

Commercial examples: Einbecker Maibock, Germany; Ayinger Maibock, Germany

Beginner suggestions

Start with no less than 8 pounds of very pale hopped extract; steep 1.5 pounds of 10-L crystal and strain into wort. Add 1 ounce of traditional German hops (Hallertauer, Tettnanger) in the last 15 minutes of the boil. Adding 1 pound of light honey also adds an interesting complexity to this style. Pitch a true Lager yeast and ferment at cool temperatures for an extended period of time.

Ja, Das Ist ein Schnitzel Bock

(Intermediate)
Brewer: Marty Nachel

Malt extract:	8.5 pounds light DME
Specialty grain:	1.5 pounds 10-L crystal malt
	0.5 pound Munich malt
Bittering hops:	1.5 ounces Hallertauer (60 mins.)
Flavoring hops:	1 ounce Hallertauer (30 mins.)
Finishing hops:	0.5 ounce Saaz (10 mins.)
Yeast:	Wyeast #2206

Misc. non-fermentable ingredients:	8 ounces malto-dextrin powder
Primary:	5 days at 50 degrees Fahrenheit
Secondary:	4 weeks at 40 degrees Fahrenheit

Typical/unusual procedures used: Aerate the wort well and pitch plenty of yeast at about 65 degrees Fahrenheit; as soon as fermentation is visible, gradually lower temperature to 50 degrees Fahrenheit.

Helles/Maibock

(Advanced)
Brewer: Marty Nachel

Base grain:	10 pounds Pilsener malt
Specialty grain:	0.5 pound CaraVienne malt
	0.5 pound CaraMunich
Bittering hops:	1 ounce Hallertau (60 mins.)
	1 ounce Hallertau (40 mins.)
Flavoring hops:	0.5 ounce Hallertauer (20 mins.)
Yeast:	Wyeast #2206

Fining agent/clarifier:	1 teaspoon Irish moss
Primary:	6 days at 60 degrees Fahrenheit
Secondary:	14 days at 45 degrees Fahrenheit

Typical/unusual procedures used: Perform a protein rest at 128 degrees Fahrenheit for 15 minutes; an intermediate rest at 145 degrees Fahrenheit for 15 minutes; and a saccharification rest at 152 degrees Fahrenheit for 60 minutes. Sparge with 168-degree Fahrenheit water.

Traditional Bock (5-6)

The northern German city of Einbeck was the first center of commercial brewing in the 13th century. Beer from Einbeck became known as Beck beer (no relation to Beck's beer). Beck beer was famous throughout the Hanseatic League of cities on the North Atlantic but completely unknown in the south of Germany. Beck beer's eventual introduction to the south took place several hundred years later, at the wedding of the Duke of Braunschweig to the daughter of a wealthy aristocrat from the south. The wedding took place in Bavaria in the early 1600s and was attended by nobility from distant states. The Bavarians embraced the beer style from the north and adopted it as the beer of choice in the state-commissioned Hofbrauhaus in Munich. The brew soon became known as Bock beer — a corruption of Beck in the Bavarian accent.

Bavarians like to downplay the Einbeck connection in favor of a local interpretation of the beer's origin. *Bock* means *billy goat,* which is the animal associated with the zodiacal sign of Capricorn that rules over the months of December and January, when brewers start making Bock beer. Yet another version suggests that the male goat is a symbol of fertility synonymous with the spring season. One thing is for sure — Bock beer is *not* what's cleaned out of the bottom of the vats once a year!

Traditional Bock beer is a hearty bottom-fermented beer with a generously malty character and burnt toffee dark-grain flavors. It has a creamy mouthfeel and the finish is lengthy and malty sweet. Hop bitterness is subdued — it's just enough to cut the cloying character of the malt. The color can run the spectrum from a deep burnt orange to mahogany. The alcohol content is usually considerable; a true German Bock beer must have a minimum alcohol content of 6.5 percent to be called a Bock.

Flavor profile: Deep copper to dark brown. No hop aroma, fruitiness, or esters are evident. The malty-sweet character predominates in aroma and flavor, with some toasted chocolate-malt character. Low bitterness, low hop flavor, and low diacetyl are okay. Medium- to full-bodied.

OG/FG:	1.064–1.072 / 1.013–1.019
ABV:	6.3–7.2
IBUs:	20–27
SRM:	14–22

Commercial example: Spaten Bock, Germany; Einbecker Ur-Bock, Germany

Beginner suggestions

Traditional Bock beers are big beers; start with no less than 8 pounds of amber extract; steep 1.5 pounds of 40-L crystal and strain into wort. Use a high-quality Lager yeast (preferably liquid) and allow a long, cool fermentation period.

RE: Bock

(Intermediate)
Brewer: Marty Nachel

Malt extract:	6 pounds pale liquid malt extract	**Flavoring hops:**	0.5 ounce Hallertau (30 mins.)
	2 pounds pale DME	**Yeast:**	Wyeast #2206
Specialty grain:	1 pound 60 L Crystal malt	**Fining agent/ clarifier:**	1 teaspoon Irish moss
	0.5 pound chocolate malt	**Primary:**	8 days at 55 degrees Fahrenheit
Bittering hops:	0.5 ounce Hallertau (60 mins.)	**Secondary:**	14 days at 45 degrees Fahrenheit
	0.5 ounce Hallertau (45 mins.)		

Basically Bock

(Advanced)
Brewer: Phil Rahn

Award won: 2nd Place, AHA Nationals

Base grain:	10 pounds Klages malt	**Yeast:**	Wyeast #2308
	4 pounds Munich malt	**Primary:**	2 months at 44 degrees Fahrenheit
Specialty grain:	2 pounds crystal malt	**Secondary:**	2 months at 65 degrees Fahrenheit
	6 ounces chocolate malt		
Bittering hops:	1 ounce Perle (60 mins.)		
	1.5 ounces Hallertauer (40 mins.)		
Finishing hops:	0.5 ounce Hallertauer (5 mins.)		

Typical/unusual procedures used: Mash at 149 degrees Fahrenheit for 2 hours.

Doppelbock (5-c)

Oddly enough, a religious order of Italian Monks invented Doppelbock. The Order of St. Francis of Paula, cloistered high in the Bavarian Alps, developed this distinctive brew to sustain themselves through periods of fasting. They named this higher alcohol double Bock *Salvator,* in honor of the Savior; thus, Paulaner Salvator was born. In reverence to the original, all subsequent German Doppelbocks are given names that end in *-ator.* Most American microbrewers continue the tradition of using the *-ator* suffix, making Doppelbocks easy to spot on a beer list or menu.

Flavor profile: Amber to dark brown. Slight fruitiness and esters are expected but no hop aroma. The malty sweetness of this beer is evident in the aroma and flavor and may be intense. Low bitterness, low hop flavor, and low diacetyl are okay. High alcohol flavor may be present. Very full body.

OG/FG:	1.072–1.096+ / 1.016–1.024+
ABV:	7.0–10.0+
IBUs:	16–26
SRM:	6–25

Commercial examples: Paulaner Salvator, Germany; Dock Street Illuminator, Pennsylvania

Beginner suggestions

Start with at least 9 pounds of pale or amber hopped extract and add additional color and complexity with specialty grain. Steep 2 pounds of 40-L crystal malt and 0.5 pound of chocolate malt and strain directly into the brewpot. Pitch a pure Lager yeast strain (preferably liquid) and ferment at cool temperatures for an extended period of time.

(Intermediate)
Brewer: Thomas Griffith

Doppelbock Two

Award won: 1st Place, AHA Nationals

Malt extract:	15 pounds Laaglander light DME	**Yeast:**	Wyeast #2206 (1 teaspoon yeast energizer)
Specialty grain:	8 ounces crystal malt	**Water treatment:**	0.5 teaspoon gypsum
	6 ounces chocolate malt	**Fining agent/ clarifier:**	1 teaspoon Irish moss
Bittering hops:	2 ounces Eroica (85 mins.)	**Primary:**	6 weeks at 48 degrees Fahrenheit
Flavoring hops:	1 ounce Tettnanger (10 mins.)	**Secondary:**	8 weeks at 58 degrees Fahrenheit
Finishing hops:	1 ounce Tettnanger (1 min.)		

(Advanced)
Brewer: Steve Dempsey

Scintillator

Award won: 1st Place, AHA Nationals

Malt extract:	3.3 BME Munich Gold	**Primary:**	1 day at 65 degrees Fahrenheit
	1 pound light DME	**Secondary:**	21 days at 47 degrees Fahrenheit
Base grain:	7 pounds Munich malt	**Tertiary:**	21 days at 38 degrees Fahrenheit
Specialty grain:	2 pounds 20-L crystal malt		
Bittering hops:	1.25 ounces Hallertauer (4.1 AAU)		
Flavoring hops:	1 ounce Tettnanger (3.8 AAU)		
Yeast:	Wyeast #2308		
Water treatment:	0.33 teaspoon gypsum		
	1.66 teaspoons calcium carbonate		
	0.33 teaspoon Epsom salt		
	0.5 teaspoon salt		

Typical/unusual procedures used: Mash at 156 degrees Fahrenheit for 2 hours.

Fun Label Ideas

"Come over to the dark side"

DARK VADER

American Dark Lager

Knoll Brewery,
Frankfort, IN

Gullywasher Lager

Cayton Family Brewery
Possum Trot, KY

Chapter 17

Mixed-Style Recipes

In This Chapter

▶ German Ale

▶ Wheat beer

▶ California Common beer

▶ Fruit and Vegetable beer

▶ Herb and Spice beer

▶ Christmas and Winter seasonal beer

▶ Smoked beer

▶ Wood-Aged beer

▶ Specialty beer

Mixed-style beers, or *hybrids*, are beers that cross the lines between conventional beer styles. These beers are fermented and aged with mixed traditions; one beer may be fermented with Ale yeast at cold temperatures, and another is fermented with Lager yeast at warm temperatures. Sometimes — depending on the whims of the brewer — they may be fermented either coolly or warmly as either Ales or Lagers.

This chapter provides beer recipes for the beer styles that don't fit neatly into the regular Ale and Lager categories. *Note:* I haven't included all of the hybrid beer styles and substyles listed on the AHA hierarchical list (on the Cheat Sheet) in this chapter. Because certain beer styles are very difficult to produce at the homebrewing level without highly advanced information, techniques, equipment, and ingredients, I decided to save you from them.

Cream Ale (6-a)

Cream Ale seems to be an American innovation. These beers are fermented at cold temperatures with either Ale yeasts or blends of Ale and Lager yeasts.

The idea behind Cream Ale is to produce a pale beer of medium gravity, ferment it with Ale yeasts, and age it cold like a Lager beer. Although the original Cream Ales were produced this way, some brewers ferment newer versions with Lager yeast or a mixture of Ale and Lager yeasts.

The cream part of the name has nothing to do with dairy products — presumably, the original brewers of Cream Ale wanted the name to suggest that this style has a creaminess about it. It doesn't.

Flavor profile: Very pale. Low fruitiness or esters are okay. Low hop flavor or aroma is also okay. Faintly sweet malt character offers a low to medium bitterness. Light-bodied and effervescent.

OG/FG:	1.042–1.055 / 1.006–1.012
ABV:	4.2–5.6
IBUs:	15–20
SRM:	2.5–5

Commercial examples: Genesee Cream Ale, New York; Little Kings Cream Ale, Ohio

Beginner suggestions

Start with a base of 5 pounds of the palest extract available and add 1 pound rice syrup directly to the brewpot. Add 1 ounce of aromatic hops with 15 minutes left in the boil. Pitch Ale yeast but keep the primary fermentation at less than 60 degrees Fahrenheit. I recommend another 2 to 3 weeks of aging at temperatures lower than 50 degrees Fahrenheit.

(Intermediate)
Brewer: Richard Schmit

Arlington Ale No. 33

Award won: 1st Place, AHA Nationals

Malt extract:	3.3 pounds John Bull light hopped extract	**Yeast:**	Wyeast #1056
	2 pounds light DME	**Misc. flavoring ingredients:**	1 teaspoon ascorbic acid
Specialty grain:	4 ounces toasted pale malt	**Fining agent/ clarifier:**	1 teaspoon Irish moss
	3 ounces crystal malt		
Flavoring hops:	0.25 ounce Cascade (10 mins.)	**Primary:**	8 days at 65 degrees Fahrenheit
	0.25 ounce Willamette (10 mins.)	**Secondary:**	2 days at 65 degrees Fahrenheit
Finishing hops:	0.25 ounce Cascade (2 mins.)		
	0.25 ounce Willamette (2 mins.)		

(Advanced)
Brewer: Rodney Howard

Colby's Cream Ale

Award won: 1st Place, AHA Nationals

Base grain:	8.5 pounds pale malt	**Finishing hops:**	1 ounce Fuggles (5 mins.)
Specialty grain:	0.5 pound Munich malt	**Dry hop:**	1 ounce Tettnanger
	0.5 pound flaked rice	**Yeast:**	Whitbread Lager (dry)
Bittering hops:	0.33 ounce Eroica (60 mins.)	**Primary:**	4 weeks at 70 degrees Fahrenheit
	0.33 ounce Eroica (45 mins.)	**Secondary:**	3 weeks at 45 degrees Fahrenheit
Flavoring hops:	0.33 ounce Galena (30 mins.)		
	0.33 ounce Galena (15 mins.)		

Typical/unusual procedures used: Mash at 156 degrees Fahrenheit for 45 minutes. After conversion, sparge with 172-degree Fahrenheit water.

Blonde Ale (6-6)

This somewhat-ambiguous style is widely popular at brewpubs (and not so much at packaging breweries) because it appeals to the many light-beer and non-beer drinkers who dine at these establishments. A *blonde* beer of any style is code for a light-colored, light-bodied beer, though blonde Ales can be — and often are — quite flavorful in spite of their lightness. No dumb blond jokes, please.

Flavor profile: Very pale. Low fruitiness or esters are okay. Low to medium hop flavor or aroma is also okay. Faintly sweet malt character offers a low to medium bitterness. Light-bodied and effervescent.

OG/FG:	1.038–1.054 / 1.008–1.013
ABV:	3.8–5.5
IBUs:	15–28
SRM:	3–6

Commercial examples: Redhook Blonde, Washington; Deschutes Cascade Golden, Oregon

Beginner suggestions

Start with a base of 5 to 6 pounds of the palest extract available (as an alternative, you can replace 1 pound of malt extract with 1 pound of rice syrup). Add 1 ounce of aromatic hops with 15 minutes left in the boil. Ferment with ale yeast — 1 week in the primary fermenter, 2 weeks in the secondary fermenter — and consider dry hopping with 1 ounce of American hops.

(Intermediate)
Brewer: Marty Nachel

Def, Dum, and Blonde

Malt extract:	5 pounds Northwestern light dry extract
Specialty grain:	1 pound 10-L crystal malt
Bittering hops:	1.5 ounces Hallertau (60 mins)
Flavoring hops:	0.5 ounce Hallertau (20 mins.)
Finishing hops:	0.5 ounce Cascade (10 mins.)
Yeast:	Wyeast #1056
Primary:	6 days at 60 degrees Fahrenheit
Secondary:	10 days at 60 degrees Fahrenheit

(Advanced)
Brewer: Joe Formanek

Little Cathy's Blonde Ale

Award won: 2nd Place, 2006 AHA Nationals

Base grain:	4 pounds Simpson's Maris Otter pale 2-row malt
	4 pounds Rahr's pale 2-row malt
Specialty grain:	1 pound Michigan Weyermann wheat malt
Bittering hops:	½ ounce Centennial (60 mins.)
	¼ ounce Centennial (30 mins.)
Flavoring hops:	¼ ounce Willamette (30 mins.)
Finishing hops:	¼ ounce Centennial (5 mins.)
	¼ ounce Willamette (5 mins.)
Yeast:	WLP002
Finings:	1 teaspoon Irish Moss (rehydrated) 15 minutes from end of boil
Primary:	5 days at 65 degrees Fahrenheit
Secondary:	7 days at 65 degrees Fahrenheit

Typical/unusual procedures used:
Perform a single infusion mash at 153 degrees Fahrenheit for 60 minutes. Boil for 75 minutes.

American Wheat (6-d)

American Wheat beers, although their ingredient profile may mirror the traditional German-style Weizen, generally contain a lower percentage of wheat malt (15 to 50 percent) and are typically fermented with a simple top-fermenting (Ale) yeast. American Wheat beers, therefore, lack the clovey phenolics, bubblegum, banana, and spicy flavors and aromatics of traditional German Weizenbiers.

Flavor profile: Golden to light amber. Low to medium fruitiness and esters; no phenolic character is evident. Malt and hop aroma and flavor are subdued; low to medium bitterness is expected. Low diacetyl is okay. Light- to medium-bodied.

OG/FG:	1.040–1.055 / 1.008–1.013
ABV:	4.0–5.5
IBUs:	15–30
SRM:	3–6

Commercial examples: Bell's Oberon Wheat, Michigan; Goose Island 312 Wheat Beer, Illinois

Beginner suggestions

Try using 5 to 6 pounds of unhopped wheat extract and add your own choice of German hops (Hallertauer, Tettnanger) to the boiling wort — 2 ounces should do it. Yeast is also an important characteristic of this style — try progressing to a liquid culture as soon as you're comfortable with the procedures required.

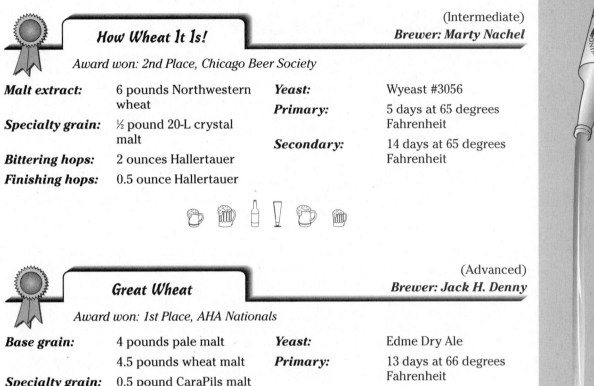

(Intermediate)
Brewer: Marty Nachel

How Wheat It Is!

Award won: 2nd Place, Chicago Beer Society

Malt extract:	6 pounds Northwestern wheat	**Yeast:**	Wyeast #3056
Specialty grain:	½ pound 20-L crystal malt	**Primary:**	5 days at 65 degrees Fahrenheit
Bittering hops:	2 ounces Hallertauer	**Secondary:**	14 days at 65 degrees Fahrenheit
Finishing hops:	0.5 ounce Hallertauer		

(Advanced)
Brewer: Jack H. Denny

Great Wheat

Award won: 1st Place, AHA Nationals

Base grain:	4 pounds pale malt	**Yeast:**	Edme Dry Ale
	4.5 pounds wheat malt	**Primary:**	13 days at 66 degrees Fahrenheit
Specialty grain:	0.5 pound CaraPils malt	**Secondary:**	(not given)
Bittering hops:	0.5 ounce Hallertauer (4.8 AAU) (60 mins.)		
	0.5 ounce Hallertauer (4.8 AAU) (40 mins.)		
Flavoring hops:	0.25 ounce Hallertauer (4.1 AAU) (20 mins.)		
Finishing hops:	0.25 ounce Hallertauer (4.1 AAU) (2 mins.)		

Note: When you're mashing malted wheat, I recommend adding a pound or two of rice hulls to the grist. Because wheat kernels are huskless, the mash can compact on itself and slow or stop the sparging and lautering procedures. Adding rice hulls helps keep the mash from compacting.

California Common Beer (7-b)

Steam beer, as it's known and marketed in the U.S., is a style that can consider itself one of the few indigenous American beers. Unfortunately, the brewery that revived the style and developed the modern recipe has also trademarked the Steam Beer name. By virtue of the fact that no other brewery produced a beer of that style in the latter part of this century, the Anchor Brewing Co. in San Francisco registered the Steam Beer designation as its own. Hence, the style itself is now known as *California Common beer.*

California Common beer has roots in British brewing traditions and, in fact, is still called Steam beer in the U.K. The Germans also developed a similar style called *Dampfbier* (literally translated as *Steam beer*). Here in the United States around the turn of the century, the style varied considerably from one brewery to the next and was also known as *swankey, small beer,* and *common.*

One of the most obviously identifiable features of Steam beer/California Common beer is its hybrid style. Whereas Ales use a top-fermenting yeast and ferment at warm temperatures, California Common beers ferment warm but use Lager yeasts designed for cold fermentation. Why the against-the-grain approach? Although artificial refrigeration wasn't in widespread use on the West Coast at the time this style was developed, the new German Lager yeast was both abundant and much less contaminated with the bacteria resident in Ale yeast cultures. Similarly, high hopping rates also helped combat spoilage and delay its unpleasant effects on the beer.

Today, precious few legitimate examples of this style are available to the consumer, although many other beers have similar profiles. All-malt amber Ales and Lagers that contain a percentage of caramel malt in the mash simulate this beer's palate. The hop bitterness you achieve by using the Northern Brewer variety of hop, along with a pungent American hop variety bouquet, also closely resembles the hop profile of this style.

Flavor profile: Light amber to copper. Medium-bodied. Has a toasted or caramel-like maltiness in aroma and flavor. Medium to high hop bitterness. Hop flavor is medium to high; hop aroma is medium. Fruitiness and esters are low. Low diacetyl is okay.

OG/FG:	1.048–1.054 / 1.011–1.014
ABV:	4.5–5.5
IBUs:	30–45
SRM:	10–14

Commercial examples: Anchor Steam, California; Old Dominion Victory Amber, Virginia

Beginner suggestions

You can easily replicate a good California Common beer by starting with 6 pounds of amber hopped extract and adding 1 ounce of Cascade hops at the end of the boil. Ferment with a Lager yeast at typical Ale temperatures (60 to 70 degrees Fahrenheit).

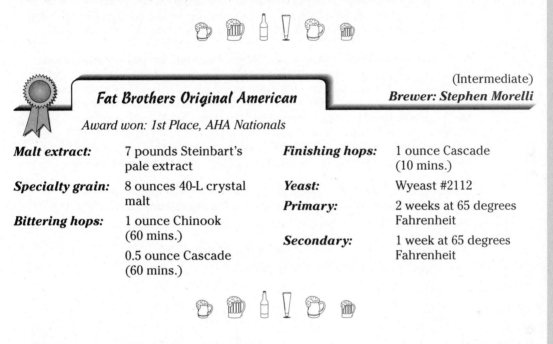

Fat Brothers Original American

(Intermediate)
Brewer: Stephen Morelli

Award won: 1st Place, AHA Nationals

Malt extract:	7 pounds Steinbart's pale extract	**Finishing hops:**	1 ounce Cascade (10 mins.)
Specialty grain:	8 ounces 40-L crystal malt	**Yeast:**	Wyeast #2112
Bittering hops:	1 ounce Chinook (60 mins.)	**Primary:**	2 weeks at 65 degrees Fahrenheit
	0.5 ounce Cascade (60 mins.)	**Secondary:**	1 week at 65 degrees Fahrenheit

Memphis Steamer

(Advanced)
Brewer: Phil Rahn

Award won: 1st Place, AHA Nationals

Base grain:	8.25 pounds Klages malt	**Dry hop:**	0.5 ounce Cascade
Specialty grain:	1.25 pounds crystal malt	**Yeast:**	Wyeast #2206
Bittering hops:	1.66 ounces Northern Brewer (60 mins.)	**Primary:**	12 days at 68 degrees Fahrenheit
	0.4 ounce Cascade (60 mins.)	**Secondary:**	10 days at 68 degrees Fahrenheit
Flavoring hops:	0.75 ounce Cascade (40 mins.)		
Finishing hops:	0.5 ounce Centennial (5 mins.)		

Typical/unusual procedures used: Mash the grains at 155 degrees Fahrenheit for 90 minutes.

Düsseldorfer-Style Altbier (7-c)

The concept of a German Ale has oxymoronic overtones. German brewers are generally recognized as the world leaders in the production of high-quality Lager beers, so imagining them creating original Ale styles may be difficult. Because neither single yeast-cell isolation nor artificial refrigeration was at anyone's disposal in the early days of brewing, brewers had to work with what they had: top-fermenting yeast strains. Thus, they created the German Ale.

One of these Ale styles is known as *Altbier.* The style is strongly associated with the city of Düsseldorf, although it also has lesser ties to Münster and Dortmund. The German word *alt,* contrary to popular belief, doesn't mean *ale* but rather *old,* a reference to Old World brewing styles. Modern-day Altbiers are fermented warm, as is common to Ale styles, but they're aged cold, as are Lagers. The Altbier profile is deep amber to dark brown in color. The hop blend is complex and can differ from one brewery to the next. German hop varieties are typically best, but American domestic varieties suffice.

Flavor profile: Medium to high maltiness. Medium to high bitterness. Very low in hop flavor with no hop aroma. Low fruitiness and esters. Light- to medium-bodied.

OG/FG:	1.046–1.054 / 1.010–1.015
ABV:	4.5–5.2
IBUs:	35–50
SRM:	13–17

Commercial examples: Pinkus Alt, Germany; Zum Uerige, Germany

Beginner suggestions

Start with 6 pounds of hopped European Lager extract. Steep 1 pound of 40-L crystal malt and add it to the brewpot. Pitch a traditional German Ale yeast (if at all possible), ferment below 60 degrees Fahrenheit, and age below 50 degrees Fahrenheit.

Alterior Motive

(Intermediate)
Brewer: Northwestern Extract Co.

Malt extract:	6.6 pounds Gold extract	**Yeast:**	Yeast Culture Kit # A-37
Specialty grain:	8 ounces 80-L crystal malt	**Primary:**	(not given); I recommend 1 week at 60 to 65 degrees Fahrenheit.
	3 ounces chocolate malt	**Secondary:**	(not given); I recommend 2 weeks at 40 to 50 degrees Fahrenheit.
Bittering hops:	1.5 ounces Saaz (60 mins.)		
Finishing hops:	0.5 ounce (15 mins.)		

League City Alt Part 3

(Advanced)
Brewers: Steve and Christina Daniel

Award won: 1st Place, AHA Nationals

Base grain:	8 pounds 2-row malt	**Primary:**	3 weeks at 50 degrees Fahrenheit
	2 pounds Munich malt	**Secondary:**	4 weeks at 32 degrees Fahrenheit
Specialty grain:	2 pounds crystal malt		
Bittering hops:	0.75 ounce Perle (90 mins.)		
Yeast:	Wyeast #2308		

Typical/unusual procedures used: Mash the grains for 1 hour at 152 degrees Fahrenheit.

Weizen/Weissbier (15-a)

Weizen beer is a spritzy Ale made by replacing some of the barley used in regular beers with a portion of wheat malt. These German-style Wheat beers have unique fruity and phenolic aromas and flavors that result from the specific strains of yeast you use to ferment them. German-style Wheat beers are alternatively known as *Weizenbier* or *Weissbier*. Of these two designations, *Weizen* (meaning wheat) is more correct than *Weiss* (which means white); these beers are typically a rich, golden color.

A traditional German Weizenbier must use at least 50 percent malted wheat, with the rest of the grist being malted barley. Weizenbier clones made elsewhere use anywhere between 25 and 75 percent wheat malt, depending on the whims of the brewer. Traditional Weizenbiers also have a dose of yeast added at bottling time for a secondary fermentation in the bottle. This state is called *Hefe-weizen* (yeast-wheat). Homebrewed Wheat beer, if bottle-conditioned (that is, primed with sugar), is automatically a Hefe-weizen. Commercially, filtered *kristalklar* (crystal-clear) Weizenbier is also widely available.

Flavor profile: Pale to golden. Very fruity and estery. Low hop flavor and aroma. Clove and banana aroma and flavor are evident; vanilla, nutmeg, smoke, and cinnamon-like phenolics are also acceptable. No diacetyl. Low bitterness levels accompany a mild sourness. Light- to medium-bodied and highly effervescent. This style may come packaged with or without yeast in the bottle (Hefe-weizen or *kristalklar*).

OG/FG:	1.044–1.052 / 1.010–1.014
ABV:	4.3–5.6
IBUs:	8–15
SRM:	2–8

Commercial examples: Schneider Weisse, Germany; Hacker-Pschorr Weisse, Germany

Beginner suggestions

You can easily make a wheat-flavored beer of sorts by using wheat malt extract. The traditional German-style Weizen, however, gets most of its character from the yeast. You can get the fruity, estery, clovey, spicy aromas and flavors typical of true Bavarian Weizenbier only by using true Weizen yeast strains (see the appendix for more information on yeast strains).

Two Year Wheat Beer

(Intermediate)
Brewer: Northwestern Extract Co.

Malt extract:	6.6 pounds Weizen extract	
Bittering hops:	1 ounce Hallertauer (30 mins.)	
Flavoring hops:	0.5 ounce Saaz (15 mins.)	
Finishing hops:	0.5 ounce Saaz (5 mins.)	
Yeast:	Wyeast #3068	

Fining agent/ clarifier: 0.5 teaspoon Irish moss

Primary: (not given) I recommend one week at 65 degrees Fahrenheit.

Secondary: (not given) I recommend two weeks at 50 to 60 degrees Fahrenheit.

Dry Ice 'n' Weizen

(Advanced)
Brewer: Dick Van Dyke

Award won: 1st Place, Kenosha Bidal Society

Base grain:	5 pounds wheat malt
	3 pounds 2-row ale malt
Specialty grain:	0.5 pound 10-L Munich malt
Bittering hops:	⅛ ounce Galena (12 AAU) (90 mins.)
	0.5 ounce Perle (8 AAU) (60 mins.)
	1 ounce Hallertauer (4.2 AAU) (60 mins.)
Finishing hops:	0.5 ounce Hallertauer (5 mins.)
Yeast:	Wyeast #3068

Fining agent/ clarifier: 1 teaspoon Irish moss at 10 minutes left in boil

Primary: 6 days at 60 degrees Fahrenheit

Secondary: 7 days at 60 degrees Fahrenheit

Note: When mashing malted wheat, I recommend adding a pound or two of rice hulls to the grist. Because wheat kernels are huskless, the mash often compacts on itself and slows or stops the sparging and lautering procedures. Adding rice hulls helps keep the mash from compacting.

Dunkelweizen (15-b)

As with other beer styles, you can find many variations on the wheat-beer theme. One such variation is Dunkelweizen. Meaning *dark wheat,* this style is to regular Weizen what Münchener Dunkel is to Münchener Helles (see Chapter 16). Plainly stated, this style is just a Weizen beer that's darkened and imbued with a mild chocolatey-caramelly flavor by the use of lightly roasted crystal or Munich malts.

Flavor profile: Deep copper to brown. Low hop flavor and aroma, although banana, cloves, and other phenolics may be present. Roasted malt and chocolate flavors are evident but no diacetyl. Medium-bodied.

OG/FG:	1.044–1.056 / 1.010–1.014
ABV:	4.3–5.6
IBUs:	10–18
SRM:	14–23

Commercial example: Hopf Dunkle Weisse, Germany; Franziskaner Dunkel Hefe weiss, Germany

Beginner suggestions

You can easily copy this beer style by starting with 5 to 6 pounds of wheat malt extract; add to that 0.5 pound of chocolate malt steeped and strained into the brewpot. Keep in mind that traditional German-style Weizenbier gets most of its character from the yeast. You can get the fruity, estery, clovey, spicy aromas and flavors typical of true Bavarian Weizenbier only by using true Weizen yeast strains (see the appendix for more on yeast strains).

Slam Dunkel

(Intermediate)
Brewer: Marty Nachel

Malt extract:	6 pounds Northwestern wheat extract	**Flavoring hops:**	0.5 ounce Hallertauer (30 mins.)
	1 pound light DME	**Finishing hops:**	0.5 ounce Hallertauer (5 mins.)
Specialty grain:	1 pound 20-L crystal malt	**Yeast:**	Wyeast #3068
	0.5 pound chocolate malt	**Primary:**	7 days at 60 degrees Fahrenheit
Bittering hops:	1.5 ounces Northern Brewer (60 mins.)	**Secondary:**	14 days at 60 degrees Fahrenheit

Dangerously Delicious Dunkel Weizen

(Advanced)
Brewer: Ray Daniels

Base grain:	4 pounds 6-row malt	**Primary:**	(not given)
	5 pounds wheat malt	**Secondary:**	(not given)
	2 pounds Munich malt		
Specialty grain:	0.25 pound chocolate malt		
Bittering hops:	1 ounce Hersbrucker (60 mins.)		
Flavoring hops:	0.5 ounce Hersbrucker (30 mins.)		
Yeast:	Wyeast #3068		
Water treatment:	1.5 teaspoons gypsum in mash		
	1.5 teaspoon gypsum in sparge water		

Typical/unusual procedures used:
Mash in at 130 degrees Fahrenheit; allow a 20-minute protein rest. Raise mash temperature to 152 degrees Fahrenheit; rest for 30 minutes. Raise temperature to 168 degrees Fahrenheit for mash out. Ferment at 65 degrees Fahrenheit.

Weizenbock (15-c)

Another variation on the Wheat beer theme is Weizenbock, which means *Wheat Bock*. This style is similar to the Bock beer style in terms of richness and alcohol content but owes much more to its Weizen origins. Made from a high percentage of wheat malt (as are all German-style Wheat beers), Weizenbock is also fermented with the traditional yeast strains that lend their telltale fruity and phenolic aromas and flavors to the beer.

Flavor profile: Amber to dark brown. Banana and clove are apparent; hop flavor and aroma are absent. Maltiness is high, bitterness is low, and no diacetyl is apparent. Dark versions have mild roast and chocolate flavors and aromas. Medium- to full-bodied.

OG/FG:	1.064–1.080+ / 1.015–1.022
ABV:	6.5–8.0+
IBUs:	15–30
SRM:	12–25

Commercial examples: Erdinger Pikantus, Germany; Schneider Aventinus, Germany

Beginner suggestions

Start with at least 8 pounds of wheat extract. Steep 0.75 pound of chocolate malt and strain into the brewpot. You can achieve the true banana-clove character of German Dunkelweizen only by using genuine liquid Weizen yeast strains.

Ein, Zwei, Drei Weizen

(Intermediate)
Brewer: Marty Nachel

Malt extract:	8 pounds Northwestern wheat malt	*Finishing hops:*	0.5 ounce Hallertauer (10 mins.)
Specialty grain:	1 pound Special "B" 221-L crystal malt	*Yeast:*	Wyeast #3068
Bittering hops:	2 ounces Hallertauer (60 mins.)	*Primary:*	8 days at 60 degrees Fahrenheit
Flavoring hops:	0.5 ounce Hallertauer (20 mins.)	*Secondary:*	14 days at 50 degrees Fahrenheit

Pale Moon Rizen Weizen

(Advanced)
Brewer: Paddy Giffen

Award won: 2nd Place, AHA Nationals

Malt extract:	3.5 pounds amber DME	*Yeast:*	Wyeast #3056
Base grain:	6 pounds wheat malt	*Primary:*	5 days at 65 degrees Fahrenheit
	3 pounds Klages malt	*Secondary:*	6 weeks at 50 degrees Fahrenheit
Specialty grain:	1.5 pounds 60-L crystal malt		
	1.5 pounds CaraPils malt		
Bittering hops:	0.5 ounce Perle (60 mins.)		
Flavoring hops:	1.25 ounce Saaz (30 mins.)		
Dry hop:	0.75 ounce Hallertauer		

Typical/unusual procedures used:
Perform a protein rest for 30 minutes at 120 degrees Fahrenheit. Raise the temperature to 152 degrees Fahrenheit for 30 minutes, then raise it to 157 degrees Fahrenheit for 30 minutes.

Fruit Beer (20)

As a beer-style category, Fruit beer is a relatively new creation, but European brewers have made beers with fruit in them for centuries. (Belgian-style Fruit Lambic is one such example.) Today, however, spurred by consumer interest, virtually every beer style known to man comes with a fruit variation.

Homebrewers wanting to emulate their favorite Fruit beer styles have the advantage of using fruit extracts and syrups rather than real fruit. These fruit flavors, easily found at well-stocked homebrew supply stores, run the gamut from cherry to blueberry to marionberry. (Hey, wasn't he the mayor of . . .?)

Flavor profile: Fruit beers often are made with an anything-goes approach. In light of this approach, I have no way to accurately describe what you may expect from one of these beers.

OG/FG:	refer to base style guidelines
ABV:	refer to base style guidelines
IBUs:	refer to base style guidelines
SRM:	refer to base style guidelines

Commercial examples: Pyramid Apricot Ale , Washington; New Glarus Belgian Red, Wisconsin.

Beginner suggestions

For Fruit beer, buy a high-quality fruit extract from your local homebrew shop and add to your base brew according to the package directions.

Cherry Ale

(Intermediate)
Brewer: David G. Hammaker

Award won: 1st Place, AHA Nationals

Malt extract:	6 pounds English pale extract	**Primary:**	2 weeks at 60 degrees Fahrenheit
Bittering hops:	0.5 ounce Bullion (45 mins.)	**Secondary:**	10 weeks at 60 degrees Fahrenheit
Finishing hops:	1 ounce Hallertauer (10 mins.)		
Yeast:	Red Star Ale (dry)		

Typical/unusual procedures used:
Pour the hot wort over the cherries in the fermenter; top off with cool water and add yeast.

Misc. flavoring ingredients: 10 pounds sweet cherries

Leftover Strawberry Ale

(Advanced)
Brewer: Dan Robison

Award won: 1st Place, AHA Nationals

Base grain:	7 pounds 2-row Klages malt	**Primary:**	7 days at 65 degrees Fahrenheit
Specialty grain:	1 pound dextrin malt	**Secondary:**	7 days at 65 degrees Fahrenheit
Bittering hops:	1.5 ounces Chinook (90 mins.)		
Finishing hops:	1 ounce Cascade (5 mins.)		
Yeast:	Wyeast #1056		

Typical/unusual procedures used: Mash the grains at 158 degrees Fahrenheit for 90 minutes. Add the frozen strawberries to the wort in the fermenter.

Misc. flavoring ingredients: 9 pounds frozen strawberries

Herb, Spice, and Vegetable Beer (21-a)

Although you don't see many Herb and Spice beers on your local beer retailers' shelves, a few do exist. If homebrewers had their say, many more would be available. The Herb-and-Spice-beer category is one of the more popular among homebrewers because it presents an almost unlimited number of choices.

Herbs and Spice beers may include lemon grass, ginger (what — you've never heard of ginger ale?), cumin, allspice, caraway, mace, pepper, cinnamon, nutmeg, and clove, among myriad others. Some *sage* advice: Take the *thyme* to peruse the spice section of your local supermarket — a *mint*-condition spiced brew may *curry* favor with the beer judges.

Vegetables in beer, on the other hand, are very few and far between — and, to my knowledge, no such thing as a vegetable extract is made for brewing — so you're pretty much limited to pumpkin and hot peppers here.

Flavor profile: Herb, Spice, and Vegetable beers are often made with an anything-goes approach. In light of this practice, I have no way to accurately describe what you may expect from one of these beers.

OG/FG:	refer to base style guidelines
ABV:	refer to base style guidelines
IBUs:	refer to base style guidelines
SRM:	refer to base style guidelines

Commercial examples: Left Hand JuJu Ginger, Colorado; Fraoch Heather Ale, Scotland

Beginner suggestions

Here's an opportunity to go a little crazy. Pick a favorite herb or spice and either add it to your beer in the brewpot (in the last 20 minutes of the boil) or during the fermentation and aging phase. *Hint:* Too little is better than too much; you can always add more to the next batch you make. Add your veggies in the secondary fermenter for best results.

Wassail While You Work

(Intermediate)
Brewer: Marty Nachel

Award won: 1st Place, Dukes of Ale Spring Thing

Malt extract:	10 pounds North-western light	**Dry hop:**	1 ounce Cascade
Specialty grain:	1 pound 40-L crystal malt	**Yeast:**	Pasteur Champagne (dry)
Bittering hops:	2 ounces Mount Hood (60 mins.)	**Misc. flavoring ingredients:**	2 sticks of cinnamon, 1 teaspoon of cloves
Flavoring hops:	1 ounce Northern Brewer (30 mins.)	**Primary:**	11 days at 60 degrees Fahrenheit
Finishing hops:	1 ounce Cascade (5 mins.)	**Secondary:**	25 days at 60 degrees Fahrenheit

Herb Alpert

(Advanced)
Brewer: Ron Page

Award won: 2nd Place, AHA Nationals

Base grain:	13.6 pounds Pilsener malt	**Misc. flavoring ingredients:**	11 chamomile tea bags, 60 dried marigold blossoms
	0.5 pound Munich malt		
Specialty grain:	0.5 pound chocolate malt	**Primary:**	1 week at 50 degrees Fahrenheit
Bittering hops:	0.5 ounce Tettnanger	**Secondary:**	3 weeks at 40 degrees Fahrenheit
Finishing hops:	0.75 ounce Mount Hood		
Yeast:	Wyeast #2206		

Typical/unusual procedures used: Add the tea bags and marigold blossoms to the fermenter with the wort.

Christmas/Winter/Specialty Spiced Beer (21-b)

Throughout history, drinkers have enjoyed beers of a somewhat higher alcohol content and richness during the winter holidays, when friends and neighbors get together to enjoy the season. Many breweries produce unique seasonal offerings that may be darker, stronger, spiced, or otherwise fuller in character than their normal beers. Spiced versions are an American and Belgian tradition, because English and German breweries traditionally don't use spices in their beers. Overall balance is the key to presenting a well-made Christmas beer; the special ingredients should complement the base beer and not overwhelm it.

Flavor profile: These winter seasonal brews are often made with an anything-goes approach. In light of this practice, I have no way to accurately describe what one may expect from one of these beers.

OG/FG:	refer to base style guidelines
ABV:	refer to base style guidelines
IBUs:	refer to base style guidelines
SRM:	refer to base style guidelines

Commercial examples: Anchor Our Special Ale, California; Harpoon Winter Warmer, Massachusetts

Beginner suggestions

Yule Ales and Winter Warmers are made to toast the holidays and the winter season. Warm spice flavors and elevated alcohol levels are pretty effective at putting a flush in your cheeks. Start with at least 7 pounds of pale malt extract and then add whatever adjunct grains or flavorings evoke the holiday spirit for you.

Anne's Choice Christmas Ale

(Intermediate)
Brewer: Philip Fleming

Award won: 1st Place, AHA Nationals

Malt extract: 3.5 pounds Munton & Fison stout kit

3.3 pounds Munton & Fison amber extract

3 pounds Munton & Fison amber DME

Bittering hops: 0.5 ounce Hallertauer (55 mins.)

Finishing hops: 0.5 ounce Hallertauer (5 mins.)

Yeast: Wyeast #1007

Misc. fermentable ingredients: 0.75 pound honey

Misc. flavoring ingredients: five 3-inch cinnamon sticks

2 teaspoons allspice

1 teaspoon cloves

6 ounces grated gingerroot

6 medium oranges — rinds only

Primary: 14 days at 60 degrees Fahrenheit

Secondary: (not given)

Typical/unusual procedures used: Simmer all the flavoring ingredients in the honey for 45 minutes; strain into the brewpot.

Chocolate Chambord Stout

(Advanced)
Brewer: Ron Page

Award won: 1st Place, AHA Nationals

Base grain: 7.5 pounds pale malt

1.5 pounds wheat malt

0.5 pound flaked barley

Specialty grain: 0.5 pound crystal malt

0.5 pound chocolate malt

Bittering hops: 1 ounce Cascade (60 mins.)

1 ounce Perle (60 mins.)

Yeast: (not given)

Misc. flavoring ingredients: 0.25 cup Hershey's cocoa powder

Chambord liqueur (see following instructions)

Primary: 3 weeks at 65 degrees Fahrenheit

Secondary: 6 weeks at 35 degrees Fahrenheit

Typical/unusual procedures used: Mash the grains at 152 degrees Fahrenheit for 1 hour. Add Hershey's cocoa powder to the wort and boil for 30 minutes. Add 1 tablespoon of Chambord liqueur to each bottle at bottling in place of priming sugar.

Smoked Beer (22-b)

The Franconian city of Bamberg, Germany, is famous for its *Bamberger Rauchbier* (Bamberg Smoke beer). This style, although very popular in northern Bavaria, is rarely produced elsewhere in the world. Many beers are said to be acquired tastes, but Rauchbier takes that description to a whole new level.

A beer gets its smoked character as a brewer kilns his malt over a wood fire (typically beechwood, but sometimes alder, apple, or cherry) or peat fire. The grain retains this smokiness and imparts this quality in the beer as it's mashed. How smoky the resulting beer is depends on how long you leave the malt to smoke and how much of the grain bill consists of smoked malt. The smoked character of the beer varies from one brewer to the next but is often assertive and always noticeable.

But the use of smoked grains isn't limited to making Rauchbier. You can imbue any existing beer style with smoke aroma and flavor just by adding smoked malt to the recipe. The trick to making a good smoked beer, however, is achieving the perfect balance between the malt and the smoke. Porter is one style that seems to be a particularly good host for smoke character. Just remember to sip the beer and not inhale it.

Flavor profile: Dark amber to dark brown. The intensity of the smoke character may be medium to high. You should notice a balance between smokiness and the expected flavor characteristics of the base beer style. Smoky flavors may range from woody to somewhat bacon-like depending on the type of malts used. Peat-smoked malt can add an earthiness. The balance of underlying beer characteristics and smoke can vary, although the resulting blend should be somewhat balanced and enjoyable. Smoke can add some dryness to the finish.

OG/FG:	refer to base beer style guidelines
ABV:	refer to base beer style guidelines
IBUs:	refer to base beer style guidelines
SRM:	refer to base beer style guidelines

Commercial examples: Aecht Schlenkerla, Germany; Alaskan Smoked Porter, Alaska

Beginner suggestions

The quickest and easiest way to add smoke character to your beer is to use a high-quality liquid smoke extract sold at most well-stocked grocery stores. The biggest drawback to using smoke extract, however, is that the most common smoke flavor is hickory. That's why it's advisable to buy traditional smoked malts from a homebrew ingredient supplier. One to three pounds steeped in a 5-gallon batch should do the trick.

Smokey the Beer (Smoked Porter)

(Intermediate)
Brewer: Marty Nachel

Malt extract:	6 pounds Northwestern dark extract
Specialty grain:	1 pound 40-L crystal malt
	0.75 pound chocolate malt
Bittering hops:	2 ounces Northern Brewer (60 mins.)
Flavoring hops:	1 ounce Fuggles (15 mins.)

Yeast:	Wyeast #1028
Misc. flavoring ingredients:	1 ounce Wright's liquid smoke
Primary:	6 days at 65 degrees Fahrenheit
Secondary:	10 days at 65 degrees Fahrenheit

Beech Beer (Rauchbier)

(Advanced)
Brewer: James Cannon

Award won: 1st Place, AHA Nationals

Base grain:	4 4.5 pounds Klages malt
	2.5 pounds smoked Klages malt
	2.25 pounds Munich malt
	1 pound Vienna malt
Specialty grain:	0.5 pound 40-L crystal malt
Bittering hops:	1 ounce Hallertauer (105 mins.)
Flavoring hops:	0.5 ounce Hallertauer (15 mins.)
Finishing hops:	0.25 ounce Hallertauer (2 mins.)
Dry hop:	0.25 ounce Saaz

Yeast:	Wyeast #2206
Primary:	28 days at 50 degrees Fahrenheit
Secondary:	28 days at 35 degrees Fahrenheit

Typical/unusual procedures used: Mash the grains at 105 degrees Fahrenheit for 20 minutes. Perform the first decoction to 125 degrees Fahrenheit for 10 minutes and the second decoction to 149 degrees Fahrenheit. Cool to 144 degrees Fahrenheit over a 30-minute period. Raise the temperature to 154 degrees Fahrenheit for 30 minutes; raise it again to 168 degrees Fahrenheit. Sparge with 168-degree Fahrenheit water.

Wood-Aged Beer (22-c)

Aging beer in wooden barrels is a traditional production method rarely used by major breweries these days, and even then usually only with specialty products. The trend is becoming more popular with modern American craft breweries looking to produce new and distinctive products. The beer is often aged in wooden casks or barrels (traditionally oaken, although other woods can be suitable) often previously used to store whisky, bourbon, port, sherry, Madeira, or wine, but you can also achieve the same effect by using wood-based additives (wood chips, wood staves, oak essence). Fuller-bodied, higher-gravity base styles are popular candidates for barrel aging because they can best stand up to the additional flavors.

Flavor profile: This varies with the base style of beer. Wood usually contributes a woody, cedary, or oaky flavor. Other flavors that may optionally be present include vanilla (from vanillin in the wood); caramel, butterscotch, toasted bread, or almonds (from toasted wood); coffee, chocolate, and cocoa (from charred wood or bourbon casks); and alcohol flavors from other products previously stored in the wood (if any). Watch for drunken termites.

OG/FG:	refer to base beer style guidelines
ABV:	refer to base beer style guidelines
IBUs:	refer to base beer style guidelines
SRM:	refer to base beer style guidelines

Commercial examples: Goose Island Bourbon County Stout, Illinois; MacTarnahan's Oak-Aged IPA, Washington.

Beginner suggestions

The quickest and easiest way to add wood character to your beer is to add liquid oak essence to your brew. Otherwise, you can add wood chips directly to your primary or secondary fermenter while your beer is fermenting or aging. Oak is the standard wood character in beer because it emulates the character found in barrel-aged wine and whisky.

Early Times Old Ale

(Intermediate)
Brewer: Marty Nachel

Awards Won: 1st Place, Chicago Beer Society 2005 Spooky Brew

Malt extract: 12 pounds Northwestern Gold extract

Specialty grain: 2 pounds 40-L crystal malt

1 pound biscuit malt

0.5 pound chocolate malt

1 pound flaked oats

Bittering hops: 2 ounces Northern Brewer (60 mins.)

Flavoring hops: 1 ounce Fuggles (15 mins.)

Yeast: Wyeast #1028

Misc. flavoring ingredients: 6 ounces toasted oak chips steeped in Kentucky whisky for 2 weeks

1 cup oak-steeped whisky

Primary: 10 days at 65 degrees Fahrenheit

Secondary: 1 month at 65 degrees Fahrenheit

Typical/unusual procedures used: Add steeped oak chips to the secondary fermenter, and allow to age for 1 month. Blend in 1 cup oak-steeped whisky at bottling.

Wood Bomb (wood-aged IPA)

(Advanced)
Brewer: Mark Merisco

Award won: 1st Place, AHA Nationals

Base grain: 12 pounds Maris Otter pale malt

Specialty grain: ½ pound 20-L crystal malt

Bittering hops: ¼ ounce Chinook (first wort hopped)

¼ ounce Chinook (60 mins.)

Flavoring hops: ½ ounce Centennial (30 mins.)

½ ounce Cascade (30 mins.)

½ ounce Cascade (20 mins.)

Finishing hops: ½ ounce Centennial (10 mins.)

¼ ounce Chinook (5 mins.)

Misc. flavoring ingredients: 3 ounces American oak chips

Yeast: Wyeast #1056

Primary: (not given)

Secondary: (not given)

Typical/unusual procedures used: Mash for 1 hour at 150 degrees Fahrenheit; boil for 90 minutes. Add American oak chips to the secondary fermenter; let age for 1 month.

Specialty Beer (23)

This category is the one that runs all over the map. Small brewers love to create Specialty beers because the process involves so much freedom. Where beer making is considered both an art and a science, Specialty beers definitely fall on the side of artistry. Although you must brew the vast majority of the other beers I've profiled within tight constraints, Specialty beers have virtually no parameters and few rules to follow.

You may as well call the Specialty-beer category the kitchen-sink category, because everything but seems to go into these beers. You name it — fruit, herbs, spices, unusual sugars, odd flavorings, and nontraditional grains all contribute unique flavors to these offerings. Unusual sugars you can find in maple sap, molasses, treacle, brown sugar, sorghum, and honey. Brewer's licorice and brewer's chocolate make for odd flavorings in beer, and nontraditional grains may include oatmeal and rye. (Sounds like a breakfast of the gods to me.)

Beers in the Specialty category can be made with unusual techniques (superheated stones in the brewkettle) or unusual adjuncts (sorghum, buckwheat), they can be regional (stronger, hoppier) interpretations of traditional styles, or they can be historical/indigenous beers (Sahti, Colonial spruce or molasses beers, Kvass). One thing Specialty beers can't be is out-of-style because this category has no style guidelines. Isn't that special?

Flavor profile: Specialty beers are often made with an anything-goes approach. In light of this approach, I have no way to accurately describe what you may expect from one of these beers.

OG/FG:	refer to base style guidelines
ABV:	refer to base style guidelines
IBUs:	refer to base style guidelines
SRM:	refer to base style guidelines

Commercial examples: Fraoch Heather Ale, Scotland; Rauchenfels Steinbiere: Germany

Beginner suggestions

Go crazy! You have no restrictions whatsoever on you in this category. The only parameter for Specialty beers is that they be drinkable!

Yule Brimmer

(Intermediate)
Brewer: Marty Nachel

Award won: 1st Place, B.O.S.S. 2005 Chicago Cup Challenge

Malt extract:	9 pounds Northwestern Gold	**Primary:**	8 days at 60 degrees Fahrenheit
Specialty grain:	2 pounds 40-L crystal malt	**Secondary:**	14 days at 60 degrees Fahrenheit

Misc. fermentable ingredients: 1 cup brown sugar

Bittering hops: 2 ounces Hallertau (60 mins.)

Yeast: Wyeast #1388

Misc. flavoring ingredients: 1 ounce dried gingerroot, 1 ounce dried orange peel

6 ounces oak chips

Typical/unusual procedures used:
Boil ½ ounce each gingerroot and orange peel in the brewpot; add the remaining gingerroot and orange peel to the beer in the secondary fermenter. Add the oak chips to the secondary fermenter as well.

Killer Winter Storm Candy Imperial Porter

(Advanced)
Brewer: Steve Kamp

Award won: 2nd Place, B.O.S.S. 2006 Chicago Cup Challenge

Base grain: 12 pounds American 2-row pale malt

2¼ pounds German Pilsner malt

Specialty grain: ¼ pound Belgian black malt

1 pound American 40-L crystal malt

½ pound American black patent malt

Misc. fermentable ingredients: ¾ pound dark molasses

1.5 pounds sucrose (see unusual procedures below)

Bittering hops: 2 ounces Hallertau Hersbrucker (60 mins.)

1 ounce Northern Brewer (60 mins.)

Yeast: Red Star Pasteur Champagne (dry)

Misc. flavoring ingredients: 8.5 ounces of anise squares, 7 ounces of cinnamon candies, 6.5 ounces of horehound drops, 7 ounces of licorice

Primary: (not given)

Secondary: (not given)

Typical/unusual procedures used:
Dissolve all candy in 1 gallon of water and add to the brewpot.

Fun Label Ideas

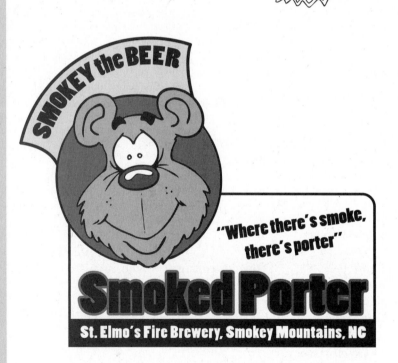

Part V
Alternative Brewing

The 5th Wave
By Rich Tennant

"It's been like this ever since he started making his own Mead."

In this part . . .

I've included two chapters on making alternative beverages using the same equipment you'd use to brew beer: Mead and Cider. Chapter 20 covers the organic movement in the homebrewing sector and the opportunities to become a green brewer.

Although all of that is about options and personal choice, Chapter 21 deals with making a beverage that addresses important dietary restrictions; gluten-free brewing is for those who have no options or choice.

Chapter 18

In-Cider Information

In This Chapter

▶ Deciding on Cider

▶ Cider-making recipes

The art of homebrewing generally denotes brewing beer in one's home. However, this definition doesn't necessarily exclude the options to make other somewhat-similar fermented beverages such as Cider. It's probably safe to say most homebrewers never try their hand at making a Cider, but they already have all the equipment they need, so why not present the information in case the occasion should arise? Well, here it is. . .

Exploring the Cider Option

Once the most popular beverage in America, Hard Cider is making a comeback of sorts, hot on the heels of the microbrewing revolution. In fact, some suggest that Cider is now where craft brews were about 20 years ago and continues to grow in interest.

Hard Cider, for the uninitiated, is a fermented beverage made from the juice of apples. (Regular, or *soft,* Cider is unfermented and therefore contains no alcohol.) Hard Cider is predominantly a British drink, although its traditions in the U.S. run deep. Its production may include optional ingredients such as white and brown sugars and various other fruits and spices, depending on the producer and the style.

Because of its combined acid and alcohol content, Cider also has a shelf life that far exceeds that of beer.

Cider-bar

The word *Cider* appears to be a derivation of the Hebrew *shekar*, which means "strong drink." The recorded history of Cider dates back to the first-century B.C. Roman soldiers under Julius Caesar, who discovered this drink while marching across the Kentish countryside in southern Britain and brought it back with them to Rome (introducing it to the rest of western Europe along the way). Following the Norman conquest of England in 1066, the consumption of Cider increased immeasurably. (Being from the north of France, the Normans had no trouble appreciating this Champagne-like beverage.) Under King Henry VIII, England made deliberate attempts to develop apple orchards for Cider-making purposes. Cider production peaked in the 1700s, only to lose ground due to the results of increased taxation of Cider in the 1800s.

In the United States, Cider was the beverage of choice among the white Anglo-Saxon Protestants who settled the original colonies, but its popularity diminished in the mid-1800s, following the arrival of millions of German and Eastern European immigrants whose preferred drink was beer. Cider lost out again to the non-alcoholic soft drinks introduced to the American populace at the turn of the century.

Comparing apples to apples

The Cider-making industry uses a wide variety of apples. At their most basic level, apples fall roughly into two categories: *bittersweet* and *culinary*. Most of us are familiar with the culinary varieties, such as Granny Smith, Jonathan, Macintosh, and Golden Delicious, but few of us know of the wide variety of bittersweet apples that go by monikers such as Northern Spy, Kingston Black, Golden Russet, and Newton Pippen. The culinary varieties are the ones cooks use in apple pies or applesauce or that you just eat plain. The bittersweet apple varieties tend to have thicker skins and elevated tannin levels (which contribute the bitterness) and higher acid contents that make them less desirable for common consumption.

The natural sugars you find in apples are mostly mono- and disaccharides, which are both highly fermentable. The breakdown is approximately 75 percent fructose, 15 percent sucrose, and 10 percent glucose.

Most brand-name Ciders are blends of the juices of different apple varieties, which creates a wider spectrum of flavors. This blending also allows the Cider producer to exercise more control over the Cider flavor — especially if one or more of the apple crops experiences a bad growing season. And blending also results in a greater consistency in the finished product. The largest Cider maker in the world (Bulmer, in England) uses 15 varieties of apples to produce the various brands it markets.

The key to making a good and enjoyable Cider is to find the correct balance between the apple character (sweetness and flavor) and the natural acidity found in Cider. Many people find the puckery tang of Cider a little too assertive. If you count yourself among them, try adding a can of frozen apple concentrate to the mix to intensify the apple flavor, or add honey or juices of other flavorful fruits to cut through the acid levels in your Cider.

Some Cider makers even blend in a small percentage of pear juice, which is less acidic, thus reducing some of the cidery bite. A Cider made from a majority of pear juice is rightly called a *Perry*.

The quality of your Cider depends greatly on your source of fermentable material — in this case, apples or apple juice. Because apple pressing is rather long and laborious, you could say it's best left to the hard-core Cider makers; the juice route is more appealing to homebrewers.

Sorting cider styles

The antiquated *Anglo* style of Cider, which originated in Britain, is generally more tannic and Ale-like because of the Cider makers' use of Ale yeasts and bittersweet apples. (The greater use of bittersweet apples is what sets English Ciders apart from North American Ciders.) The Anglo style is also more costly because it requires longer fermentations. The newer Continental style, popular in the United States, is generally sweeter and more like sparkling wine.

And speaking of sparkling wine, you can render Ciders and Perries with various levels of carbonation from *still* (uncarbonated) to *sparkling* (highly carbonated). The level of mild carbonation in between still and sparkling is called *petillant,* which isn't to be confused with petulant (or flatulent, for that matter!)

According to competition guidelines set by the American Homebrewers Association, you can produce Cider in any of the following styles:

✔ Standard Cider and Perry (Category 27)

- *Common Cider* (27-a) is made from culinary/table apples, with wild or crab apples often used for acidity/tannin balance.

- *English Cider* (27-b) is made with bittersweet and bitter-sharp apple varieties cultivated specifically for cider making.

- *French Cider* (27-c) is made with bittersweet and bitter-sharp apple varieties cultivated specifically for cider making. Note that traditional French procedures use small amounts of salt and calcium compounds (calcium chloride, calcium carbonate) to aid the process of pectin coagulation. You must use these additives sparingly, however, unless you want your cider to taste salty.

The main difference between English and French ciders is that the French use a slow or *arrested* fermentation, which leaves more apple flavor and sweetness. Some French cider makers even add apple juice after fermentation for a richer, sweeter apple flavor.

- *Common Perry* (27-d) is made from culinary/table fruit (pears and apples).

- *Traditional Perry* (27-e) is made from pears grown specifically for that purpose instead of for eating or cooking. (Many *perry pears* are nearly inedible.)

✔ Specialty Cider and Perry (Category 28)

- *New England Cider* (28-a) is a cider made with characteristic New England apples for relatively high acidity, with adjuncts such as white or brown sugars or molasses to raise alcohol levels.

- *Fruit Cider* (28-b) is made with other fruits or fruit juices added (for example, blueberry). Note that a cider made from a combination of mostly apple juice and a little pear juice would be entered in this category because it's neither a standard cider nor a perry.

- *Apple Wine* (28-c) is simply a cider with a substantial amount of added sugar to achieve a higher alcohol content than a common cider.

- *Other Specialty Cider and Perry* (28-d) is an open-ended category for cider or perry with other adjuncts such that it doesn't fit any of the categories above. This includes the use of spices and/or other sweeteners.

Even though these style descriptions mention actual fruit, you can easily substitute high-quality natural fruit juice.

Ciders of any style may also range from sweet to dry, depending on the types of apples you use, as well as the yeast strain you use to ferment the juice. Furthermore, you may also serve Cider *draft style,* which is pasteurized and filtered, or in the more natural *farmhouse style,* which is traditionally served unfiltered from a cask.

If you're looking for a few commercial Ciders for comparison tasting, try the three most popular brands in the U.S.: Woodchuck, Seven Sisters Wild Horse, and Cider Jack. Two lesser-known brands, Ace and Hornsby's, come out of California. The leading non-U.S. brands include Woodpecker, Strongbow, and Blackthorn, all from the U.K.

Making Cider

Although the various Cider style categories open to homebrewers at competitions are evidence of its acceptance and appeal, Cider making is still catching on with homebrewers. This may be because Cider's tart taste isn't to everyone's liking, but it may just be that many homebrewers are unaware of how easy Cider is to make. Technically, only one ingredient is necessary to make Cider: apples (or apple juice)! No water, no yeast — just the forbidden fruit.

Okay, I'm misleading you just a bit. Apples (and freshly squeezed apple juices), like grapes, *do* come complete with their own resident wild yeasts, but for better control over the Cider-making process, I recommend you destroy these uninvited apple yeasts by heating the juice to at least 180 degrees Fahrenheit, and then choose and add the proper yeasts. As far as water goes, apple juice naturally contains a high percentage of water and therefore doesn't require dilution.

Before you embark on your Cider-making journey, be sure to check out the secondary fermentation procedures in Chapter 11. Cider making is very similar to beginner extract brewing (see Chapter 10) except for the secondary fermentation process.

Because the amount of apple juice you buy represents the finished batch size (remember, you're not diluting), you must heat all of your apple juice. This restriction means you either have to get a brewpot that can hold 5 gallons of liquid, or you have to heat your apple juice a couple gallons at a time until it's all heated. I don't recommend reducing your batch size because a lot of damaging airspace may be left in your primary and secondary fermenters that can cause oxidation problems later. The easy answer to this dilemma, if you choose to pursue small-batch brewing, is to simply buy smaller fermenters and carboys.

The first place to shop for apple juice is at your local grocer. Most large grocery stores carry at least a few different brands of apple juice and Cider. But brand names aren't as important as product contents. Juice that's sugar-free and preservative-free is best.

Some serious Cider makers prefer to buy their apple juice fresh from the local farmers' market or at roadside stands. This practice is fine, but keep in mind that this juice (which often comes as soft Cider) isn't pasteurized, and you need to stabilize it before you pitch yeast into it. You also need to use such juice quickly because unpasteurized and preservative-free apple juice soon begins fermenting on its own! I don't recommend boiling unfiltered apple juice; the easiest way to stop wild and unintentional fermentations is to mix sulfur dioxide in the juice, which you can do simply by adding one crushed Campden tablet to the *must* (unfermented liquid). Winemakers use Campden tablets regularly, and most homebrew supply shops stock them.

If you boil unfiltered apple juice, a semipermanent haze forms in the liquid. *Fruit pectin* causes this discoloration, and after it sets (or *gels*), the only way to remove it is by filtration. (It doesn't affect the taste, however, and is hardly worth the effort of filtering out.)

You can greatly enhance Cider (like some beer styles) with the addition of fruits or fruit flavors, some spices, or even some other fermentable sugars such as honey or brown sugar. Cider also benefits from long periods of aging (anywhere from a couple of months to several months), so adding some more complex flavorings to your Cider is no big deal. You can add some of these directly to the brewpot, and you should add some to the secondary fermenter (see Chapter 8 for flavoring ideas and procedures).

Cider Considerations: Recipes

With the following Cider recipes, you can produce an interesting libation appropriate for special occasions, competition, or just for sipping with friends. An added bonus is that you don't have to buy any extra equipment — your beer-brewing equipment is all you need.

Although making Cider is no more difficult than is brewing an extract beer, you should be familiar with secondary fermentation procedures before attempting these recipes (see Chapter 11). Because of this relative ease of brewing, I haven't broken these recipes out into beginner, intermediate, and advanced levels.

Common Cider (27-a)

You make *Common Cider* without the addition of adjunct sugars or flavorings. In England, where the Cider tradition began, Ale yeasts are preferable over Champagne or other types; this use results in fruitier Ciders with more residual sweetness. Traditional Ciders should be light-bodied with a crisp apple flavor.

Rotten to the Corps

(Intermediate)
Brewer: Denny Lake

Apple Juice:	5 gallons (preservative-free)	**Primary:**	8 days at 65 degrees Fahrenheit
Yeast:	Nottingham dry Ale yeast	**Secondary:**	21 days at 65 degrees Fahrenheit
Nutrient:	2 ounces yeast nutrient		

Typical/unusual procedures used: Add priming sugar only at bottling for sparkling Cider.

New England-Style Cider (28-a)

New England-Style Cider is a very natural style, so spontaneous wild yeast fermentations are okay. Because of the addition of white and brown sugars, New England-Style Cider also sports elevated alcohol levels (8 to 14 percent). Medium- to full-bodied, New England-Style Cider offers a pronounced apple aroma and flavor, ending with a throat-warming finish.

Pride and Jay

(Advanced)
Brewer: Jay Lubinsky

Apple Juice:	5 gallons (unpasteurized, preservative-free)	**Primary:**	10 days at 65 degrees Fahrenheit
Yeast:	none added (spontaneously fermented)	**Secondary:**	14 days at 65 degrees Fahrenheit
Misc. fermentable ingredients:	5 cups granulated white cane sugar		
	0.5 cup dark-brown sugar		
Flavoring ingredients:	1.5 teaspoons grape tannin		
	10 ounces raisins		
	6 ounces oak chips		

Typical/unusual procedures used:
Use apple juice immediately. Boil and cool 5 cups of white sugar with 5 cups of apple juice. Add sugar, juice, and tannin to rest of juice. Let ferment naturally. After fermentation subsides, add the raisins and let sit about 10 days or until fermentation subsides again. Transfer to the secondary fermenter. Boil the oak chips in a little water for 10 minutes; add to the Cider. Let sit for a week or two, depending on desired oakiness. Bottle and age for 3 months.

Specialty Cider (28-d)

As in the Specialty Beer category, *Specialty Ciders* run all over the map — you may use any and all adjuncts and yeast (and you often do). At least 75 percent of the fermentable material should consist of apple juice.

Big Apple Punch

(Advanced)
Brewer: Philip Curcio

Apple Juice: 4.5 gallons

Yeast: Pasteur Dry Champagne

Misc. fermentable ingredient: 1 pound light honey

Flavoring ingredient: 1 750-ml bottle of raspberry liqueur

Primary: 14 days at 65 degrees Fahrenheit

Secondary: 30 days at 65 degrees Fahrenheit

Typical/unusual procedures used: Heat the apple juice and honey together and cool; pitch the yeast. Add the raspberry liqueur to the secondary fermenter while racking the Cider to the carboy.

Chapter 19

A Meading of the Minds

In This Chapter

▶ Appreciating Mead

▶ Mead-making recipes

Although the product of homebrewing is usually beer, you can apply the same equipment and techniques to other tasty purposes as well — specifically, making Mead. Many homebrewers never take a shot at making a Mead, but in this chapter I give you the lowdown on Mead and its origins, as well as some recipes, in case you ever get the Mead wanderlust.

Mulling Over the Mead Option

Mead is a simple fermented beverage made from honey and water; it's also one of the more natural and uncomplicated beverages known to man. Despite its simplicity, however, Mead is intoxicatingly enjoyable — pun intended, of course — and when well made, it can rival the finest Champagnes in the world.

Throughout the millennia, Mead was believed to have curative, restorative, and aphrodisiac qualities; how's that for an uncomplicated beverage? The concept of a honeymoon derives from the ancient belief that drinking honey wine (Mead) for one full moon (28 days) was a way to increase fertility among newlyweds.

The honey bunch: Appreciating honey

To understand and appreciate Mead is to understand and appreciate honey. Mead is, after all, a simple dilution of honey in water fermented with yeast.

Bees, of course, produce honey. After the energetic honeybee collects nectar from flowers, it partially digests and regurgitates it in the form of honey. The bees store the honey in their hexagonal honeycombs, which are also made from bee excretions. (If that doesn't make you appreciate honey, nothing will!)

The Meady muse

Mead is one of the most sublime beverages known to man, but it's most often referred to as the "nectar of the gods." Historically, Mead has had strong ties to Norse Vikings, English kings, and Celtic roustabouts (and all the sacking and pillaging ascribed to them). Mead is often the subject of poetic, even lyrical verse, and it features prominently in ancient mythology and other classic literature such as the *Rig-Veda*, the *Odyssey, Beowulf,* the *Kalevala,* and the *Heimskringla* (Norse King Sagas). Pliny, Plutarch, Homer, Chaucer, Pepys, Shakespeare, Rabelais, and Washington Irving all mention it in their works as well. One notable work that doesn't mention Mead is the Bible, presumably because of Mead's close association with pagan gods.

Honey is highly fermentable because it's mostly sugar. The quantities of natural sugars in honey vary from one variety to the next, but all honeys contain a mixture of fructose, glucose, and sucrose sugars. A small percentage of honey content is made up of unfermentable stuff such as aromatic oils, gums, resins, fats, acids, and the bees' digestive enzymes — yum! Taken as a whole, pure and natural honey is a healthy potion containing a handful of minerals such as iron, potassium, and phosphorus and vitamins A, B, C, and K. Unfortunately, the more processed the honey is, the fewer of these goodies you're likely to find in it.

The natural sugars you find in honey are mostly mono- and disaccharides, both highly fermentable — very similar to what you'd find in fruit juice. What are vastly different, however, are the flavor and viscosity of honey when compared to fruit juice.

Estimates reveal over a thousand different kinds of honey in the world, each with a different color and flavor (though these differences may be miniscule). Most commercially produced honeys are blends of various types, which tends to foster homogeneity among them. Lighter honeys such as clover, alfalfa, and wildflower are good for Mead making because their flavor contribution is mild. Dark honeys, on the other hand, can be rather aggressive and even harsh-tasting. For Meads with some taste complexity, pure *varietal*, or single-source, honey is highly desirable. Varietal honeys are those derived primarily from a single blossom. The downside is that most of the varietal types are also fairly scarce and, therefore, often more expensive.

Here are some varietal honeys that produce very tasty Mead:

- Orange blossom
- Mesquite
- Fireweed
- Tupelo

Many brand-name Meads are typically made from a homogenous blend of honeys, which pretty much guarantees consistency between batches. Those Meads made from varietal honey usually broadcast that fact on their labels.

The honey-brew list: Mead styles

As previously mentioned, traditional Mead is rather uncomplicated and pretty easy to make. Things start to get interesting when you use a single variety of honey or start adding various adjunct sugars, spices, and flavorings to your Mead.

Just so you don't get lulled into a false sense of familiarity with this honey-based libation, brewers also divide Mead into substyles. Fermenting plain honey and water produces traditional Mead, but by simply adding other flavorings and fermentable sugars, you can produce different styles of Mead. Here's a breakdown of Mead substyles:

- *Braggot* is Mead made with a portion of fermentable ingredients derived from malted grain. In other words, braggot is part beer. (This style is occasionally called *brackett*.)
- *Cyser* is Mead to which you add apple juice. (I guess that would make it a cider-cyser.)
- *Hippocras* is a spiced *pyment* (a Mead made with grape juice and spices).
- *Melomel* (also called *Mulsum*) is Mead to which you add fruit juices other than apple or grape.
- *Metheglin* is Mead to which you add herbs and spices. *Gruit* is the common term that refers to a mixture of herbs and spices used to flavor Meads.
- *Morat* is Mead to which you add mulberries.
- *Pyment* (also called *Clarré* by the French) is Mead to which you add grape juice.

According to the American Homebrewers Association competition guidelines, brewers can make Mead at home in any of the following styles:

- Traditional Mead (Category 24)
  - Dry Mead (24-a)
  - Semi-sweet Mead (24-b)
  - Sweet Mead (24-c)
- Melomel (fruit Mead) (Category 25)
  - Cyser (25-a) (apple Melomel)

- Pyment (25-b) (grape Melomel)
- Other Fruit Melomel (25-c)

✔ Other Mead (Category 26)

- Metheglin (26-a) (spiced Mead)
- Braggot (26-b) (barley Mead)
- Open Category Mead (26-c)

All Meads, regardless of style, should exhibit these three qualities:

✔ **Sweetness:** *Sweetness* simply refers to the amount of residual sugar in the Mead; a Mead may be *dry, semi-sweet,* or *sweet.* Sweet Meads shouldn't be cloyingly sweet or have a raw, unfermented honey character. Sweetness is independent of strength; body is related to sweetness, but dry Meads can still have some body. Dry Meads don't have to be bone dry.

One of the keys to making a good and enjoyable Mead is to achieve the correct balance between the honey (sweetness and flavor) and the acidity in the Mead. Like brewers who use bitter hops to balance the natural grain sweetness of beer, Mead makers need something to offset the cloying taste of syrupy sweet Mead. You can add powdered or liquid acids, such as citric, malic, and tartaric acids, to Mead for flavor balance and complexity. Well-stocked homebrew shops sell Acid Blend packets that contain this exact mix of citric, malic, and tartaric acids.

Occasionally, due to a low original gravity or overly aggressive yeasts, Mead can come out much drier than you intended. If your Mead turns out this way, you can always add a little more honey directly to the Mead at bottling time to sweeten it up. To avoid the possibility of exploding bottles, however, you need to make sure all the yeast remaining in solution is 100 percent dead by using potassium sorbate (according to package directions) to prevent renewed fermentation. Obviously, this tip applies only to uncarbonated (*still*) Meads (see the next bullet).

✔ **Carbonation:** A Mead may be still, petillant, or sparkling. Still Meads don't have to be totally flat — they can have some very light bubbles. *Petillant* Meads are lightly sparkling and can have a moderate, noticeable amount of carbonation. *Sparkling* Meads aren't gushing but may have a character ranging from mouth-filling to an impression akin to Champagne or soda pop. (Making a petillant or sparkling Mead is a simple matter of adding additional fermentable sugar to the Mead at bottling time. Check out Chapter 13 for more on bottling and carbonation.)

✔ **Strength:** A Mead may be categorized as *hydromel, standard,* or *sack strength. Strength* refers to the alcohol content of the Mead (and therefore to the amount of honey and fermentable ingredients used to make the Mead). Stronger Meads have a greater honey character and body (as well as alcohol content) than weaker Meads, although this isn't a strict rule.

Meager Meads

Why isn't Mead more popular and available today? Several factors have probably affected the decline of Mead. One possibility is that wine simply overtook it in popularity; grapes are, and have always been, far more abundant than honey, and the scarcity of any commodity directly affects its price on the free market. As to why more commercial wineries don't produce Mead, it's probably as simple as a lack of awareness and demand on the part of the consumer.

And the amount of time required for the proper fermentation and aging of Mead can be excruciatingly long (but worth every month). The leading source of Mead in the United States today is the hobbyists (homebrewers and home winemakers) who make it in their kitchens and basements. Of the relatively few commercial Meaderies in the United States, most of them are wineries that have ventured into the Mead-making arena.

The vast majority of commercially made Meads you encounter are likely middle-of-the-road Meads: standard, semi-sweet, and still. Unfortunately for the non-brewing consumer, commercial Mead is nowhere near as widely available as beer or wine — availability depends greatly on your local purveyor of adult beverages.

If you're looking for a few commercial Meads for comparison tasting, try scouting out Chaucer Mead, Lurgashall Mead, White Winter Mead, Redstone Mead, Rabbit's Foot Mead, or Jadwiga Mead.

Sweet Success: Making Magnificent Mead

Although homebrewing competitions have accepted Mead with open arms (and categories), Mead making is still not very common among homebrewers. This unpopularity may stem from the fact that Mead is an acquired taste, but perhaps the main obstacle is that many homebrewers are unaware of how easy Mead is to make. After all, all you really need to make Mead is honey.

Okay, that statement is a bit deceptive. To make a *tasty* Mead, you need to dilute the honey with water and pitch it with yeast, but these are minor points. Technically, unpasteurized honey may even spontaneously ferment if left in an unsealed container. I don't think it would taste very pleasant, though.

Choosing your honey

As you're shopping for honey, check out the honey aisle of your local grocery store. Most large grocery stores carry at least a few different brands of honey, but keep in mind the vast majority of commercial honeys are blended and homogenized — they're all virtually the same. You may want to travel that extra mile or spend that extra dollar to purchase a specialty or varietal honey from a specialty food store, a roadside food stand or farmers' market, or a local beekeeper.

Some hard-core Mead makers prefer to buy their honey closer to the source — at the local farmers' market or at roadside stands. Keep in mind that this honey often isn't pasteurized (or even filtered), and you need to stabilize it before you pitch yeast into it. The quickest way to kill unwanted wild yeast or bacteria is to mix sulfur dioxide into the *must* (unfermented honey and water dilution); you can do this by adding one crushed Campden tablet to the must. Winemakers and Mead makers use Campden tablets regularly, and most homebrew supply shops stock them.

Boiling your honey to kill of any resident bacteria is also an option, but be careful: Boiling may also kill off a lot of the delicate aromatics of the honey, too. The best way to boil safely is to pour the honey into water that's already boiling and immediately turn off the heat. Stir well.

Sometimes raw honey begins to crystallize within its jar or container, which makes it difficult to pour out. I've found that microwaving the container for a few seconds causes the honey to quickly revert to its syrupy form.

Mead-iocre? Not! Fermenting your Mead

The brewer has a fair amount of control over the fermentation process; some sweet Mead yeasts aren't very alcohol-tolerant and cease fermenting before they've consumed all the available sugars. On the other hand, liquid culture dry Mead yeasts or Champagne yeasts are very alcohol-tolerant and consume as much available sugar as they can. Given honey's high degree of fermentability and some yeast strains' alcohol tolerance, your Mead could conceivably end up with a final gravity of 0.999 or lower, which is even less dense than water.

Most Meads start with original gravities greater than 1.080 and ferment down to final gravities below 1.020. This level of attenuation results in alcohol levels above 9 percent, which is equivalent to most table wines. For the homebrewer, it takes about 12 pounds of honey in a 5-gallon batch to get to this starting gravity point, but it's not unheard of for Mead makers to use as many as 15 to 18 pounds of honey in a 5-gallon batch. Figure on a dilution rate of 2½ to 3 pounds of honey per gallon of water to achieve the appropriate starting gravity.

Progress report: Progressive Mead

Another way (one that lives in legend as far as I know because no one I associate with has tried it) to make a high-gravity Mead is called *Progressive Mead*. The idea is that you brew a Mead of regular gravity and strength in a smaller batch size to leave room in your fermentation vessel. After the initial fermentation subsides, you boil more, undiluted honey, cool it, and mix it with the existing Mead as you rack it over to the secondary fermenter. Along with the fresh dose of honey, you may need more yeast and yeast nutrient, too.

Because it's progressive, you don't have to stop at a second helping of honey. As the legend goes, you can continue adding more honey in this fashion until you run out of space in your fermenter (or your yeasts die of alcohol toxicity).

At high original gravities, however, yeasts have a tough time staying motivated. It helps to make sure you've aerated the must before you pitch the proper amount of yeast. In order to keep fermentation moving along, you may need to rouse the yeast by agitating the fermenter or by racking the Mead over to another vessel. Adding fresh, healthy yeast to a Mead already in the secondary fermenter isn't out of the question, either.

Consider using a yeast nutrient to aid in fermentation. Yeast nutrient is a blend of vitamins, minerals, amino acids, nitrogen, zinc, and other trace elements designed to help wine and Mead ferment completely.

Don't be surprised if your primary Mead fermentations continue for two weeks to a month. Secondary fermentations typically last months rather than weeks. Three to six months is the norm, but nine to twelve months isn't out of the ordinary for extremely high gravity Meads or those with lots of flavor components that benefit from aging and melding, such as bold fruit flavors or aggressive spices. Some Mead makers who are fans of oak-aged white wines such as Chardonnay can throw toasted oak chips into the secondary fermenter as they rack the Mead into it.

Before you dive headlong into Mead making, take a look at the secondary fermentation procedures in Chapter 11. Check out Chapter 10 as well; Mead making is very similar to beginner extract brewing except for the secondary fermentation process.

Finally, you're not just stuck with plain old honey-and-water Meads; like a lot of beer styles, you can jazz up your Mead by adding spices, fruits or fruit flavors, or even other fermentable sugars like brown sugar. Because Mead benefits from long periods of aging (anywhere from a couple of months to several months), adding more complex flavorings to your Mead is no problem: Chuck 'em in the brewpot or the secondary fermenter. (See Chapter 8 for flavoring ideas and procedures.)

1 Mead a Drink: Mead Recipes

These Mead recipes, like the Cider recipes in Chapter 18, allow you to create a tasty, competition-worthy concoction perfect for special occasions (even if that occasion is Wednesday). As a bonus, you don't even need any new equipment; your beer-brewing gear is perfect.

Because Mead brewing is pretty low-key, these recipes don't offer separate beginner, intermediate, and advanced levels. Be aware, however, that even after you've bottled your Mead, it may not reach its peak flavor potential for another 2 to 6 months.

Traditional Mead (24-a)

Traditional Mead is one of the least-complicated Meads to make. It's a simple mix of honey and water that you can ferment to various levels of sweetness. The following recipe (Lindisfarne Libation) is on the dry end of the sweetness scale.

	Lindisfarne Libation		(Intermediate) **Brewer: Marty Nachel**
Honey:	12 pounds wildflower (unpasteurized)	**Primary:**	16 days at 65 degrees Fahrenheit
Yeast:	Pasteur Champagne (dry)	**Secondary:**	21 days at 65 degrees Fahrenheit
Nutrient:	2 ounces yeast nutrient	**Typical/unusual procedures used:** Add the yeast nutrient to the must in primary fermenter.	

Open Category Mead (26-c)

An Open Category Mead is one that combines elements of two or more other Mead categories, or one that simply doesn't fit the style description of any other Mead category. These Meads are often made with an "anything goes" attitude.

(Intermediate)

Winter Holiday Sweet Mead

Brewer: Tim Reiter

1st Place, First Round, 2001 AHA Nationals

Honey:	14 pounds wildflower	**Clarifying agent:**	3 teaspoons Sparkolloid
Apple Juice:	4 gallons (unpasteurized, preservative-free), chilled	**Primary:**	10 days at 65 degrees Fahrenheit
		Secondary:	14 days at 65 degrees Fahrenheit
Yeast:	Red Star Cote des Blanc (dry)		

Misc. fermentable ingredients: 2 pounds dark brown sugar

Flavoring ingredients: 0.5 ounce cinnamon stick

Typical/unusual procedures used: Heat the honey, brown sugar, and cinnamon in 1 gallon of water in the brewpot. Cool with chilled apple juice and pitch rehydrated yeast. After primary fermentation is complete, stir in rehydrated Sparkolloid. Bottle or keg after 2 weeks.

Pyment (grape melomel) (25-b)

Pyments, or grape melomels, are perfect Meads for wine lovers since these are made with a mixture of honey, water, and grape juice. The ingredient mixtures and the grape juice type are all up to the Mead maker (you).

Concord Grape Sweet Mead

(Advanced)
Brewer: Tim Reiter

3rd Place Best-of-Show, Chicago Beer Society Spooky Brew 2001

Honey: 15 pounds generic honey

Yeast: Red Star Cotes de Blanc (dry) rehydrated

Misc. fermentable ingredient: 4 gallons Concord grape juice (preservative-free), chilled

Clarifying agent: 2 teaspoons Sparkolloid

Primary: 10 days at 65 degrees Fahrenheit

Secondary: 14 days at 65 degrees Fahrenheit

Typical/unusual procedures used: Heat 1 gallon of water to 150 degrees Fahrenheit. Add the honey and stir frequently to dissolve. Pour the chilled grape juice from high above the fermenter so it splashes on the bottom of the fermenter and aerates thoroughly. Add the honey/water mixture similarly and stir vigorously. Pitch rehydrated yeast. After primary fermentation is complete, stir in rehydrated Sparkolloid. Bottle or keg after 2 weeks.

Chapter 20

Going Green: Being an Eco-Friendly Homebrewer

In This Chapter

▶ Being an environmentally conscious brewer

▶ Brewing organically

*W*ith all the talk these days of greenhouse gasses, carbon emissions, ozone holes, and melting glaciers, the concept of green products and practices are gaining steam (which isn't necessarily a green energy source). *Green* (for those of you who may have just awakened from a coma) generally refers to anything that's ecologically or earth-friendly. And it's not just car manufacturers who are becoming earth-conscious; even the international brewing industry is turning green, so to speak, and homebrewers everywhere are also doing their little part. This chapter takes a look at those products and practices that juxtapose the concepts of brew and green. Solar-powered brew kettle, anyone?

Brewing Green Beer: It's Not Just for St. Patrick's Day Anymore

Very few people begin homebrewing out of necessity because commercial beer is readily accessible to just about everyone everywhere. But rather than simply buy a product out of convenience, these brewers make the conscious choice to spend their money, time, and effort on a pastime that isn't inherently easy or convenient. Now, with this same dedication and conviction, many homebrewers are making the choice to spend additional money, time, and effort to pursue the same hobby with the added challenges of brewing in a way that many consider socially conscious. Ecologically friendly brewing isn't necessarily cheaper or easier, but, on the other hand, some aspects of eco-friendliness can actually conserve resources — including your money.

Green with envy

Commercial breweries are leading the way within the industry by employing green practices specific to their operations. Not only are these methods helping the breweries' bottom lines, but they're also gaining positive attention from local governments and the media. Some inspirational examples:

✔ The Mad River Brewing Company received an award from its home town of Blue Lake, California, for reducing its solid wastes by a whopping 97 percent.

✔ The Sierra Nevada Brewing Company of Chico, California, was honored by Governor Arnold Schwarzenegger and awarded a $2.4-million rebate by the local gas and electric company for installing an energy-efficient power plant that lightened the load on the municipal power grid while significantly reducing air emissions.

✔ In 2003, Brooklyn Brewery in Brooklyn, New York, was the first business in New York City to operate on 100 percent wind-generated electricity.

✔ The New Belgium Brewery in Fort Collins, Colorado, following its own mission statement of "Ethical and Environmental Responsibility," has won several awards for its dedication to environmental ethics. The employee-owned brewery produces 100 percent of its own energy through the use of wind turbines and a unique *cogeneration* process by which bacteria produce methane gas. (A couple of beers and a bowl of chili usually work for me.)

✔ In Australia, the Foster's brewing conglomerate is adopting a new brewing technology that produces energy via brewery waste products. Called a *Microbial Fuel Cell,* this device feeds on organic substances like sugar, starch, and alcohol found in brewery waste water, which it then turns into Watts and stores in a battery that can power various electrical components within the brewery. In addition to creating energy, the technology also leaves clean water and non-polluting carbon dioxide as by-products.

Using the oft-repeated mantra of "Reduce, Reuse, Recycle" as a starting point, homebrewers have different avenues on which to begin their walk toward eco-friendliness. Ultimately, each individual brewer has to decide which of these practices is workable within his or her own circumstances. The following sections provide some ideas to get you started in your quest to become a green brewer.

Reduce

The first step in brewing green is reducing your usage of anything that's not eco-friendly. Here are some ways to make brewhouse reductions:

✔ **Your energy usage:** Gas heat is typically more economical to use than electrical heat and typically costs energy companies less to produce. Wherever possible, consider brewing with propane gas on high-BTU so-called turkey-cooker burners.

Always allow for proper ventilation when using high-BTU propane burners. These are best used outdoors, away from flammable structures.

✔ **Your energy needs:** *Jacketing* (insulating) metal mash tuns, sparging vessels, and brewpots conserves heat. Not only will you save energy, but you'll also likely attain higher temperatures more quickly and sustain them longer.

✔ **Your usage of non-organic brewing ingredients:** Non-organic farming adds tons of toxic chemicals to the earth's soil and water each year. See the "Organically Speaking" section later in this chapter for more on organic issues.

Try growing your own organic hops at home. See Chapter 26 for more details on this process.

✔ **Your reliance on cleansers and sanitizers that aren't environmentally friendly:** You can't always avoid using environmentally *un*friendly cleansers and sanitizers, but reducing their use helps.

Two highly recommended environmentally friendly products are B-Brite, which is a no rinse, non-toxic all-purpose cleanser, and biodegradable Five Star PBW (Powdered Brewery Wash).

✔ **Your electricity usage:** If you use a refrigerator exclusively for your homebrew, you can save a considerable amount of energy by investing in a temperature controller (see Chapter 27). Most refrigerators maintain a temperature range of 30 to 40 degrees Fahrenheit. If you raise the temperature just 10 degrees, you can save enough each month on electricity to pay for 1 batch of beer each year! And if you have a home kegging system, a refrigerator tap can also help save energy. By dispensing your brews from outside the refrigerator, you don't have to open the door as frequently, which significantly cuts down on the amount of energy needed to keep your brews cold.

Reuse

Another way to brew green is to reuse as much as you can to avoid contributing more waste to the environment. Here are some things you can reuse in your home brewery:

✔ **Your cleaning and sanitizing solutions:** It's not unreasonable to keep and reuse cleaning and sanitizing solutions that are only lightly used. Consider disposing of them only after several uses; it won't affect their power.

I know one conservative homebrewer who cleans all ten of his beer kegs one at a time by pouring the same sanitizing solution from one to the next over a period of a few hours.

✔ **Your cooling water:** This can be the water you use to cool your brewpot in the sink or the water that flows through your wort chiller. Think of both sources as usable water for cleaning dishes, for watering house plants, for mopping floors, for filling the dog's water bowl — whatever! The water that flows from wort chillers isn't only drinkable, it's also already heated. Consider pointing the chiller outflow hose into a clothes washing machine, or just use it to clean your home brewery when you're done brewing.

The water that emerges from a chiller immersed in a pot of just-boiled wort may initially be as hot as 160 to 180 degrees Fahrenheit. So let it cool a bit before you give Sparky a bath.

✔ **Your yeast:** It reproduces by itself, for Pete's sake! As I discuss in Chapter 26, you can re-propagate your yeast and keep a yeast bank in your fridge.

Recycle

Another way to brew green is to recycle as much as you can to reduce your contribution to the world's landfills. Here are some things in your home brewery that you can recycle:

✔ **Your plastic and glass:** When plastic equipment is no longer suitable for brewing or when beer bottles or carboys break, don't just throw them in the garbage. Both are likely recyclable, which means they won't add unwanted and unnecessary volume to a garbage dump somewhere.

When I decide that a large volume plastic vessel is no longer usable for brewing, I demote it to serving as a holding tank for reusable sanitizing solution. This practice guarantees that I always have some at the ready for that last-minute sanitizing of something I may have overlooked.

✔ **Your grain:** If you're a gardener, grain makes an excellent addition to compost piles. If you know anyone who owns any barnyard animals, spent grain is also a great food source for horses, cows, pigs, and so on. And you can always make high-fiber homemade bread with spent brewing grains.

Organically Speaking

Brewing organic beer is really not as difficult as you may think, especially with the rapidly spreading interest in organic foods and ingredients. Organically grown ingredients for beer making are slowly but surely trickling down from the commercial brewing sources to homebrew supply shops. Rest assured, as the interest in organic beer grows, so too will the availability of organic ingredients.

Keep in mind, though, that you won't find any real financial incentive for brewing organic beer. This is but one of many steps toward becoming a green brewer; the real incentive to brew organically is rooted in the deep satisfaction of knowing that you're not placing an added burden on the environment. A commitment to sustainable agriculture and the environment are what brewing organic beer is really all about.

And, in case you're concerned, the process of brewing organic beer is no different from brewing regular beer; you're simply switching from non-organic ingredients to organic ingredients. The only caveat to this generalization is that if you're serious about maintaining high organic standards, organic ingredients and beer should never come in contact with any piece of equipment that you previously used to store, brew, or ferment non-organic ingredients and beer unless you first thoroughly cleaned and sanitized it to remove traces of all the verboten pesticides and fertilizers.

Why use organic ingredients?

The following are some important — and somewhat opinionated — considerations about organic brewing:

- ✔ **Brewing organically allows you to brew better beer.** Beer made with organic ingredients tends to be much clearer without requiring chemicals or fining agents, which in turn results in a cleaner taste.

  On average, organic malts have a lower protein content, which results in reduced haze problems in your finished beer. Also, organic malts leave no chemical deposits that may interfere with fermentation.

- ✔ **Brewing organically can contribute to your overall health and well-being.** By using organic ingredients, you can avoid consuming the often-toxic chemicals farmers and food processing companies use.

- ✔ **Brewing organically contributes to a better world.** Organic farming reduces erosion, soil nutrient depletion, water shortages, and pollution by not using chemicals to fertilize crops or to fight pests and diseases. Per acre, organic farming also provides more agricultural jobs than conventional farming.

By using organically grown ingredients to make your beer, you're automatically improving its purity. You're also supporting the organic farming industry, which contributes to the amount of land farmed in a sustainable and chemical-free way.

Beware of the urban myth that organic beers are less likely to produce hangovers due to their lack of chemicals — not true! Now where'd I put the aspirin?

Perhaps you'd like to peruse our list of non-toxic beers?

Beer	Brewery	Country
Stone Mill	Anheuser-Busch	USA
Wild Hop	Anheuser-Busch	USA
Organic ESB	Lakefront	USA
Woody Organic IPA	Roots Organic	USA
Laurelwood Free Range Red Ale	Hopworks	USA
Fish Tale Amber Ale	Fish	USA
Naughty Nellie's Golden Ale	Pike	USA
Henry Weinhard's Premium Amber	Miller**	USA
Foret	DuPont	Belgium
Golden Promise	Caledonian	UK
Organic Best Ale	Samuel Smith	UK
Jade	Benifontaine	France
Pinkus Alt	Pinkus-Müller	Germany

**Brewed for Miller Brewing Company by Full Sail Brewing Company

Tracking the trend

The recent movement toward organic farming and the production of organically grown foods is well documented. Domestic sales of organic food and drink grew from $1 billion in 1990 to $14 billion in 2006, according to the U.S. Department of Agriculture (USDA). It seems natural, then, that beer would also follow the trend — and it has. By 2005, organic beer ranked with coffee as the fastest-growing organic beverage. (Hmmm, pesticide-free caffeine or pesticide-free alcohol — take your pick.) As of 2006, organic beer still represents less than 1 percent of U.S. beer sales, but those sales doubled to $19 million between 2003 and 2005, according to the Organic Trade Association.

The modern organic beer movement traces its roots to Brauerei Pinkus-Müller in Münster, Germany, where the first all-organic beer was brewed in 1979 as the result of the brewer's disappointment in the declining quality of conventional malt at the time. He found organic malt to be a superior substitute, and the brewery switched to all-organic brewing a little over a decade later. Germany alone now boasts about 30 organic breweries. Pinkus-Müller's organic beers eventually influenced brewmasters abroad. In 1997, the USDA established the National Organic Program, which opened the door for Morgan Wolaver to found the first all-organic brewing company, Wolaver's Organic Ales, in Santa Cruz, California.

The worldwide brewing industry is making huge strides on the organic beer sector, but American commercial brewers are lagging a bit behind. Perhaps more brewers in the U.S. would make organic beers today if it weren't for the many challenges they face. For example, the organic certification process can be expensive and burdensome, and some of the raw ingredients can be difficult to secure in bulk. It can also be expensive to maintain separate equipment for organic brewing. Luckily, most homebrewers have an easier time of it (for starters, you don't have to be certified). But if you're more interested in drinking organic beer than making it, check out the nearby "Perhaps you'd like to peruse our list of non-toxic beers?" sidebar.

Certifiably nuts: Determining what's really organic

Simply put, the United States Department of Agriculture (USDA) standards for organic beer are the same as those for organic foods: ingredients must be grown without toxic pesticides or synthetic fertilizers in soil free from chemicals for at least three years, and genetically modified ingredients (GMOs) are a no-no. Keep in mind this Organic Certification process is kind of a work in progress. USDA regulations are likely to continue changing and modifying in the future.

A GMO is a *Genetically Modified Organism*. GMOs are common in food production, including genetically modified corn that may appear in the brewing industry. The certified-organic label is a guarantee that the product doesn't contain GMOs.

I should add that this description is *over*-simply put. Although this may all sound pretty straightforward, the specifics regarding how organically grown ingredients affect brewing processes and exactly how to define organic ingredients make this topic anything but simple. Check out the "It's not organic till the USDA signs" sidebar for all the boring details.

Unless you've memorized the entire list of the USDA's organic certifications, what you read on product labels ranges from vague at best to outright confusing at worst. The four basic building blocks of beer are grain (typically malted barley), hops, yeast, and water, and the following sections tell you what you need to know about selecting organic versions of each.

It's not organic till the USDA signs

In order for a beer to qualify for organic certification, the USDA requires that 95 percent of the ingredients used be organic. In other words, it must contain 95 percent organic ingredients, with the other 5 percent being non-organic ingredients on the USDA National List, provided that organic equivalents aren't commercially available in sufficient quantity. Are you still with me?

Currently, the National List only contains five items: corn starch, water-extracted gums, kelp, unbleached lecithin, and pectin. Besides hops, there are an additional 38 ingredients currently under consideration for inclusion on the National List.

This is how the USDA breaks down its organic certifications according to Product Composition:

✔ A raw or processed agricultural product sold, labeled, or represented as "100 percent organic" must contain, by weight or fluid volume, 100 percent organically produced ingredients.

✔ A raw or processed agricultural product sold, labeled, or represented as "organic" must contain, by weight or fluid volume, not less than 95 percent organically produced raw or processed agricultural products. Any remaining product ingredients must be organically produced, unless not commercially available in organic form, or must be nonagricultural substances or non-organically produced agricultural products produced consistent with the National List.

✔ Multi-ingredient agricultural products sold, labeled, or represented as "made with organic (specified ingredients or food group[s])" must contain, by weight or fluid volume, at least 70 percent organically produced ingredients produced and handled in accordance with USDA organic specifications.

Thirsty yet? Read your labels carefully. . .

In 1997, Seven Bridges Homebrewing Cooperative became a homebrew pioneer by becoming the first supplier to offer quality organic ingredients to homebrewers. It has since grown to become the world's most complete resource for certified organic homebrewing ingredients. It's the only certified organic homebrew retailer in the United States, which guarantees that all of its organic products are fully documented and carry the USDA organic seal. Check out http://www.breworganic.com for more information or to order products online.

Water

In terms of volume, water makes up about 95 percent of beer. Assuming you've got average filtered water, you don't have to worry about organic issues with it (and water isn't considered an ingredient by the USDA anyway).

Grain

Next up is the grain. Malted barley is the primary source of beer flavor and character, followed by wheat, corn, rice, oats, rye, and so on. All of these grains — malted or unmalted — now grow both organically and non-organically, so obviously, you need to be careful in choosing the grain you use to make organic beer. And in addition to the standard organic regulations against pesticides, herbicides, and fertilizers, watch out for grains tainted with GMOs.

To keep this stuff out of your beer, the best place to start brewing organic beer is with organic malt. Many brewers consider organic grain difficult to work with when compared to non-organic grain. Non-organic malt is easy to handle because of the uniformity in the barley kernels, and, unfortunately, uniformity falls victim to organic practices. Other than this disadvantage, you can substitute organic malts pound-for-pound in your favorite recipes. One big plus is that organic malts have a slightly higher conversion rate than conventional malts, so you can consider reducing the amount of organic grain in your recipe by 1 or 2 percent. Specialty malts are pretty much interchangeable.

The heading of organic malt also encompasses extracts produced with organic ingredients. As of now, only one organic malt extract is available to homebrewers. Fortunately, it's a pale, unhopped extract, which gives you a lot of leeway in your recipe formulation.

For homebrewers and beer lovers who may have grain-related food allergies, you can also find a small variety of gluten-free grains available, including buckwheat, millet, and quinoa. See Chapter 21 for more on gluten-free brewing.

Hops

Hops constitute the next-largest percentage of brewing ingredients, but their certification, status, and viability are currently in a state of flux (I think that's near Rhode Island). Yes, you can get organically grown hops, but not in great quantities; hops are subject to a variety of diseases and other growth-related problems. Quite a bit of confusion also surrounds the need for organic hops in the first place. Most small organic brewers insist on using them to make their products 100 percent organic, or at least to make their beers USDA Organic Certified (95 percent organic ingredients). Larger breweries argue that because hops constitute less than 5 percent of the total ingredient profile of their beers, beers brewed with non-organic hops still qualify for organic certification. And the debate rages on. . .

Hops are notoriously difficult to grow organically because they're subject to many diseases such as wilt, mildew, and hop mites. (See Chapter 5 for more on hops.) This is why no large-scale commercial hop grower in the United States has taken the risky leap to organic hop production. Currently, most of the few organic hop varieties available in the U.S. are imported from New Zealand, Germany, and the U.K. Of course, this scarcity affects the brewers' bottom lines as well; imported organic hops are 20 to 30 percent more expensive than conventional domestic hops.

Yeast

Finally, yeast is the last puzzle piece. Yeast itself is organic, but the liquid medium in which you propagate it will have an effect on its organic certification. If the grain-based wort was produced from non-organically grown grain, the yeast is considered non-organic. Eco-friendly homebrewers can also get specially packaged yeast; ask your homebrew supplier about their selection of organic yeast.

Adjuncts

Those brewers who like to use adjunct sugars in their beers can rest assured their interests are being looked after as well. In addition to organic rice syrup, brewers may also find cane sugar, corn sugar, and malto-dextrin in the organic market.

Be aware that corn is one of the most genetically modified crops, and the USDA has no labeling requirements for GMOs. Because of this ambiguity, you can't be sure that any corn product, including corn sugar, is free from GMOs. To completely avoid GMOs, use a substitute for corn sugar such as malt extract or organic cane sugar.

More-intrepid brewers can also find a wide variety of organically grown herbs and spices. If you can't get these from your favorite homebrew supplier, your average organic food store probably stocks them.

Chapter 21

Gluten-Free Brewing

In This Chapter

▶ Discovering gluten

▶ Dealing with gluten intolerance

▶ Brewing gluten-free beer

*I*magine going the rest of your life without beer; what a depressing thought! Unfortunately, some very real physical conditions make beer consumption difficult for many people. Luckily, beer made without gluten-filled products provides a glimmer of hope for these folks. For sufferers of gluten intolerance, brewing their own beer at home presents an opportunity to continue enjoying their favorite beverage without the risks normally associated with their condition. Honestly speaking, beers made from gluten-free grains aren't likely to match regular beer for taste and quality. But to someone facing a lifetime beer-drinking restriction (gasp!), gluten-free beer is like manna from Heaven — made without gluten, of course. This chapter is all about brewing these gluten-free beers at home. Don't worry: The processes are largely the same; you just have to be more careful about the ingredients you choose.

Getting to Know Gluten

As I detail in Chapter 4, brewers have used many different grains to brew beer over the millennia. Barley is the most popular because of its many positive attributes and contributions toward making good beer. Wheat runs a close second in grain preference, distantly followed by rye. The problem with these grains — at least for people who suffer from *celiac disease*—is they all contain gluten.

Gluten, which is a combination of the proteins *gliadin* and *glutenin*, is responsible for triggering an autoimmune reaction in the small intestines of people with celiac disease. That reaction can be very debilitating, causing the sufferer great discomfort and possibly long-term disruption to the function of their small intestine. This means they don't get the nutrients they need out of their food and may experience a range of other health issues as well. The only treatment available to people with gluten intolerance is a lifelong avoidance of products that contain gluten. That means no regular beer in their diets. (Check out the "More about celiac disease" sidebar for more information.)

Gluten helps make bread dough very elastic (so the yeast can make it rise) and gives the bread its characteristic chewiness. As a component of barley, wheat, and rye, gluten gives beer a thickness and chewiness as well.

In response to the growing demand for gluten-free beers in the commercial market, several breweries around the world introduce new gluten-free products each year (see the nearby "No disputin' gluten-free beers" sidebar for a list). England even hosts an international gluten-free beer festival each year.

Because "gluten-free" constitutes a health claim, current U.S. beer label regulations don't allow the term "gluten-free" to appear on any beer sold in the United States. Look for an ingredient listing of grains that don't contain gluten.

From Intolerant to Tolerable: Brewing Gluten-Free Beer at Home

Let me set the record straight here: Gluten-free beers don't taste exactly like regular beers. Compared to regular brewing, the ingredients available for gluten-free beer are limited, so you have to use your imagination when formulating your gluten-free beer recipes. I address this topic in greater detail a bit later.

Readying your equipment

One of the first considerations for the at-home brewer is making sure their equipment doesn't cause cross-contamination. In other words, if you've previously brewed regular beer in the equipment, you need to redouble your cleaning efforts. This includes everything from your grain mill (if you brew all-grain) to your brewpot, your fermenters, your transfer hoses, your bottles, and every piece of equipment in between. Don't take chances here; even the minutest traces of gluten can make a celiac sufferer ill. See Chapter 3 for details on proper cleaning and sanitation practices.

Substituting safe ingredients

The next consideration is where to obtain the appropriate ingredients for brewing gluten-free beer. Start with the easiest parts: Neither water nor hops play any part in gluten-free brewing, so don't worry about these ingredients. Just brew with what's readily available. The main ingredient concern is the fermentable grain or starch you plan to substitute for the glutinous barley or wheat you use to brew typical beers.

More about celiac disease

Celiac Disease is also known as *gluten-sensitive enteropathy*, *gluten intolerance*, or *celiac sprue*. Gluten intolerance is an auto-immune response some people's bodies have to gluten; this reaction damages the lining of the small intestine. The result is that nutrients quickly pass through the small intestine instead of being absorbed.

Estimates show that 1 in every 133 people in the United States may be affected by this chronic, inherited disease that can ultimately lead to malnutrition if not treated. The disease is permanent, and damage to the small intestine will occur every time a sufferer consumes gluten, even if he or she doesn't experience any symptoms.

The following list spells out the prohibited grains (and their derivatives) that celiac sufferers need to avoid:

- ✔ Barley or barleymalt

- ✔ Malt or malt flavoring

- ✔ Malt vinegar

- ✔ Rye

- ✔ Wheat (including durum, semolina, kamut, and spelt)

- ✔ Triticale (sometimes used in brewing)

Although sorghum and buckwheat are the most commonly substituted gluten-free grains (check out the "Sorghum and buckwheat" sidebar), you have plenty of options when you're looking for safe grains and starches:

- ✔ Sorghum
- ✔ Buckwheat
- ✔ Rice
- ✔ Corn
- ✔ Soybeans

- ✔ Potato
- ✔ Beans
- ✔ Tapioca
- ✔ Quinoa
- ✔ Millet

Note: Although consuming uncontaminated oats in moderation (1 cooked cup a day) is considered safe for the average celiac sufferer, health professionals are concerned that most oats may be cross-contaminated with glutinous grains.

The following sections suggest other safe ingredient substitutes.

Sorghum and buckwheat

Sorghum is a valuable food source in its native northeast Africa. It's a vigorously growing grass that tolerates the African climate very well, which makes it a common ingredient in African beer. Buckwheat, which traces its roots (no pun intended) to central and western China, is actually an herb. Its nuts are milled, separating the edible interior (called *groats*) from its outer husk. The groats are then roasted and used as a grain. Buckwheat blossoms are also full of nectar, which makes them popular on beekeeping farms. Hmmm, now I'm thinking Mead. . .

Extract-ly what you need

Fortunately for the extract brewer, a couple of products on the market make life easier for the celiac sufferer. At least one major maltster in the U.S. markets white sorghum syrup. Pound-for-pound, this syrup is equivalent to regular malt extract, and you can use it in the same way. Be sure to read labels, however; in at least one of these products, processors add simple sugars (white cane sugar, honey) during production. This added sugar creates a more-fermentable beer, which typically results in a drier beer.

This point is where your imagination kicks in. In order to keep your beer sweet and flavorful, consider adding flavorings, adjuncts, herbs, and spices to keep it interesting. Try using corn or rice syrup, molasses, treacle, brown sugar, or fruit juices and the like to make your gluten-free brew unique.

Gluten-free but flavorful

Yet another way to enhance your beer with grain-like flavors without any concern about gluten is to roast your buckwheat or sorghum. If you like roasty-toasty flavors in your beer or you want to make your brew a little darker, consider roasting some raw sorghum or buckwheat grain in your oven and steeping it in your wort as you would a specialty malt. Simply spread about a pound of grain on a pizza tin (or similar apparatus) and roast for 10 to 30 minutes at 350 degrees Fahrenheit (depending on the degree of toastiness you desire). You can use this roasted grain immediately or store it refrigerated in a sealable sandwich bag. You can use anywhere between a ¼ pound and a full pound in a single batch for more complex beer flavor and overall character.

Depending on your source of gluten-free grains, be aware that some grains may be sold as seed and not intended for human consumption. This seed may be treated with junk you don't want to be drinking in your beer later on.

Brewing gluten-free beers from all grain

For you all-grain brewers who want to try your hands at making gluten-free beer, listen up. . .er, uh, read carefully. This undertaking has a degree of difficulty above and beyond brewing regular all-grain beers. The first consideration here is finding the right grains in sufficient quantity at a reasonable price. You also have to make sure they're the malted variety. As always, start with your local purveyor of homebrew supplies. If your favorite homebrew shop doesn't stock them, you should be able to find many gluten-free grains in better supermarkets or health-food stores. If not, try searching for them online. Finding the right grains can be somewhat expensive but well worth the price and effort for someone who can't drink beer otherwise.

As always, when making beer from all grain you must first mash your grain. One of the main challenges in mashing gluten-free grains is that they're low in *diastatic power*. In other words, they lack the requisite enzymes for conversion. (Check out Chapter 12 for more on mashing procedures.) You might want to consider adding amylase enzyme to your mash water — about 1 teaspoon per 5 gallons of water. (See Chapter 9 for more information about enzymes.)

Another issue with gluten-free grains is that many of them—including sorghum — are huskless. This deficiency means you need to add about ½ pound of rice hulls to your mash in order to lauter and sparge efficiently.

If you choose to forego mashing and attempt to gelatinize your gluten-free grains, be aware that the gelatinization temperature of the starches in most gluten-free grains is higher than that of regular brewing grains. With sorghum, corn, and rice, the gelatinization temperature is about 180 degrees Fahrenheit, but these grains contain fewer required enzymes to convert the starches to soluble sugars. Adding an amylase enzyme preparation (about 1 teaspoon per 5 gallons of water) is helpful in this regard.

Armed with this knowledge, formulating a recipe for gluten-free beer is no different from any other regular beer. Simply substitute your favorite gluten-free grain for barley or wheat. For yeast suggestions, check out the next section.

Last, but not yeast

The last of the four principal beer ingredients is yeast. Yeast by itself isn't harmful to people with celiac disease. Therefore, you can use dry yeast to ferment any gluten-free beer as long as you rehydrate it in plain water (with no malt products). What is harmful to celiac sufferers is the liquid medium in which commercial yeast is propagated; the base solution of this medium is typically wort derived from barleymalt.

So if you make a liquid yeast starter at home, it must be gluten-free, too. If you use a normal yeast strain, you need to plate out the yeast on a petri dish or slant and then propagate the culture from a single yeast colony by using molasses or sorghum syrup as your culture media. As always, you must carry out all these processes in a very sterile environment.

At yeast someone cares

Due to an increase in celiac disease, gluten intolerance, and wheat and barley allergies, production of gluten-free products is one of the fastest-growing sectors in the food industry. At least one yeast laboratory has responded to the need for specialty brewing yeast: Wyeast's gluten-free yeast is a natural extension of the demand for gluten-free beer.

After months of research and development, Wyeast Laboratories now offers two of its most popular liquid yeast strains in gluten-free form. Yeast vitality, cell count, and recommended pitching rates are comparable to Wyeast's current popular products.

Wyeast 1272 GF American Ale II and Wyeast 2206 GF Bavarian Lager are now available to craft brewers by special order. Check with your local homebrew shop for more details.

Part VI
Putting Your Brew to the Test

"Oh, come on, you're just drinking it!
You're not even tasting it..."

In this part . . .

Anyone who makes anything — whether homebrewed beer or crocheted sweaters — wants a second opinion (or at least objective feedback) on how well the product turns out. These chapters help you to objectively evaluate your own beers as well as find out where to go for reliable outside feedback.

Okay, this part is about treating your beer and yourself right, too.

Chapter 22

Storing and Pouring

• •

In This Chapter

▶ Storing, aging, and conditioning your beer

▶ Pouring and drinking your brew

▶ Choosing beer glassware

▶ Washing and storing your glasses

• •

*B*eer drinkers don't typically have to face the prospect of storing large quantities of beer for long periods of time, but you're a homebrewer now, and the rules are different. With each batch of brew you make, you produce the equivalent of slightly more than two cases of bottled beer. And this stuff isn't just any beer; it's homemade, it's unpasteurized, and it's technically alive. (Remember: Some yeast is still at work in each bottle.) This kind of beer requires — and deserves — a little more attention. How you store and pour your homebrew can make a world of difference in how it tastes. In this chapter, I give you the lowdown on the proper storage of your homebrew, as well as some pouring techniques and tips for glass selection. I also discuss the pros and cons of different glass-cleaning methods.

Storing Your Suds

Average commercial-beer drinkers don't need to concern themselves with the correct storing of beer because they usually purchase and consume it within a couple of days (if not hours). For homebrewers, however, this issue is worthy of attention; after all, they've put a lot of time and effort into their finished product.

The term *finished product* (when used in conjunction with homebrew) is actually a misnomer. As long as live yeast is in the bottle, the beer is never really a finished product — it continues to change over time.

How do I store it?

Unlike wine bottles, homebrew bottles don't need to be stored horizontally. Wine is stored this way to keep the cork from going dry — which is not a problem with bottle caps. Actually, keeping your beer bottles standing upright minimizes the beer's contact with any oxygen that has also been sealed in the bottle with the beer.

What's most important about storing your homebrew is making sure the beer is in a location in your home that's cool and dark, because both heat and light can destroy beer flavor.

Where do I store it?

For the first two weeks after you bottle your brew, you want to store it in a cool (50+ degrees Fahrenheit), dark location while it silently *conditions* (clarifies and carbonates). Back away from the fridge — it's too cold for this brief conditioning phase. Your brew eventually becomes clearer, and the carbonation level gradually increases. To satisfy your curiosity, you may want to open a bottle every couple of days during this time to keep tabs on your beer's progress. Or you can simply give a bottle a little jiggle and see whether bubbles emerge from the beer.

After you've conditioned your brew to your liking, you need to store it in the coolest and darkest place possible (without freezing it) to stunt the yeast activity within the bottle and to protect it from those elements that will cause your beer to deteriorate, such as heat and light.

Your best storage bet is an Alpine cave, but a spare fridge or cool, dark spot in your basement is sufficient. I realize that not everyone has the luxury of a spare refrigerator or even a basement, so, forgoing these possibilities, a crude beer cellar is better than nothing at all — consider using a ground-level interior closet, a crawl space, or even an abandoned root cellar. Hey, if you've got little to work with, you need to be flexible. And the closer you can get to serving temperature (42 to 48 degrees Fahrenheit), the better.

The two most important criteria for this beer cellar are that it be cool and that it be dark. You want to factor in accessibility at some point; what good is an effective beer cellar if it effectively keeps you from easily getting a beer?

You *don't* want to use a garage for storing your beer. Garages, unless thermostatically controlled, experience wide temperature fluctuations on a daily basis, and they usually get way too hot or way too cold (depending on your geographic location and the time of year). But a spare fridge in your garage, well, now you're talking!

How long do I store it?

By and large, you want to consume homebrewed beer fresh, typically within three months of bottling. However, a handful of beer styles not only stand up well to storage but actually improve with short-to-long-term aging. The styles that fit this category are all high-gravity beers: Barley Wines, strong Ales, Imperial Stouts, Triple Bocks, some of the Belgian Trappist styles, and especially Meads. Although many beers are still good after several months, the hardiest beers are likely to improve over a number of years.

Pouring Procedures

The simple act of serving a beer doesn't need to be done with a flourish, but it does go a bit beyond drinking beer straight out of the bottle. This fact is especially true when serving homebrewed beer.

Correct presentation of any beer automatically includes glassware or even plastic ware (as long as it's clean). Appearances aside, the underlying concept here is that, by pouring out the beer, you release much of the pent-up carbonation. This frothing effervescence creates the beer's head, releases the brew's aromatic bouquet, and lessens its carbonic bite.

Speaking of aromatic bouquet, less gas trapped in the liquid means less gas trapped in your intestinal tract.

Out of the bottle. . .

With homebrew, most people — even most homebrewers — prefer to leave the yeast dregs in the bottle. (These can taste pretty nasty.) Mastering this pouring technique requires patience, timing, and a steady hand — especially if you're pouring your beer into more than one glass. Not to belabor the point, but careful pouring has a lot less to do with clear beer than it does with clear air — live yeast continues the fermentation process within your digestive system, which often results in excess, um, flatulence. Be aware that jostling your bottles of homebrew causes the yeast sediment to cloud up the beer. Either handle the bottles gently or allow the yeast to resettle to the bottom of the bottles.

Absolutely nothing is wrong with drinking the yeast sediment, which is actually high in the water-soluble B-complex vitamins — unless you have something against bloating and gas. Apparently this is not a problem for fans of hefe weizen, which is traditionally served *mit Hefe,* or with the yeast.

Of course, you don't have to worry about clean pouring if you choose to filter your homebrew. (See Chapter 27 for more about filtering.)

The best way to pour a beer is to just plop it right down the middle of the glass, and starting with a glass large enough to hold the full contents of the bottle really helps. A huge head forms immediately, so you may want to slow the pour or tilt the glass slightly as the beer nears the top. You also want to be a little less aggressive when pouring Wheat beers or any brew that includes wheat malt as a heading agent, as well as any homebrew that's getting on in age. A true head is at least 1 inch thick, or two fingers in depth.

One of the finer points of beer presentation that too many drinkers often overlook is the correct serving temperature. Most beers are served much too cold for serious appreciation. The average refrigerator is set to keep things chilled to around 38 degrees 40 degrees Fahrenheit. I can think of at least three reasons not to serve your beer this cold:

- ✔ The colder the beer, the less carbonation it releases and the smaller the head.

- ✔ The less carbonation a beer releases, the less aroma it gives off.

- ✔ These temperatures numb the palate to the point that it can't discern many of the beer's flavor nuances (which explains why American mass-market beers are best served just above the freezing mark).

Although you must make a little extra effort and plan ahead to serve beers at their correct temperatures, the rewards are great. Drinking beer at the correct temperature enables you to smell and taste all that the beer has to offer. Serve most Lagers between 42 and 48 degrees Fahrenheit and most Ales between 46 and 52 degrees Fahrenheit. Authentic Stouts can be served as warm as 55 degrees Fahrenheit, which is *British cellar temperature.* Most high-gravity Barley Wines and strong Ales are best lightly chilled or at room temperature, like a snifter of brandy.

To save time as you clean and sanitize your bottles for your next brew, always rinse each bottle thoroughly after you empty it and then store it upside down. If you drink your homebrew from a keg, always clean and rinse the keg thoroughly after it's empty, too. See Chapter 14 for keg cleaning instructions.

. . . and into the glass

Stylish beer glassware serves primarily as a commercial product enhancement. Beyond visuals, however, the various shapes and sizes of beer glasses play an even more meaningful role. Specialized beer glassware enhances the aromas of the beer — for example, glasses that are deep or that curve inward toward the top are very effective in capturing and concentrating a beer's aromas.

The act of pouring beer into a glass (known as *decanting*) also enables carbonation to escape from the beer and lets the beer warm a bit if you've served it too cold. Decanting also allows you to pour a clearer beer if you're not partial to the yeast sediment in a homebrewed beer.

In the realm of tradition, many beer styles actually have a glassware style dedicated to them. A Pilsener beer, for example, belongs in any of the many tall, stemmed, or hourglass-shaped Pilsener-style glasses. A Stout, on the other hand, is perfectly at home in a simple pint glass. The nice thing about beer glassware, however, is that you're not bound by any hard-and-fast rules.

General rules on beer glassware suggest that simple beers can be served in simple glasses; well-aged and expensive beers deserve the regal treatment. Figure 22-1 shows you several different types of beer glasses; the following list helps you decide what to put in them:

- Aromatic Trappist Ales and Belgian Fruit beers for thin, stemmed glasses
- Rich and spirituous Barley Wines, Old Ales, and Imperial Stouts for small, brandy-snifter-type glasses (or even cordials)
- Aromatic beers such as Witbier for wide-bowled glasses

Beer flute

Berliner
Weisse-style
goblet

Duvel-style
flared tulip
glass

Faceted dimpled mug
(English style)

Thistle glass

Pilsener glass

English pub glass

Figure 22-1:
A wide
range of
beer
glasses lets
you choose
the right one
for your
beer style.

  ✔ Light, spritzy, and aromatic beers for tall, narrow glasses

  ✔ Wheat beers for thick glasses (which help keep the beer cooler longer)

  ✔ Strong beers for deep, tulip-shaped glasses

The following list demystifies a few of the many specific glass styles that you may encounter anywhere today, as well as their suggested uses:

  ✔ **Beer flute:** This slim and dainty glass with a stem and base can be used for Pilseners and similar beers; however, it's meant for beers that emulate wines, such as Belgian Fruit beers. Flutes emphasize the aromatics of beer.

  ✔ **Dimpled pint mug:** This glass used to be the standard drinking vessel in British pubs. It has slowly and quietly given way to the straight-sided pint glass, which is easier to store on crowded pub shelves. Wherever you may find it, the pint mug is well suited to English Ales and Bitters.

  ✔ **Goblet:** Used almost exclusively for Berliner-style Weissbiers, this glass has a chalice-like appearance, with a wide, shallow bowl and a heavy stem and foot. This shape discourages excessive head formation; additionally, the drinker's nose fits inside the glass's mouth, which enhances the aromatic experience.

  ✔ **Pilsener:** Pilsener glasses come in a variety of styles. The more elegant ones are tall, footed, wafer-thin glasses that hold 10 or 12 ounces. The more common versions are usually either hourglass shaped or tumblers that are slightly flared at the top. These ordinary Pilsener glasses hold between 8 and 12 ounces and were designed specifically for Pilsener beers.

  ✔ **Pint glass:** The pint glass is probably the most pedestrian and inter-changeable beer glass. The standard shaker (so called because bartenders like to use this glass for shaking mixed cocktails) pint glass is a thick glass that tapers outward toward the top and holds 16 ounces of beer. (Before you say "duh!" read on.) You can also find an *imperial pint glass* that holds 20 ounces of beer, but it's not common in the U.S. This style of pint glass is perfect for any style of beer.

  Pint glasses of both sizes can be found with *sleeves* — bulges near the top of the glass that protect its lip from nicking if the glass tips over. The sleeve also enables you to stack the glasses one inside the other without them becoming wedged. Another style of pint glass is a slightly curvaceous version of the standard pint called a *pub glass*.

  ✔ **Thistle:** Thistle glasses help intensify a beer's aroma. The silhouette of the thistle glass is exactly what the name implies: it resembles a thistle flower. Drinkers use this uniquely-shaped glass almost exclusively for strong Scottish Ales. (The thistle is the symbol of the Scottish Crown.) However, this affectation is attributed to the Belgians, who developed a fondness for this style of beer after Scottish soldiers stationed in Belgium during World War I brought their strong Scottish Ale with them.

- ✔ **Tulip:** Tulip-shaped glasses are very effective in capturing the aromatic qualities of beer. The tulip glass also closely resembles its name; these glasses often have a flared opening to enable the drinker to sip the beer and the foam at the same time, creating a creamy mouthfeel. Many drinkers favor tulip glasses for strong Belgian beers.

- ✔ **Weizenbier glass:** The Weizenbier is a tall, shapely, wide-rimmed glass that holds at least 18 ounces. It's ideal for holding a half liter of Wheat beer (and the beer's towering head).

So do you need to run out and buy a dozen different sets of beer glassware to consume correctly? Not at all. Beer drinking should be enjoyable, and a great part of that enjoyment is comfort. Choose a beer-glass style that's comfortable to use, and enjoy using it — often. I recommend having a set of standard 16-ounce pint glasses on hand, as well as a set of more elegant tulip glasses to show off your proud brews.

Dirty Deeds: Cleaning Beer Glassware

After you've made your choice in glassware, commit yourself to keeping the glasses clean. No matter which beer goes in which glass, one thing is for sure — keeping your beer glassware absolutely free of dust, oily fingerprints, lipstick, and soapy residue is crucial. All these potential contaminants can have a detrimental effect on the beer.

The phrase *beer clean* describes a particular level of cleanliness. This term isn't just lip service — beer glasses need to be spotlessly clean in order to present the beer in its best light. The beer betrays any shortcomings in the cleansing and rinsing practices.

Even though a glass looks clean, it may not be. As you're rinsing, look at how the water drains off the glass. If the water sheets off the glass, the glass is beer clean; if the water breaks up, streaks, or spots, the glass is still dirty. When pouring, check for bubbles that appear on the bottom or sides of the glass below the head — these indicate invisible soap residue, grease, or dust. (Cracks and chips also attract bubbles.) Soap residues and dust in a glass can cause a beer to go flat quickly, and any fats or grease can break down and destroy the surface of the head.

The most reliable way to check for a beer-clean glass is to pour a beer into the glass, allowing a good head to form. After the beer stands for a few minutes, the head should remain firm and compact. If you didn't properly clean the glass, the foam breaks up, leaving large fish-eye bubbles.

Depending on your level of seriousness, you can clean beer glassware in a number of ways. The best thing to do is to rinse your beer glasses thoroughly in hot water right after you use them. This task may seem a bit compulsive, but it's very effective at keeping your glasses residue-free. Some drinkers are so averse to cleaning their beer glasses in soapy water that a hot-water rinse is as far as they want to go.

Check out both sides to this argument: One camp says that household dishwashing soaps are scented and can be hard to rinse off. The other camp (the one I belong to) says that if you use very small amounts of unscented dishwashing liquids and follow up immediately with a hot water rinse, you don't do any damage.

I can give you a better (and more compulsive) way to clean your glasses. Draw a sink full of hot water and add a couple of heaping tablespoons of baking soda. Use a clean dishcloth to reach the deepest recesses of the glass. Pay particular attention to the rim, making sure that you remove any lipstick or lip balm. The dishwasher itself can't do a better job.

Finally, be wary of running your glasses through the dishwasher. Food particles don't always rinse and drain out of the dishwasher after each cycle, and they could end up in your beer. Regardless of how you choose to clean your glasses, always follow with a good hot rinse and then air-dry them in a dish drainer.

Never towel-dry beer glasses. The towel can leave traces of soap, body oil, and especially lint on the glasses.

At the professional or commercial level, where governmental regulations apply, health departments require chemical sanitizers or sterilizers, including products made with *trisodium phosphate* (TSP). Commercial establishments generally use a glass-cleaning compound that's odorless, sudsless, non-fat based, and free-rinsing.

Storing Your Steins

The storing of your glassware is just as important as its cleaning. A poor storage location can make your cleaning efforts all for naught. Make sure you store air-dried glasses away from unpleasant odors, grease, or smoke coming from restrooms, kitchens, or ashtrays. If possible, store the glasses upside down in a breakfront, credenza, or similar, relatively dust-free environment.

Don't store glassware in the freezer. The glasses can pick up odors from food in the freezer, and frozen glasses are uncomfortable to hold. (They also leave a nasty water ring wherever you set them down.) Your homebrew deserves better.

Chapter 23

You Can't Judge a Bock by Its Cover: Evaluating Beer

In This Chapter

▶ Focusing your senses on the beer

▶ Evaluating beer objectively and subjectively

▶ Speaking homebrew-ese

Drinking beer shouldn't be a one-dimensional experience, although it can be if you let it. Consuming beer or wine (or even food, for that matter) is an activity that you need to approach as a full-sensory experience. The more of your senses you involve, the more you remember of the experience (positive or otherwise).

If you cook a barbecued steak for dinner, you don't just see the meat cooking on the grill; you also hear the sizzling of its juices, and you smell its tantalizing aromas wafting through the air. As you taste the steak, you not only savor the flavor, but you also describe the steak in a tactile manner — saying that it's moist and tender or dry and tough as leather (especially if you eat at my house).

Now transfer these mental notes to tasting beer. This chapter tells you how.

Because of all the senses and nuances involved in evaluating beer, a special beer lingo has evolved to help describe the entire beer experience. (Notice that I didn't say beer-*drinking* experience — the beer experience involves more than simply tasting!) I cover these special kinds of words later in this chapter.

Tuning In to Your Beer

As you pour a beer into a glass, listen to the splashing of the liquid and the fizzing of the escaping carbonation. See the fine bubbles race upward through the liquid, only to get lost in a blanket of dense foam. Watch the head rise and swell up over the lip of the glass. Breathe in the full bouquet of aromas emanating from the beer. Taste the many flavors of the malt, hops, and other ingredients. Feel the viscosity of the beer and the prickly effervescence of the carbonation on your tongue and palate. Even after you swallow, you can continue to discern the various flavors and textures of the departed beer.

When you find that you give each beer you drink this kind of attention, congratulations are in order: You've made the first step in the painless transition from plain old beer drinker to beer evaluator. This change in outlook means that you're tuning in to your beer; you're no longer just drinking it — you're *experiencing* it. As a homebrewer, this experience is a useful tool. The more you pay attention to the beers you drink, the better you become at picking up different aromas, flavors, and sensations. Your finely tuned sensory organs can then help you fine-tune your own homebrew.

Most beer drinkers find themselves simply enchanted by beer. Recognizing and identifying the beer's attributes helps you understand the basis for your enchantment. However, like most human objects of desire, beer can also have some negative traits in addition to the good ones. Rating a friend or lover according to a checklist is rather callous, but evaluating a beer by this method is not only acceptable, I highly recommend it.

Evaluating One Sense at a Time

You want to get all or as many of your senses as possible involved in the beer experience. Your sight, naturally, is the first sense to transmit an image of the beer to your brain. However, because the aromatics of the beer are very *volatile* (meaning that they're fleeting), you need to give your nose the opportunity to register the olfactory data first. Your sense of smell can also become desensitized as it becomes accustomed to the smell wafting from your glass, so taking the opportunity to appreciate a beer's fragrance at first contact is very important. After you give your sense of smell its turn, you can take a visual snapshot of the beer; follow this visual by taking in the taste and aftertaste, and then take time for reflection. In correct order, the sequential steps to experiencing beer are as follows:

1. **Smell**

2. **Look**

3. **Taste**

4. **Aftertaste**

5. **Reflect**

The following sections explore each of these experiences in more detail.

The nose knows

The fact that your nose is located above your mouth is no fluke of nature. A quick look anywhere in the animal kingdom confirms this statement. The strategic location of the nose enables you to detect questionable odors emanating from potentially digestible items before you eat or drink them. This nasal early-warning system safeguards man and beast alike from unknowingly ingesting anything that may be detrimental to their health.

Nothing about beer should have you fearing for your health and well-being (shameless overconsumption notwithstanding), but whether you need it as a warning system or not, your ability to smell is of great importance as you drink. A full third of your ability to taste is directly connected to the olfactory functions. Even as you taste beer, you also smell it in the *retronasal passage* at the back of the throat. Flavor relies on aroma, and the human nose can detect thousands of aromas. Overlooking this fundamental aspect of the beer-evaluation process would be negligent.

Alcoholic-beverage evaluators discuss the aromatic properties of their respective drinks by using the word *nose*. Nose, appropriately enough, is also the word they use to describe the total olfactory experience, which includes aroma *and* bouquet. (To distinguish between these terms, think of *aroma* as if it were a sound and *bouquet* as the volume level or intensity of that sound.) Beer connoisseurs also use the word *nose* interchangeably as a noun and verb: "He nosed his beer studiously," or "She commented on the beer's pungent nose."

So what kinds of aromas can you as beer evaluators expect to encounter? You face both positives and negatives. The positives are those smells that you expect to find in a correctly made beer of a particular style, and the negatives are odors that indicate flaws in the beer. Somewhere in between are the aromas that you don't expect to find that don't necessarily indicate problems. These smells are aromas that don't belong to the style of beer you're evaluating — they aren't necessarily bad, but stylistically speaking, they're incorrect.

Each beer style comes with its own aroma and flavor profile; the following sections offer only general parameters.

Positive aromas

Positive aromas result from the fermentation process and accentuate or underline the main ingredients in the beer. The following list describes several of these aromas:

✔ The first (and usually most obvious) aroma you encounter is the *malt character* of the beer. This aroma can run from perfumy-sweet to rich and caramelly, depending on the beer style. Ales tend toward fruity and buttery (or butterscotchy) aromas that you can trace to warm fermentations and certain yeast strains. Depending on how dark the beer is, roasty, toasty, or chocolatey aromas may also emanate from the specialty grains you added to the beer during brewing.

✔ The second most obvious aroma you may encounter is the *hop character* of the beer. This aroma, of course, depends on hops: What variety and quantity of hops the brewer used, when she added the hops to the boiling beer, and whether she added aromatic hops to the beer during the secondary fermentation phase. (See the discussion on dry hopping in Chapter 11.) Common descriptors for these hop aromas are herbal, spicy, grassy, floral, piney, citrusy, and occasionally cheesy (as well as Sleepy, Grumpy, and Doc). You may very well get a whiff of the hops even before you smell the malt — it all boils down to the individual beer style and recipe.

✔ Positive aromas that directly result from the fermentation process may include fruity esters, *diacetyl* (a buttery smell) in small quantities, and nuttiness. You may even detect alcohol in the beer's nose.

After you home in on the particular aromas in the beer, try to gauge their intensities. Although lots of beer styles feature many of the same aromatics, the different components vary in intensity.

Negative aromas

Negative aromas may include plastic-like and cooked–vegetable odors, rotten eggs, skunkiness, paint-thinner, olives or pickles, and wet dog, among other scents. (Makes ya kinda thirsty, doesn't it?) I detail the possible causes of each of the preceding aromas in Chapter 24.

You can inadvertently create negative aromas (and flavors) in any one of the following four ways:

✔ You may have used flawed ingredients to make the beer. Stale hops or moldy grain may inadvertently find their way into a brewpot now and again. (As the brewer, you need to exercise strict quality control over your ingredients.)

✔ You may be guilty of procedural mistakes — for example, steeping the grain at too high a temperature, oversparging the mash, or fermenting at too high a temperature.

✔ Wild fermentations by rogue bacteria or wild yeast may contaminate a batch anytime between cool down of the wort and bottling (or kegging) the beer.

> ✔ The way in which you store your bottled or kegged beer may affect the beer's aroma (as well as the length of time you age it). See Chapter 22 for more on proper storage techniques.

Make sure you carefully follow all the directions in sanitizing, brewing, and storing your beer to help ensure that your homebrew has positive aroma and bouquet.

Seeing is beer-lieving

Sight is the most trusted sense you have. Experts in such matters say that you base 75 percent of your perception of the world on sight; maybe that's why many beer drinkers fall into the trap of making hasty judgments of beer based on what they see. In terms of beer evaluation, the eyes may not lie, but they can only tell half-truths. A beer that looks dark, rich, strong, and roasty may be just plain dark. And what can your eyes tell you about taste or smell? Nothing — and that's the point: Your eyes can tell you only about the beer's appearance, and nothing else.

What should you look for in a beer? You can discern three things about a particular beer by using your eyes:

- ✔ **Color:** The colors that make up the various styles run the spectrum from pale straw to golden, amber, copper, orange, red, brown, and black — and everything in between. No one color is necessarily better than the other; each is the result of stylistic differences.

- ✔ **Clarity:** Many beer drinkers (Americans in particular) obsess over clear beer. If their Old Frothy isn't crystal clear, they refuse to drink it. With homebrew, however, even perfectly aged and clarified beer may again become cloudy if it's not handled correctly; you don't need to do much to disturb the yeast sediment on the bottom of the bottle.

  Commercial beer is crystal clear only because of filtering equipment and techniques developed in the 19th century. Most brews throughout history have been anywhere from hazy to murky. The source of this turbidity was the organic ingredients used in the beer-making process — especially the yeast. The particulate matter that clouded the beer was also what helped make the beer the nutritious drink that it was (and still is).

- ✔ **Head retention:** Head retention can tell a short story about the beer in hand. All beers should be able to form and keep a head; the latter is as important as the former. The head should form quickly and be very tightly knit. The head may also take on a "rocky" appearance if sufficient proteins (from the grain) are present. If a brew can't form a proper head, it may have any one of a number of problems. (See Chapter 24 for more information on these problems.)

In good taste

Here's where I get down to the basics of beer consumption. Regardless of how a beer looks and smells, if it doesn't taste good, it hasn't fulfilled its obligation. Before delving into this subjective topic, take a closer look at the primary tasting receptor in the human body: the tongue.

The four principal tastes that the tongue differentiates are salty, sour, sweet, and bitter. As shown in Figure 23-1, the tongue has been mapped to show that the tip of the tongue is where the sweet receptors are predominately located; the sides of the tongue are largely responsible for tasting sourness and saltiness; and the very back of the tongue detects bitterness. Flavor receptors are also located at the back and on the roof of the mouth, independent of the tongue.

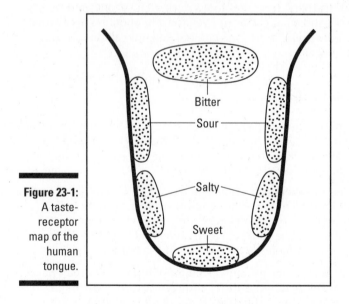

Bitter

Sour

Salty

Sweet

Figure 23-1:
A taste-receptor map of the human tongue.

Two tastes for the price of one

Beer tasting should be delineated between the first taste sensation experienced by the tip of the tongue (*foretaste*) and the *midtaste* or *true taste,* in which the beer displays its taste attractions completely. (The aftertaste I address separately in the following section.) The foretaste and midtaste should blend together mildly and harmoniously so as not to discourage further drinking.

As is true of the aroma, the foretaste is of the sweet malt — this time, the result of the tongue's sweet-sensing region up front. With most adjunct-laden brews (those made with a lot of rice or corn), the sweetness is delicate and perfumy and only vaguely tastes of true malt flavor, mainly because of the lightening effect of the adjunct grain used. The fewer adjuncts you use, the more the rich, caramelly maltiness of the barley shows through. (See Chapter 9 for more information on brewing with adjuncts.)

As you use more specialty grains in brewing — roasted ones in particular — the beer's flavor becomes more *layered,* or complex. With the exception of crystal malt, these specialty grains rarely add sweetness — only the flavors of the individual grain. These specialty malts create a mosaic of toasty, roasty, nutty, toffee, and coffeelike flavors that meld into the finished brew. A lot of these flavors register in the middle and at the back of the tongue. Some of the more highly roasted malts add a dry, astringent taste that the tongue perceives as being bitter, much like strong or stale coffee, or grape tannin in wine. Certain beers may exhibit a slight tartness that you detect between the midtaste and the aftertaste.

Normally, sour flavors constitute a flaw in beer, but in several Belgian beers and at least one German beer, sourness is actually a prerequisite for the style. For the sake of a general rule, certain Ales may have some sourness; Lagers, however, definitely should not. Generally speaking, *lactic* sourness (which is more of a mild tartness) is preferable over *acetic* sourness (which is vinegary) unless you specifically intend the latter.

Hops can make their taste presence known in one of two ways: *Hop flavor* or *hop bitterness.* (The terms are mutually exclusive.) Hop flavor is distinctive and usually tastes a lot like its aroma — grassy, piney, floral, citrusy, herbal, cheesy, and so on; you normally experience it at midtaste. Hop bitterness, on the other hand, is rather one-dimensional; you mostly experience it at the back of the tongue and in the aftertaste.

Some of the positive flavors that you can attribute to fermentation include fruitiness, diacetyl (buttery, butterscotchy), and alcohol. The fruity and buttery character you usually find only in Ales or warm-fermented beers. Brewers usually consider Lagers that exhibit these traits to be incorrectly fermented and out of character. You should find an obvious alcohol taste only in beers that have concentrations higher than 7 or 8 percent by volume.

On the negative side of the ledger is a long list of unpleasant flavors that you may experience. From the harsh astringency of boiled grain to the rubbery taste of autolyzed yeast, brewers and beer drinkers alike need to be on the lookout for these palate-destroyers. Other defective flavors include cidery aldehydes, medicinal phenolics, bloody metallics, "poopy" enterics, and dozens of equally unappetizing tastes. (See the section "Relaying the Results: Homebrew Lingo, Jargon, and Vernacular" later in this chapter.)

After you home in on the various flavors, try to gauge their intensity. Most beer styles share common flavors, but the intensity of each fluctuates according to style.

Aftertaste can be a good thing!

The *aftertaste,* also called the *finish,* is one of the most important and enjoyable aspects of the beer-drinking experience, one that chiefly affects the decision whether to take another drink. American commercial beer drinkers have been brainwashed into believing that beer is not supposed to have an aftertaste and that beers that do are bad. What a shame! Imagine dining on succulent (and expensive) Maine lobster tail dipped in pure, drawn butter, only to have the flavor disappear from your mouth the second you swallow. That flavor memory is what aftertaste is all about.

Many facets of the beer (including its faults) become more obvious in the aftertaste. The aftertaste is where you want to evaluate the various taste components of the beer, especially their harmony and balance.

Certain beer styles strive to accentuate malt over hops and vice versa, but no one ingredient should completely dominate the other.

The aftertaste is a good time to assess the *body* and tactile quality of the beer. In beverage evaluation, body refers to the weighty feel or thickness of a product. A light beer you describe as light-bodied; an India Pale Ale you may describe as medium-bodied; and a Doppelbock you describe as full-bodied. Other, more colorful descriptors, such as *wimpy, thin, voluptuous, massive,* and *robust* are more effective at getting the point across.

The tactile aspect of beverage evaluation is *mouthfeel.* You don't want to confuse taste and mouthfeel with one another — *taste* you interpret by way of the taste buds, and *mouthfeel* is the sensory experience of the whole inside of the mouth and throat. (That is, you don't taste cold; you feel it.) A light Lager beer you may describe as effervescent and watery, and a Stout you may describe as soft and chewy.

Astringency runs a fine line between taste and mouthfeel — and between hops and grain, for that matter. *Astringency* is like the mouthfeel of a grape skin (recognized as tannin in wine) or of strong tea. Hops contribute bitterness to the beer. Grain can also contribute its own bitterness in the form of *astringents.* This astringency straddles the fence between the "husky" flavor of the grain and a harsh, dry, or powdery mouthfeel. Very often, people who experience grain astringency wrongly attribute that experience to the hops. The key to distinguishing between hop bitterness and grain astringency is two-sided: You usually experience hop bittering farther back on the tongue, and grain astringency tends to affect the roof of the mouth (the soft palate) more than hop bitterness does.

You also experience alcohol most keenly in the aftertaste, not just in terms of flavor but in its warming sensation in the throat. This sensation can run from searing heat to menthol-like cooling. As is the case with brandy or cognac, the alcohol sensation is one of the understated pleasures of a high-octane brew.

From Observations to Reflections

The *reflection* is essentially your overall impression of the beer. The difference here is that you made (or should have made) all the previous assessments objectively. Reflection is the time to take into account all those objective observations and then form a subjective opinion about the beer. Here's where you do your accounting and weigh all the checks and balances. If you're judging the beer according to a particular beer style, you need to evaluate it according to style guidelines rather than by personal preferences. If, however, you're judging strictly by matter of personal taste, you can simply go with a thumbs up or a thumbs down.

Here, again, the budding homebrewer faces another choice: objective versus subjective analysis. Not a difficult choice, not a life-changing one, but one to challenge your enthusiasm and your commitment to increasing your brewing expertise. Are you satisfied with the back-patting of your beer-guzzling buddies, or are you interested in getting legitimate and unbiased feedback on your brews? If you are, I suggest that you check out Chapter 25 for the lowdown on homebrew competitions.

Relaying the Results: Homebrew Lingo, Jargon, and Vernacular

If you're like most other homebrewers, after you're comfortably established in your new hobby you want to seek out and interact with your fellow enthusiasts — those who share your passion for brewing. The exchange of information on any specific subject generally requires a common language, and, just your luck, beer evaluation also has such a language. This little-known patois is absolutely necessary for professionals within the industry as a quality-control vocabulary, as well as for professionals outside the industry who evaluate brewers' products. Homebrewers also have a vested interest in this language.

One of the best illustrations of the beer vocabulary is the internationally recognized Beer Flavor Wheel developed by a gent named Dr. Morton Meilgaard, who headed up a group of technologists from the American Society of Brewing Chemists. On Dr. Meilgaard's wheel are 14 major categories covering every aspect of beer evaluation (see Figure 23-2). Notice that, although you can register taste in seven of these categories, you can register aroma in 12 of them; the only two categories that your nose can't detect are salty and bitter.

These 14 categories further break down into 44 first-tier terms (terms such as *bitter, salty,* and *fruity*). Not listed here (for reasons of simplicity) are more than 80 second-tier terms and hundreds of comments, synonyms, and definitions that provide an in-depth (read: *professional*) understanding of correct beer evaluations.

Notice that some of the descriptors for aroma and flavor can be considered both good and bad — these run according to stylistic parameters. Musty aromas and flavors, for example, are acceptable in some bottle-conditioned Ales but are wholly inappropriate for a German Lager.

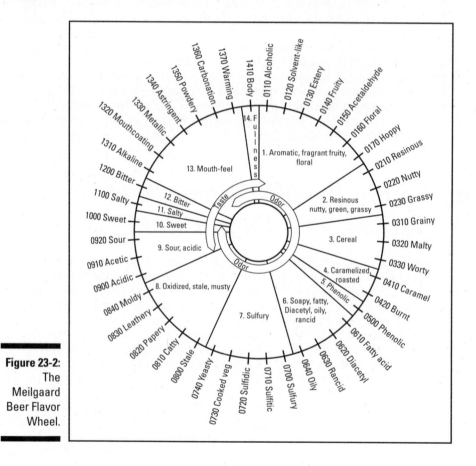

Figure 23-2:
The
Meilgaard
Beer Flavor
Wheel.

Chapter 24

Troubleshooting

In This Chapter

▶ Fixing your fermentation

▶ Solving flavoring problems

▶ Correcting aroma woes

▶ Resolving appearance issues

*J*ust as everyone is a beginner once, everyone is also likely to make a mistake at least once. Making mistakes is actually an inevitable part of the homebrewing process; the key is to figure out what the problem is and then not repeat it. Identifying these goof-ups is the first step on the road to both quality and consistency in homebrewing.

Occasionally, adverse things happen to homebrewed beer that are difficult to understand and even more difficult to describe; the purpose of this chapter is to help you troubleshoot — in standard homebrew lingo — any problems that may occur during your homebrewing adventures. You may even want to read this chapter prior to brewing a batch just to reacquaint yourself with the many pitfalls of homebrewing as well as ready yourself with an appropriate reaction to any problem that may arise.

Fermentation Lamentations

Like naive and optimistic young parents, homebrewers sometimes have unrealistic visions of how perfect everything will be and often take for granted that things will happen exactly as expected. One good example is adding yeast to sweet, sugary wort. Many brewers assume the yeast hungrily consumes whatever they feed it, finishes eating at an appropriate time, and then takes its scheduled nap. Then reality strikes. Reality, in this case, is represented by the following list of fermentation problems.

Fermentation problems occur quite frequently — sometimes your fermentation gets off to a slow start, and sometimes it never wants to stop. The following sections describe what you should do if you ever face one of these situations.

No fermentation

Your fermentation never started? First, make sure it actually hasn't. Judging fermentation by the bubbles (or lack thereof) coming out of the airlock can sometimes be deceiving. Look at the beer (if it's in a glass fermenter) or peek through the airlock hole in the lid (if it's in a plastic fermenter). Do you see any foam or a ring of brownish scum around the fermenter? If so, the beer is fermenting or has fermented. Use your hydrometer to check the gravity. The beer is typically done fermenting if the final gravity is ⅓ to ¼ of the original gravity. For example: A 1.045 beer ferments down to 1.015 to 1.012 or below. If after 24 to 48 hours fermentation has truly not begun — or you're just not sure — try adding more yeast.

Situations like this one give you good reason to keep a packet of dry yeast in the fridge for emergencies.

Be mindful of sanitary practices; how or when the beer ferments doesn't mean a thing if you contaminate the whole batch in the process. (See Chapter 3 for more advice on sanitation.)

If fermentation still hasn't begun after you add more yeast, you may have made one of the following mistakes:

- ✔ **You didn't rinse the sanitizer from the fermenter.** Sanitizer residue can kill yeast, too.

- ✔ **You put the fermenter in a place that's too cold.** Leave it at 64 to 72 degrees Fahrenheit for Ales.

- ✔ **You used old or dead yeast.** The yeast contained in ingredient kits is often so old that it's useless — always buy fresh yeast that has been kept refrigerated.

- ✔ **You rehydrated the yeast improperly by using water that was too hot (more than 110 degrees Fahrenheit).** Also, don't leave the yeast in the rehydration water too long; 30 minutes is plenty.

- ✔ **You used good yeast but shocked it with sudden changes in temperature or by adding it to wort that was too cold (under 70 degrees Fahrenheit) or too hot (over 110 degrees Fahrenheit).**

- ✔ **You didn't use enough yeast.** Pitch 10 to 15 grams of dry yeast, or use 1 package of ready-to-pitch liquid yeast per 5 gallons of beer. (See Chapter 6 for more information on RTP yeast.)

Slow-starting or stuck fermentations usually mean under-pitching of yeast, underaerated wort, or both. To correct these problems in the future, pitch a larger volume of yeast and make sure you properly aerate the wort before pitching.

High-gravity worts (those with a specific gravity of 1.056 or higher) need even more yeast and aeration for proper fermentation.

Stuck fermentation

What if the fermentation started well but seems to have become stuck? Again, looks can be deceiving — use your hydrometer to find out whether your fermentation is actually stuck or simply finished! Remember that you want the final hydrometer reading to be ⅓ to ¼ of the original gravity.

If the gravity is below 1.020, your brew has probably fermented out as much as it's going to. Some recipes contain lots of unfermentable sugars.

If the fermentation is truly stuck and the wort still has a high gravity reading, do one (or more) of the following to help restart the fermentation process:

- **Add more fresh yeast or a different strain of yeast.**

- **Try to rouse the yeast with a sanitized spoon.** Mix the yeast off the bottom to wake it up and get it to start fermenting again.

- **If all else fails, bottle or keg the beer (kegging being the safer of the two options).** If you're bottling the beer, cut back the priming sugar to less than ½ cup to reduce the chance of exploding bottles. Chapters 13 and 14 have more information about bottling and kegging.

If the batch's alcohol level is above 7 percent, the yeast may have reached its limit for alcohol tolerance. Try adding a yeast with higher alcohol tolerance, like champagne yeast. (Champagne yeast also ferments cleanly, with no off flavors.)

Never-ending fermentation

If you have a beer that has been fermenting in the primary fermenter for more than 14 days, consider these possibilities:

- **Is the temperature too low?** (60 degrees Fahrenheit for Ales and 40 degrees Fahrenheit for Lagers may be too low.) Ale yeast works very slowly at these temperatures (if at all); try warming the beer up to get it to finish fermenting.

- **Are you making a Lager?** Lagers typically take 10 to 14 days to ferment at proper temperatures (see the preceding bullet).

✔ **Do you have a wild yeast contamination?** Rogue yeasts are capable of fermenting sugars that pure beer yeast can't, so fermentation can appear to go on forever. If your beer actively ferments for over 3 weeks, it's probably contaminated, and your brew may be doomed. Smell and taste the beer and decide for yourself whether to keep it or toss it.

✔ **Did you rack into your secondary fermenter too soon?** If you're using a two-stage fermentation system, you may have racked the beer into the secondary fermenter too early. Never rack beer until vigorous fermentation is done (which usually takes a minimum of 5 days). By racking to a secondary vessel too early, you remove the beer from most of the yeast. What little yeast is left has to carry on the rest of the fermentation duties. Racking later is generally better than racking sooner. Try adding more yeast. See Chapter 11 for more on secondary fermentation.

In Bad Taste: Off Flavors and Aromas

Flavor is a complex combination of smell and taste. Sometimes, it can be difficult to tell whether the strange character of your beer is due to something you taste or smell. Pinpointing these flavors is the first step to fixing problems in your brew.

In the following sections, I give you a rundown of some common flavor and aroma defects, with possible causes and remedies (and Chapter 23 includes more evaluative information). Also check out the quick-reference troubleshooting tables at the end of this section.

Butter/butterscotch flavors

Buttery or butterscotchy flavors indicate the presence of a compound called *diacetyl*. Diacetyl occurs naturally in most warm fermentations but also dissipates naturally throughout the course of a proper fermentation cycle. Very obvious diacetyl flavor may indicate other problems, such as extremely warm fermentation temperatures, unhealthy yeast, underoxygenated wort, or bacterial contamination.

Homebrewers can reduce diacetyl levels in their beer by allowing a *diacetyl rest* at the end of primary fermentation. Yeast can reduce diacetyl levels in beer; the key is to not rack the beer over to a secondary fermenter for 2 to 3 days after initial fermentation has subsided to allow the yeast time to rid the beer of the diacetyl.

Many beer styles in the Ale family — especially those from Britain — can exhibit noticeable diacetyl flavors. The presence of diacetyl in any Lager beer, however, indicates a flaw.

It's sometimes difficult to distinguish between the caramelly flavors created by caramel malts (caramel is made by heating butter and sugar) and the buttery flavor derived from diacetyl. Novice judges beware!

Sour/tart flavors

Sourness in the average beer is usually a sure sign of a bacterial contamination. These bacteria can produce lactic acid or acetic acid (found in vinegar), and these acids can range from the mild tartness of grapefruit to the mouth-puckering tanginess of lemons.

The bacteria that creates lactic acid is *lactobacillus,* and the bacteria that creates acetic acid is *acetobacter.*

You can easily prevent beer spoilage by increasing your cleaning and sanitizing efforts. Be especially suspicious of any scratched plastic equipment that may be harboring bacteria; you may need to replace that equipment. Also, be careful when handling grain around sanitized equipment — grain dust harbors bacteria that can travel airborne for long distances. All bacteria tend to multiply faster than yeast; this speed means if bacteria are present in your yeast cultures, they can increase dramatically every time you repitch the yeast. In this case, replace your yeast culture.

In many beer styles — mostly Belgian styles — sour flavors aren't only acceptable, they're expected. Even the most famous stout in the world (Guinness) undergoes a mild lactic fermentation (brewers sour a small portion of the beer and then blend it back into the rest of the batch).

Medicinal/plastic/smoky flavors

These flavors comprise part of a class of compounds called *phenols.* Phenolic flavors can come from wild yeast. The best cure is to improve your sanitation procedures and/or to replace your yeast culture.

Before knocking yourself out trying to eliminate *all* phenolic flavors, be aware that some beer styles actually include phenolics as part of their taste and aromatic profiles. These styles include Bavarian Weizenbier, some Belgian Ales, and most Smoked beers.

Chlorine can also give rise to these flavors, forming what are called *chlorophenols.* Always use dechlorinated water (preboiled or carbon-filtered), and be sure that you thoroughly rinse any bleach off of your equipment after sanitizing.

Papery/cardboard/sherry-like flavors (oxidation)

It's important not to aerate finished beer during the bottling process, and oxidation is why. (See Chapter 13 for bottling procedures.) Oxygen in finished beer is where these flavors come from. Remember the following:

- ✓ **Be careful when siphoning.** To avoid splashing or foaming, stir priming solution very carefully.

- ✓ **Don't aerate hot wort, either.** The oxygen comes back to haunt you later. (Aerate cooled wort only at pitching time.)

- ✓ **If you keg, use CO_2 to purge all vessels of oxygen.**

- ✓ **If you top-up fermenters with water, use boiled and cooled water.** This process removes oxygen from the water.

- ✓ **Fill bottles to the highest reasonable level.** This process minimizes air contact with the beer. Shoot for 1 inch from the bottle opening.

Oxygen-absorbing caps are available for bottles if you want to pay the higher cost. For all the good that these caps do, they aren't a cure for sloppy beer/wort handling.

Dry/puckering mouthfeel (astringency)

Sometimes, you may experience a dry, puckering sensation (similar to chewing on a grape skin) in your beer's finish; you typically feel this on the back sides of the tongue and on the back of the roof of your mouth. This *astringency* is caused by compounds called tannins.

The most common cause of astringency is improper handling of grains (see bulleted list below). If you're not careful, tannins can be extracted from the grains and washed into the wort.

The following steps can help you keep the tannin extraction from malt husks to a minimum:

- ✓ **When milling malt, don't overcrack the grain.** Fine husk particles can easily get into the wort.

- ✓ **Don't oversparge grains.** By the time you extract the last bit of sugar, you've also extracted a good amount of tannins. Limit sparging to 2 quarts of water per pound of grain.

✔ **Don't use sparge water over 168 degrees Fahrenheit.** Exceeding this temperature extracts tannins in large quantities.

✔ **Try to acidify your sparge water (less than 7.0 pH).** Alkaline pH (greater than 7.0) can also extract tannins from grains. You can also add gypsum to the sparge water to keep the mash pH and wort pH low. (The best pH for sparge water is between 5.0 and 6.0.)

Harshness/hotness

Occasionally, a beer may taste harsh or have a mouthfeel that's best described as *hot*. Many factors can cause a harsh tasting beer.

✔ **Excessive hopping rates can create a bitter harshness in your beer.**

✔ **Beers made with hard or chalky water can taste harsh.** See Chapter 7 for more on dealing with hard water.

✔ **High fermentation temperatures can produce *fusel alcohol,* which creates a hot, solvent-like sensation.** Try not to exceed a fermentation temperature of about 75 degrees Fahrenheit.

✔ **Overcarbonated beers can have an unpleasant, prickly harshness on the palate.** Contaminated and overprimed beers are usually excessively carbonated.

Metallic flavor

Sometimes a metallic taste in your brew is the result of oxidation, but you can typically trace it back to iron utensils or equipment. Try to use copper or stainless-steel vessels for boiling. If you use enamelware pots, make sure that the ceramic surfaces aren't chipped. Also, if you can taste iron in your water, you can taste it in your beer. If this is the case, you need to consider buying your brewing water bottled.

Skunk aroma

Skunky smelling beer is the unfortunate result of storing beer in direct light for extended periods of time. Sunlight has the most detrimental effect, but fluorescent and incandescent light can also destroy beer aroma. Beer that smells skunky is referred to as *light-struck.*

Sulfury odors

Certain sulfury (hydrogen sulfide) odors can emanate from yeast and can smell like rotten eggs, burned matches, rubber, and so on. The source is usually yeast that's breaking down (a process called *autolysis*). The key to keeping these odors from occurring is to rack your beer promptly after primary fermentation. Certain Lager yeasts also naturally produce these odors; changing yeast strains or (in the case of Lagers) proper aging can sometimes correct the problem.

Vegetal flavors and aromas

Occasionally, you may taste or smell a cornlike character in your beer. This quality comes from a compound called *dimethyl sulfide* or DMS.

DMS comes from the malt or, more specifically, the heating or boiling of the wort. Pale malts also produce more DMS than darker malts. Typically, DMS is driven off in the steam of the boil, but after you turn the heat off, DMS can still creep up in the wort. If you cool your wort too slowly, you trap large quantities of DMS in the beer. So the best preventative measure is to cool your wort as quickly as possible to keep DMS at a minimum.

One important point is that some DMS is part of the flavor profile of Lager beers due to the fact that Lager malts produce larger amounts of DMS. Although you can expect some DMS in Lagers, you certainly don't need to purposely create it. If you use Lager malts, you still have plenty of DMS in your beer.

Certain bacteria also create DMS. When this happens, very large amounts of DMS are typically present. These bacteria can also produce other flavors and odors that are reminiscent of vegetables, such as cooked cauliflower and broccoli. To minimize these off flavors, cool the wort and pitch the yeast as soon as possible.

Flavor and Aroma Therapy Quick References

So your beer stinks, huh? Well, if you're speaking literally rather than figuratively, the following table is for you. If your beer doesn't smell quite right, the problem can be any number of things. For this reason, Table 24-1 gives you some symptoms, the corresponding beer lingo, and then (most important) some possible sources of the problem.

Table 24-1	Beer Aroma Troubleshooting List	
If Your Beer Smells Like	*The Proper Term Is*	*The Source May Be*
Adhesive bandages	Phenolic	Bacterial contamination; residue from a sanitizing agent (Note: This odor is expected of certain beer styles)
Apple cider	Acetaldehyde	Refined sugar in the recipe or bacterial contamination
Baby diapers	Enteric	Bacterial contamination
Banana	Banana esters	Certain Ale yeast strains, particularly Bavarian Weizenbier and Belgian Strong Ales
Barnyard	Enteric	Bacterial contamination
Bubblegum	Bubblegum	Certain Ale yeast strains, particularly Belgian Strong Ales and Bavarian Weizenbier
Butter/butterscotch	Diacetyl	Bacteria; certain yeast strains; warm fermentation; short aging
Cardboard or paper	Oxidized	Contact with air; old, stale beer
Cauliflower or Cooked cabbage	Vegetal	Bacterial contamination
Cloves	Phenolic	Certain yeast strains, such as those in Bavarian Weizenbier
Cooked corn	DMS (dimethyl sulfide)	Poor grain quality; bacterial contamination
Cooking sherry	Oxidized	Contact with air; long and warm fermentation
Green apple	Acetaldehyde	Refined sugar in the recipe; bacterial contamination
Leather	Oxidized	Contact with air; old, stale beer
Marker	Phenolic	Bacterial contamination; residue of sanitizing agent
Matches (burnt) or Sulfur	Hydrogen sulfide	Natural by-product of fermentation that's normally flushed out with the production of carbon dioxide

(continued)

Table 24-1 *(continued)*

If Your Beer Smells Like	The Proper Term Is	The Source May Be
Mold	Moldy	Sanitation problem; leaking package seal
Nail polish remover	Solvent-like	Esters produced during high-temperature fermentations
Olives (green or black) or Pickles	Acetic	Acetobacteria contamination
Paint thinner	Solvent-like	Fusel alcohols produced during high-temperature fermentations
Rotten eggs	Hydrogen sulfide	Natural by-product of fermentation that's normally flushed out with the production of carbon dioxide
Rubber	Hydrogen sulfide	Yeast autolysis
Skunk	Light-struck	Damage from light
Smoke	Phenolic	Use of dark or smoked grains that evoke this aroma
Soap	Soapy	Residue from sanitizing agents
Vinyl upholstery	Phenolic	Bacterial contamination; residue from sanitizing agents
Wet dog	Musty	Bacterial contamination; lengthy aging of bottle-conditioned beer

If your brew tastes odd (or even *bad*), check out Table 24-2 for help discerning the most common off flavors, their correct names, and their possible sources.

Table 24-2   Beer Taste Troubleshooting List

If Your Beer Tastes Like	The Proper Term Is	The Source May Be
Blood	Metallic	Iron in water supply; contact with metals
Butter/butterscotch	Diacetyl	Certain yeast strains; warm fermentations
Cardboard	Oxidized	Contact with air; old, stale beer

If Your Beer Tastes Like	The Proper Term Is	The Source May Be
Cauliflower or Cooked cabbage	Vegetal	Bacterial contamination
Chalk	Astringent	Overfermentation; misuse of grain
Cooked corn	DMS (dimethyl sulfide)	Poor grain quality; bacterial contamination
Cooking sherry	Oxidized	Contact with air; long, warm fermentation
Green apple	Acetaldehyde	Use of refined sugar; bacterial contamination
Harsh	Astringent	High hop bitterness; misuse of grain.
Olives or Pickles	Acetic	Acetobacteria contamination
Powdery	Astringent	Lack of sweetness; grain astringency
Salt	Salty	Use of brewing salts, especially sodium chloride and magnesium sulfate
Smoke	Phenolic	Use of dark or smoked grains that evoke this flavor
Soap	Soapy	Residue of sanitizing agents
Sour milk	Lactic	Lactic fermentation (which is intentional in some beer styles such as Berliner Weisse)
Sulfur	Hydrogen sulfide	Natural by-product of fermentation; can also be attributed to certain grains such as 6-row pale malt
Tin can	Metallic	Iron in water supply; contact with metals

Conditioning and Appearance Problems

Once your beer is done fermenting, you need to condition it. *Conditioning* is an added aging process during which the beer is naturally clarified and recarbonated. As simple as the process seems, things don't always work out the way they should. The appearance of your beer may mean a lot to you, and color and clarity can influence how drinkers perceive it. This section addresses problems that may occur with the conditioning and appearance of your brew.

Flat out of gas

What if your beer is flat? If you can still feel the CO_2 bubbles on your tongue, but the beer just isn't holding a head, your beer isn't the problem — the dirty glass is. See Chapter 22 for more on proper glass-cleaning techniques.

If you can't even feel the carbonation, check these potential problems:

- ✔ **Did you age the beer enough?** Typically, your beer needs at least 2 weeks to carbonate properly in the bottle. Lagers take even longer because of the cold storage. After you bottle your beer, be sure to keep the bottles at 66 to 70 degrees Fahrenheit for 2 weeks for proper conditioning. Don't store your beer cold until after this conditioning period is over.

- ✔ **Did you prime the beer with the proper amount of corn sugar?** Always use ½ to ¾ cup of corn sugar per 5 gallons of beer (but never more). And be sure that you thoroughly mix the priming sugar solution into the wort — pour the dextrose and water mixture into the bottling bucket before you drain the beer into it.

- ✔ **Did you thoroughly rinse your equipment?** Make sure you rinse all the equipment of sanitizer residue. Any residue can shock or kill the yeast necessary to carbonate the beer.

- ✔ **Did you tightly seal your bottles?** Prior to bottling, check all your bottles and caps for cracks, chips, or imperfections. These flaws let CO_2 escape from the bottles. Improperly seated caps can also be the culprit.

Thar she blows! Overcarbonated beers

Got beer that foams and gushes? Again, check the priming rate. (See Chapter 13 for more on priming.) Also, be sure that your beer has fully fermented before you bottle it. Any residual unfermented sugar left in the beer causes your brew to become overcarbonated.

Another cause of overcarbonation can be contamination. Certain wild yeasts and bacteria consume sugars that beer yeast can't. This occurrence produces copious amounts of CO_2. The excess carbonation comes out of solution quickly and produces gushing. Remember to sanitize bottles, caps, and so on, and always boil your priming solutions.

In a haze: Cloudy beers

The average beer drinker is accustomed to crystal-clear, filtered beers. If your beer tastes good but has a haze, don't worry about it — most of the time the haze does not affect the flavor. Some beers, like unfiltered wheat beers, are cloudy by nature.

Eventually, most haze (especially yeast) settles out if given enough time. However, if you really need clear beer, you can try some clarifying products. Check out Chapter 9 to find out more about clarifying and fining agents.

Chill haze is a phenomenon caused by chilling your beer. A clear beer at room temperature becomes hazy when refrigerated. The haze doesn't affect the flavor and eventually settles out on its own. The beer also clears up if you allow it to warm up again.

Like anything else, fining agents have their drawbacks. Any time you remove something you want to get rid of (yeast, haze), you can also inadvertently remove something you don't want to get rid of (body, head retention). Be careful about improper use or overuse of finings.

Poor head, bad body

Do you need better body and head retention in your beers? Proteins in your beer are responsible for a great body and a head to go with it (and who doesn't want that?). If you don't use any grains in your beer, you need to. Incorporating ½ to 1 pound of crystal malt or CaraPils malt (per 5-gallon batch) into your wort helps. (See Chapter 4 for more information about malts.) Adding flavorless malto-dextin powder to your wort also works like a charm (use 4 to 8 ounces per 5 gallons).

Chapter 25

Homebrew Competitions

In This Chapter
▶ Entering homebrew competitions
▶ Becoming a beer judge

*J*ust as amateur chefs and bakers compete in chili cook-offs and pie bake-offs, homebrew competitions provide a competitive platform for people who like to make beer. Back in 1985, a dozen such competitions may have been held across the country, attracting a couple hundred entries; now a couple hundred competitions attract thousands of entries every year. These competitions are held at the local, regional, and national level and offer awards of varying sizes to the winners.

Because homebrew competitions now have so much at stake, the American Homebrewers Association (AHA) in Boulder, Colorado, in conjunction with the Home Wine and Beer Trade Association (HWBTA), saw the need to establish a Beer Judge Certification Program (BJCP) to standardize judging and scoring procedures. (For more information regarding the BJCP and how to become a beer judge, check out the section "Becoming a Barrister of Beer" later in this chapter.) After establishing the BJCP, the AHA created a sanctioning program that guaranteed uniform rules and operations at all AHA sanctioned events.

Today, the homebrewing community considers any competition that doesn't request and receive an AHA sanction a maverick event. Neither judges nor contestants are quick to participate in nonconformist events — judges because they don't earn BJCP judging points, and contestants because they aren't guaranteed a respectable level of competency from the judges. In this chapter, I give you the lowdown on AHA-sanctioned beer competitions, including how they're run and how you can enter. If simply entering isn't enough involvement for you, I also cover how you can become a beer judge.

What's Involved in Homebrewing Competitions?

The general format for an AHA-sanctioned event goes something like this: The event's sponsor picks a calendar date far in advance of the competition, both for positioning purposes (so that it doesn't coincide with any other competitions) and for advertising purposes (to enable homebrewers to plan their entries ahead of time and to make sure that enough judges can attend). A homebrew club (or several clubs together) usually sponsors the event, but retail stores — and especially homebrew shops — may also sponsor such an event. The sponsor must also reserve a location at which to hold the competition and actively solicit donations toward prizes.

Closer to the day of the event, the sponsor contacts qualified judges and coaxes and cajoles them into attending. (Judges rarely receive any compensation for their participation.) Meanwhile, word of the event spreads to potential competitors via popular press, direct mail, Internet postings, and word-of-mouth. Customarily, all competitors must submit their entries at least one week in advance of the event so that the beer has time to settle and the competition committee can correctly register all entries. After the committee logs in the brews by beer style and category, they store the entries in cool conditions until the event.

The typical AHA-sanctioned event may have as many as 28 major classifications and another 50 subcategories open to entries. The major classifications include beer, Cider, Mead, and even sake. If the competition committee doesn't receive enough entries to fill a certain category, it pairs those entries with other, similar categories and instructs the judges to judge them separately according to style — for example, the judges would judge German-Style Pilseners and Bohemian-Style Pilseners together in the same grouping but differently according to their individual style.

How are the entries judged?

On the day of the event — or the first day, in the case of larger, multi-day competitions — the sponsor readies the location, assembles the panel of judges, and hands out judging assignments. *Stewards* — people who help the competition run smoothly (often beer judge trainees) — make sure that all judges have the correct judging forms and score sheets, appropriate writing implements, drinking water, and something to cleanse the palate between beers (usually French bread or unsalted crackers).

The standard AHA scoring format uses a 50-point system. The aroma scores 0 to 12 points; the appearance, 0 to 3; the flavor, 0 to 20; the body, 0 to 5; and the overall impression, 0 to 10. The score sheet also addresses beer quality according to "Stylistic Accuracy, Technical Merit, and Intangibles." with check boxes (but no extra points)

At a sanctioned event, a common practice is to have all the participating judges evaluate a *calibration beer* as a way of tuning up their palates before moving on to the actual competition beers. Every judge gets a sample of the same calibration beer, usually a commercially made product. After all the judges evaluate the calibration beer (according to its style), they turn in their score sheets. The competition director tabulates the judges' scores, announces the average score, and reminds judges who scored higher or lower than the average to calibrate themselves up or down to achieve balanced scores with the other judges.

The competition committee pairs the event's judges according to their stylistic preferences and/or level of knowledge. (If a judge has no experience with Australian Aboriginal Ale, for example, that judge has no business judging that category.) No fewer than two judges ever judge a brew together.

After tasting the brew and writing their remarks on the score sheet, the judges usually discuss the beer's attributes together. Although judges are at liberty to disagree with one another on the finer points, their scores should always reflect a shared opinion of the beer within a 5-point margin. (A huge disparity in scores indicates a bias or fundamental lack of knowledge on the part of one or both judges.) The brewers always receive these score sheets shortly after the event.

In the name of fairness and objectivity, only the competition committee members, who are responsible for registering and logging in the entries, know the identities of the individual brewers. Judges aren't privy to any information that divulges the brewers' identities.

After all the beer categories are judged and the score sheets tabulated, the best beer from each category goes on to the Best-of-Show round. The competition committee hand-picks the most senior and experienced judges (from a pool of those who don't have a brew competing for the Best of Show) to adjudicate the beers at this level. Judges use no score sheets; they choose the two or three beers that best represent their respective categories by process of elimination. The final three beers left standing receive first-, second-, and third-place honors, based on the judges' evaluations. (Some competitions choose up to four or five Best-of-Show beers.)

The prizes at homebrewing competitions nowadays are nothing to sneeze at. Generally speaking, the larger the competition is, the more valuable the prizes are. The national competitions, especially the one hosted by the AHA, are exceptionally generous, thanks to the donations that large breweries and allied businesses worldwide make.

How do I enter a homebrew competition, and what are the rules?

To enter a homebrew competition, you first need to find out where and when the competitions take place. You can find this information at various locations on the Internet. The standard eligibility requirement is simple: The beer must be genuine homebrewed beer made *in the home*. Beyond this standard rule, individual competitions may set the entry requirements and rules and regulations, including those described in the following list:

- **Competition entry fee:** The entry fee is a nominal amount to help defray the costs of hosting competitions. In addition to prizes (which may or may not be donations), competition committees must find a location for the event, which often comes at a price; they must provide food for the judges and stewards (who don't receive payment for their services); and they must cover the costs for mailings in advance of the event and again for mailings of score sheets and prizes after the event. Entry fees generally run from $5 per entry up to $15 per entry, depending on the event. Most events also give price breaks to brewers who submit more than, say, four or five entries.

- **Bottle size limits:** These limits are to keep all entries somewhat uniform. Typical bottle size requirements are from 12 to 16 ounces (in green or brown glass). If sponsors didn't impose limits on submission size, storage or refrigeration problems could result. Unusually sized or odd-shaped bottles can also compromise brewer anonymity.

- **Number of bottles per entry:** Most competitions require two or three bottles per entry and for a good reason: One bottle is for the first round of judging; if a particular beer takes first place in its category, it moves on to the Best-of-Show round, at which point the judges sample a fresh bottle. A third bottle is to cover for any breakage that may occur in shipping and handling. If no breakage occurs, the leftover beer becomes the well-earned property of the host club. (Now *that's* some incentive to sponsor a competition!)

- **Category and classification:** The AHA keeps a composite listing of some 20-odd major beer styles and their taste profiles, along with a multitude of lesser substyles. (See the recipe chapters in this book for more on these profiles.) These standards are respected throughout the home-brewing community. All AHA-sanctioned events use AHA beer style guidelines for judging purposes, but each event reserves the right to pick and choose which categories to judge at each event — make sure that you read the competition category rules carefully.

✔ **Entry deadline:** As I mention in the section "What's Involved in Homebrewing Competitions?" earlier in this chapter, the customary deadline is one week before the competition to give participants time for registration and cataloging, as well as to provide time for the beer to settle. Each competition committee, however, has the right to set a deadline as it sees fit.

How do I send my beer?

Anyone familiar with the U.S. postal laws knows that sending alcoholic beverages through the mail is illegal. Some package shipping services, however, deliver homebrewed beer to a designated location "for analysis only." (Like the U.S. Postal Service, these companies also make international deliveries.) Only once in many years of shipping homebrew this way was I ever questioned about the contents of my parcel or its purpose. Just make sure you pack the bottles well, using wadded newspaper or Styrofoam packing peanuts. Line the inside of the box with a plastic bag and place the bottles and packing material inside the liner. Some competitions recommend double-boxing for extra protection.

Make sure that you fill out all the necessary forms and attach them to bottles, where appropriate — and don't forget to include the entry fee!

Many homebrewers who live close to the competition location drop off their brews at the designated location and save themselves the shipping costs.

Becoming a Barrister of Beer

So you think you want to become a beer judge? You think that the job sounds like an easy gig? You think you'd get to drink a lot of free beer? The answer to the first question may be "Yes," but the answer to the second two is "No!" — conditionally speaking, of course. You do reach a point where the good aspects of the job far outweigh the bad, but becoming a certified beer judge is no cake walk. If you think you're qualified just because you drink beer, think again.

What it takes to become a beer judge

Becoming good at judging beer takes time, practice, experience, perseverance, and a genuine desire to excel at the task. The following list describes in detail what developing these characteristics requires:

How's my brewing?

Sending your homebrewed beer to a sanctioned competition can be a very gratifying aspect of homebrewing. Beyond winning nice ribbons and prizes, however, competitions offer homebrewers clear and objective evaluations of their beers by competent and knowledgeable beer judges. For each brew that you send to a sanctioned competition, you're guaranteed to receive all the judges' score sheets in return. These score sheets go beyond assigning a simple numerical score to your brew; because of their training, BJCP judges offer intelligent and coherent feedback on your beer. Although some of what they say about your brew may be guesswork, the judges' comments may also point out important negative attributes in your beer and in your brewing technique that may help you improve not only your beer but also your enjoyment of homebrewing. This information alone is often worth the entry fee.

✔ **Time:** No one becomes an expert at anything overnight. Just because you've been drinking Old Foamy for years (since you were legally old enough, of course) doesn't qualify you for anything but a loyal-customer award and a rebate coupon. You need to spend time taste-testing and absorbing all the style parameters of various beers. The more you read, taste, and practice, the quicker you develop the skills you need to be a good beer judge. (Depending on your level of dedication, you can achieve judgeship within a year.)

✔ **Practice:** Even good and experienced judges need to practice beer judging. You must put your evaluation skills to the test regularly to stay sharp and in tune. You don't need to practice just at actual competitions either; regular evaluation of your own homebrews or store-bought beer accomplishes the same goal.

✔ **Experience:** A good beer judge has a deep and profound knowledge of beer styles and has personally tasted hundreds of different brands from different countries and breweries in a quest for this experience. And although you can conceivably become a beer judge without being a homebrewer, you'd miss a fundamental part of what the game is all about. Every certified beer judge I know is a homebrewer.

✔ **Perseverance:** Beer-judging opportunities don't always come to you. Some travel and a significant contribution of personal time are imperative to progress within the system. No one pays you for this honor, and no one reimburses you for your expenses.

✔ **Genuine desire:** If you can't drink Barley Wine (a rich, thick, alcoholic Ale) for three hours before lunch, if you can't stomach beer from 9 a.m. till 5 p.m., if you can't handle tasting brews for two or maybe even three days straight, you may want to take up stamp collecting instead of beer judging. And by the way, you get no guarantees that everything you judge is gonna taste good!

I can never forget one particular national competition during which a table of judges had to evaluate a garlic beer. That stuff was so potent they had to open the windows before judging could continue!

Your enthusiasm is undiminished? Your resolve unflagging? Good; you may find a place in the Beer Judge Certification Program. And because this program is the only one of its kind in the United States (with members in Canada), you have no alternative choices if you really want to become a beer judge. However, the Association of Brewers, parent organization of the American Homebrewers Association, is currently sharing information with brewing groups in Europe and Asia. It's just a matter of time before countries in these regions develop their own beer judging organizations.

At the time I became a beer judge in the spring of 1986, I was one of only 70 across the country and the first one in the state of Illinois. Today, over 2,000 judges from every state in the Union — and Canada — are in the BJCP.

Advancing to supreme quart justice

The BJC Program was established in 1985 to educate already-knowledgeable people in correct procedural judging techniques and to standardize scoring methods. After a judge candidate proves her knowledge and ability by passing an entrance exam at a certain level, she may progress through the program by earning experience points for judging, stewarding, and organizing competitions. The number of points she receives depends on what position (organizer, judge, steward) she holds in a competition and how large the competition is (as measured by the number of entries). As she accumulates experience points, she can advance to the next level (assuming that she achieves a minimum exam score for that next level). I describe these levels in the following list:

- **Apprentice Judge:** The BJCP added this level (originally called *Novice judge*) in 1995 to recognize anyone who fails to achieve the minimum score of 60 on the program entrance exam. This level serves as an encouragement for inexperienced judges to continue to work within the system and improve on their judging skills.

- **Recognized Judge:** This level requires a minimum test score of 60 percent. You need no judging experience points to start at this level.

- **Certified Judge:** This level requires a minimum test score of 70 percent and at least 5 experience points.

- **National Judge:** This level requires a minimum test score of 80 percent and at least 20 experience points.

- **Master Judge:** This level requires a minimum test score of 90 percent and at least 40 experience points.

✔ **Grand Master Judge:** This level requires a minimum test score of 90 percent, at least 100 experience points, and an additional point total based on special services performed on behalf of the BJCP.

Note: Retaking the test to achieve a higher score isn't only allowed — it's encouraged!

One other position is that of *Honorary Master Judge*. This position is a temporary designation bestowed by the BJCP on certain persons widely known for their judging skills and mastery of the craft who may not have fulfilled the official requirements of that level.

The BJCP program still requires an entrance exam, and the test *isn't* free. Your first shot costs 50 bucks, and the cost for any repeats lowers to $30 — or you can take either the essay or tasting portions of the test separately for $15. (How do you think the organization pays for administrative costs?) The BJCP administers the exam throughout the country on many dates throughout each year. The frequency is determined by the number of requests for the exam in a given region and the availability of qualified proctors. (Proctoring the exam is one way Grand Master Judges can earn their service points.) For more and updated information, contact the Beer Judge Certification Program at the following Web site: www.bjcp.org.

Scoring and evaluating beer

From a professional-standards perspective, you must judge beer, like wine, according to its style. To judge a hearty vintage Cabernet Sauvignon against a field of young and fruity Beaujolais wines wouldn't be at all fair. Likewise, you can't compare a Bock beer to a group of Brown Ales. You must judge each wine and each beer on its own merits and against wines and beers of like style. This type of judging is standard procedure in the various amateur and commercial beer competitions that take place across the United States, including the widely acclaimed Great American Beer Festival in Denver.

For a person to critically evaluate beer this way, a reasonable understanding of beer styles and an ability to be fair and objective is integral to the process. Anyone who takes upon himself the task of evaluating beers should do so with at least a modicum of respect for the beer and a maximum of responsibility for the personal critique. The correct evaluation of beer requires the taster to follow certain rules of fairness. A clean palate is essential to a valid taste assessment of beer. (Judging beer immediately after eating raw onions or garlic chip dip, for example, is a definite no-no.) But you also want to avoid judging beer on an empty stomach (to lessen the possibility of inebriation).

Yet another problem inherent to taste evaluations that involve any product containing alcohol is the fact that alcohol itself deadens the various sensory systems of the human body — especially the palate. Thus, palate fatigue becomes a problem. *Palate fatigue* is what occurs if you taste too many beers, especially of like style, one after the other. It's also the main reason why wine tasters spit out the wine instead of swallowing it. Beer tasters, on the other hand, are just too appreciative to waste a good thing by following that example.

Part VII
The Part of Tens

The 5th Wave   By Rich Tennant

In this part . . .

This part provides a barrelful of unrelated but fun, helpful, and interesting topics about brewing beer. Wanna
get more personally involved in your brewing? Read
Chapter 26. Are you a gadget freak (or do you have a
bunch of cash burning a hole in your pocket)? Check out
Chapter 27. Got some questions about beer and brewing?
Head to Chapter 28.

Chapter 26

Ten (or so) Ways to D.I.G.I.B.I.Y. (Do It, Grow It, Build It Yourself)

In This Chapter

▶ Banking your yeast

▶ Manipulating those grains

▶ Growing hops (in leaps and bounds)

▶ Building the equipment you need

*H*omebrewers who are really into their hobby inevitably continue to discover more and experiment more, simultaneously expanding their horizons and their own control over their craft. This chapter is for those intrepid individuals who intend to immerse themselves deeply in new homebrewing techniques, as well as for the rest of you who just have lots of idle hours on your hands.

Banking Yeast

Yeast is the logical first choice for advanced involvement in the control over your beer's ingredients. *Yeast banking, ranching,* or *farming* — call the procedure what you want — is all about culturing your own pure yeast strains and keeping them on hand for future use in your home brewery. The basic idea behind yeast banking is that you keep several pure, live yeast cultures — in bulk quantity — on hand for inoculating your future brews. In short, if you bank your own yeast, you have the type of yeast you want when you want it and in sufficient quantities for pitching into your new brew.

As is true of homebrewing itself, you can do your yeast banking on various levels. At the frugal end, you can use mason jars and cheap wine carafes for storing yeast. At the extravagant end, expensive glass beakers and flasks lend a high-tech look to your unfinished basement. The way you decide to go all depends on your approach.

Before moving on, remember that sanitizing techniques either make or break your foray into yeast banking. If you aren't willing and able to practice absolutely *aseptic* (pristinely sanitary) yeast-handling techniques, maybe you should just throw the towel in now. (See Chapter 3 for more on proper sanitation procedures.)

Preparing to open your own bank

When starting up your yeast bank, you should keep it simple. The average homebrewer probably doesn't use more than a half-dozen different strains in a year's time. For each strain you intend to bank, you need the following equipment:

- At least one holding tank (for example, a mason jar, wine carafe, or glass flask). Call this slurry the *mother culture.* As you continue to propagate the yeast, you need more vessels.

- A rubber stopper to fit the holding tank (and any other vessels you add later).

- An airlock (for each vessel). See Chapter 2 for a discussion of airlocks.

Additional items you need on hand include isopropyl alcohol and sterile cotton balls for sanitizing yeast-handling equipment (butane lighters also come in handy to sterilize, or *flame,* the openings of beer-bottle holding tanks); dry malt extract to feed the yeast; pure clean water (the same as you brew with); and the yeasts! Although your goal is self-sufficiency, you still need to start with pure yeast cultures from a reliable yeast supplier.

Consider using self-stick labels to identify each strain if you're banking more than one. One yeast strain doesn't look a whole lot different from another, and confusion may undermine your efforts.

Creating yeast

Follow the directions in Chapter 12 for making a yeast starter culture, because that's basically what you're doing. The difference is that after the yeast completes its mini-fermentation in its holding tank, you can either repeat the procedure in a larger vessel (such as a half-gallon apple-cider jug) with more wort, or you can subdivide the yeast into several vessels of the same size. Using one large vessel is cheaper and easier than using several smaller ones, but the risk of contamination is lower if you separate the mixture into several vessels and open them one at a time rather than reopen the large one every time you need to pitch a brew. Regardless of how you store them, keep all your yeast cultures refrigerated until you need them.

As you're boiling the wort you intend to use as yeast food, make a larger batch and store the excess sterile wort in sanitized and capped beer bottles for future use. (Keep these bottles refrigerated, too.)

Handling Grain

Grain handling is an area of homebrewing into which very few homebrewers venture — and probably smartly so, because grain growing and malting procedures require vast amounts of land, equipment, capital, and expertise. This task, therefore, is best left to the farmers and maltsters who can provide you with high-quality product much more quickly and cheaply than you can possibly produce yourself.

You can, however, manipulate your grains in some small (and very tasty) ways. Roasting and smoking are a couple of the methods that can give you more control over your brew.

Roast-a-rama

Why would you want to roast your own grains? Again, it's a control issue (or lack of a social life). Roasted grains give your beer complexity by imbuing it with various toasty, roasty, and nutty flavors (which isn't to say that you can't just buy these same grains at the local homebrew supplier).

To roast your own grains, start with a couple of pounds of *unground* pale malt (Ale or Lager malt is fine) and follow these steps:

1. **Preheat the oven to 350 degrees Fahrenheit.**

2. **Spread the grain out thinly on a cookie sheet or a pizza tin.**

3. **Place the grain tin on the highest oven rack, set a timer, and watch the grain closely.**

At increments of ten minutes or so, your grain should progress through a spectrum of gold, amber, copper, and brown colors. (The exact timing of these changes depends greatly on individual oven efficiency.) You need to monitor the color-to-taste relationship by periodically (and very carefully) tasting the grain as it's roasting.

You're always better off underroasting your grain than overroasting it. Take good notes regarding your procedures and use them as guidelines for the next time around.

If the grain is moist as it goes into the oven, the roasting enhances its aroma development. You can moisten the grain by briefly wetting it with a plant mister and allowing it to absorb the moisture for about an hour prior to roasting.

After you've roasted the grain to your satisfaction, allow it to cool sufficiently, put it into a sealed plastic bag, and leave it alone to mellow over a week's time before brewing with it.

Smoke 'em if you got 'em

Instead of just roasting your grains in an oven, you can opt to smoke them on a grill. You can imbue your grain (and beer) with a variety of smoky aromas and flavors by burning various types of wood in a barbecue grill or meat smoker. Put your malt (the same type of grain I describe in the preceding section) on something that enables the smoke to waft up through the grain.

One cost-effective smoking method is to buy some disposable aluminum roasting or pizza tins and poke holes in their bottoms; *do not* allow flames to touch these tins — they're designed for use in low-flame and low-heat applications and can melt in an instant. If you want to get a little more sophisticated, buy an all-steel strainer (no plastic handles or flammable parts) with a flat bottom. You probably don't want to use this utensil for anything else but smoking grain.

How long you smoke your grain depends on how much grain you're smoking, the intensity of the fire, the intensity of the smoke, and your tolerance for smoky grain. You need at least a half-hour to imbue the grain with some smoky character. After the grain has cooled, you're best off allowing it to mellow for about a week before using it; keep it stored in a plastic self-sealing bag.

Some wood choices you can use for smoking grain include alder, apple, beech, hickory, maple, pear, pecan, and oak; each variety brings its own qualities to the fire. Alder, for example, gives malt a sweet, delicate woodiness, and pecan is more pungent, intense, and spicy. Don't forget that you can use spicy mesquite chips or peat for that sharp creosote character found in some Scotch whiskies.

Di-vine Intervention: Growing Hops

Although only a minority of homebrewers grow hops, hop-growing certainly does have its advocates.

Homebrewers not only benefit from the bounty of the commercial hop-processing trade, but they can also now take advantage of the much smaller but equally satisfying glut of hop rhizomes. (A *rhizome* is a root cutting — the easiest way to start a new hop plant.) You can purchase hop rhizomes through many homebrew suppliers, although they're usually available only very early in the growing season. (That's late Fe*brew*ary through early April, of course.)

Here we grow!

You can successfully grow hops just about anywhere between the 40th and 50th parallels north and south of the equator. As long as the hops receive plenty of moisture and ample sunlight, they can thrive.

You need to plant the rhizomes at least a couple weeks after the winter thaw, in a hole about 6 inches deep (and similar in diameter) within a small mound of dirt. Cover the root cutting with loamy soil and pack tightly. Make sure that the location of the plant drains well because molds are quick to attack hop leaves. If you plant two or more hop varieties, space them at 2-yard intervals. (That's 3-foot spaces, not your neighbors' yards.) Because hops are climbing vines, you need to rig up a trellis or a network of stakes and twine that fans out from each hop plant. (Locate the stake close to the hop root.) Check out the section on building a hop trellis later in this chapter for directions. Any rig lower than 8 feet high is hardly worth the effort, because hops can easily grow to greater than 20 feet high. (This lofty stature can present a challenge to the homebrewer at harvest time.)

As the hop shoots begin to emerge in late March or early April, clip all but the four healthiest bines. (For some odd reason, hop vines are called *bines*. Why? Who knows? Maybe the brewer who named them had too much of his own brew or was a lousy speller.) This clipping concentrates the plant's energies. As they grow upward on their own, they start to droop under their own weight — this point is when you need to train them on the twine. Wrap the plants loosely around the twine in a clockwise direction, coming up the twine (unless you live in the Southern Hemisphere, in which case you want to train them in a counterclockwise direction coming up). This positioning is important because the bines follow the sun from east to west every day as they grow. During peak growing season, healthy hop plants can grow as much as a foot each day.

To ensure a good, healthy plant and an abundant harvest, I always treat my hop plants to a biweekly application of water-soluble, all-purpose plant food.

Pick a hop, any hop

Harvest season begins sometime in August and may continue into October, depending on climatic conditions. As the hop flowers grow in size, sporadically check the development of the *lupulin glands*. You can find these glands by gently pulling the soft, leafy petals back against the stem; the yellow lupulin glands are at the base of each petal near the stem. As the season wears on, the hop flowers puff up slightly and the lupulin glands begin to swell. (Of course, how much is a swell if you're talking about something the size of a pinhead?)

If the hops begin to burn in the sun or turn brown, you'd best pick them soon. If you allow the hops to deteriorate, you lose the freshness edge of growing your own hops.

Not all the hops mature at the same pace; you need to pick on several different occasions before the season ends. Checking the plant once a week should be fine unless the weather is particularly hot, cool, wet, or dry. If you pick on a regular weekly schedule, you usually have your hop-drying device emptied just in time for the next batch of freshly picked hops.

Drying and storing your hops

Each time you pick some hops, you need to dry them before storing them. Air-drying is fine, but how long this process takes depends on the humidity levels in the air. I usually dry my hops for a week to make sure that they're as dry as possible

The dried hops should feel light and crumbly in your hands; in fact, the individual leaves may fall off the stem easily. Store them in self-sealing zipper-type sandwich bags (in the size of your choice). Attach self-stick labels to each bag, noting the variety (if you grow more than one) and the date you picked the hops. (You can also just mark the bag with a grease pencil.) You may want to weigh each bag, although quantity isn't really important until brewing day. Store all your hops in your freezer to keep them as long as possible.

Building Brewing Equipment

This section explains ways for you to take control of your brewing process by making your own equipment rather than buying it, thus enabling you to take more personal control over your spending processes as well.

Chillin' out: Immersion wort chillers

An *immersion wort chiller* is a very effective piece of equipment that's relatively easy and not incredibly expensive to make yourself (refer to Figure 12-2 earlier in the book). The basic idea behind the immersion wort chiller is to cool down your wort quickly (without subjecting your brew to contamination) so that you can pitch your yeast and start fermentation as soon as possible.

Start with a coil of copper tubing purchased at your local hardware store. This tubing should have a minimum inside diameter of ⅜ inches and be at least 25 feet long. The longer and wider the tubing is, the more effective it is, but I don't recommend exceeding ½ inch in diameter or 40 feet in length. (And this extreme size is necessary only for full wort boils — see Chapter 12 for more information on that process.) The circumference of the coil itself should be about two-thirds the diameter of your brewpot, and the coil height should equal the height of your brewpot. (You can fashion the coil's dimensions yourself by simply constricting or expanding the coil by hand.) Along with this tubing, you also need a regular garden hose (with a threaded end you can attach to a faucet) you can cut up into shorter pieces. To make bends in the copper tubing without kinking it, use an inexpensive manual spring-type tubing bender (available at most hardware stores). Make sure that you buy a couple expansion clamps for the hose connections.

By working with only the first and last foot or two of each end of the copper tubing, you leave the majority of the coil intact. With the copper coil standing on end, bend the top end of the tubing straight up from the coil and add a 90-degree outward bend. To this end, attach a section of garden hosing (with the faucet attachment here) and tighten the two sections together by using a clamp. With the coil still standing on end, pull the bottom end of the tubing up through the middle of the coil to the same height as the first end and give it a 90-degree outward bend. To this bottom end, attach another length of garden hose and tighten the two together by using a clamp. Just rinse the chiller off, hook it up to a faucet, and, voilà! You're good to go.

Tuns of fun: Lauter tun

A lauter tun is absolutely necessary for effective sparging of all-grain brews. Making your own is simple. Typically, all you need are two 5-gallon plastic buckets, one of which must have a spigot. If you have a bottling bucket from your beginner homebrewing days, you're halfway home. Buy a second food-grade plastic (HDPE) bucket that fits into your bottling bucket. Using a ⅛-inch drill bit, cover the entire bottom of the second bucket with holes ¼ inch apart. After you finish, make sure that you remove all plastic burrs inside the bucket and out.

By placing the second bucket inside your bottling bucket, you've got an effective straining system that enables you to draw off the wort through the spigot while the grain is held back (which is the fundamental concept behind the lauter tun); see Figure 26-1. One important consideration in setting up your double-bucket lauter tun: You need to keep the bottoms of the inside and outside buckets less than 2 inches apart. A larger space messes with the flow of wort through the grain bed and may also aerate the hot wort and contribute to oxidation problems down the line.

Figure 26-1:
Assembling your own lauter tun.

Another slightly more difficult way of making a larger-capacity lauter tun is by using a plastic cooler — the type people use for picnicking or camping. You can use both the rectangular ice-chest design and the upright circular types. I recommend a 10-gallon minimum capacity. The idea is to build a small manifold out of half-inch copper tubing (with the help of 90-degree elbows and T connectors) that rests on the bottom of the coolers and draws off the wort through the cooler's drain hole.

For the rectangular cooler, you must connect and feed a series of four or five long parallel tubes into a short perpendicular tube at the drain end of the cooler. This end tube must then connect to a spigot or stopcock on the outside of the cooler for flow control. For the circular cooler, the best design is the shape of an *X,* with one leg connecting directly through the drain hole to the stopcock or spigot on the outside of the cooler.

If you need to seal the opening where the copper tubing exits the cooler, use the silicone caulk you typically use for bathroom applications. The silicone doesn't harm your beer.

For the tubing to drain correctly and channel the wort to the opening in the cooler, you must first slit or cross-cut the copper tubing with a hacksaw. You need to make several cuts about halfway through the tubing (you're not trying to cut pieces off) about every half inch or so apart. You also need to cap the open ends of the tubing so that no grain escapes with the wort. After you complete the slit-cutting, make sure you brush and rinse off any copper burrs. (Try wet-sanding with emery cloth.) Position the manifold tubes in the cooler with the slots facing downward.

You don't need to solder the parts together; copper fittings are normally snug enough to maintain connections. And by not making the connections permanent, you can more easily disassemble the manifold for cleaning purposes.

Pot o' plenty: Large-volume brewpot

Instead of buying a huge and expensive stock pot from a restaurant supply outlet, do what hundreds of homebrewers do — fashion one out of a real beer keg. This approach works well for several reasons:

- Beer kegs are stainless steel, just like brewpots.
- Buying a used beer keg is much cheaper than buying an equivalent-sized stock pot.
- The most common American beer keg (half-barrel) has a capacity of 15.5 gallons, which is more than enough for a full batch of homebrew. Even 50- and 30-liter European beer kegs are roomy enough.

The beer kegs that work best are the straight-sided Sanke kegs. The advantages to the Sanke keg are that no bung hole is cut in the side of the keg and it has built-in handles at the rim. Because Miller and Anheuser-Busch use these kegs extensively, you should have no difficulty finding them. After you get your hands on one, you need to find someone who does stainless steel welding. (If you're not in the trade, avoid doing the work yourself.) Stainless steel is a very hard metal, requiring specialized saw blades and drill bits. Make sure that someone trained in TIG (*tungsten inert gas*) *welding,* also known as *heliarc welding,* does the work for you; you can't weld stainless steel with regular mild-steel material. Unless you have good connections with people in the trade, you're going to fork over between $25 and $50 an hour for this kind of work. Fortunately, the work you need done doesn't entail much (and it's still cheaper than buying a new brewpot). You need to have your welder saw off and grind down the lid of the keg (at least to the point that it's no longer capable of ripping human flesh), and you want to have him or her attach a spigot near the bottom of the keg.

Cold feat: Lagering cellar

To brew authentic Lager beers, you need the capability to *lager* your beer, which means you need to store it in a cold environment for relatively long periods of time. Not many homebrewers have the means to do this because lagering requires time, space, energy, and money — four things that aren't always in great supply at the amateur level.

If you don't already have one, consider investing in a dedicated beer fridge. Because most refrigerators are designed to keep foods very cool (cooler than a lagering cellar should be), you need to buy one more item that enables the fridge to warm up a bit: an external thermostat. This *fermostat* controls the interior temperature of your beer fridge by shutting the refrigerator off at the temperature you designate. You can purchase this device through most homebrew suppliers and can hook it up in a matter of minutes. Again, effective lagering temperatures should remain fairly constant between 40 and 50 degrees Fahrenheit depending on the beer style.

Another way to capitalize on this concept is to build an enlarged beer cellar that includes removing the door of a refrigerator and attaching a large wooden box (complete with a utility or access door) in its place. Crafted of heavy plywood sheathing and lined with thick insulating material such as Styrofoam, this box offers a two- or threefold increase in the fridge's capacity with very little increase in electrical usage. How big you make this box depends on your needs and space constraints. Let your imagination run wild!

Chapter 27

Ten Gizmos That Can Make Your Brewing Easier

In This Chapter

▶ Gadgets

▶ Gizmos

▶ Brewing software

*I*n the ever-expanding world of homebrewing, hundreds — perhaps thousands — of people are trying to build a better mousetrap (although what good a mousetrap is to a homebrewer, I may never know). Someone is always coming up with new and better ways to make beer at home. Tremendous changes have taken place in the two decades that I've been brewing my own beer, and, undoubtedly, more fascinating and time-saving inventions are sure to appear in the future.

This chapter gives you an idea of the types of items available to make your brewing easier and more convenient. These gadgets aren't absolutely necessary for making good beer, and a few of them can put a real dent in your pocketbook. Whether you decide to buy them is just a question of how far you want to go with your hobby. You can purchase most — if not all — of these thingies at your favorite homebrew supply store.

Digital Thermometer and pH Meter

If you're practicing mashing techniques, you're already well aware of the need for thermometers and pH testing papers. Investing in digital equipment just makes the job a little bit easier and a lot more accurate. An appropriate digital thermometer costs anywhere between $15 and $25, and the pH meter will set you back $50 to $70.

Wort Aeration System

This system is a very effective way of aerating your wort to create a better environment for yeast respiration cycles. A pump sends ordinary air through a sterile filter and delivers it to the beer by way of a *beer stone* that diffuses oxygen into the beer. (This device isn't unlike the aerators that fish tanks use.) You can also find fully contained wort aeration systems that include a small canister of 99.9 percent pure compressed oxygen and an easy-to-sanitize stainless-steel diffusion stone. A wort aeration system will run you $30 to $50.

Auto Siphon

A couple of different kinds of auto siphons are available, but they mostly vary only by length and diameter. These gizmos help eliminate the risk of contamination and start siphon flows quickly and easily during racking and bottling procedures. You can expect to pay somewhere between $10 and $15 for an auto siphon.

Counterpressure Bottle Filler

This device allows homebrewers who keg their beer to transfer the beer into glass bottles without losing the beer's carbonation. This capability is important to kegging brewers who want to send bottles of their beer to competitions or to those who filter their homebrew. (See the following section for more information on the beer filter.) The bottle filler itself will cost you $50 to $60, but remember that it also requires a CO_2 system (tanks, gauges, hoses, fittings), which will increase your total cost. See Chapter 13 for more information on bottling; check out Chapter 25 for more on entering homebrew competitions.

Beer Filter

Beer filters do exactly what they say they do: They remove yeast and particulate matter, creating a clearer beer. To filter homebrew, however, you must force the liquid through the filter under pressure, which requires a CO_2 system and a minimum of two pressure vessels such as soda kegs. If you filter all the yeast from the beer, however, bottle-priming by using corn sugar is no longer an option, and you may need to artificially carbonate your beer. Homebrewers have a choice between the *plate* type of filter (about $50) and the *cartridge* type ($70). I vote for the more-convenient cartridge type. Remember that because this gadget requires a CO_2 system, the cost of whichever option you choose will go up. See Chapter 13 for more on bottling.

Germicidal Lamp

This hand-held germ eliminator is portable and battery-powered, and it can kill 99.9 percent of surface bacteria with a 10-second exposure. It's great for use as a dry sanitizer for all kinds of brewing and non-brewing equipment and will set you back $25 to $30.

Wort Transfer Pump

These electrical/mechanical devices take racking to whole new level by eliminating the need to siphon. These pumps can be magnetic, diaphragm, or peristaltic, but they all do the same thing: make your life easier. Making your life richer may be another story: You'll need to plunk down $130 to $150 for one of these babies. *Note:* Like all electrical devices used with or near liquids, always plug these pumps into a GFI- (Ground Fault Interrupter) protected outlet.

Refractometer

Using a refractometer is the quick and easy way to measure the sugar content of any liquid such as unfermented wort (beer) or must (mead or wine). To convert degrees Brix (the refractometer's measuring scale) to Specific Gravity, multiply the Brix reading by .004 and add a whole number 1 (example: a Brix reading of 10 equals 1.040). Expect to pay between $50 and $60 for a refractometer.

Mashing Sparge Arm

This self-powered rotating sparge arm produces an evenly distributed, rain-like spray that doesn't bore holes in the mash. This sparger is made of brass and comes complete with a handy holding bracket. It's available in various diameters to fit various sparging vessels and costs between $30 and $40.

Brewing software

Nineteenth-century brewing and 21st-century technology are on a collision course. The result? Computer software for homebrewers.

At the risk of sounding like a brewing bumpkin, not only do I not own brewing software, I probably wouldn't know what to do with it if I had it. I'd been formulating my own beer recipes (some of which I include in Part IV of this book) for several years prior to the introduction of brewing software. I didn't need it then, and I don't need it now. You, however, may find it all very fascinating and useful.

Because this material represents a stretch of the technological turnpike that I don't travel, here's a passing glance at some of the brewing software that exists out there.

✔ Pro Mash "Brewing Software for the Discriminating Brewer": www.promash.com

✔ BrewWizard "The Brewers Encyclopedia": http://members.aol.com/brewwizard/bwiz-cal.html

✔ BeerSmith "Take the Guesswork out of Brewing": www.beersmith.com

✔ Strangebrew Homebrewing Software: www.strangebrew.ca/

✔ SUDS Homebrewing Software: www.oldlib.com/suds/

Counterflow Wort Chiller

At first glance, you may think that this piece of equipment is redundant. Unlike the immersion-type wort chiller mentioned in Chapter 2, however, the *counterflow* wort chiller is a quicker and more efficient means of cooling hot wort. Cold water in an outer hose flows in an opposite direction from the hot wort flowing within the inner copper tubing. This product runs anywhere from $80 to $150.

Chapter 28

Just the FAQs: Ten (or so) Frequently Asked Questions

In This Chapter
▶ Cost questions
▶ Time questions
▶ Supplies questions
▶ Legality questions
▶ Methodology questions

People unfamiliar with the art and craft of homebrewing always seem to have the same questions. Here's a sampling of their oft-repeated queries, along with my answers to them.

How Much Is Taking Up Homebrewing Going to Cost?

At the beginner level, the minimum amount of equipment you need to brew beer correctly is going to run you in the vicinity of $70. This setup is relatively bare-bones in nature, but it's enough to get you up and running. Eventually, you want to acquire more and better equipment as you become more familiar and comfortable with the processes and procedures. (I know some home-brewers who've spent in excess of $1,000 on their home breweries.)

How Much Does the Average Batch of Beer Cost?

The average batch of homebrewed beer is 5 gallons, or 53.3 12-ounce bottles of beer. At the beginner level, the ingredients for a typical batch run about $30 to $35. The amount you actually pay fluctuates because of many factors, including where you shop for your ingredients (don't forget shipping charges for mail order), whether you buy top- or bottom-of-the-line ingredients, and the style of beer you like to brew. Big-bodied, alcoholic beers require more fermentable ingredients than do light-bodied, watery beers. (Barley Wines can cost as much as 100 percent more to make than Pale Ales.)

And because extract brewers pay a premium for the convenience of using processed malt syrups, efficient all-grain brewers can produce beer more cheaply.

Where Can I Buy Homebrewing Supplies?

Homebrew supply shops are commonplace these days. Whereas they were once located in clandestine little holes-in-the-wall, you can now find homebrew suppliers anywhere from old factory buildings to modern strip malls. Even some craft breweries and liquor stores have set aside unused floor space for retail homebrew-supply sales.

And, of course, you may have heard of this little thing called the Internet? I understand quite a few sites out there are just waiting for you to click and order (check out the Cheat Sheet for places to start your search).

How Long Does Making a Batch of Homebrew Take?

At the beginner level, the actual brewing process takes only about two hours, including setup and cleanup. On the day you bottle your beer, schedule at least three hours, including setup and cleanup.

At the extreme short end of the process, you can conceivably drink your beer within three weeks of brewing it, but most experienced homebrewers like their beers to age and mellow for as long as four to six weeks. Initial fermentation needs to last at least five to seven days. A maturation period in a secondary fermenter lasts at least a week, probably two. After you bottle your beer, you want to set aside another two weeks for the beer to carbonate and clarify correctly.

Is Homebrewed Beer Better Than Commercially Made Beer?

Is it automatically better? No. Is it generally better? Not necessarily. Does the potential exist to make homebrew that's better than commercially made beer? Very emphatically, YES! It's been my experience that homebrewers have the ability to make some of the best beer in the world, if they're committed enough to try. I know because I've made some great beers and I've had the pleasure of tasting many truly outstanding world-class beers at homebrewing competitions (one of the perks of being a beer judge).

How Do You Carbonate Homebrew?

One of the natural functions of yeasts during fermentation is to produce carbon dioxide. After the initial phase of fermentation is complete, you can prime your beer by using a small (but exact) measure of highly fermentable sugar as you bottle it. The yeast cells that remain in the solution feed on these sugars and create the appropriate level of CO_2 carbonation within the sealed bottle. Check out Chapter 13 for more bottling information.

How Do I Add Alcohol to Homebrew?

You don't need to add alcohol to homebrew because the yeast naturally produces the alcohol during fermentation. Yeast cells feed on the natural malt sugars in the liquid, producing ethyl alcohol and carbon dioxide in return.

Can I Distill Homebrew into Whiskey?

Yes and no. Yes, distilling homebrew is technically feasible, but no, distilling any alcoholic beverage in a private residence is not at all legal in the United States — anytime or anywhere (unless, of course, you've registered your still with the appropriate governmental agencies).

Can I Sell Homebrew?

Not legally (in the United States). Attempting to sell an untaxed, unregulated alcoholic beverage is a violation of several state and federal laws — just ask Al Capone. Unless you want the FBI knocking on your door, I don't recommend it.

Why Shouldn't I Age Beer in the Plastic Primary Fermenter?

You have two good reasons not to age beer in a plastic primary fermenter. First, the beer would sit on all the yeast sediment and protein fallout from the fermented beer and would eventually pick up off flavors. Second, even HDPE (high-density polyethylene) food-grade plastic is permeable by oxygen molecules over a long period of time; glass and stainless steel, however, are completely impermeable.

Do I Have to Worry About Things Blowing Up in My House?

Tales of explosions while homebrewing are mostly old wives' tales. Any explosions that may occur while making beer at home are usually nothing more than excess carbon dioxide being vented from enclosed vessels such as fermenters, carboys, and bottles. The worst thing about these eruptions is the mess they leave for you to clean up.

Appendix

Ingredients:
The Building Blocks of Beer

In This Appendix

▶ Malts, grains, and producers

▶ Hop varieties, origins, and other descriptive information

▶ Dry and liquid yeast strains

*H*ere it is, folks: a veritable smorgasbord of ingredient info. In this appendix, I look at various kinds of malts and base, adjunct, and specialty grains and give you an overview of the companies that produce them. I also list several different kinds of hops and what you need to know about them before you chuck them into your brewpot. Finally, I provide yeast strains produced by a couple of the industry's heavy hitters, complete with descriptions and attenuation information. Dig in!

Malt: Grainy Names and Extract Excerpts

Here's a glimpse at the world of cereal grains used in the realm of professional brewing and widely available at the homebrew level. First up is a list of grain producers whose products are commonly used by professional brewers but may also be found at the homebrewing level. Following that list is a type-specific list of grain. In this second list, I've included the various grain types, divided by their usage (base grain, specialty grain, adjunct grain) and other details such as their Lovibond ratings and whether they require mashing. Finally, you find a semi-comprehensive list of malt extract brands that produce a wide variety of beer kits for the extract homebrewer.

You'll notice here and elsewhere when shopping for brewing grains that many of the grain names are *branded*, meaning the malting companies market them by specific names. Also of note: Whenever you see a grain with the prefix *cara-*, it simply denotes a caramel malt (also known as crystal malt).

Producers of grains

The following list includes many of the top producers of grain for the brewing industry worldwide. These company names are widely known in the commercial brewing arena and are becoming more familiar and sought-after at the homebrewing level.

Briess: This Wisconsin-based maltster is one of the primary suppliers of brewer's grain to the microbrewing industry, particularly in the Midwestern U.S. In addition to the wide range of malted grains that the company produces, Briess also markets a full line of liquid and dry malt extracts called CBW, or Concentrated Brewer's Wort.

Crisp Malting: This English malthouse in County Norfolk, England, exports its distinctive Maris Otter brand of 2-row, pale, and crystal malts to North America. Maris Otter is a barley variety renowned by U.K. brewers.

Dingemans: The Dingemans family has produced an extensive range of basic ingredients for the demanding Belgian and European brewer since 1875. The result is an outstanding line of brewer's and specialty malts used not only in Pilsen type beers but also in Trappist, Abbey, and White beers.

Durst: An authentic German malt producer located in the fatherland of beer, Durst began as a family-owned country brewery and malthouse 170 years ago. It sold its first malt exports in 1924 and has since expanded into an international supplier producing 157,000 U.S. tons of malt each year.

Gambrinus Malting: This small Canadian maltster produces some of the finest 2-row malt in the world. Gambrinus Malting also produces malts not made by other well-known maltsters, such as the almost-forgotten *bruhmalt,* a pale malt that imbues the beer with a honeyed aroma and flavor.

Great Western Malting: Many consider Great Western Malting's 2-row pale malt to be the best in the U.S; many of the biggest microbrewers on the West Coast use this base grain.

Hugh Baird: Located in the U.K., the Hugh Baird Malting Company is one of the world's best suppliers of specialty malts and authentic 2-row British Pale Ale malt.

Meussdoerffer: Since 1852, the name Meussdoerffer has exemplified products of excellent quality made in accordance with the strict traditional rules of the Bavarian purity law. Cargill Malt introduced the excellent malts of Meussdoerffer to the North American brewery market.

Paul's Malt: Paul's Malt originated in the first half of the 19th century on the east coast of England, where its headquarters still reside today. Today, Paul's Malt is a modern company and the U.K.'s largest maltster, producing in excess of 500,000 British tons of malt per year.

Rahr Malting: Rahr Malting Co. is a family owned company that has been in business since 1847. It produces and distributes malt and industry-related brewing supplies. Rahr's malt production plants are located in Shakopee, Minnesota, and Alix, Alberta.

Schreier: This small maltster from Wisconsin is one of the small malting houses distributed by the American conglomerate Cargill.

Simpson's: Established in 1866 by corn merchant James Parker Simpson, Simpson's is still the largest totally independently family-owned malting company in the U.K. The company manufactures a wide range of quality malts, including specialty roasted malts, for the brewing, distilling, and food industries.

Weyermann: The 118-year-old malthouse housing Mich. Weyermann & Co. KG Malzfabrik is a protected historic site. But behind the red-brick turn-of-the-century building in Bamberg, Germany, lies the modernized heart of the world's leading manufacturer of specialty brewing malts. For over a century, Mich. Weyermann has been providing specialty malts to breweries large and small on virtually every continent of the world.

The international conglomerate Con-Agra owns Canada Malting, Great Western Malting, Hugh Baird, and others, making it the world's largest maltster. Similarly, the American malting conglomerate Cargill imports and distributes Paul's Malt, Muessdoerffer, Gambrinus, and Schreier.

Types of grains

This section provides you with details about a variety of base, specialty, and adjunct grains available to the homebrewer. I've listed Lovibond ratings and the need for mashing procedures, along with a ton of background information on each individual grain. This is by no means an exhaustive listing — many more grains are available in the market.

Base grains

Base grains denote all the malted grains (barley, wheat, rye, etc.) used to make beer. Brewers must mash all base grains order to create the wort that becomes beer through the magic of fermentation. Beginner and intermediate homebrewers can simply use malt extract to create their wort.

Type of barley grain: 2-row (domestic)
Degrees Lovibond: 1.8
Mashed: Yes
Description: You can use 2-row malt as the base malt for all Lager and Ale styles. Although it yields a slightly higher maltose (malt sugar) extract than 6-row malt, it also costs more per pound. However, 2-row malt tends to give a smoother, less grainy-flavored beer. Two-row malt also tends to have fewer proteins and yield a lighter color than 6-row malt.

Type of barley grain: 2-row Lager
Degrees Lovibond: 1.4
Mashed: Yes
Description: The American brewing industry loves this low-protein 2-row malt. Because of 2-row's lower enzyme content, the addition of higher-enzyme 6-row malt is often recommended (enzymes are what are needed to break down the grain's complex malt sugars during the mashing phase).

Type of barley grain: 6-row Lager (domestic)
Degrees Lovibond: 1.8
Mashed: Yes
Description: Six-row malt is less expensive to use than 2-row malt and is also more readily available. You can use this grain as the base for all Lager and Ale styles. It has a thicker husk and higher protein content than 2-row malt. Six-row malt also has more enzymes, which makes it a good choice to use in conjunction with adjunct grains or wheat malt.

Type of barley grain: Pale Ale malt
Degrees Lovibond: 3
Mashed: Yes
Description: You can use Pale Ale malt as a base malt or in conjunction with regular 2-row malt to impart a richer malt flavor and additional color. Pale Ale malt is a 2-row variety that's kilned longer and usually better-modified, giving it a more pronounced flavor than regular 2-row malt. It's also deeper in color, which can add golden hues to your wort. The enzymes in Pale Ale malt can support the use of nonenzymatic specialty malts.

Type of barley grain: Mild Ale malt
Degrees Lovibond: 3
Mashed: Yes
Description: This grain is a lightly kilned pale malt that provides a subtle nutty flavor. British brewers favor Mild Ale malt for mild Ales and Bitters.

Type of barley grain: Pilsener
Degrees Lovibond: 1.2
Mashed: Yes
Description: Two-row Pilsener malt is the palest malt available. You can use it as a base malt for any Lager recipe. High-enzyme levels allow for mashing of large percentages of (nonenzymatic) adjunct grains.

Type of barley grain: Dextrin malt
Degrees Lovibond: 1.5
Mashed: No
Description: Dextrin malt adds body, head retention, and beer stability without influencing flavor. (Dextrins occur naturally in malt and are one contributor to the body of beer.) The nonfermentables contained in dextrin malt are perfect for balancing the body and flavor of dark-colored beers. One maltster in particular (Briess) has its own trade name (CaraPils). You can simply steep dextrin malt and strain it into the brewpot.

Type of barley grain: CaraVienne
Degrees Lovibond: 20
Mashed: Yes/No
Description: This term was coined by the old DeWolf-Cosyns maltster for that company's medium-colored crystal malt. You can steep or mash CaraVienne.

Type of barley grain: CaraMunich
Degrees Lovibond: 55
Mashed: Yes/No
Description: This term was coined by the old DeWolf-Cosyns maltster for that company's dark-colored crystal malt, which has an assertive, malty flavor. You can also steep or mash CaraMunich.

Type of barley grain: Vienna malt
Degrees Lovibond: 4
Mashed: Yes
Description: You can use the lightly kilned Vienna malt in place of standard pale malt as a base malt for your brew. This malt type contributes a slightly maltier, grainy flavor and a deeper golden color than standard base malt does. Increased enzymes are sufficient to support large quantities of specialty or adjunct malts in the mash. For Pilsener beer, use Vienna malt for between 10 and 30 percent of the total malt in your recipe for color and malty flavor. For amber Vienna-Style Lager beers, I suggest between 60 and 90 percent Vienna malt, along with a percentage of low-Lovibond crystal malt.

Type of barley grain: Light Munich
Degrees Lovibond: 10
Mashed: Yes
Description: Munich malt is a Lager malt that has been lightly kilned to provide a pronounced grainy flavor without adding nonfermentables or affecting the foam stability and the body. Small amounts of this Lager malt added to the grist can improve the malty flavor and give a richer color to low-gravity brews. You can improve Amber and Märzen beers if Munich malt comprises between 5 and 15 percent of the malt in your recipe, although the more robust Bock beers and Dark Lager beers may require 10 to 30 percent Munich malt.

Type of barley grain: Dark Munich
Degrees Lovibond: 20
Mashed: Yes
Description: Similar to Light Munich malt, Dark Munich malt is kilned to a slightly higher degree, providing a modest color increase toward the orange and deep copper hues. For Bock beers and Dark Lagers, Dark Munich malt needs to account for only 5 to 7 percent of the total amount of malt in the recipe to achieve the malty, grainy flavors characteristic of these styles.

Type of wheat grain: Malted Wheat
Degrees Lovibond: 2.5
Mashed: Yes
Description: Wheat grain is completely different from barley grain in both appearance and composition. Unlike barley, the kernels of wheat have no husks. Malted wheat gives a malty flavor that you can't get by using just raw wheat. (See the "Specialty grains" section for more information on unmalted wheat.) For Weizenbier, use between 50 and 75 percent wheat malt; for Berliner-Style Weissbier, use between 25 and 35 percent wheat malt. You can also use small portions of wheat malt (0.5 to 1.5 percent of total grist) in all beer styles to aid in head retention.

Specialty grains

Specialty grains denote all the malted and unmalted grains (barley, wheat, rye, oats, etc.) you can add to the wort to give the finished beer a wide variety of colors and flavors that base grains don't provide. Both *all-grain brewers* (those who mash their grains to create their wort) and *extract brewers* (those who create their wort from malt extract) can use specialty grains effectively.

Type of specialty grain: Wheat (unmalted)
Degrees Lovibond: 2.5
Mashed: No
Description: Brewers use unmalted wheat exclusively for flavoring and for head retention because it contributes no fermentable sugars or sweetness. The use of unmalted wheat, such as in Kölschbier and Witbier, often results in an unavoidable protein haze in the beer.

Type of specialty grain: Crystal malt
Degrees Lovibond: 10–120
Mashed: No
Description: Also called *caramel malt,* this grain undergoes the kilning process while the grain kernels are still moist. This process causes the starches to convert to sugars and the sugars to crystallize within the grain husk (thus the *crystal malt* designation). Crystal malts are kilned to various Lovibond colors, usually in increments of 10 degrees. Crystal malt contributes color, caramel flavor, body, stability, and head retention to beer. The

higher the Lovibond number, the darker the color and the more sweet caramelly flavor the grain contributes to the beer. Crystal malt may be made from 2-row or 6-row barley.

Type of specialty grain: Special "B"
Degrees Lovibond: 221
Mashed: Yes/No
Description: This very dark crystal malt was unique to the Belgian maltster DeWolf-Cosyns. (Special "B" is a trade name). It provides a very highly caramelized and chocolatey-nutty flavor. Therefore, you can substitute Special "B" for chocolate malt if you want to avoid roast grain bitterness. You can steep or mash Special "B," and it's great in Brown Ales, Porters, and Belgian specialty styles. One pound in a 5-gallon batch goes a long way.

Type of specialty grain: Victory Malt
Degrees Lovibond: 25
Mashed: Yes
Description: Victory Malt is a fully modified product designed to contribute a warm, nutty, toasty flavor and a deep golden to brown color to beer. For Amber Ales, I suggest 2 to 5 percent of total grist; for Porter, 5 to 10 percent; and for nut Brown Ales, 10 to 15 percent.

Type of specialty grain: Biscuit Malt
Degrees Lovibond: 25
Mashed: Yes
Description: This grain is a lightly roasted 2-row pale malt designed to contribute a baked-bread flavor to beer.

Type of specialty grain: Special Roast
Degrees Lovibond: 50
Mashed: Yes
Description: Special Roast is a malted specialty grain that contributes a biscuity flavor to beer, which is particularly well suited to English Ales. Use between 2 and 5 percent total grist for Amber Ales and between 5 and 10 percent for Brown Ales and Porters.

Type of specialty grain: Chocolate malt
Degrees Lovibond: 350
Mashed: No
Description: Chocolate malt is kilned to a dark brown color (but not as dark as black malt). And, as its name suggests, chocolate malt can imbue beer with dark brown color and a dry, chocolatey flavor, a pleasing color and flavor combination that's very complementary in Brown Ales, Dark Lagers, Porters, and Stouts. A small amount of chocolate malt goes a long way, so don't use more than the amount of chocolate malt required to make 10 percent of the total grist.

Type of specialty grain: Black malt
Degrees Lovibond: 500
Mashed: No
Description: This malted grain is kilned to high temperatures, giving a black, charred appearance to any beer in which it's used in even modest proportions. The acrid, sometimes smoky flavor of black malt is a prime characteristic of Porters and Stouts. Up to 10 percent of the recipe for these styles may be black malt.

Type of specialty grain: Roasted Barley
Degrees Lovibond: 500
Mashed: No
Description: Roasted Barley, unlike most other brewhouse grains, is unmalted. A slow roasting process gives this grain a sharp roasted, almost acrid flavor without charring the grain. Only small amounts of roasted barley (3 to 7 percent) are necessary to give its dark color and dry, roasty, coffeelike flavors to Stouts and Porters.

Type of specialty grain: Rye Malt
Degrees Lovibond: 4
Mashed: Yes
Description: Of all the malted grains, rye is probably the most difficult to classify. Rye doesn't comply with the German Purity Law because it's not barley — nor is wheat, for that matter. But unlike wheat, rye is never used as a base grain (more than 50 percent of the grist). Because rye is used only as a flavoring grain, it seems to belong with the specialty grains. I recommend that rye malt make up no more than 20 percent of any recipe. Rye also comes in flaked (pregelatinized) form. Flaked rye gives a higher extract yield than conventional malted rye because the complex sugars in pregelatinized grain are easier for the enzymes to break down during mashing.

Type of specialty grain: Smoked malt
Mashed: Yes/No
Description: This is malted barley that has been smoked over wood — usually beechwood but occasionally a peat fire. Beechwood-smoked malt is most popular in traditional German Rauchbier, and peat-smoked malt is common in traditional Scottish Ales. In either case, the smoked malt transfers its smoky qualities to the beer as you steep or mash the grain.

Adjunct grains

The previous sections cover base grains, which are malted and must be mashed to make beer, and specialty grains which can be malted or unmalted and don't require mashing to add color and flavor to beer. This section provides a list of *adjunct grains,* which can be malted or unmalted and can be used as either a base grain or specialty grain (and two of these "grains" come as syrups).

Type of adjunct grain: Rice
Degrees Lovibond: 0
Mashed: Yes
Description: You can use rice as a whole grain, in its flaked (pregelatinized) form, or in a prepared syrup. You need to cook whole rice in a cereal cooker to gelatinize the starches. After cooking, mash the rice with enzyme-rich barley malt. You can add flaked rice directly to the mash and rice syrup directly to the brewkettle. As you can see by the Lovibond rating, rice adds virtually no color whatsoever to the beer. To keep its beers very pale, megabrewer Anheuser-Busch uses rice in place of a portion of barley malt.

Type of adjunct grain: Corn
Degrees Lovibond: 0
Mashed: Yes
Description: You can use corn as a whole grain, as flaked maize (pregelatinized corn), or in a prepared syrup. Like rice, you need to cook whole corn in a cereal cooker to gelatinize the starches, and then mash it with enzyme-rich barley malt. You can add flaked maize directly to the mash and corn syrup directly to the brewkettle. As you can see by the Lovibond rating, corn adds virtually no color whatsoever to the beer, so big commercial brewers around the world use corn in place of a portion of barley malt to keep their beers very pale.

Type of adjunct grain: Oats
Degrees Lovibond: 2.2
Mashed: Yes
Description: Like rice and corn, you can use oats as a whole grain, as flakes (pregelatinized), or in processed form. You must mash malted oats with enzyme-rich barley malt, but you can also throw processed oatmeal into the mash with the rest of the grain just to add texture and flavor to the beer. Try using unmalted oats, in the form of flakes, for flavoring and improved head retention.

Malt extract brands

Following is an alphabetical list of malt-extract brand names and their countries of origin. This list is simply to help beginners become familiar with brand names so that they can make informed choices on appropriate malts for their desired beer styles. In other words, if I intended to brew a Pale Ale, I wouldn't choose an extract brand produced in Germany. Conversely, if I wanted to brew a lager, I wouldn't choose a kit made in the U.K.

Brand Name	Country of Origin	Brand Name	Country of Origin
Alexander's	U.S.	John Bull	U.K.
Bierkeller	Germany	Laaglander	Netherlands
Black Rock	New Zealand	Morgan's	Australia
Brewferm	Belgium	Mountmellick	Ireland
Coopers	Australia	Munton's	U.K.
Edme	U.K.	Northwestern	U.S.
Geordie	Scotland	Superbrau	Germany
Glenbrew	Scotland	Telfords	Scotland
Ireks	Germany	Weyermann's	Germany
Ironmaster	U.K.		

Top Hops: Hop Varieties and Descriptions

The world of hops is a fairly big one — one that continues to grow every year. Because of this scope, the discussion of hop varieties can be a fairly confusing subject. This section, which you should use in conjunction with Chapter 5, is designed to help you make decisions about which hops you should use in your brews.

You typically base your primary hop-choosing decision on the alpha-acid content of the hop variety — this characteristic tells you the *bittering potential* of the hop variety, or how much bitterness a particular variety may add to your beer. You make a secondary decision in regards to the hops' aromatic potential (which isn't measured by a numerical score; I discuss it in the description). Finally, you may want to take into consideration the hops' stability rating; this rating tells you how well the variety holds up in storage, which can be important if you buy your hops in bulk and need to store them over longer periods of time.

One final note: a handful of these varieties are now being grown organically and are becoming more accessible to homebrewers. Check with your favorite homebrew supplier for availability.

Type of hop: Admiral
Origin: U.K.
Alpha: 11.5–14.5
Noble (Yes/No): No
Stability: Fair
Description: This very new English variety of hop is relatively high in alpha acids, but it has proven itself to be very versatile as a kettle hop because it can replace both high-alpha varieties and dual-purpose (flavoring/bittering) hops.

Type of hop: Ahtanum
Origin: U.S.
Alpha: 7.0–9.0
Noble (Yes/No): No
Stability: Good
Description: This hop is used primarily for aroma and moderate bittering in American Ales, and is appreciated for its citrus zest character. This variety's unusual name is derived from an area near Yakima, Washington, where the first hop farm in the United States was established in 1869!

Type of hop: Amarillo
Origin: U.S.
Alpha: 8.0–11.0
Noble (Yes/No): No
Stability: Good
Description: This relatively new variety offers an intense floral/citrus character that's ideal for American Ales and IPA styles. It's similar to Cascade, but with more of an orange/tangerine aroma and flavor rather than grapefruit.

Type of hop: Aurora
Origin: Slovenia
Alpha: 8.0–10.0
Noble (Yes/No): No
Stability: Good
Description: Bred from the Northern Brewer hop variety at Zalec in Slovenia to provide a higher-alpha complement to Styrian Goldings, this variety has become known as Super Styrian. The alpha content of the Aurora variety is fairly high, but it's still a versatile kettle hop. Its bittering characteristics are similar to the Northern Brewer, but without the harshness.

Type of hop: Cascade
Origin: U.S.
Alpha: 4.5–7.0
Noble (Yes/No): No
Stability: Fair
Description: This U.S.-bred hop is a seedling of the English Fuggles variety. The Cascade is a mild hop with good soft bittering properties and a very distinctive citrus aroma. The lemony-grapefruity aromatics of this variety are the hallmarks of a craft brew from the American West Coast.

Type of hop: Centennial
Origin: U.S.
Alpha: 9.5–11.5
Noble (Yes/No): No
Stability: Poor
Description: Formerly called CFJ-90, the Centennial is a relatively new American variety that's still in the experimental stage. It's a cross between Brewer's Gold and an undistinguished American variety grown in Washington State. Though a relatively high-alpha hop, its flavor is rather floral.

Type of hop: Challenger
Origin: U.K.
Alpha: 6.5–8.5
Noble (Yes/No): No
Stability: Good
Description: Released for commercial production in 1972, the Challenger is a granddaughter of the venerable Northern Brewer and a cousin of the Target variety. The Challenger was developed in the U.K. but is also grown in small quantities in Belgium and France. A fruity, spicy hop, the Challenger is a versatile kettle hop for all types of beer.

Type of hop: Chinook
Origin: U.S.
Alpha: 12.0–14.0
Noble (Yes/No): No
Stability: Good
Description: The Chinook is bred in the U.S. and is a cross between a Peltham Golding and an undistinguished American variety. It's a disease-resistant hop variety used to replace the Bullion and Bramling varieties. Use this very high-alpha hop in modest amounts because its bittering can be somewhat coarse, and its aromatics smell like potent grapefruit.

Type of hop: Cluster
Origin: U.S.
Alpha: 5.5–8.5
Noble (Yes/No): No
Stability: Excellent
Description: This variety is one of a few *traditional* American hops, with selected clones being propagated to improve yields. As a kettle hop, it's fairly

low in alpha acids and is gradually being replaced as new, higher-alpha varieties are introduced. The Cluster has a strong aroma but provides well-balanced bitterness with standard kettle additions.

Type of hop: Columbus
Origin: U.S.
Alpha: 13.5–15.0
Noble (Yes/No): No
Stability: Good
Description: This American-bred hop is one of a few *super-alpha* varieties similar in some respects to the Centennial. Although you can use it as an aroma hop, it's rarely explored by homebrewers.

Type of hop: Crystal
Origin: U.S.
Alpha: 6.0–8.0
Noble (Yes/No): No
Stability: Good
Description: This new variety is a *triploid seedling* (incapable of forming seeded cones) developed from the genetics of at least three different hop varieties, including the Hallertauer, Cascade, and Brewer's Gold. Its floral-perfumey character makes it a good choice for late kettle additions, particularly for Lagers.

Type of hop: First Gold
Origin: U.K.
Alpha: 6.5–8.5
Noble (Yes/No): No
Stability: Fair
Description: The First Gold is a new, experimental English hop variety. This variety is similar to Goldings for its aromatics but also has a higher alpha content than traditional aroma hops. As such, it's suitable as a general kettle hop and has late-addition and dry-hopping capabilities in all beer styles.

Type of hop: Fuggles
Origin: U.K.
Alpha: 4.0–5.5
Noble (Yes/No): No
Stability: Good
Description: First propagated in County Kent by Richard Fuggle in 1875, this variety is perhaps the most famous and revered of English hops. This robust hop contributes all the essential characteristics of flavor, aroma, and balanced bitterness to Ales. Brewers frequently blend the Fuggles with Goldings to improve drinkability by adding roundness and fullness to the flavor. Because it's a relatively low-alpha hop, a high-hopping rate is necessary to achieve desired bitterness levels. The Fuggles is also used as a distinctive dry hop.

Type of hop: Galena
Origin: U.S.
Alpha: 12.0–14.0
Noble (Yes/No): No
Stability: Fair
Description: A derivative of the Brewer's Gold variety, the Galena hop rapidly became the dominant high-alpha hop in the U.S. As a kettle hop, it gives a strong and somewhat floral flavor and balanced bitterness. Because it has a low oil content, the Galena offers very little in aromatic qualities.

Type of hop: Goldings (Kent)
Origin: U.K.
Alpha: 4.5–6.5
Noble (Yes/No): No
Stability: Good
Description: The Goldings variety is actually a grouping of traditional English hop varieties that have been cultivated in southern England for centuries. Recognized as having the most-typical English aroma and a distinctive flavor, this hop is in demand for late-addition usage as well as for dry hopping Ales. The Goldings is also useful for late-hopping Lagers if you require a delicate aroma.

Type of hop: Goldings (Styrian)
Origin: Slovenia/U.S.
Alpha: 4.0–6.0
Noble (Yes/No): Yes
Stability: Good
Description: Grown in Slovenia (mainly in the Savinja Valley around Zatec), this variety is genetically the same as the Fuggles but has developed distinctive flavor characteristics peculiar to that environment. Styrian Goldings impart a distinctive, mild bitter flavor, somewhat richer than the English Goldings variety. Try using this hop for late kettle additions and for dry hopping.

Type of hop: Hallertauer
Origin: Germany
Alpha: 4.5–6.0
Noble (Yes/No): Yes
Stability: Good
Description: Respected as one of the Noble hop varieties, this type is named for the Hallertau region in Germany where it's grown. The Hallertauer became quite popular due to its fine flavoring and aromatic properties. This hop is the predominant European Lager hop.

Type of hop: Hallertau Hersbrucker
Origin: Germany
Alpha: 4.5–5.5
Noble (Yes/No): Yes
Stability: Fair

Description: Grown in the Hersbruck area near Nürnberg, this variety now dominates hop production in the Hallertau region. The Hersbrucker, with its greater tolerance to wilt, began to overtake the venerable Hallertauer hop, until it, too, was displaced by newer aroma varieties. The Hersbrucker's fine bittering and flavoring is suitable for all mild-flavored Lager beers. I also recommend it for late kettle additions.

Type of hop: Hallertau Mittelfruh
Origin: Germany
Alpha: 3.5–5.5
Noble (Yes/No): Yes
Stability: Fair
Description: This hop provides a classic Hallertauer flavor profile with mild spicy character and is great for European style lagers and German Pilsners. The name refers to this variety's middle-early season ripening. The Hallertau Mittelfruh has been largely replaced with other Hallertau varieties.

Type of hop: Liberty
Origin: U.S.
Alpha: 3.5–6.0
Noble (Yes/No): No
Stability: Fair
Description: Released for general cultivation as recently as 1991, this Hallertauer seedling is being planted in increasing quantities, particularly in Washington State. The Liberty hop variety has many similarities to the Hallertauer and provides good, flavorful bittering with a fruity/floral character.

Type of hop: Lublin
Origin: Poland
Alpha: 3.0–5.5
Noble (Yes/No): No
Stability: Fair
Description: Also known as the Lubelski, this Czech hop clone offers many of the same brewing attributes of the respected Saaz variety. The Lublin is virtually unknown in the U.S.

Type of hop: Magnum
Origin: Germany
Alpha: 10.0–12.5
Noble (Yes/No): No
Stability: Good
Description: Bred during the 1980s in Germany's Hallertau region from the American Galena hop and a German cultivar, this hop is the first of what is being called the super-alpha variety. It combines high alpha with a good yield, and its area of cultivation is increasing substantially. The Magnum has excellent bittering quality with acceptable aromatic properties. It's useful for all types of beer, but make sure that you use it sparingly. Imported Magnum hops are sometimes referred to as German Magnum, and domestically grown versions are called Yakima Magnum.

Type of hop: Mount Hood
Origin: U.S.
Alpha: 4.0–6.5
Noble (Yes/No): No
Stability: Fair
Description: The Mount Hood hop variety is named for the famous volcano in Oregon. Like the Liberty hop, the Mount Hood is also a Hallertauer seedling, showing characteristics of both the parent plant and the Hersbrucker variety. The Mount Hood imparts a clean and soft bitterness to beer, with a distinct herbal aroma.

Type of hop: Newport
Origin: U.S.
Alpha: 12.0–14.0
Noble (Yes/No): No
Stability: Good
Description: Newport is a very new super alpha hop with an earthy, slightly resinous aroma sometimes described as newly mown hay. Because of this hop's high alpha acid content, I would limit its use to very high gravity beers.

Type of hop: Northdown
Origin: U.K.
Alpha: 7.0–10.0
Noble (Yes/No): No
Stability: Good
Description: The Northdown is also a descendant of the Northern Brewer. This hop has a very mild, clean, neutral flavor that can be used in all types of beer. The high level of oil in the Northdown makes it a desirable dry hop for full-bodied Ales.

Type of hop: Northern Brewer
Origin: U.K.
Alpha: 7.5–9.0
Noble (Yes/No): No
Stability: Fair
Description: The Northern Brewer was bred in England in the early 1930s and exported to Germany via Belgium. In Germany, it has been the dominant bittering hop, although it's now being outclassed by some new varieties. Strong, robust, and sometimes coarse, Northern Brewer hops provide a good bitter character if used early in the boil.

Type of hop: Nugget
Origin: U.S./Germany
Alpha: 12.0–14.0
Noble (Yes/No): No
Stability: Good
Description: Released for general cultivation in 1982, the Nugget variety is a Brewer's Gold derivative. This high-alpha hop is grown in the Pacific Northwest and Germany. Nugget hops impart a pleasant, mild bittering to beer, along with a subdued aromatic contribution.

Type of hop: Perle
Origin: Germany/U.S.
Alpha: 6.0–9.0
Noble (Yes/No): No
Stability: Good
Description: Raised from the Northern Brewer variety, Perle hops were quickly accepted in the Hallertau region and are now grown in significant quantities in the U.S. Perle hops are similar in contribution to the Hallertauer variety in imparting fine flavoring and aromatics, sometimes with floral/fruity effects.

Type of hop: Pride of Ringwood
Origin: Australia
Alpha: 8.0–10.0
Noble (Yes/No): No
Stability: Fair
Description: This hop variety is grown in the Victoria and Tasmania regions of Australia and is the dominant variety grown there. This hop is primarily a bittering variety because poor stability affects the hop's aromatic properties. As with all hops grown in Australia, this variety is a pesticide-free crop, which makes it attractive to those brewers who want to use organic ingredients.

Type of hop: Saaz
Origin: Czechoslovakia
Alpha: 3.0–6.0
Noble (Yes/No): Yes
Stability: Fair
Description: The true Saaz hops are grown in the hopyards around the Bohemian towns of Zatec and Louny in the Czech Republic. The Saaz hop is prized for its very fine, noble aroma and slightly spicy/peppery flavor. This variety is the traditional hop used in Pilsener-type beers.

Type of hop: Santiam
Origin: U.S.
Alpha: 6.0–7.0
Noble (Yes/No): No
Stability: Good
Description: The Santiam is an aromatic variety crossbred from Swiss Tettnanger, German Hallertauer, and American Cascade varieties. It can be used for both Lagers and Ales and is considered similar to, but better than, the discontinued Ultra variety.

Type of hop: Simcoe
Origin: U.S.
Alpha: 12.0–14.0
Noble (Yes/No): No
Stability: Good
Description: You can use the Simcoe for both aroma and bittering. It has a wonderful pine-floral character that blends well with Amarillo, Cascade, and Centennial varieties in American-style Ales.

Type of hop: Spalt
Origin: Germany
Alpha: 4.5–7.0
Noble (Yes/No): Yes
Stability: Fair
Description: Grown only in the Spalt region of Germany (southwest of Nürnberg), this variety has been in production for many generations. It has long been considered one of the finest of the Noble aromatic varieties. Most often used as a late-kettle-addition hop, the Spalt imbues beer with a fine, traditional, noble aroma, similar in quality to Tettnanger.

Type of hop: Target
Origin: U.K.
Alpha: 10.0–12.5
Noble (Yes/No): No
Stability: Fair
Description: This cousin of the Challenger variety is primarily an English hop but is also grown in parts of Germany and Belgium. With its strong English flavor and good bittering qualities, you can use this hop in all types of beer. The high oil content of the Target hop makes it a logical choice for dry hopping. The Target produces floral aromas.

Type of hop: Tettnanger
Origin: Germany
Alpha: 4.0–5.0
Noble (Yes/No): Yes
Stability: Fair
Description: Originally grown only in the Tettnang area of Germany (near the Bodensee), considerable quantities of this hop are now produced in the U.S. The traditional Tettnanger hop has long been regarded as one of the finest original aroma hops of Germany. The German variety offers a delicate, noble aroma, and the American-grown variety tends to be slightly coarser. Tettnanger hops are often used for late kettle additions.

Type of hop: Vanguard
Origin: U.S.
Alpha: 5.0–6.0
Noble (Yes/No): No
Stability: Good
Description: Originally crossbred in 1982 with American hop and Hallertau Mittelfruh parentage, this cultivar was released for commercial use in 1997. It's prized for its aromatic properties, and you can substitute it for Hallertau varieties.

Type of hop: Warrior
Origin: U.S.
Alpha: 15.0–17.0
Noble (Yes/No): No
Stability: Good
Description: A bittering hop of recent origin, you can also use this super-high-alpha hop for late kettle hop additions. Expect aggressive bittering as well as a unique, interesting citrus and spice character.

Type of hop: Willamette
Origin: U.S.
Alpha: 4.5–7.0
Noble (Yes/No): No
Stability: Fair
Description: The Willamette variety was developed in Oregon in the 1970s as a seedling of the Fuggles variety. Initially grown to be a Fuggles-replacement variety, the Willamette is now the dominant aroma hop grown in the Pacific Northwest. Mild, full bodied, and sometimes spicy, the rounded bittering and flavor characteristics of the Willamette deliciously mimic its precursor the Fuggles.

Yeast: Dry and Liquid

This section lists all the liquid-yeast strains available from two major liquid-yeast suppliers to the homebrewing industry; I've identified their products not only by the brand name but also by a beer-style-specific identifying code number. I've also included many other well-known freeze-dried-yeast suppliers.

You also find a beer style table designed to help you choose an appropriate liquid-yeast strain to produce any beer style you have in mind. In this table, I identify the recommended yeast strains by their code numbers.

Note that I also include a few Mead and Cider yeasts in some of these lists for your convenience.

Some liquid-yeast-culture suppliers list the rate of *attenuation* of the yeast. This rate refers to the percentage of sugar that you can expect a particular strain to eat during fermentation. (I've listed these rates of attenuation wherever the information was available.) What this rate of attenuation means to you as a brewer is that you can choose a yeast strain according to how dry or sweet you like your beers.

Table A-1 gives you the most popular dry yeast brands arranged according to Ale, Lager, and Belgian beer styles.

Table A-1	Dry Beer Yeast by Brand Name	
Dry Ale Yeast	*Dry Lager Yeast*	*Dry Belgian Yeast*
Cooper's	Amsterdam Lager	Brewferm Blanche
Doric	Superior Lager	Safbrew T-58
Edme	Brewferm Lager	
Munton's	Saflager S-23	
Nottingham		
Safale S-04, US-05		
Safbrew S-33		
Whitbread		
Windsor		

You can use these dry yeasts for fermenting both Cider and Mead:

- ✔ Epernay Cotes des Blanc
- ✔ Lalvin K1-V1116
- ✔ Lalvin 71B-1122
- ✔ Lalvin ICV-D47
- ✔ Red Star Montrachet
- ✔ Red Star Pasteur Champagne
- ✔ Red Star Premier Cuvee

Liquid top-fermenting yeast (Ales)

All the following yeast culture descriptions were supplied by the yeast producer Wyeast Laboratories (P.O. Box 146, Odell, OR 97044; 541-354-1335).

Wyeast product number: 1007
Style of yeast: German Ale
Description: Ferments dry and crisp, leaving a complex but mild flavor. Produces an extremely rocky head and ferments well down to 55 degrees Fahrenheit. Apparent attenuation: 73 to 77 percent

Wyeast product number: 1028
Style of yeast: London-Rich
Description: Minerally profile. Bold and crisp, with some diacetyl production.
Apparent attenuation: 73 to 77 percent

Wyeast product number: 1056
Style of yeast: American
Description: Widely known as Chico yeast for its use at Sierra Nevada Brewing
Company in Chico, California. Ferments dry and finishes soft, smooth, and
clean. An American classic. Apparent attenuation: 73 to 77 percent

Wyeast product number: 1084
Style of yeast: Irish
Description: Slight residual diacetyl and fruitiness. Great for Stouts. Clean,
soft, smooth, and full bodied. Apparent attenuation: 71 to 75 percent

Wyeast product number: 1098
Style of yeast: British
Description: A Whitbread strain. Ferments crisp and dry. Slightly tart, fruity,
and well balanced. Ferments well down to 65 degrees Fahrenheit. Apparent
attenuation: 73 to 77 percent

Wyeast product number: 1272
Style of yeast: American II
Description: Fruitier and more prone to *flocculation* (where the yeast clumps
together and drops to the bottom of the fermenter) than #1056. Slightly
nutty, soft, and clean, with a slightly tart finish. Apparent attenuation: 72 to
76 percent

Wyeast product number: 1275
Style of yeast: Thames Valley
Description: Produces classic British Bitters. Rich, complex flavor profile —
clean, light malt character, low fruitiness and esters; well balanced. Apparent
attenuation: 72 to 76 percent

Wyeast product number: 1335
Style of yeast: British II
Description: Typically used for British and Canadian Ale fermentation profile.
Crisp finish, clean, and fairly dry. Apparent attenuation: 73 to 76 percent

Wyeast product number: 1318
Style of yeast: London III
Description: Great malt and hop profile. Fruity, light, soft, balanced palate.
Finishes slightly sweet. Apparent attenuation: 71 to 75 percent

Wyeast product number: 1728
Style of yeast: Scottish
Description: Ideally suited for Scottish-Style Ales and high-gravity Ales of all
types. Apparent attenuation: 69 to 73 percent

Wyeast product number: 1338
Style of yeast: European
Description: From Munich. Full-bodied, complex strain. Finishes very malty. Apparent attenuation: 67 to 71 percent

Wyeast product number: 3056
Style of yeast: Bavarian Wheat
Description: A blend of top-fermenting Ale and Wheat beer yeast strains. Produces mildly estery and phenolic Wheat beers. Apparent attenuation: 73 to 77 percent

Wyeast product number: 1099
Style of yeast: Whitbread Ale
Description: The original Whitbread from England. Mildly malty and slightly fruity. Not as tart as #1098 and much more prone to flocculation. Apparent attenuation: 68 to 72 percent

Wyeast product number: 1187
Style of yeast: Ringwood Ale
Description: Distinct fruit esters and high flocculation. Provides malty flavors with diacetyl overtones. Apparent attenuation: 68 to 72 percent

Wyeast product number: 1332
Style of yeast: Northwest Ale
Description: One of the classic strains from the northwest U.S. Produces a malty and mildly fruity Ale with depth and complexity. Apparent attenuation: 67 to 71 percent

Liquid bottom-fermenting yeast (Lagers)

All the following yeast culture descriptions were supplied by the yeast producer Wyeast Laboratories (P.O. Box 146, Odell, OR 97044; 541-354-1335).

Wyeast product number: 2007
Style of yeast: Pilsen
Description: A classic American Pilsener strain. Smooth, malty palate. Ferments dry and crisp. Apparent attenuation: 71 to 75 percent

Wyeast product number: 2035
Style of yeast: American
Description: Not a Pilsener strain. Bold, complex, and aromatic, with slight diacetyl production. Apparent attenuation: 73 to 77 percent

Wyeast product number: 2042
Style of yeast: Danish
Description: A rich Dortmund style with a crisp, dry finish. Soft profile accentuates hop characteristics. Apparent attenuation: 73 to 77 percent

Wyeast product number: 2112
Style of yeast: California
Description: Particularly well suited to producing 19th-century West Coast beers. Retains its Lager characteristics up to 65 degrees Fahrenheit. Produces malty, brilliantly clear beers. Apparent attenuation: 67 to 71 percent

Wyeast product number: 2124
Style of yeast: Bohemian
Description: Pilsener yeast from Weihenstephan, Germany. Ferments clean and malty, with rich residual maltiness in full-bodied Pilseners. Apparent attenuation: 73 to 77 percent

Wyeast product number: 2206
Style of yeast: Bavarian
Description: Used by many German brewers to produce rich, full-bodied malty beers. Apparent attenuation: 73 to 77 percent

Wyeast product number: 2247
Style of yeast: Danish II
Description: Clean, dry flavor profile. Often used in aggressively hopped Pilsener beers. Very mild flavor, mild sulfur production, dry finish. Apparent attenuation: 73 to 77 percent

Wyeast product number: 2272
Style of yeast: North American
Description: Traditional culture used to make many American and Canadian Lagers and light Pilseners. Apparent attenuation: 70 to 76 percent

Wyeast product number: 2278
Style of yeast: Czech Pils
Description: Classic Pilsener yeast from the birthplace of Pilsener beer. Sulfur produced during fermentation dissipates with proper *conditioning* (aging). Apparent attenuation: 70 to 74 percent

Wyeast product number: 2308
Style of yeast: Munich
Description: Unique strain of yeast capable of producing fine Lager beers. Very smooth, well-rounded, and full-bodied profile in the Bavarian style. Apparent attenuation: 73 to 77 percent

Wyeast product number: 2000
Style of yeast: Budvar
Description: Rich malt profile, finishes malty but dry, crisp, and well balanced. Hop character comes through in the finish. Apparent attenuation: 71 to 75 percent

Wyeast product number: 2001
Style of yeast: Urquell
Description: Very clean and dry with a full mouthfeel and subtle malt character. Very clean finish. Apparent attenuation: 72 to 76 percent

Advanced liquid yeast (Ales)

All the following yeast culture descriptions were supplied by the yeast producer Wyeast Laboratories (P.O. Box 146, Odell, OR 97044; 541-354-1335).

The following list describes yeast cultures Wyeast considers advanced because the production of these beer styles is generally more difficult or involved than those styles listed previously.

Wyeast product number: 1214
Style of yeast: Belgian Abbey
Description: Top-fermenting, Abbey-style yeast suitable for high-gravity beers. Very estery. Apparent attenuation: 72 to 76 percent

Wyeast product number: 1388
Style of yeast: Belgian Strong Ale
Description: Robust-flavored yeast with moderate to high alcohol tolerance. Fruity nose and palate. Dry, tart finish. Apparent attenuation: 73 to 77 percent

Wyeast product number: 1762
Style of yeast: Belgian Abbey II
Description: High-gravity yeast with distinct warming character from ethanol production. Slightly fruity with dry finish. Apparent attenuation: 73 to 77 percent

Wyeast product number: 1968
Style of yeast: Special London
Description: Also known as London ESB. Rich, malty character and balanced fruitiness. Some diacetyl production. Excellent strain for cask-conditioned Ales. So conducive to flocculation that additional aeration and agitation are necessary to complete fermentation. Apparent attenuation: 67 to 71 percent

Wyeast product number: 2565
Style of yeast: Kölsch
Description: Hybrid strain with Ale and Lager characteristics. Develops excellent maltiness with subdued fruitiness and a crisp finish. Ferments well at moderate (50 to 60 degrees Fahrenheit) temperatures. Apparent attenuation: 73 to 77 percent

Wyeast product number: 3068
Style of yeast: Weihenstephan Wheat
Description: Unique top-fermenting strain from one of the oldest breweries in the world. Produces the spicy Weizen character rich with clove, brown spices, vanilla, and banana aromas and flavors. Best results achieved if fermentation temperatures are held around 68 degrees Fahrenheit. Apparent attenuation: 73 to 77 percent

Wyeast product number: 3278
Style of yeast: Belgian Lambic blend
Description: Belgian Lambic-Style yeast blend with lactic bacteria for souring of the wort. Rich, earthy aroma and acidic finish. Suitable for gueuze, Fruit beers, and faro. Apparent attenuation: 65 to 75

Wyeast product number: 3333
Style of yeast: German Wheat
Description: Subtle, fruity flavor profile for Wheat Beers. Sharp, tart crispness and a fruity, sherry-like palate. Apparent attenuation: 70 to 76 percent

Wyeast product number: 3787
Style of yeast: Belgian Trappist
Description: Trappist-style yeast good for unique high-gravity Ales (ideal for Biere de Garde). Robust yeast creates phenolic character. Alcohol tolerance up to 12 percent. Ferments dry with rich ester profile and malty palate. Apparent attenuation: 75 to 80 percent

Wyeast product number: 3942
Style of yeast: Belgian Wheat
Description: From Belgium. Estery yeast with low phenol production. Apple- and plum-like nose with dry finish. Apparent attenuation: 72 to 76 percent

Wyeast product number: 3944
Style of yeast: Belgian Witbier
Description: A tart, slightly phenolic character capable of producing distinctive Witbiers and Grand Cru styles. Alcohol-tolerant. Apparent attenuation: 72 to 76 percent

Wyeast product number: 3463
Style of yeast: Forbidden Fruit
Description: Sourced from an old Belgian brewery and ideal for the production of Wits and classic Grand Cru styles. Phenolic profile with subdued fruitiness. Apparent attenuation: 73 to 77 percent

Wyeast product number: 3522
Style of yeast: Belgian Ardennes
Description: A classic Belgian Ale yeast. Phenolic flavor develops with increased fermentation temperatures along with mild fruitiness and complex spicy character. Apparent attenuation: 73 to 77 percent

Wyeast product number: 3274
Style of yeast: Belgian Saison
Description: Produces an Ale with spicy and complex aromatics. Very tart and dry finishing crisp with mild acidity. Apparent attenuation: 76 to 80 percent

Liquid top-fermenting yeast (Ales)

All the following yeast culture descriptions were supplied by the yeast producer White Labs (5564 Trade St., San Diego, CA 92121; 858-693-3441).

White Labs product number: WLP001
Style of yeast: California Ale Yeast
Description: This yeast is famous for its clean flavors, balance, and ability to be used in almost any style of Ale. It accentuates the hop flavors and is extremely versatile. Apparent attenuation: 73 to 80 percent

White Labs product number: WLP002
Style of yeast: English Ale Yeast
Description: A classic ESB strain from one of England's largest independent breweries. This yeast is best suited for English-style Ales including Milds, Bitters, Porters, and English-style Stouts and leaves a beer very clear with some residual sweetness. Apparent attenuation: 63 to 70 percent

White Labs product number: WLP004
Style of yeast: Irish Ale Yeast
Description: This is the yeast from one of the oldest Stout-producing breweries in the world. It produces a slight hint of diacetyl, balanced by a light fruitiness and slight dry crispness. Great for Irish Ales, Stouts, Porters, Browns, Reds, and a very interesting Pale Ale. Apparent attenuation: 69 to 74 percent

White Labs product number: WLP005
Style of yeast: British Ale Yeast
Description: This yeast is a little more attenuate than WLP002. Like most English strains, this yeast produces malty beers. Excellent for all English-style Ales including Bitter, Pale Ale, Porter, and Brown Ale. Apparent attenuation: 67 to 74 percent

White Labs product number: WLP007
Style of yeast: Dry English Ale Yeast
Description: Clean, highly flocculent, and highly attenuate yeast. This yeast is similar to WLP002 in flavor profile, but is 10 percent more attenuate. This eliminates the residual sweetness and makes the yeast well suited for high-gravity Ales. It also reaches terminal gravity quickly. You can reach 80 percent attenuation even with 10 percent ABV beers. Apparent attenuation: 70 to 80 percent

White Labs product number: WLP008
Style of yeast: East Coast Ale Yeast
Description: You can use the Brewer Patriot strain of this yeast to reproduce many of the American versions of classic beer styles. It has a neutral character similar to WLP001, but with less attenuation, less accentuation of hop

bitterness, increased flocculation, and a little tartness. It's very clean, has low esters, and is great for Golden, Blonde, Honey, Pale, and German Alt-style Ales. Apparent attenuation: 70 to 75 percent

White Labs product number:
WLP011http://www.whitelabs.com/beer/strains_wlp011.html
Style of yeast: European Ale Yeast
Description: This malty, Northern European-origin Ale yeast has low ester production and a clean profile. It produces little to no sulfur, and low attenuation helps contribute to the malty character. Good for Alt, Kölsch, malty English Ales, and Fruit beers. Apparent attenuation: 65 to 70 percent

White Labs product number: WLP013
Style of yeast: London Ale Yeast
Description: This dry, malty Ale yeast provides a complex, oaky ester character to your beer. Hop bitterness comes through well. This yeast is well suited for classic British Pale Ales, Bitters, and Stouts; it doesn't flocculate as much as WLP002 and WLP005. Apparent attenuation: 67 to 75 percent

White Labs product number: WLP023
Style of yeast: Burton Ale Yeast
Description: From the famous brewing town of Burton-on-Trent, England, this yeast is packed with character. It provides delicious subtle fruity flavors like apple, clover honey, and pear and is great for all English styles, IPAs, Bitters, and Pales and excellent in Porters and Stouts. Apparent attenuation: 69 to 75 percent

White Labs product number: WLP028
Style of yeast: Edinburgh Scottish Ale Yeast
Description: Scotland is famous for its malty, strong Ales. This yeast can reproduce complex, flavorful Scottish-style Ales and can be an everyday strain, similar to WLP001. Hop character isn't muted with this strain as it is with WLP002. Apparent attenuation: 70 to 75 percent

White Labs product number: WLP029
Style of yeast: German Ale/Kölsch Yeast
Description: From a small brewpub in Cologne, Germany, this yeast works well in Kölsch and Alt-style beers and is good for light beers like Blond and Honey. It accentuates hop flavors much like WLP001. The slight sulfur produced during fermentation disappears with age and leaves a super-clean, Lager-like Ale. Apparent attenuation: 72 to 78 percent

White Labs product number: WLP041
Style of yeast: Pacific Ale Yeast
Description: This is a popular Ale yeast from the Pacific Northwest that clears from the beer well and leaves a malty profile. It's fruitier than WLP002 and good for English-style Ales including Milds, Bitters, IPAs, Porters, and English-style Stouts. Apparent attenuation: 65 to 70 percent

White Labs product number: WLP051
Style of yeast: California Ale V Yeast
Description: This strain from Northern California is fruitier than WLP001 and slightly more flocculent. Attenuation is lower, resulting in a fuller-bodied beer than WLP001. Apparent attenuation: 70 to 75 percent

White Labs product number: WLP060
Style of yeast: American Ale Yeast Blend
Description: This blend celebrates the strengths of WLP001: It's clean, boasts a neutral fermentation and versatile usage, and adds two other strains that belong to the same clean/neutral flavor category. The additional strains create complexity in the finished beer. This blend tastes more Lager-like than WLP001. It accentuates hop flavors and bitterness — but not to the extreme of WLP001 — and produces slight sulfur during fermentation. Apparent attenuation: 72 to 80 percent

White Labs product number: WLP080
Style of yeast: Cream Ale Yeast Blend
Description: This is a blend of Ale and Lager yeast strains that work together to create a clean, crisp, light American-Lager-style Ale. You can perceive a pleasing estery aroma from the Ale yeast contribution, and hop flavors and bitterness are slightly subdued. The Lager yeast produces slight sulfur during fermentation. Apparent attenuation: 75 to 80 percent

White Labs product number: WLP099
Style of yeast: Super High Gravity Ale Yeast
Description: This yeast from England can ferment up to 25 percent alcohol. It produces an ester character that increases in higher-gravity beers, although malt character dominates at lower gravities. Apparent attenuation: >80 percent

Specialty/Belgian yeast

All the following yeast culture descriptions were supplied by the yeast producer White Labs (5564 Trade St., San Diego, CA 92121; 858-693-3441).

White Labs product number: WLP300
Style of yeast: Hefeweizen Ale Yeast
Description: This famous German yeast is a strain used in the production of traditional, authentic Wheat beers. It produces the banana and clove nose traditionally associated with German Wheat beers and leaves the desired cloudy look of traditional German Wheat beers. Apparent attenuation: 72 to 76 percent

White Labs product number: WLP320
Style of yeast: American Hefeweizen Ale Yeast
Description: This yeast is used to produce the Oregon-style American Hefeweizen. Unlike WLP300, this yeast produces a very slight amount of the banana and clove notes. It produces some sulfur but is otherwise a clean-fermenting yeast that doesn't flocculate well, producing a cloudy beer. Apparent attenuation: 70 to 75 percent

White Labs product number: WLP380
Style of yeast: Hefeweizen IV Ale Yeast
Description: This yeast produces a crisp, drinkable hefeweizen with a strong clove and phenolic aroma and flavor with minimal banana. It also promotes refreshing citrus and apricot notes. It's less flocculent than WLP300, and sulfur production is higher. Apparent attenuation: 73 to 80 percent

White Labs product number: WLP400
Style of yeast: Belgian Wit Ale Yeast
Description: Slightly phenolic and tart, this is the original yeast used to produce Wit in Belgium. Apparent attenuation: 74 to 78 percent

White Labs product number: WLP500
Style of yeast: Trappist Ale Yeast
Description: Found in one of the few remaining Trappist breweries remaining in the world, this yeast produces the distinctive fruitiness and plum characteristics. Excellent yeast for high-gravity beers, Belgian Ales, Trappist dubbels, and tripels. Apparent attenuation: 75 to 80 percent

White Labs product number: WLP530
Style of yeast: Abbey Ale Yeast
Description: Use this yeast to produce Trappist-style and high-gravity beers, Belgian Ales, dubbels, and tripels. It's similar to WLP500 but is less fruity and more alcohol-tolerant (up to 15 percent ABV). Apparent attenuation: 75 to 80 percent

White Labs product number: WLP550
Style of yeast: Belgian Ale Yeast
Description: Saisons, Belgian Ales, Belgian Reds, Belgian Browns, and White beers are just a few of the classic Belgian beer styles that you can create with this yeast strain. Phenolic and spicy flavors dominate the profile, with less fruitiness than WLP500. Apparent attenuation: 78 to 85 percent

White Labs product number: WLP565
Style of yeast: Belgian Saison I Yeast
Description: This slightly sweet classic Saison yeast from Wallonia produces earthy, peppery, and spicy notes. With high-gravity saisons, brewers may want to dry the beer with an alternate yeast added after 75 percent fermentation. Apparent attenuation: 65 to 75 percent

White Labs product number: WLP568
Style of yeast: Belgian Style Saison Ale Yeast Blend
Description: This blend melds Belgian-style Ale and saison strains that work in harmony to create complex, fruity aromas and flavors. The blend of yeast strains encourages complete fermentation in a timely manner and creates phenolic, spicy, earthy, and clove-like flavors. Apparent attenuation: 70 to 80 percent

White Labs product number: WLP570
Style of yeast: Belgian Golden Ale Yeast
Description: This versatile yeast from East Flanders can produce light Belgian Ales to high gravity-Belgian beers (12 percent ABV). A combination of fruitiness and phenolic characteristics dominate the flavor profile. Some sulfur is produced during fermentation, which will dissipate following the end of fermentation. Apparent attenuation: 73 to 78 percent

White Labs product number: WLP575
Style of yeast: Belgian Style Ale Yeast Blend
Description: This blend of two Trappist-type yeasts and one Belgian-Ale-type yeast can be used for Trappist-type beers or a myriad of Belgian-type beers. Apparent attenuation: 74 to 80 percent

Bottom-fermenting yeast (Lagers)

All the following yeast culture descriptions were supplied by the yeast producer White Labs (5564 Trade St., San Diego, CA 92121; 858-693-3441).

White Labs product number: WLP800
Style of yeast: Pilsener Lager Yeast
Description: This classic Pilsener strain from the premier Pilsener producer in the Czech Republic is somewhat dry with a malty finish. It's best suited for European Pilsener production. Apparent attenuation: 72 to 77 percent

White Labs product number: WLP802
Style of yeast: Czech Budejovice Lager Yeast
Description: This Pilsener Lager yeast from Southern Czech Republic produces dry, crisp Lagers with low diacetyl production. Apparent attenuation: 75 to 80 percent

White Labs product number: WLP810
Style of yeast: San Francisco Lager Yeast
Description: Use this yeast to produce the California Common-style beer. A unique Lager strain that can ferment up to 65 degrees Fahrenheit while retaining Lager characteristics, it can also ferment down to 50 degrees Fahrenheit for production of Märzens, Pilseners, and other-style Lagers. Apparent attenuation: 65 to 70 percent

White Labs product number: WLP820
Style of yeast: Oktoberfest/Märzen Lager yeast
Description: This yeast produces a very malty, Bock-like style that doesn't finish as dry as WLP830. This yeast is much slower in the first generation than WLP830, so consider using a larger starter in the first generation or scheduling a longer lagering time. Apparent attenuation: 65 to 73 percent

White Labs product number: WLP830
Style of yeast: German Lager Yeast
Description: This yeast is one of the most widely used Lager yeasts in the world. It's very malty and clean and great for all German Lagers, Pilseners, Oktoberfests, and Märzens. Apparent attenuation: 74 to 79 percent

White Labs product number: WLP833
Style of yeast: German Bock Lager yeast
Description: Originating in the Alps of southern Bavaria, this very versatile Lager yeast produces a beer that's so well balanced between malt and hop character that it has gained tremendous popularity for use in Classic American-style Pilseners. The excellent malt profile makes it well suited for Bocks, Dopplebocks, and Oktoberfest-style beers, and it's also good for Helles-style Lager beer. Apparent attenuation: 70 to 76 percent

White Labs product number: WLP838
Style of yeast: Southern German Lager Yeast
Description: This yeast is characterized by a malty finish and balanced aroma. It's a strong fermenter and produces slight sulfur and low diacetyl. Apparent attenuation: 68 to 76 percent

White Labs product number: WLP840
Style of yeast: American Lager Yeast
Description: This yeast is used to produce American-style Lagers. It's dry and clean with a very slight apple fruitiness, and sulfur and diacetyl production are minimal. Apparent attenuation: 75 to 80 percent

White Labs product number: WLP940
Style of yeast: Mexican Lager Yeast
Description: From Mexico City, this yeast produces clean Lager beer with a crisp finish. It's good for Mexican-style light Lagers as well as dark Lagers. Apparent attenuation: 70 to 78 percent

Suggested strains for specific beer styles

Tables A-2, A-3, and A-4 give you popular beer styles and the Wyeast and White Labs code numbers for the yeasts appropriate to each style.

Table A-2	Ales	
Beer Style	**Wyeast Code Numbers**	**White Labs Code Numbers**
English-style Pale Ale/Bitters	1028, 1968, 1099	002, 005, 013
American-style Pale Ale	1056, 1028, 1338	001, 008, 041
Brown Ale/Mild	1028, 1338, 1984	002, 005, 007
Scottish Ale	1728, 1056, 1084	023, 028
Scottish Strong (Scotch) Ale	1728, 1056, 1187	002, 028
English Strong Ale	1968, 1028, 1098	002, 005, 028
Porter	1084, 1028, 1056	002, 005, 013
Dry Stout	1084, 1007, 1028	004, 005, 007
Sweet Stout	1968, 1338, 1056	004, 013, 028
Imperial Stout	1084, 1056, 1728	004, 013, 099
Barley Wine	1728, 1084, 1056	013, 099
Altbier	1007, 1338, 1056	029, 080, 820
Kölschbier	2565, 1007, 1338	029, 080
Belgian Ale (Dubbel, Tripel, Abbey)	1214, 3944, 3522	530, 550, 575

Table A-3	Lagers	
Beer Style	**Wyeast Code Numbers**	**White Labs Code Numbers**
Bohemian-style Pilsener	2000, 2007, 2001	800, 802
German-style Pilsener	2007, 2000, 2001	800, 802, 830
American-style Pilsener	2035, 2007, 2278	810, 840, 940
Münchner-style Helles (Pale Lager)	2308, 2206, 2124	820, 830, 838
Dortmunder/European-style Export	2206, 2308, 2035	820, 830, 838

Beer Style	Wyeast Code Numbers	White Labs Code Numbers
Märzen/Oktoberfest/Vienna	2206, 2278, 2308	820, 833, 838
Munich Dunkel (Dark Lager)	2206, 2308, 2035	820, 830, 838
Bock/Doppelbock	2124, 2278, 2007	820, 833, 838
California Common (Steam Beer)	2112, 1332	001, 051, 810

Table A-4	Wheat Beers	
Beer Style	**Wyeast Code Numbers**	**White Labs Code Numbers**
American Wheat	1007, 1056	320, 380
Bavarian Weizenbier	3068, 3056	300, 380, 550
Belgian Witbier	3944, 3463	400, 550

Mead and cider yeast

All the following yeast culture descriptions were supplied by the yeast producer.

Wyeast #4766 Cider: Crisp and dry fermenting yeast with big, fruity finish. Creates a nice balance for all types of apples, pears, and other fruits. Allows fruit character to dominate the profile.

Wyeast #4184 Sweet Mead: One of two strains for mead making. Leaves 2 to 3 percent residual sugar in most Meads. Rich, fruity profile complements fruit Mead fermentation. Use additional nutrients for Mead making.

Wyeast #4632 Dry Mead: Best choice for dry Mead. Used in many award-winning Meads. Low foaming with little or no sulfur production. Use additional nutrients for Mead making.

White Labs WLP715 Champagne Yeast: Classic yeast, used to produce champagne, Cider, dry Meads, dry wines, or to fully attenuate Barley Wines/strong Ales. Neutral.

White Labs WLP720 Sweet Mead/Wine Yeast: A wine yeast strain that's less attenuate than WLP715, leaving some residual sweetness. Slightly fruity and will tolerate alcohol concentrations up to 15 percent. A good choice for sweet Mead and Cider, as well as Blush wines, Gewürztraminer, Sauternes, and Riesling.

White Labs WLP775 English Cider Yeast: Classic Cider yeast. Ferments dry, but retains fruit flavor. Produces sulfur during fermentation, but this will disappear in first two weeks of aging. Can also be used for wine and high-gravity beers.

Index

• Numerics •

1-4-U, 2-4-ME S.B., 161
2-row barley, 44
2-row malt, 364
3-D (Duisberg, Dortmund, Düsseldorf) Export, 217
6-row barley, 44
6-row malt, 364
50-point system, 335

• A •

AAUs (alpha acid units), 58–60
Abbey Ale yeast, 389
abbey beer, 198
ABV (alcohol by volume), 24, 71–72
ABW (alcohol by weight), 24, 71–72
acetaldehyde, 327, 329
acetic aromas and taste, 328–329
acetobacter bacteria, 323
Acid Blend packets, 276
acid tests, 96
acidic pH, 75
Activator packs, 69
additives, 92–93
adjunct grains, 45, 47, 368–369
adjunct-laden brews, 314
adjuncts, 81–84, 292
Admiral hops, 371
advanced liquid yeast, 384–385
aftermash procedures, 133–134
aftertaste, 316
aging process, 13
AHA (American Homebrewers Association), 3, 11, 333
Ahtanum hops, 371

Ain't Monkin' Around Dubbel, 199
airlock, 19, 21, 27
airspace, 140
alcohol by volume (ABV), 24, 71–72
alcohol by weight (ABW), 24, 71–72
alcohol content, 105, 321
Ale recipes
   American Amber Ale (10-b), 168–169
   American Brown Ale (10-c), 170–171
   American India Pale Ale (IPA) (14-b), 191–192
   American Pale Ale (10-a), 166–167
   Baltic Porter (12-c), 178–179
   Belgian Dark Strong Ale (18-e), 204–205
   Belgian Golden Strong Ale (18-d), 202–203
   Belgian Pale Ale (16-b), 196–197
   Brown Porter (12-a), 174–175
   Dry Stout (13-a), 180–181
   Dubbel (18-b), 198–199
   English India Pale Ale (IPA) (14-a), 189–190
   English-Style Barley Wine (19-b), 208–210
   Extra Special/Strong Bitter (E.S.B.) (8-c), 160–161
   Foreign-Style Stout (13-d), 184–185
   Imperial India Pale Ale (IPA) (14-c), 192–194
   Imperial Stout (13-f), 186–188
   Irish Red Ale (9-d), 162–163
   labels, 210
   Northern English Brown Ale (11-c), 172–173

   Old Ale (19-a), 206–207
   Robust Porter (12-b), 177
   Strong Scotch Ale (9-e), 164–165
   Sweet Stout (13-b), 182–183
   Tripel (18-c), 200–201
   White (Wit)(16-a), 194–196
Ale yeast, 64, 66
Ales, 44, 392. *See also* Ale recipes
alfalfa honey, 274
alkaline pH, 75
all-grain brewing, 128–132
alligator seed, 194
all-malt extracts, 49
allspice, 89
alpha acid content, 55–56
alpha acid units (AAUs), 58–60
alpha-amylase, 119
Altbiers, 242
Alterior Motive, 243
alternative primers, 146–147
Amarillo hops, 371
Amber Waves, 169
American Ale Yeast Blend, 388
American Amber Ale (10-b), 168–169
American Brown Ale (10-c), 170–171
American Dark Lager (4-a), 222–223
American Hefeweizen Ale yeast, 389
American Homebrewers Association (AHA), 3, 11, 333
American hops, 61
American II yeast, 381
American India Pale Ale (IPA) (14-b), 191–192
American Lager yeast, 391
American Pale Ale (10-a), 166–167

American Premium Lager (1-c), 212–213
American Society of Brewing Chemists, 317
American Wheat (6-d), 238–239
American yeast, 381, 382
Americas, 44
ammonia, 35
amylase enzyme, 92
Anglo style, 267
anise, 89
Anne's Choice Christmas Ale, 255
antibacterial agents, 75–76
antioxidant, 96
aphrodisiacs, 272
apple juice, 269–270
Apple Wine (28-c), 268
apples, 266–267
Apprentice Judge, 339
Arlington Ale No. 33, 235
aroma hops, 56, 60
aromas, 311–313, 327–328. *See also* flavors and aromas
arrested fermentation, 268
Arvidson, Dennis and Cindy, 221–222
ascorbic acid, 95
aseptic techniques, 344
Ashman, Todd, 173
Asia, 44
Association of Brewers, 339
astringency, 316, 324–325, 329
attenuation rate, 379
Aurora hops, 371
auto siphon, 354
autolysis, 111, 325

• *B* •

bacteria, 34–35
bad body, 331
ball fittings, 150
Balling scale, 24
Baltic Porter (12-c), 178–179
Bamberg Smoke beer, 256
Bamberger Rauchbier, 256
banana esters aromas, 327

banking yeast, 343–345
barley, 5, 43–44
Barley Wines, 145, 208, 358
barleymalt. *See* malts
base grains, 363–366
base malted grain, 45
Basically Bock, 229
batch sizes, 3, 131–133
bathtub booze, 1
Bavarian brewers, 64
Bavarian Weizenbier, 246
Bavarian Wheat yeast, 382
Bavarian yeast, 383
Beck beer, 228
Beech Beer, 257
beer
  aromas, 327–328
  calibration, 335
  cloudy, 331
  commercial, 11
  filters, 354–355
  flutes, 305, 306
  green, 45
  kegs, converting to brewpots, 351
  kitchen-sink category, 260
  nonalcoholic, 72
  non-toxic, 288
  organic, 286–287
  styles, HBUs for, 60
  taste, 328
  transparent, 91
  yeast, 34, 63
beer clean, 307
Beer Flavor Wheel, 317
beer gravity, 58
Beer Judge Certification Program (BJCP), 333, 339–340
beer stone, 66, 354
bees, 273
Belgian Abbey, 197, 202–203
Belgian Abbey yeast, 384
Belgian Ale yeast, 389
Belgian Ardennes yeast, 385
Belgian candi sugar, 84
Belgian Dark Strong Ale (18-e), 204–205
Belgian Golden Ale yeast, 390
Belgian Golden Strong Ale (18-d), 202–203

Belgian Lambic blend yeast, 385
Belgian Pale Ale (16-b), 196–197
Belgian Saison yeast, 385
Belgian specialty beers, 34
Belgian Strong Ale yeast, 384
Belgian Trappist yeast, 385
Belgian Wheat yeast, 385
Belgian Witbier, 87
Belgian Witbier yeast, 385
Belgian Yeast, 388–390
bench-cappers, 23, 141
bentonite, 94
Berliner Weisse, 145
Berliner Weisse-style goblet, 305
Best-of-Show round, 335
beta-amylase, 119
bicarbonate, 77
Biere Blanche, 194
Big Apple Punch, 272
bines, 347
Biscuit Malt, 367
bitter taste receptors, 314
bittering hops, 56, 58–61, 110
bittering potential, 370
bitterness, 108
bitters. *See* Extra Special/Extra Strong Bitter
bittersweet apples, 266
BJCP (Beer Judge Certification Program), 333, 339–340
Black malt, 368
blackstrap molasses, 83
bleach, 36
Bliss, Brian, 203
Blonde Ale (6-b), 236–237
Bock beer, 228
Bockmore, Jerry, 165–166
body, 316
Bohemian yeast, 383
Bohemian-Style Pilsener (2-b), 218–219
boiling, 34, 56, 110
Boobs Barley Wine, 209
BOPs (Brew On Premises), 13
Boston Beer Company, 16
bottle brushes, 20, 22

bottle cappers, 20, 23, 141
bottle caps, 15, 39, 147–148, 324
bottle holders, 39
bottle rinsers, 20, 22
bottled water, 76, 78–79
bottles
  choosing, 135–136
  cost of, 20
  exploding, 276
  glass, 22
  size requirements for competitions, 336
  soaking, 138
bottling
  crowns, 147–148
  kegged beer, 142–144
  priming, 144–147
  process, 136–142
bottling buckets, 22, 349
bottling tubes, 20, 22, 140
bottom-fermenting yeast, 390–391
bouquet, 311
Boyce, Chuck, 209
bracteole, 52
braggot, 275
branding, 361
Brass Baltics Imperial Porter, 179
Brew On Premises (BOPs), 13
brew spoons, 19–20
brewer's chocolate, 260
brewer's licorice, 186, 260
brewing. *See* homebrewing
brewing purists, 146
brewing software, 356
brewing timeline, 14
Brewmistress I.P.A., 189–190
Brewpots, 17, 19, 20
brewpubs, 12
Bridge House Bitter, 161
Briess, 362
British Ale yeast, 386
British ales, 79
British cellar temperature, 304
British II yeast, 381
British yeast, 381
British-style Ales, volumes for, 156

Brix reading, 355
brix scale, 49
Brockington, David and Melinda, 185, 187–188
Brooklyn Brewery, 284
Brown Porter (12-a), 174–175
brown sugar, 83
bruhmalt, 362
Brune Dream, 205
brushes, 20, 22, 26–27
bubblegum aromas, 327
bubblers, 21
buckwheat, 295, 296
Budvar yeast, 383
Burko, Robert, 197
Burton Ale yeast, 387
Burton salts, 79, 92
Burtonizing, 79
Burton-on-Trent beers, 79
butane lighters, 344
butter flavors, 322–323
butterscotch flavor, 322–323
Butt-Scratcher, 213
Buxton Brown of Derbyshire County, 173

• **C** •

calcium, 77
calcium carbonate, 31, 77, 268
calcium chloride, 31, 268
calcium sulfate, 78
calibration beers, 335
California Ale V yeast, 388
California Ale yeast, 386
California Common beer (7-b), 240–241
California yeast, 383
Campbell, Jim, 165
Campden tablets, 278
canes, 27
cannabis plant, 52
Cannon, James, 257
cappers, 20, 23, 141
caps, 15, 39, 147–148, 324
caramel malts, 109, 323, 361, 366–367
CaraMunich, 365
CaraPils malt, 331
CaraVienne, 365

caraway, 89
carbohydrates, 44
carbon dioxide (CO_2), 54, 63–64, 142, 149–150
carbon filters, 76
carbonate, 77
Carbonater cap, The, 142–143
carbonation, 145, 154–156, 330
carboy brushes, 26–27
carboys, 26–27
cardamom, 89
cardboard cases, 138
cardboard flavors, 324
carrageen, 94
cartridge type filters, 355
Cascade hops, 372
caustics, 35
CBW (Concentrated Brewer's Wort), 362
Cedar Mountain Brown Ale, 171
celiac disease, 293, 295
Centennial hops, 372
cereal grains, 44, 122
Certified Judge, 339
chalk. *See* calcium carbonate
chalky water, 325
Challenger hops, 372
Champagne yeasts, 278
chemistry of water, 74
Cherry Ale, 251
chill haze, 331
Chinook hops, 59, 372
chloride, 77
chlorine, 36, 75, 150
chlorophenols, 76, 323
chocolate, 85, 260
Chocolate Chambord Stout, 255
chocolate malt, 172, 367
Christmas/Winter/Specialty Spiced Beer (21-b), 254–255
Cider, 71, 265–272
Cider yeast, 393–394
cinnamon, 89
Cistercian monks, 198
citric acid, 96
clarifying, 93–95, 112, 141

clarity, 313
Clarré, 275
Classic Dry Stout, 180
Classic Irish-style Dry Stout, 180, 182
cleaning. *See also* sanitation
   bottles, 38–39
   ecology and, 285
   glassware, 307–308
cleansers, 35–37
clover honey, 274
cloves, 89
Cluster hops, 372–373
CO_2 (carbon dioxide), 54, 63–64, 142, 149–150
Coal Porter, 175
cogeneration process, 284
Colby's Cream Ale, 235
color, 108, 313
colored glass, 136
Columbus hops, 373
commercial beer, 11
Common Cider (27-a), 267, 270–271
Common Perry (27-d), 268
competitions
   50-point system, 335
   bottle size requirements, 336
   entries, 334–337
   judges, 337–340
   from keg to bottle for, 143–144
   overview, 333–334
   prizes, 335
   Samuel Adams LongShot, 16
   score sheets, 338
   soda bottles and, 143
   sponsors, 334
   swing-top bottles and, 142
compost piles, 286
compressed carbon dioxide gas cylinders, 147
Concentrated Brewer's Wort (CBW), 362
conditioning
   appearance problems, 330–331
   recommended length of time for, 13

secondary fermentation, 111–115
storage, 302
tertiary fermentation, 115–116
contamination, 33
Continental Lager, 214
Continental style, 267
conversion process, 118
coolers, 350
cooling water, 286
Coors Brewing Company, 162
copper finings, 94
copper tubing, 349
coriander, 89
corn, 44, 46, 369
corn sugar, 330
corn syrup, 83
costs, 19–20, 29, 358
cotton balls, 344
counterflow wort chillers, 32, 356
counterpressure bottle fillers, 143–144, 354
cracking, 46, 109
craft breweries, 12
Cream Ale (6-a), 234–235
Cream Ale Yeast Blend, 388
Cream City Abbey Ale, 197
cream liqueurs, 147
Cream Stout, 86, 182
Crisp Malting, 362
cross-contamination, 294
crowns, 15, 39, 147–148
Crystal hops, 373
crystal malt, 109, 331, 366–367. *See also* caramel malts
culinary apples, 266
Curcio, Philip, 272
cysers, 275
Czech Budejovice Lager yeast, 390
Czech Pils yeast, 383

• *D* •

D & J Stout, 183
Dad's Beer, The, 167
Dampfbier, 240

Dangerously Delicious Dunkel Weizen, 247
Daniel, Christina, 243
Daniel, Steve, 171, 213, 223, 243
Daniels, Ray, 247
Danish II yeast, 383
Danish yeast, 382
Dark Vader Lager, 223
decanting, 141, 305
decoction, 122
Def, Dum, and Blonde, 237
degrees Plato, 24
demarara sugar, 84
Dempsey, Steve, 231
Dennis, Tom, 179, 205
Denny, Jack H., 239
density, 24, 58. *See also* gravity
Dextrin malt, 365
dextrose, 82, 84, 139, 145–146
diacetyl, 312, 322, 327, 328
diastatic power, 297
Dickenson, Norman, 217
dietary restrictions, 5
D.I.G.I.B.I.Y. *See* do it, grow it, build it yourself
digital thermometers, 353
Dilldine, Jim, 171
dimethyl sulfide (DMS), 326–327, 329
dimpled pint mug, 306
Dingemans, 362
dip tubes, 153
disaccharides, 266, 274
dishwashers, 38
distilled water, 78
DME (dry malt extract), 50, 146
DMS (dimethyl sulfide), 326–327, 329
do it, grow it, build it yourself (D.I.G.I.B.I.Y)
   equipment, 348–352
   grain, 345–346
   hops, 343–348
   yeast, 343–345
Dominion Day Oktoberfest, 221
Doppelbock (5-c), 230–231
Doppelbock Two, 231

Dortmunder/European-Style Export (1-e), 216–217
dough-in, 128
Do-Well Trappist Tripel, 201
draft style Cider, 268
drilled rubber stoppers, 19, 22
dry beer yeast, 380
Dry English Ale yeast, 386
dry hopping, 54, 112, 160
Dry Ice 'n' Weizen, 245
dry malt extract (DME), 50, 146
dry mead, 276
Dry Stout (13-a), 180–181
dry yeast, 67–68
dry/puckering mouthfeel, 324–325
dual gauge tank regulators, 150
Dubbel (18-b), 198–199
Dudley Brewright Amber Ale, 169
Duisberg, Dortmund, Düsseldorf (3-D) Export, 217
Dunkelweizen (15-b), 246–247
Durst, 362
Düsseldorfer-Style Altbier (7-c), 242–243

• E •

Early Times Old Ale, 259
East Coast Ale yeast, 386
East Kent Goldings hops, 55
ecological/enviromental issues
  organic brewing, 286–292
  overview, 283–284
  recycle, 286
  reduce, 284–285
  reuse, 285–286
Edinburgh Scottish Ale yeast, 387
Egypt, 44
Ein, Zwei, Drei Weizen, 249
electrical heat, 284
elm, 52
endosperm, 44
energizers, yeast, 71
energy usage, 284

English Ale yeast, 386
English Cider (27-b), 267
English India Pale Ale (IPA) (14-a), 189–190
English Kent hops, 194
English pub glass, 305
English-Style Barley Wine (19-b), 208–210
enteric aromas, 327
enterobacteria, 76
entire, 174
Entirely Yours, 175
entries, 334–337
enzymes, 44
Epsom salt, 78
equipment
  for advanced brewers, 28–32
  for beginning brewers, 19–25, 100
  cleaning, 37–38
  gluten-free brewing and, 294
  immersion wort chillers, 348–349
  for intermediate brewers, 25–28
  kegging, 149–151
  lagering cellar, 351–352
  large-volume brewpot, 351
  lauter tun, 349–351
  overview, 12–13, 17
  retailers, 18
E.S.B. See Extra Special/ Strong Bitter
esoteric brews, 85–87
Ester the Molester, 203
estery, 64
ethanol, 63
European Ale yeast, 387
European hops, 61
European Lagers, 156
European yeast, 382
evaluating brew
  aromas, 311–313
  homebrew vocabulary, 317–318
  overview, 309–310
  reflections, 317
  seeing, 313
  taste, 314–316
Exchequer Pale Ale, 189
exotic flavorings, 85–87

exploding bottles, 276
external thermostats, 352
Extra Special/Strong Bitter (E.S.B.) (8-c), 160–161
extracts. See also malts
  gluten-free brewing, 294–296
  hop, 53
  liquid smoke, 87, 165, 256–257
  oak chips/oak, 86

• F •

faceted dimpled mug, 305
FAQs (frequently asked questions), 357–360
farmhouse style Cider, 268
farming yeast, 343
Fat Brothers Original American, 241
faucets, 23
fermentable sugars, 66
fermentation
  alcohol content, 71–72
  cycles, 65
  defined, 13
  dry yeast, 67–68
  fungi, 63–64
  hydrometer readings of, 136
  liquid yeast, 68–69
  mead and, 278–279
  never-ending, 321–322
  no fermentation, 320–321
  overview, 63, 111, 319
  priming ingredients, 144
  propagating yeast, 69–70
  secondary, 111–115
  stuck, 321
  tertiary, 115–116
  variables, 65–67
  yeast energizers and nutrients, 71
fermenters, 17, 21, 27
fermostats, 352
FG (final gravity), 24, 105
fill level, 140
filtering water, 74
filters, 76, 354–355
final alcohol potential, 24
final gravity (FG), 24, 105
finings, 93–95

finish, 316
finished product, 301
finishing hops, 56, 110
First Gold hops, 373
first runnings, 123
First Wort Hopping (FWH), 56, 126
Flabby Abbey Not-So-Grande Reserve, 204
flaming, 344
flat beer, 330
flavoring hops, 56, 110
flavorings, 84–90
flavors and aromas
  butter/butterscotch flavor, 322–323
  chart, 326–329
  dry/puckering mouthfeel, 324–325
  harshness/hotness, 325
  medicinal/plastic/smoky flavor, 323
  metallic flavor, 325
  papery/cardboard/sherry-like flavors, 324
  skunk aroma, 325
  sour/tart flavors, 323
  sulfury odors, 326
  vegetal flavors and aromas, 326
Fleming, Philip, 255
flocculation, 65, 381
fluorescent light, 325
fluoride, 76
foam control, 92
food-grade plastic, 21, 360
food-grade sanitizers, 36
Forbidden Fruit yeast, 385
force carbonating, 154
Foreign-Style Stout (13-d), 184–185
foretaste, 314
Formanek, Joe
  Hannah's Ambrosia Imperial I.P.A., 193–194
  Little Cathy's Blonde Ale, 237
  Veronica's Nectar I.P.A., 191–192
Fountainhead Black Magic, 187

French Cider (27-c), 268
frequently asked questions (FAQs), 357–360
freshness scale, 58
fructose, 82
fruit, 86, 87, 146–147, 270
Fruit Beer (20), 250–251
Fruit Cider (28-b), 268
Fuggle, Richard, 373
Fuggles hops, 373
full-wort boils, 32, 128
fully modified malts, 120
fungi, 34–35
funnels, 26
fusel alcohol, 325
FWH (First Wort Hopping), 56, 126

• G •

GA (Gravity Adjustment) factor, 58
Galena hops, 374
Gambrinus Malting, 362
garages, 302
gas heat, 284
gas inflow line, 150
gaskets, 142, 152–153
gelatin, 94
gelatinization, 46, 297
Genetically Modified Organisms (GMOs), 289
George Killian Lett's Irish Ale, 162
German Ale yeast, 380
German Ale/Kölsch yeast, 387
German Bock Lager yeast, 391
German Lager yeast, 240, 391
German Light Lagers, 214
German Purity Law, 368
German Wheat yeast, 385
German-Style Helles Bock/Maibock (5-a), 226–227
German-style Weizenbier, 246
germicidal lamp, 355
germs, 35
GFI (Ground Fault Interrupter) outlets, 355
Giffen, Paddy, 175, 181, 249
gingerroot, 89

Give Me Liberty, or. . . Else, 167
glass bottles, 22
glass carboys, 26–27, 139
glassware, 136, 307–308
gliadin protein, 293
gloves, 35, 36
glucose, 82
gluten intolerance, 293
gluten-free brewing
  from all grain, 296–297
  equipment and, 294
  overview, 293–294
  substituting safe ingredients, 294–296
  yeast, 297–298
gluten-free grains, 291
glutenin protein, 293
gluten-sensitive enteropathy, 295
GMOs (Genetically Modified Organisms), 289
goblets, 306
goggles, 35, 36
Goldings hops, 374
Goliath Imperial Pale Ale, 193
grain astringency, 316
grain mills, 26, 28, 31
Grain of Paradise, 194
Grain-n-Beerit, 217, 219
grains
  adjunct, 368–369
  base, 363–366
  gluten-free, 291
  gluten-free brewing from, 296–297
  kilning and milling, 46
  malted, 363
  malting, 44
  mashing, 45
  mixing with other grains, 45–46
  organic brewing and, 290–291
  overview, 43–44
  producers of, 362–363
  recyling, 286
  roast-a-rama, 345–346
  smoking, 346
  specialty, 108–109, 366–368
Grand Master Judge, 340

grape melomels, 282
gravity
  Barley Wine and, 208
  defined, 108
  hydrometers and, 24
  of Meads, 278
Gravity Adjustment (GA)
    factor, 58
Great American Beer Festival
    in Denver, 340
Great Western Malting, 362
Great Wheat, 239
green beer, 45
Griffith, Thomas, 231
grinders, 28
grist, 120
groats, 296
Grolsch bottles, 142
Ground Fault Interrupter
    (GFI) outlets, 355
gruit, 275
Guinness Stout, 180
Gullywasher, 213
gushers, 146
gypsum, 31, 78

● **H** ●

Hallertau Hersbrucker hops,
    375
Hallertau Mittelfruh hops, 375
Hallertauer hops, 55, 374
Hammaker, David G., 251
hands-on/off steps, 13
hangovers, 287
Hannah's Ambrosia Imperial
    I.P.A., 193–194
Hard Cider, 265
hard water, 76–77, 119–120,
    325
harshness, 325
harvesting yeast, 133–134
HBUs. *See* Homebrew
    Bitterness Units
HCU (Homebrew Color
    Units), 48
HDPE (high-density
    polyethylene), 21, 360
Head Brewers, 15
head retention, 313
heading compound, 92

heather tips, 90
Hefe-weizen, 244
Hefeweizen Ale yeast, 388
Hefeweizen IV Ale yeast, 389
heliarc welding, 351
Helles, 215
Helles Lager, 214
Helles/Maibock, 227
hemp, 52
Herb, Spice, and Vegetable
    Beer (21-a), 252–253
herbs, 90
Herrold, Ross, 225
high kraeusen, 65, 114
high-density polyethylene
    (HDPE), 21, 360
high-gravity beers, 145
high-gravity worts, 69
highly carbonated beers, 156
hippocras, 275
hobbies, 1, 18
Holland, Matthew, 219
Home Wine and Beer Trade
    Association (HWBTA),
    333
Homebrew Bitterness Units
    (HBUs), 59, 60
Homebrew Color Units
    (HCU), 48
homebrewing
  advanced
    all-grain brewing, 128–131
    batch sizes, 131–133
    harvesting yeast, 133–134
    mashing procedures,
      118–124
    overview, 117–118
    partial mashing, 124–127
  alternative brewing, 5
  beginner, 99–105
  clubs, 13, 334
  equipment, 12–13
  feedback, 5
  ingredients, 5, 14–15
  intermediate, 107–111
  overview, 11
  supply shops, 18
  timeline, 13–14
honey
  boiling, 278
  choosing for mead, 277–278

defined, 82–83
  overview, 273–275
honeybees, 273
Honorary Master Judge, 340
Hooligan's Red, 163
hop bitterness, 315
hop character, 312
hop cones, 52
hop extract, 53
hop flavor, 315
hop flowers, 52–54
hop oils, 54
hop processors, 53
hop rhizomes, 347
hop zones, 55
hoplets, 53
hops
  Admiral, 371
  Ahtanum, 371
  Amarillo, 371
  American, 61
  aroma, 56, 60
  Aurora, 371
  bittering
    boiling times for, 110
    calculating AAUs, 59
    chart, 60–61
    defined, 56
    overview, 58
    utilization factor, 58–59
  Cascade, 372
  Centennial, 372
  Challenger, 372
  Chinook, 59, 372
  choosing, 347–348
  Cluster, 372–373
  Columbus, 373
  Crystal, 373
  dry hopping, 54, 112, 160
  drying and storing, 348
  East Kent Goldings, 55
  English Kent, 194
  European, 61
  extracts, 53
  First Gold, 373
  First Wort Hopping (FWH),
    56, 126
  flavoring, 56, 110
  flowers of, 52–54
  freshness, 57–58
  Fuggles, 373

hops *(continued)*
  Galena, 374
  Goldings, 374
  growing, 347
  Hallertau Hersbrucker, 375
  Hallertau Mittelfruh, 375
  Hallertauer, 55, 374
  hybrids, 55
  late-kettle, 56
  Liberty, 375
  Lublin, 375
  Magnum, 375
  Mount Hood, 55, 376
  Newport, 376
  noble, 56
  Northdown, 376
  Northern Brewer, 59, 376
  Nugget, 376
  Olympic, 55
  organic brewing and, 291
  overview, 51
  oxidized, 57
  Perle, 377
  Pride of Ringwood, 55, 377
  replacement, 61
  Saaz, 55, 377
  Santiam, 377
  Simcoe, 377
  stability of, 58
  stale, 56
  Super Styrian, 371
  Target, 378
  Tettnanger, 378
  Vanguard, 378
  varieties, 60–61, 109–110
  Warrior, 379
  whole-leaf, 53
  Willamette, 379
hotness, 325
How Wheat It Is!, 239
Howard, Rodney, 235
Hugh Baird Malting Company, 362
Humulus Lupulus, 52
husks, 44
HWBTA (Home Wine and Beer Trade Association), 333
hybrids, 55. *See also* mixed-style recipes
hydrogen sulfide, 327–329
hydrolyzed cornstarch, 82

hydromel strength Mead, 276
hydrometer readings, 104–105
hydrometers
  ABV versus ABW, 71
  with cylinder, 20
  liquid density and, 24
  taking fermentation readings with, 136
  triple-scale, 23

• I •

IBUs (International Bitterness Units), 59
immersion wort chillers, 30, 32, 131, 348–349
Imperial India Pale Ale (IPA) (14-c), 192–194
imperial pint glass, 306
Imperial Porter. *See* Baltic Porter
Imperial Stout (13-f), 186–188
incandescent light, 325
India Pale Ale, 186
Indiana Pale Ale, 191
infusion mashing, 120
ingredients. *See also* yeast
  basic, 5
  flawed, 312
  gluten-free brewing and, 294–296
  hops, 370–379
  intermediate brewers and, 108–111
  malt, 362–370
  organic, 287–288
  priming, 144
innovation, 3
International Bitterness Units (IBUs), 59
invert sugar, 83, 85
iodine-based sanitizers, 36
Iodophor, 150
IPA. *See* American India Pale Ale; English India Pale Ale; Imperial India Pale Ale
Irish Ale yeast, 386
Irish moss, 94
Irish Red Ale (9-d), 162–163

Irish yeast, 381
Irish-style Stout, 180
isinglass, 94–95
iso-alpha acids, 53
isomerization, 53
isopropyl alcohol, 344

• J •

Ja, Das Ist ein Schnitzel Bock, 227
Jack the Sipper, 207
jacketing, 285
Janowiak, John, 221
Jealous Wit, 195
judges
  levels of, 339–340
  requirements for, 337–339
juniper berries, 89

• K •

Kamp, Steve, 163, 193, 261
kegging
  carbonating procedures, 154–156
  converting kegs to brewpots, 351
  equipment, 149–151
  from keg to bottle for competition, 143–144
  plastic bottles and, 142–143
  sanitizing and racking procedures, 151–154
  tapping procedures, 156
kettle adjuncts, 79
kettle caramelization, 162, 168
kettle hops, 56. *See also* bittering hops
kettle-coagulant, 94
Killer Winter Storm Candy Imperial Porter, 261
kilning, 46–47, 108
Kinvig, Dennis, 175
kitchen
  faucets, 23
  scales, 26, 28, 31
  strainers, 26, 27
kitchen-sink category beer, 260

kits, 49, 99
Klasinski Baltic, 179
Kölsch yeast, 384
kristalklar, 244

● ***L*** ●

lab immersion thermometers, 26, 28, 31
labels
  for ale recipes, 210
  for lager recipes, 232
  for mixed-style recipes, 262
  self-stick, 344, 348
lactic acid, 96
lactic taste, 329
lactobacillus bacteria, 323
lactose, 82, 86
Lady of the Morning, 225
lag time, 66
Lager recipes
  American Dark Lager (4-a), 222–223
  American Premium Lager (1-c), 212–213
  Bohemian-Style Pilsener (2-b), 218–219
  Doppelbock (5-c), 230–231
  Dortmunder/European-Style Export (1-e), 216–217
  German-Style Helles Bock/Maibock (5-a), 226–227
  label ideas, 232
  Märzen/Oktoberfest (3-b), 220–222
  Münchner-Style Helles (1-d), 214–215
  Munich Dunkel (4-b), 224–225
  overview, 211
  Traditional Bock (5-b), 228–229
Lager yeast, 64, 66
lagering cellar, 351–352
Lagers
  chart, 392–393
  European, 156
  secondary fermentation and, 112
Lake, Denny, 271

lapping, 156
large-volume brewpots, 30, 351
Larsen, Rich, 201, 209
Late Hop Essence, 54
late-kettle hops, 56
lauter tun, 30, 123, 128, 349–351
lautering, 126, 133–134
layered taste, 315
League City Alt Part 3, 243
League City Dark, 223
Leftover Strawberry Ale, 251
Liberty hops, 375
licorice, 86, 186, 260
light molasses, 83
light-struck, 325, 328
liqueurs, 87, 146–147
liquid culture dry Mead yeasts, 278
liquid density, 24
liquid malt extract, 50
liquid smoke extract, 87, 165, 256–257
liquid yeast
  bottom-fermenting, 382–383
  cultures, 111
  versus dry yeast, 67–69
  top-fermenting, 380–382, 386–388
Little Cathy's Blonde Ale, 237
London Ale yeast, 387
London III yeast, 381
London-Rich yeast, 381
London-style Stout, 182
London-Style Sweet Stout, 86, 184
LongShot Variety Pack, 16
Lovibond scale, 48
Lubinsky, Jay, 271
Lublin hops, 375
lupulin glands, 52, 347
lye, 36

● ***M*** ●

Macke's Son Stout, 183
Mad River Brewing Company, 284
magnesium, 77
magnesium sulfate, 78

Magnum hops, 375
malic acid, 96
malignant hyperthermia, 110
Malt, Cargill, 362
malt character, 312
malt syrup, 14, 43
malted wheat, 366
malto-dextrin, 93, 331
maltose, 44
maltose sugars, 43, 146
malts
  2-row, 364
  6-row, 364
  Biscuit, 367
  Black, 368
  caramel, 109, 323, 361, 366–367
  CaraPils, 331
  chocolate, 172, 367
  Crisp, 362
  crystal, 109, 331, 366–367
  Dextrin, 365
  extracts, 47–50, 369–370
  fully modified, 120
  grains
    adjunct, 368–369
    base, 363–366
    kilning and milling, 46–47
    mashing, 45
    mixing with other grains, 45–46
    overview, 44
    producers of, 362–363
    specialty, 366–368
  non-organic, 291
  organic, 291
  overview, 43
  Pale Ale, 364
  Paul's, 363
  peat-smoked, 256
  Pilsener, 364
  Rye, 368
  Smoked, 368
  Victory, 367
  Vienna, 365
maltsters, 44
maple syrup, 83
Maris Otter brand, 362
Märzen/Oktoberfest (3-b), 220–222
mash tun, 45

mashing
  aftermash or mash-outs,
    122–124
  cereal grain, 122
  defined, 28, 45
  gluten-free grains, 297
  overview, 118
  partial mashing, 124–127
  types, 120–122
  variable of, 119
  water and, 119–120
mashing brewpots, 30
mashing sparge arms,
  355–356
mash-outs, 133–134
mason jars, 343
mass-market beer, 11
Master Judge, 339
maturation period, 359
Meads
  fermenting, 278–279
  history of, 274
  honey, 273–278
  overview, 273
  petillant, 276
  Progressive, 279
  recipes, 280–282
  sack strength, 276
  semi-sweet, 276
  sparkling, 276
  standard strength, 276
  sweet, 276
  yeast, 393–394
medicinal flavors, 323
Meilgaard Beer Flavor Wheel,
  318
Meilgaard, Dr. Morton, 317
melomel, 275
Meltdown Lager, 215
Memphis Steamer, 241
meniscus effect, 24
Merisco, Mark, 259
Mesopotamia, 44
metallic taste, 325, 328, 329
metals, 78
metheglin, 275
Meussdoerffer, 362
Mexican Lager yeast, 391
microbes, 34
Microbial Fuel Cell, 284
microbreweries, 1, 12

midtaste, 314
Milk Stout, 86
Miller, Dave, 215
millet, 44
milling, 46–47, 109
mineral ions, 77–78
mineral salts, 77
mint, 90
mixed-style recipes
  American Wheat (6-d),
    238–239
  Blonde Ale (6-b), 236–237
  California Common Beer
    (7-b), 240–241
  Christmas/Winter/Specialty
    Spiced Beer (21-b),
    254–255
  Cream Ale (6-a), 234–235
  Dunkelweizen (15-b),
    246–247
  Düsseldorfer-Style Altbier
    (7-c), 242–243
  Fruit Beer (20), 250–251
  Herb, Spice, and Vegetable
    Beer (21-a), 252–253
  labels, 262
  overview, 233
  Smoked Beer (22-b),
    256–257
  Specialty Beer (23), 260–261
  Weizenbock (15-c), 248–249
  Weizen/Weissbier (15-a),
    244–245
  Wood-Aged Beer (22-c),
    258–259
MLC (Moe, Larry, and Curly)
  Barley Wine, 209–210
molasses, 83, 186
mold spores, 34
moldy aromas, 328
monosaccharides, 266, 274
morat, 275
Morelli, Stephen, 241
mother culture, 344
Mount Hood hops, 55, 376
mouthfeel, 43, 316
mulsum, 275
multistep infusion mashing,
  121
Münchner-Style Helles (1-d),
  214–215

Munich Dunkel (4-b), 224–225
Munich malts, 365–366
Munich Pale Lager, 224
Munich yeast, 383
musty aromas, 328

• N •

Nachel, Marty
  1-4-U, 2-4-ME S.B., 161
  3-D (Duisberg, Dortmund,
    Düsseldorf) Export, 217
  Amber Waves, 169
  Brass Baltics Imperial
    Porter, 179
  Buxton Brown of Derbyshire
    County, 173
  Dark Vader Lager, 223
  Def, Dum, and Blonde, 237
  Dubbel Trubbel, 199
  Early Times Old Ale, 259
  Ein, Zwei, Drei Weizen, 249
  Exchequer Pale Ale, 189
  Flabby Abbey Not-So-
    Grande Reserve, 204
  Give Me Liberty, or. . . Else,
    167
  Grain-n-Beerit, 219
  Gullywasher, 213
  Helles/Maibock, 227
  How Wheat It Is!, 237
  Indiana Pale Ale, 191
  Ja, Das Ist ein Schnitzel
    Bock, 227
  Jack the Sipper, 207
  Lindisfarne Libation, 280
  Macke's Son Stout, 183
  Pugnacious Porter, 177
  RE: Bock, 229
  Slam Dunkel, 247
  Smokey the Beer (Smoked
    Porter), 257
  TransPorter, 177
  Tripel Play, 201
  Wassail While You Work, 253
  Why'd You Kilkenny?, 163
  Wit or Witout You, 195
  Yule Brimmer, 261
  Yulebrew '92, 185
National Judge, 339

National Organic Program, 289

natural clarifying agents, 51

natural maltose sugars, 43

Netherlands, 198

neutral pH, 75

New Belgium Brewery, 284

New England Cider (28-a), 268, 271

New Stout II, 185

New Years Day, 181

Newport hops, 376

nitrogen-barrier bags, 57

noble hops, 56

nonalcoholic beer, 72

non-organic ingredients, 285, 287

non-organic malt, 291

non-toxic beers, 288

North American microbrewing industry, 60

North American yeast, 383

North, Brian and Linda, 183, 215

Northdown hops, 376

Northern Brewer hops, 59, 376

Northern English Brown Ale (11-c), 172–173

Northwest Ale yeast, 382

Northwestern Extract Co.
 Alterior Motive, 243
 Belgian Abbey, 197, 202–203
 Dudley Brewright Amber Ale, 169
 Jealous Wit, 195
 St. James Gate Stout, 181
 Two Year Wheat Beer, 245

Novice judge, 339

Nugget hops, 376

• O •

oak chips/oak extract, 86

oats, 295, 369

odors. *See* aromas

off flavors. *See* flavors and aromas

OG (original gravity), 105

Oktoberfest/Märzen Lager yeast, 391

Ol' Brown Bear Brown Ale, 173

Old Ale (19-a), 206–207

Old Alt Ale, 207

Olympic hops, 55

Open Category Mead (26-c), 281

orange peel, 87

organic brewing
 adjuncts and, 292
 grain and, 290–291
 hops and, 291
 ingredients, 287–288
 malt and, 291
 overview, 286–287
 tracking trend, 288–289
 USDA certification, 290
 water and, 290
 yeast and, 292

original gravity (OG), 105

overcarbonation, 325, 330

overroasting, 345

oversparging, 324–325

oxidation, 148, 324–325

oxidized aromas, 327

oxidized hops, 57

oxidized taste, 328

oxygen-absorbing caps, 148, 324

oxygen-barrier bags, 57

• P •

Pacific Ale yeast, 387

Pacific Coast Brewing Company, 47

Page, Ron, 253, 255

palate cleansers, 334

palate fatigue, 340

Pale Ale malt, 364

Pale Ales, 160, 358

Pale Moon Rizen Weizen, 249

papery flavors, 324

partial mashing, 124–127

parti-gyle brewing, 123

pathogens, 35

Paulaner Brewery, 214

Paul's Malt, 363

PBW (Powdered Brewery Wash), 285

peak fermentation, 65

peat-smoked malt, 256

pectin, 116, 270

Peek Under the Kilt Ale, A, 165

pellets, 53

percarbonates, 35, 36

Perle hops, 377

permanent hardness, 77

Perries, 267

petillant carbonation, 267

petillant Meads, 276

pets, 15, 110

pH balance
 acidic, 75
 adjusting levels, 126
 of mash water, 120
 mashing and, 119
 neutral, 75
 of sparge water, 325
 water composition and, 73

pH meters, 353

pH papers, 30

phenolic aromas, 327, 328

phenolic taste, 329

phenols, 323

phosphoric acid, 96

Pilsen yeast, 382

Pilsener beer, 79

Pilsener glasses, 305, 306

Pilsener Lager yeast, 390

Pilsener malt, 364

Pilsner Urquell, 218

pin lock fittings, 150

pint glasses, 305–306

pitching, 13, 65, 66

plastic bottles, 142–143

plastic flavors, 323

plastic, food-grade, 21, 360

plastic funnels, 26

plastic hose, 19, 22

plate type filters, 355

plugs, 53

polypropylene glycol alginate, 93

Polyvinylpolypyrrolidone (PVPP), 95

Porter beer, 174

postal scales, 26, 28, 31

potassium sorbate, 276

pouring, 303–307

Powdered Brewery Wash
(PBW), 285
precipitation, 76–77, 92
prehopped malt extract, 49
preservative-free apple juice,
270
preservatives, 92–93
pressure per square inch
(psi), 155
pressure relief valves, 147
pressurized carbon dioxide
tank, 150
Pride and Jay, 271
Pride of Ringwood hops, 55,
377
primary fermenters, 19, 21,
139
primers
alternative, 146–147
choosing, 145–146
overview, 144–145
priming buckets, 20
priming ingredients, 144
priming vessels, 22
prizes, 335
Product Composition, 290
Progressive Mead, 279
proofing, 102
propagation, 69–70, 113
protein rest, 121
proteins, 44
psi (pressure per square
inch), 155
pub glasses, 306
Pugnacious Porter, 177
pungent floral/herbal
aroma, 51
purists, 47, 146
PVPP (Polyvinyl-
polypyrrolidone), 95
pyments, 275, 282

• Q •

Quadrupel Trappist ale, 200
quality
acid test, 96
additives and preservatives,
92–93
clarification, 93–95
overview, 91

• R •

racking, 27, 116, 151–154
racking tubes, 26, 27
Rahn, Phil, 229, 241
Rahr Malting Co., 363
ranching yeast, 343
Rauchbier, 257
raw oats, 46
raw wheat, 46
RE: Bock, 229
Ready-to-Pitch (RTP) yeast,
69
recipes
Ale
American Amber Ale
(10-b), 168–169
American Brown Ale
(10-c), 170–171
American India Pale Ale
(IPA) (14-b), 190–192
American Pale Ale (10-a),
166–167
Baltic Porter (12-c),
178–179
Belgian Dark Strong Ale
(18-e), 204–205
Belgian Golden Strong Ale
(18-d), 202–203
Belgian Pale Ale (16-b),
196–197
Brown Porter (12-a),
174–175
Dry Stout (13-a), 180–181
Dubbel (18-b), 198–199
English India Pale Ale (IPA)
(14-a), 188–190
English-Style Barley Wine
(19-b), 208–210
Extra Special/Strong Bitter
(E.S.B.) (8-c), 160–161
Foreign-Style Stout (13-d),
184–185
Imperial India Pale Ale
(IPA) (14-c), 192–194
Imperial Stout (13-f),
186–188
Irish Red Ale (9-d),
162–163
Northern English Brown
Ale (11-c), 172–173

Old Ale (19-a), 206–207
Robust Porter (12-b),
176–177
Strong Scotch Ale (9-e),
164–166
Sweet Stout (13-b),
182–183
Tripel (18-c), 200–201
White (Wit)(16-a), 194–196
batch size, 3
Cider
Common Cider (27-a),
270–271
New England-Style Cider
(28-a), 271
Specialty Cider (28-d), 272
Lager
American Dark Lager (4-a),
222–223
American Premium Lager
(1-c), 212–213
Bohemian-Style Pilsener
(2-b), 218–219
Doppelbock (5-c), 230–231
Dortmunder/European-
Style Export (1-e),
216–217
German-Style Helles
Bock/Maibock (5-a),
226–227
Märzen/Oktoberfest (3-b),
220–222
Münchner-Style Helles
(1-d), 214–215
Munich Dunkel (4-b),
224–225
Traditional Bock (5-b),
228–229
Mead
Open Category Mead
(26-c), 281
Pyment (grape melomel)
(25-b), 282
Traditional Mead (24-a),
280
mixed-style
American Wheat (6-d),
238–239
Blonde Ale (6-b), 236–237
California Common Beer
(7-b), 240–241

Christmas/Winter/ Specialty Spiced Beer (21-b), 254–255
Cream Ale (6-a), 234–235
Dunkelweizen (15-b), 246–247
Düsseldorfer-Style Altbier (7-c), 242–243
Fruit Beer (20), 250–251
Herb, Spice, and Vegetable Beer (21-a), 252–253
Smoked Beer (22-b), 256–257
Specialty Beer (23), 260–261
Weizenbock (15-c), 248–249
Weizen/Weissbier (15-a), 244–245
Wood-Aged Beer (22-c), 258–259
Recognized Judge, 339
recycling, 286
reduce, 284–285
Reed, Rande, 187
refiner's syrup, 84
refractometer, 355
refrigeration, yeast and, 344
refrigerators, 285
registration, 337
Reiter, Tim, 281, 282
relief valves, 152
replacement hops, 61
retailers, homebrew supply, 18
retronasal passage, 311
returnable-type bottles, 135
reuse, 285–286
rhizome, 347
rice, 44, 46, 369
rice hulls, 297
rice syrup, 83
rice syrup solids, 83
Ringwood Ale yeast, 382
roasted barley, 46, 368
roasting, 296, 345
Robison, Dan, 251
Robust Porter (12-b), 177
Rose's Russian Imperial Stout, 187–188
Rotten to the Corps, 271

RTP (Ready-to-Pitch) yeast, 69
rubber stoppers, 27
Russia, 185
rye, 47
Rye Malt, 368

• S •

S. carlsbergensis, 64
Saaz hops, 55, 377
Saccharomyces cerevisiae, 64
Saccharomyces uvarum, 64
sack strength Mead, 276
salt, 31
salty taste, 314, 329
Samuel Adams LongShot competition, 16
San Francisco Lager yeast, 390
sanitation
  battling bacteria (and fungi), 34–35
  bottle cleanliness, 38–39
  cleansers and sanitizers, 35–37
  defined, 34
  equipment cleaning practices, 37–38
  overview, 33–34
sanitation process, 37–38
sanitizers, 35–37
  fermentation and, 320
  food-grade, 36
  iodine-based, 36
sanitizing
  bottle caps, 39
  ecology and, 285
  equipment, 137
  importance of, 15
  kegs, 151–154
Santiam hops, 377
scales, 26, 28, 31
Schmit, Richard, 235
Schreier, 363
Scintillator, 231
score sheets, 338
scoring, 340
Scotch Ale, 145, 165–166
Scotch whiskies, 164

Scottish yeast, 381
sealing bottles, 330
seasonal brews, 254
second runnings, 123
secondary fermentation
  advantages, 112–113
  for Mead, 279
  overview, 111–112
  procedure, 113–115
secondary fermenters, 27, 139, 359
secondary ions, 78
sedimentation phase, 65
seed, 52
self-reproducing, 63
self-stick labels, 344, 348
semi-sweet mead, 276
session beer, 174
Seven Bridges Homebrewing Cooperative, 290
shelf-life, 50
sherry-like flavors, 324
Shilling designation, 164
Sierra Nevada Brewing Company, 284
sight, evaluating brew by, 313
Silica gel, 95
Simcoe hops, 377
Simpson, James Parker, 363
Simpson's, 363
single gauge tank regulators, 150
Single Trappist ale, 200
siphon hose, 154
siphoning, 115
six-pack holders, 138
skunk aroma, 325
Slam Dunkel, 247
sleeves, 306
smack packs, 69
small beer, 240
SmartCap Pure Seal, 148
smoke extract, liquid, 87, 165, 256–257
smoke flavor, 87
Smoked Beer (22-b), 256–257
Smoked malt, 368
Smokey the Beer (Smoked Porter), 257
smoking, 345

smoky flavors, 323
soaking, 37, 138
soap-and-water cleaning, 33
soapy aromas, 328
soapy taste, 329
soda bottles, 143
soda keg setup, 151
sodium, 77
sodium chloride, 31, 78
sodium metabisulphite, 36
soft Cider, 265
software, 356
solvent-like aromas, 328
sorghum, 295, 296
sorghum syrup, 83
sour flavors, 323
sour taste, 314
Southeast Texas Northern
      Brown Ale, 171
Southern German Lager
      yeast, 391
Spalt hops, 378
sparge, 120
sparge bags, 26, 28
sparge water, 325
sparging, 133–134
sparkling carbonation, 267
sparkling Meads, 276
Sparkolloid, 95
Special "B", 367
Special London yeast, 384
Special Roast, 367
Specialty Beer (23), 260–261
Specialty Cider (28-d), 272
specialty grains, 45, 178
   cracking, 109
   malt and, 366–368
   milling, 109
specialty yeast, 388–390
Specific Gravity, 355
specific gravity scale, 24
spectrophotometers, 48
spices, 88–89
spiciness, 51
spigots, 139
sponsors, 334
spruce essence, 86
SRM (Standard Reference
      Method) scale, 48

St. James Gate Stout, 181
stability, hop, 58
stainless steel, 37, 150
stainless steel soda kegs, 150
stale hops, 56
standard measure, 72
Standard Reference Method
      (SRM) scale, 48
standard strength Mead, 276
starter culture, 344
starter kits, 18–19
starting point, 19
steam beer, 240
steam distillation, 54
steeping, 109, 117
steins, 308
step infusion mashing, 121
sterilization, defined, 34
stewards, 334
still carbonation, 267
stock pots, 30
stoppers, 27
storage
   during conditioning phase,
      141
   DME, 50
   hops, 348
   how, 302
   how long, 303
   overview, 301
   pellets, 53
   steins, 308
   where, 302
Stout Porter, 180
Stouts, 83
strainers, 26, 27
straws, 137
strength, 276
Strong Scotch Ale (9-e),
      164–166
Stu Brew, 225
stuck runoff, 128
sucrose, 82
sugars
   adjunct, 82–84
   fermentable, 66
   natural maltose, 43
   sources of, 145
sulfate, 77

sulfury odors, 326
sunlight, 325
Super High Gravity Ale yeast,
      388
Super Kleer KC Finings, 95
Super Styrian hops, 371
supply shops, 18
swankey, 240
sweet gale, 90
sweet Mead, 276
Sweet Stout (13-b), 182–183
sweet taste, 314
swing-top bottles, 22, 142
syrups, 43, 83–84, 146

• T •

table salt, 78
table sugar, 82
Tallman, Stu, 225
tank plugs, 153
tank regulators, 150
tanks, carbon dioxide, 150
tannin, 86, 92
tapping, 156
Target hops, 378
tart flavors, 323
tartaric acid, 96
taste, 314–316, 328
temperature correction
      scale, 24
temperatures
   fermentation, 66
   mashing and, 119
   for serving beer, 304
temporary hardness, 76
ten-forty eight, 105
ten-twelve, 105
terminal gravity, 24
tertiary fermentation,
      111–115
Tettnanger hops, 378
Thames Valley yeast, 381
Theresienwiese, 220
thermometers
   cost, 26
   digital, 353
   lab immersion, 26, 28, 31

thermostats, 352
Thistle glasses, 305, 306
three-stage fermentation, 111–115
thriftiness, 15, 19
throwaway bottles, 135
TIG (tungsten inert gas) welding, 351
timeline, homebrewing, 13–14
tinted glass, 136
tongue, 314
top-fermenting strain, 64
trace metals, 78
Traditional Bock (5-b), 228–229
Traditional Mead (24-a), 280
Traditional Perry (27-e), 268
translucent liqueurs, 147
transparent beer, 91
TransPorter, 177
Trappist abbey breweries, 68
Trappist beer, 198
treacle, 84
Tripel (18-c), 200–201
triple-scale hydrometers, 23
triploid seedling, 373
trisodium phosphate (TSP), 36, 137, 152, 308
troubleshooting
  conditioning and appearance problems, 330–331
  fermentation, 319–322
  off flavors and aromas, 322–329
true taste, 314
TSP (trisodium phosphate), 36, 137, 152, 308
tulip glasses, 307
tungsten inert gas (TIG) welding, 351
turbinado sugar, 84
twist-off bottles, 136
Two Year Wheat Beer, 245
two-handle-style cappers, 141
two-stage fermentation, 111–115
type-100 hoplets, 53

• U •

ullage, 140
under-oxygenated wort, 103
underroasting, 345
unfermented beer, 72
unfiltered apple juice, 270
uniform bottles, 136
unpasteurized apple juice, 270
unpasteurized honey, 278
unsulfured dark molasses, 186
urban myths, 287
Urquell yeast, 383
U.S. Department of Agriculture (USDA), 288–290
utility faucets, 23
utilization factor, 58–59

• V •

Van Dyke, Dick, 161, 167, 189–190, 207, 245
Vanguard hops, 378
vanilla, 87, 89
varietal honey, 274
vegetal flavors and aromas, 326
Veronica's Nectar I.P.A., 191–192
Victory Malt, 367
Vienna malt, 365
vinous, 206
viscosity, 43, 49
volatile aromatics, 310
volumes, 156

• W •

Ward, Bob, 209
Warrior hops, 379
Wassail While You Work, 253
water
  antibacterial agents, 75–76
  bottled, 78–79
  chalky, 325
  chemistry of, 74
  cooling, 286
  distilled, 78
  in European cities, 75
  gravity of, 24
  hard, 76–77, 119–120, 325
  mineral ions, 77–78
  organic brewing and, 290
  overview, 73
  pH balance, 75, 120, 325
  trace metals, 78
water treatments, 211
wee heavy, 164
Weihenstephan Wheat yeast, 384
Weizenbier glasses, 307
Weizenbock (15-c), 248–249
Weizen/Weissbier (15-a), 244–245
Weyermann & Co., 363
wheat, 44
Wheat Beer, 194, 392–393
Wheat Bock, 248
Whirlfloc, 95
Whitbread Ale yeast, 382
White (Wit)(16-a), 194–196
White beer, 194
white finings, 94–95
White Labs WLP715 Champagne Yeast, 393
White Labs WLP720 Sweet Mead/Wine Yeast, 394
White Labs WLP775 English Cider Yeast, 394
white sorghum syrup, 296
white sugars, 84
whole-leaf hops, 53
Why'd You Kilkenny?, 163
Wika, Jamie, 199, 209
wild yeast, 322
wildflower honey, 274
Willamette hops, 379
wine carafes, 343
wineries, 277
Winter Warmers, 254
Wit or Witout You, 196
Witbier, 194
Wolaver, Morgan, 289

Wood Bomb (wood-aged IPA), 259

Wood-Aged Beer (22-c), 258–259

wort, 13, 17, 66, 76, 103, 128, 286, 354, 355

Wyeast #4184 Sweet Mead, 393

Wyeast #4632 Dry Mead, 393

Wyeast #4766 Cider, 393

Wyeast Labs, 68

Wyeast's gluten-free yeast, 298

• Y •

yeast
  adjustments in, 110–111
  advanced liquid, 384–385
  banking, 343–345
  bottom-fermenting, 390–391
  dry, 67–68
  energizers, 71, 93
  fermentation problems and, 320
  gluten-free brewing and, 297–298
  growth phase, 65
  harvesting, 133–134
  liquid
    bottom-fermenting, 382–383
    overview, 68–69
    top-fermenting, 380–382, 386–388
  mead and cider, 393–394
  nutrients, 71, 93, 279
  organic brewing and, 292
  overview, 379–380
  pitching, 13
  propagating, 69–70
  re-propagating, 286
  reusing, 134
  specialty/belgian, 388–390
  strains, 108, 391–393
  sugar consumption, 25
  wild, 322
Yellow Dogs Pilsener, 219
Yule Ales, 254
Yule Brimmer, 261
Yulebrew '92, 185

BUSINESS, CAREERS & PERSONAL FINANCE

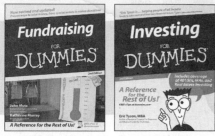

0-7645-9847-3

0-7645-2431-3

Also available:

✔Business Plans Kit For Dummies
0-7645-9794-9

✔Economics For Dummies
0-7645-5726-2

✔Grant Writing For Dummies
0-7645-8416-2

✔Home Buying For Dummies
0-7645-5331-3

✔Managing For Dummies
0-7645-1771-6

✔Marketing For Dummies
0-7645-5600-2

✔Personal Finance For Dummies
0-7645-2590-5*

✔Resumes For Dummies
0-7645-5471-9

✔Selling For Dummies
0-7645-5363-1

✔Six Sigma For Dummies
0-7645-6798-5

✔Small Business Kit For Dummies
0-7645-5984-2

✔Starting an eBay Business For Dummies
0-7645-6924-4

✔Your Dream Career For Dummies
0-7645-9795-7

HOME & BUSINESS COMPUTER BASICS

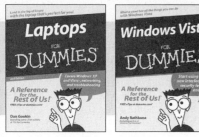

0-470-05432-8

0-471-75421-8

Also available:

✔Cleaning Windows Vista For Dummies
0-471-78293-9

✔Excel 2007 For Dummies
0-470-03737-7

✔Mac OS X Tiger For Dummies
0-7645-7675-5

✔MacBook For Dummies
0-470-04859-X

✔Macs For Dummies
0-470-04849-2

✔Office 2007 For Dummies
0-470-00923-3

✔Outlook 2007 For Dummies
0-470-03830-6

✔PCs For Dummies
0-7645-8958-X

✔Salesforce.com For Dummies
0-470-04893-X

✔Upgrading & Fixing Laptops For Dummies
0-7645-8959-8

✔Word 2007 For Dummies
0-470-03658-3

✔Quicken 2007 For Dummies
0-470-04600-7

FOOD, HOME, GARDEN, HOBBIES, MUSIC & PETS

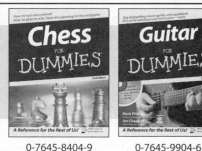

0-7645-8404-9

0-7645-9904-6

Also available:

✔Candy Making For Dummies
0-7645-9734-5

✔Card Games For Dummies
0-7645-9910-0

✔Crocheting For Dummies
0-7645-4151-X

✔Dog Training For Dummies
0-7645-8418-9

✔Healthy Carb Cookbook For Dummies
0-7645-8476-6

✔Home Maintenance For Dummies
0-7645-5215-5

✔Horses For Dummies
0-7645-9797-3

✔Jewelry Making & Beading For Dummies
0-7645-2571-9

✔Orchids For Dummies
0-7645-6759-4

✔Puppies For Dummies
0-7645-5255-4

✔Rock Guitar For Dummies
0-7645-5356-9

✔Sewing For Dummies
0-7645-6847-7

✔Singing For Dummies
0-7645-2475-5

INTERNET & DIGITAL MEDIA

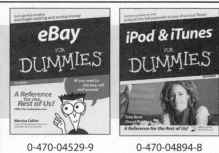

0-470-04529-9

0-470-04894-8

Also available:

✔Blogging For Dummies
0-471-77084-1

✔Digital Photography For Dummies
0-7645-9802-3

✔Digital Photography All-in-One Desk Reference For Dummies
0-470-03743-1

✔Digital SLR Cameras and Photography For Dummies
0-7645-9803-1

✔eBay Business All-in-One Desk Reference For Dummies
0-7645-8438-3

✔HDTV For Dummies
0-470-09673-X

✔Home Entertainment PCs For Dummies
0-470-05523-5

✔MySpace For Dummies
0-470-09529-6

✔Search Engine Optimization For Dummies
0-471-97998-8

✔Skype For Dummies
0-470-04891-3

✔The Internet For Dummies
0-7645-8996-2

✔Wiring Your Digital Home For Dummies
0-471-91830-X

* Separate Canadian edition also available
† Separate U.K. edition also available

Available wherever books are sold. For more information or to order direct: U.S. customers visit www.dummies.com or call 1-877-762-2974.
U.K. customers visit www.wileyeurope.com or call 0800 243407. Canadian customers visit www.wiley.ca or call 1-800-567-4797.

SPORTS, FITNESS, PARENTING, RELIGION & SPIRITUALITY

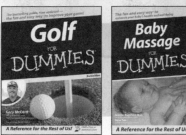

0-471-76871-5

0-7645-7841-3

Also available:
- Catholicism For Dummies
  0-7645-5391-7
- Exercise Balls For Dummies
  0-7645-5623-1
- Fitness For Dummies
  0-7645-7851-0
- Football For Dummies
  0-7645-3936-1
- Judaism For Dummies
  0-7645-5299-6
- Potty Training For Dummies
  0-7645-5417-4
- Buddhism For Dummies
  0-7645-5359-3

- Pregnancy For Dummies
  0-7645-4483-7 †
- Ten Minute Tone-Ups For Dummies
  0-7645-7207-5
- NASCAR For Dummies
  0-7645-7681-X
- Religion For Dummies
  0-7645-5264-3
- Soccer For Dummies
  0-7645-5229-5
- Women in the Bible For Dummies
  0-7645-8475-8

TRAVEL

0-7645-7749-2

0-7645-6945-7

Also available:
- Alaska For Dummies
  0-7645-7746-8
- Cruise Vacations For Dummies
  0-7645-6941-4
- England For Dummies
  0-7645-4276-1
- Europe For Dummies
  0-7645-7529-5
- Germany For Dummies
  0-7645-7823-5
- Hawaii For Dummies
  0-7645-7402-7

- Italy For Dummies
  0-7645-7386-1
- Las Vegas For Dummies
  0-7645-7382-9
- London For Dummies
  0-7645-4277-X
- Paris For Dummies
  0-7645-7630-5
- RV Vacations For Dummies
  0-7645-4442-X
- Walt Disney World & Orlando
  For Dummies
  0-7645-9660-8

GRAPHICS, DESIGN & WEB DEVELOPMENT

0-7645-8815-X

0-7645-9571-7

Also available:
- 3D Game Animation For Dummies
  0-7645-8789-7
- AutoCAD 2006 For Dummies
  0-7645-8925-8
- Building a Web Site For Dummies
  0-7645-7144-3
- Creating Web Pages For Dummies
  0-470-08030-2
- Creating Web Pages All-in-One Desk
  Reference For Dummies
  0-7645-4345-8
- Dreamweaver 8 For Dummies
  0-7645-9649-7

- InDesign CS2 For Dummies
  0-7645-9572-5
- Macromedia Flash 8 For Dummies
  0-7645-9691-8
- Photoshop CS2 and Digital
  Photography For Dummies
  0-7645-9580-6
- Photoshop Elements 4 For Dummies
  0-471-77483-9
- Syndicating Web Sites with RSS Feeds
  For Dummies
  0-7645-8848-6
- Yahoo! SiteBuilder For Dummies
  0-7645-9800-7

NETWORKING, SECURITY, PROGRAMMING & DATABASES

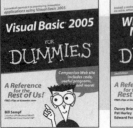

0-7645-7728-X

0-471-74940-0

Also available:
- Access 2007 For Dummies
  0-470-04612-0
- ASP.NET 2 For Dummies
  0-7645-7907-X
- C# 2005 For Dummies
  0-7645-9704-3
- Hacking For Dummies
  0-470-05235-X
- Hacking Wireless Networks
  For Dummies
  0-7645-9730-2
- Java For Dummies
  0-470-08716-1

- Microsoft SQL Server 2005 For Dummies
  0-7645-7755-7
- Networking All-in-One Desk Reference
  For Dummies
  0-7645-9939-9
- Preventing Identity Theft For Dummies
  0-7645-7336-5
- Telecom For Dummies
  0-471-77085-X
- Visual Studio 2005 All-in-One Desk
  Reference For Dummies
  0-7645-9775-2
- XML For Dummies
  0-7645-8845-1